COVID-19 and International Business

The COVID-19 pandemic has induced a crisis grasping the world abruptly, simultaneously, and swiftly. As a critical juncture, it ignited a change of era for international business. This book illustrates how governments have dealt with the pandemic and the consequent impacts on international business. It also explores the disrupted operations and responses of businesses as their worldwide interconnectivity has been seriously threatened.

The book discourses multidirectional aspects of the effects of COVID-19 on international business, ranging from the juxtaposing forces disrupting globalization and installing a change of era through decoupling of technological, production and knowledge flows to its stimulating aspects to the strategic response on business, industry and state levels. The book contains 30 chapters that offer a multidimensional interpretation of impacts of COVID-19 on international business theory and practice.

Employing the latest state of knowledge on the topic, the book is aimed at international business audience – scholars, students and managers who need to understand better the nature, scope and scale of the impacts of the pandemic on international business.

Marin A. Marinov is Professor of International Business at Aalborg University, Denmark.

Svetla T. Marinova is Professor of International Business and International Marketing at Aalborg University, Denmark.

Routledge Frontiers in the Development of International Business, Management and Marketing

Series Editors: Marin Marinov and Svetla Marinova

For more information about this series, please visit:
https://www.routledge.com/business/series/RFDIBMM

COVID-19 and International Business
Change of Era

Edited by Marin A. Marinov and
Svetla T. Marinova

NEW YORK AND LONDON

First published 2021
by Routledge
52 Vanderbilt Avenue, New York, NY 10017

and by Routledge
2 Park Square, Milton Park, Abingdon, Oxon, OX14 4RN

*Routledge is an imprint of the Taylor & Francis Group, an
informa business*

Library of Congress Cataloging-in-Publication Data
A catalog record for this title has been requested

ISBN: 978-0-367-62324-1 (hbk)
ISBN: 978-1-003-10892-4 (ebk)

Typeset in Sabon
by MPS Limited, Dehradun

Contents

List of Figures

List of Tables

Editors

Dr. Marin A. Marinov obtained his PhD degree in Management and is Professor of International Business at Aalborg Business School of Aalborg University, Denmark. He has taught and done extensive research on both sides of the Atlantic as well as in Asia in countries including Austria, Bulgaria, China, Finland, France, Germany, Portugal, Spain, Sweden, the United Kingdom and the United States among numerous others. His research interests include the phenomenon of internationalization, multinational firms and business development in general and in emerging economies in particular, as well as business policy and strategy. The publications he has done include numerous books with world leading publishers, many book chapters, as well as numerous scholarly articles in renowned academic journals such as *European Journal of Marketing, International Marketing Review* and *Journal of Marketing Management*, among many others. He is on the editorial boards of several well-known scholarly journals and has consulted for numerous multinational firms and national governments worldwide on business and educational matters. He is joint Series Editor with Routledge of the book series *Routledge Frontiers in the Development of International Business, Management and Marketing* and with Palgrave Macmillan of the book series *Palgrave Studies of Internationalization in Emerging Markets*.

Dr. Svetla T. Marinova obtained her MBA degree from the University of Warwick, the United Kingdom, and her PhD degree in International Business from Copenhagen Business School, Denmark. She is Professor of International Business and International Marketing at Aalborg Business School of Aalborg University, Denmark, where she is Head of the International Business Center. She has a rich teaching experience from numerous major universities worldwide and has conducted extensive research. Her research revolves around a variety of aspects related to firm internationalization and the role of institutions, strategy of multinational firms from developed and emerging economies, as well as value creation and value capture from business activities. Having published many books with world famous publishers, numerous book chapters as well as many scholarly papers in leading academic journals such as *Journal of World Business, International Business Review, Management and Organization Review, International Marketing Review* and many others, she is also on the editorial review boards of numerous leading scholarly journals. She is joint Series Editor with Routledge on the books series *Routledge Frontiers in the Development of International Business, Management and Marketing* and with Palgrave Macmillan, on the books series *Palgrave Studies of Internationalization in Emerging Markets.*

Contributors

Dr. Ahmad Arslan is Associate Professor at the Department of Marketing, Management and International Business of Oulu Business School, University of Oulu, Finland. Previously, he worked at several universities in the U.K. and Finland. His research is published in respected academic journals including *British Journal of Management, International Business Review, International Marketing Review, International Journal of Organizational Analysis, Journal of Business Research, Scandinavian Journal of Management, Journal of Strategic Marketing, Journal of Organizational Change Management and Production Planning & Control,* among others. He has contributed book chapters to several edited books and is member of the editorial boards of several academic journals.

Dr. Bilge Aykol is Associate Professor of Marketing at the Faculty of Business of Dokuz Eylül University in Izmir, Turkey. Her research interests are in international marketing and purchasing, relationship marketing, as well as experiential consumption. Her articles have appeared in *Journal of World Business, Journal of International Marketing, International Business Review, Management International Review, Industrial Marketing Management, Psychology & Marketing, Journal of Consumer Behavior, Journal of Global Marketing* and others.

Dr. William W. Baber has combined education with business throughout his professional career. His experience is from the U.S.; from supporting business starter ups in Japan; and from teaching in Canada, Europe and Japan. He is Associate Professor at Kyoto University, Japan, and delivers courses at the University of Vienna, Austria, and the University of Jyväskylä, Finland. He is lead author of the 2020 book *Practical Business Negotiation,* has published articles in journals as *Journal of Small Business and Enterprise Development* and *European Business Review,* among others, and conducts research in business negotiation, acculturation and business models. He received his PhD degree in 2016 from the University of Jyväskylä.

Dr. **Paolo Barbieri** is Assistant Professor of Management at the Department of Management of the University of Bologna, Italy. His research is on management of value systems, supplier relations and global value chains. He collaborates with scholars from the U.S., France and Denmark. He received his PhD degree in Managerial Engineering from the University of Padua, Italy. He has published papers in the *Journal of Operations Management, Journal of Purchasing and Supply Management, International Journal of Operations and Productions Management* and several other journals.

Albachiara Boffelli is esearch Fellow at the University of Bergamo, Italy, and doctoral candidate in a joint program between the University of Bergamo and the University of Pavia, Italy. Her research is on manufacturing relocation, more specifically reshoring, sustainability, new technologies and supply chains. She has published articles in the following journals: *International Journal of Production Economics, Journal of Purchasing and Supply Management, Operations Management Research* and *Journal of Manufacturing Technology Management.*

Dr. **Jorge Carneiro** is Associate Professor of Strategy and International Business) at Fundação Getulio Vargas (FGV) São Paulo School of Business Administration, Brazil. He is member of the board of AIB-LAC (Academy of International Business, Latin America and Caribbean chapter) and of the Governance Committee of Amcham Brazil and served as chair member of the Board of the European International Business Academy. He is also member of the editorial advisory boards of several academic journals. He has published articles in *International Business Review, Journal of Business Research, Multinational Business Review, Journal of International Entrepreneurship*, among others. Prior to his academic career, he accumulated extensive professional experience in the oil and gas industry and at dotcom companies.

Dr. **Jonas Eduardsen** is Associate Professor at Aalborg Business School of Aalborg University, Denmark. His PhD degree is from Aalborg University. His research interests are in firm internationalization with a special focus on firm internationalization, the relationship between internationalization and performance and the approaches for improving firm performance in foreign markets. He has published book chapters and articles in journals, namely, *International Business Review, International Journal of Business Environment* and *European Journal of International Management.*

Dr. **Stefano Elia** is Associate Professor of International Business at Politecnico di Milano, Italy. He was Research Fellow at the University of Reading and the University of Leeds, both in the United Kingdom, and Shanghai Jiao Tong University, China, and participated in many research projects. His research interests are in multinational firms from emerging economies, offshoring of business services, reshoring of manufacturing activities, micro-foundation of international business, new technologies and internationalization. He has published in academic journals such as *Journal of International Business Studies, Journal of Economic Geography, Economic Geography, Journal of World Business, Global Strategy Journal, Journal of Business Research, Journal of International Management, Management International Review, International Business Review, Journal of Purchasing and Supply Management,* and others.

Dr. Maria Elo is Associate Professor at the University of Southern Denmark, Odense, Denmark, Professor at the Belt and Road Institute of International Business at Shanghai University, China, and Adjunct Professor at Åbo Akademi, Finland. Her research interests are in international business, entrepreneurship and migration. She has published three books, book chapters and papers in academic journals such as *International Journal of Entrepreneurship and Small Business, European Journal of International Management* and *Journal of Family Business Management.*

Dr. Pantelitsa Eteokleous is Post-Doctoral Researcher at the University of Cyprus. Her research interests are in corporate social responsibility, ethics, entrepreneurship, supply chain management and international marketing. She has published in the *International Marketing Review* journal and book chapters.

Dr. Maria Tereza Leme Fleury is Professor of International Strategy and Director of Fundação Getulio Vargas (FGV), São Paulo School of Business Administration, São Paulo, Brazil. She is Fellow of the Academy of International Business and serves as its Vice President. She was a Research Fellow and Visiting Professor at several renowned institutions including the IFM at Cambridge University, the Institute of Development Studies and the University of Sussex, all in the United Kingdom and several others. She has served as a member of the editorial boards of several journals and published many books and articles in journals such as *Journal of International Business, Journal of World Business, Journal of Business Research, Journal of International Management* and others.

Dr. Luciano Fratocchi is Professor of Management Engineering at the University of L'Aquila, Italy. He received his PhD degree in Business Management from the University of Bologna, Italy, and was a Visiting Professor at the Department of Business Studies, the University of Uppsala, Sweden. His research is on back-shoring and near-shoring. He has published papers in *Industrial Marketing Management, International Journal of Production Economics, Journal of Purchasing* and Supply Management, *Journal of World Business, International Business Review, Supply Chain Management: An International Journal, Industrial Management & Data Systems, Journal of Global Operations and Strategic Sourcing,* and others. He is Area Editor of *Operations Management Research.*

Dr. Ismail Gölgeci is Associate Professor at Aarhus University, Denmark. His research interests include international marketing strategy, global supply chain management, sustainability and innovation. His research is published in *Journal of International Business Studies, Industrial Marketing Management, Journal of Business Research, International Business Review, International Marketing Review,* and *Supply Chain Management: An International Journal, Production Planning & Control,* among others. He is on the editorial review boards of *Journal of Business Research* and *Review of International Business and Strategy* and served as guest editor at *Industrial Marketing Management* and *European Journal of Marketing.*

Dr. Marian Gorynia is Professor of International Business at the Department of International Competitiveness of Poznań University of Economics and Business in Poland, to which he was Rector from 2008 till 2016. His research includes international business, strategic management and industrial organization. He has published extensively in scholarly journals including *Eastern European Economics, Russian and East European Finance and Trade, Journal of Transnational Management, Journal of East-West Business, Journal for East European Management Studies, Competitiveness Review, International Business Review, Economics and Business Review,* among others as well as 20 books and numerous book chapters. He has served on the editorial boards of several journals and was a member of the Board of the European International Business Academy and of the International Management Development Association. He is Chair of the Scientific Council of the Polish Economic Society.

Dr. Shuquan He is Professor at Shanghai University, China. He is Vice General-Secretary of the Shanghai Society of World Economy and the Shanghai Society of International Trade. His research interests include international economics, international business, with a focus on marketing and strategy, world economy with a focus on China and other emerging economies, international trade with a focus on global value chains. He has published numerous papers in important Chinese and international academic journals. His PhD degree is from Wuhan University, China.

Dr. Matteo Kalchschmidt is Professor at the University of Bergamo, Italy. He conducts research in the field of innovation and management of production and logistics systems, with a focus on supply chain management and manufacturing strategies. He has published book chapters and articles in scientific journals as *Journal of Purchasing and Supply Management, Journal of Manufacturing Technology Management, International Journal of Production Economics, International Journal of Production Research* and others. He is Vice-Chancellor of Internationalization and International Relations at the University of Bergamo. He is a member of editorial boards of several scientific journals and Editor-in-Chief of *Operations Management Research: Advancing Practice through Theory.*

Dr. Sardana Islam Khan is Lecturer at Central Queensland University, Australia. She has received her PhD degree from La Trobe University, Australia. Her research interests include international human resource management, offshoring and overseas sweatshops, work system performance, among other areas. She has published in journals as *Personnel Review, Journal of Developing Areas, International Journal of Economics and Management, International Business Research,* among others. For her research, she was awarded several international prizes. She has reviewed for academic journals.

Dr. Zaheer Khan is Professor of International Business at Kent Business School of the University of Kent, the United Kingdom. His work is on global technology management with a focus on emerging economy firms in knowledge transfer via foreign direct investment, capability development and formation of alliances. His work has appeared in scholarly journals, including *Journal of International Business Studies, Journal of World Business, Global Strategy Journal, International Business Review, British Journal of Management,* among many others.

Dr. Minnie Kontkanen is Lecturer at the University of Vaasa, Finland. Her research includes the internationalization of small- and medium-sized firms, international marketing strategies and sustainability. She has published chapters in books and papers in journals such as *Journal of Transnational Management* and *Journal of Strategic Marketing.*

Dr. Andrei Kuznetsov is Professor of International Corporate Social Responsibility (CSR) at Lancashire School of Business and Enterprise and Deputy-Director of the Lancashire Institute for Economic and Business Research at the University of Central Lancashire, the United Kingdom. His doctorate is in Economics, and Political and Social Sciences. Apart from CSR, his research interests include cross-cultural management, corporate governance, responsible business practices in international business contexts and institutional analysis. He has published of books, book chapters and articles, including publications in *Journal of International Business Studies, Business Ethics Quarterly, Thunderbird International Business Review,* among others.

Dr. Olga Kuznetsova is Reader in Comparative Business Studies at Manchester Metropolitan University, the United Kingdom. Her research focuses on comparative management and business practices, participatory economy and alternative business models, hybrid organizations, organizational and behavioral change and transforming business environments. Her work addresses relations between business and society and is concerned with the formation of corporate social responsibility agenda by organizations. She has published in international journals, including *Journal of Comparative Economics, Journal of International Business Studies, International Social Science Journal*, among others. She is Associated Editor of the *Encyclopedia of the Sustainable Development Goals: Transforming the World We Want.*

Laurent Lacroix is university lecturer and international consultant, having worked as sales and marketing manager for 15 years before starting his own business. He has specialized in sales techniques, marketing, supply chain management, international strategic management, circular economy and geopolitics of raw materials. He is PhD candidate defending his thesis in 2020 in management science. He worked in France, Germany, Luxembourg, Spain, the United Arab Emirates, the United Kingdom, the United States, among other countries.

Dr. Jorma Larimo is Professor of International Marketing at the University of Vaasa, Finland. He is Vice Dean of the School of Marketing and Communication and Head of the Doctoral Program of Business Studies at the University of Vaasa. His research interests include internationalization of small and medium-sized firms and foreign entry strategies of multinational companies and their performance. Presently, he focuses his research on divestment and relocation analysis. He has edited books and published papers in journals including *International Business Review, Journal of International Business Studies, Journal of International Marketing, Management International Review, Journal of World Business*, among others. He is member of the editorial boards of five international scholarly journals.

Dr. Marina Latukha is Professor of Organizational Behavior and Human Resource Management at the Graduate School of Management, the Saint Petersburg State University, Russia. She received her PhD degree and Doctoral degree from Saint Petersburg State University and graduated from several postdoctoral programs at leading European and U.S. business schools including Harvard Business School, Haas School of Business, London Business School and HEC School of Business. She has published articles in academic journals as *Human Resource Management, The International Journal of Human Resource Management, Journal of Business Research, Thunderbird International Business Review*, among others. Her research interests include international and strategic human resource management, talent management and emerging economy multinationals.

Dr. Jean Paul Lemaire is Emeritus Professor at ESCP Business School, Paris campus, France. His research focus is on cross-border corporate expansion and the impact of the changes of the international environment on regions, economic sectors and organizations. His particular interests are in emerging and fast growing economies. He has frequently taught as invited faculty and has published in French and English books, book chapters and academic papers in journals including *International Business Review*, *The Journal of Investment Management*, among others. He is member of many national and international academic associations and is the founder and first President of Atlas AFMI (Association Francophone de Management International) to which he is Honorary President.

Dr. Leonidas C. Leonidou is Professor of Marketing at the University of Cyprus and Professorial Research Fellow at Leeds University Business School, the United Kingdom. His research interests are in international marketing/purchasing, relationship marketing, strategic marketing, socially responsible marketing and marketing in emerging economies. He has published extensively in these fields. His articles have appeared in scholarly journals, such as *Journal of Marketing*, *Journal of International Business Studies*, *Journal of the Academy of Marketing Science*, *Journal of World Business*, *Journal of International Marketing*, *Management International Review*, *International Business Review*, *International Marketing Review*, *Journal of Business Research*, *Industrial Marketing Management*, *Psychology & Marketing*, *European Journal of Marketing* and others. He has published books and book chapters. He is on the editorial boards of numerous prestigious academic journals.

Dr. Kari Liuhto is Professor of International Business at the University of Turku, Finland. He obtained his PhD degree from the University of Glasgow, the United Kingdom, and the degree of Doctor of Science from the University of Turku. He is Director of the Pan-European Institute and the Centrum Balticum Foundation. Dr. Liuhto is Editor-in-Chief of *Baltic Rim Economies* review. His research focuses on investment, international economics and trade policy of emerging economies. He has published books, book chapters and articles in *Transnational Corporations*, *Journal of East-West Business*, *Europe Asia Studies*, *Journal of Business Economics and Management*, among others.

Dr. Anikó Magasházi is Researcher at the Institute of Advanced Studies in Kőszeg, Hungary. She received her PhD degree from Corvinus University, Hungary. Her research interests include globalization and regional development, global production networks of mutational corporations and their impacts on economic and social development in Central Europe and Southeast Asia. She has published papers in *Society and Economy in Central and Eastern Europe* and *Central European Business Review.*

Dr. Snejina Michailova is Professor of International Business at the University of Auckland, New Zealand, received her PhD degree from Copenhagen Business School, Denmark. Her research is in international business, general and knowledge management. She has published in academic journals including *Academy of Management Review, Academy of Management Executive, California Management Review, critical perspectives on international business, Global Strategy Journal, Journal of International Business Studies, Journal of Knowledge Management, Journal of Management Studies, Journal of World Business, International Business Review, Management International Review, Organizational Dynamics* and *Organization Studies.* She has published books and served as Editor Europe for the *Journal of World Business* and Co-Editor-in-Chief of *Critical Perspectives on International Business.* She is Consulting Editor at *Journal of International Management.*

Dr. Eric Milliot is Professor of Management Science at the University of Nantes, France, and has served as the President of Atlas AFMI (Association Francophone de Management International). He is Deputy Editor-in-Chief of the journal *International Management* and Director of the Atlas Series at Vuibert Publishing House in Paris, France. His research is primarily on strategic and organizational systems development by international companies. He has published several books, book chapters and numerous academic articles. He has taught worldwide in countries including Australia, Brazil, Bulgaria, Cameroun, China, Egypt, India, Lebanon, Madagascar, Mauritius, Morocco, the United States, among other.

Dr. Winfried Müller is the Chief Financial Officer and member of the board of a large international bank located in Munich, Germany. Prior to his current position, he held numerous key international posts in different areas of banking, finance and risk management. He worked and lived in Hong Kong, mainland China and Italy. His PhD degree is from the University of Gloucestershire, the United Kingdom, and MA degree from Reutlingen University ESB European Business School, Reutlingen, Germany.

Dr. Sophie Nivoix is Associate Professor of Finance at the University of Poitiers, France. She is Treasurer of Atlas AFMI (Association Francophone de Management International), an academic association of international management. Her research interests include risk and return of firms listed in the stock markets in Europe and Asia. She has published numerous book chapters and academic papers in journals such as *Applied Financial Economics, Asia Pacific Business Review, Journal of Economic Integration* and co-edited several books, including the recent book titled *Economic Transitions and International Business* with Routledge in 2019. She has delivered lectures in China, India, Lebanon and Poland.

Dr. Arto Ojala is Professor of International Business at the University of Vaasa, Finland. He is also Adjunct Professor at the University of Tampere, Finland, and the University of Jyväskylä School of Business and Economics, Finland. His research is in international business, information systems and entrepreneurship. He also researches digital transformation of technology companies, and its impact on business and pricing models. He has published in *Journal of World Business, International Business Review, Journal of International Marketing, International Marketing Review, Journal of Small Business Management, Information Systems Journal, IEEE Software*, among others. He received his PhD degree from the University of Jyväskylä, Finland, in 2008.

Dr. Andrei Panibratov is Professor of Strategic and International Management at Saint Petersburg State University, Russia. His research interests are in the internationalization of emerging economy firms, Russian outward foreign direct investments, China-Russia economic relationships and Russian multinationals. He has published books and book chapters, series of case studies and many articles in *International Business Review, Multinational Business Review, International Journal of Emerging Markets*, among others. He is on the editorial boards of several academic journals. He has served as consultant for the World Bank, Helsinki Metropolitan Development Corporation, as well as Russian and international firms. He is National Representative of Russia and Board Member of the European International Business Academy. His MBA degree is from the University of Wales, the United Kingdom; PhD degree in Economics from the Saint Petersburg State University; and Doctor in Economics degree from the Moscow State University of Management, Russia.

Dr. Jaqueline Pels is Professor of Marketing at the University Torcuato Di Tella Business School in Buenos Aires, Argentina. She is Director of the Inclusive Business Think Tank (ENI-Di Tella). Her research interests include emerging economies, international business, marketing theory, relationship and networking marketing. Her publications have appeared in top international journals including *Journal of the Academy of Marketing Science, Marketing Theory, Journal of Business Research, Journal of Business and Industrial Marketing, European Journal of Marketing, Journal of Relationship*

Marketing, among numerous others. She has served on the editorial boards of several leading academic journals.

Dr. Serge Rey is Professor of Economics at the University of Pau and Pays de l'Adour, France, and Dean of the Social Sciences and Humanities College there. His research interests include international macroeconomics, more specifically international trade and international finance, economic convergence, economics of the exchange rate and applied econometrics. He has published in leading academic journals, as *The Annals of Regional Science, Applied Economics, Economics Bulletin, Economics and Statistics, Economic Modelling, International Economics, Journal of Economic Integration, Pacific Economic Review,* among others.

Dr. Arnold Schuh is Director of the Competence Center for Emerging Markets & Central and Eastern Europe (CEE) and Assistant Professor at Vienna University of Economics and Business, Austria. He is Adjunct Associate Professor at Carlson School of Management, University of Minnesota, the U.S., and Honorary Professor at Corvinus University, Hungary. His core research is on marketing and strategic management in CEE and other emerging economies. Currently, he focuses on the challenges of multinational firms in CEE, competitiveness of firms from CEE and China's Belt and Road Initiative. He has published books, many book chapters and papers in *Central European Business Review, Journal of World Business, European Journal of Marketing, Journal of East-West Business,* among others.

Dr. Dmitrij Slepniov is Associate Professor at Aalborg Business School of Aalborg University, Denmark. His MSc degree is from London School of Economics, the United Kingdom, and PhD degree from Aalborg University. Prior to starting his academic career, he held key positions at the Confederation of Lithuanian Industries. His research interests include global operations and innovation, global value chains, upgrading of emerging market firms, servitization and service design. He has published papers in journals as *European Journal of Development Research, Journal of Manufacturing Technology Management, Operations Management Research,* among others. His international experience includes teaching and research in collaboration with industry in China, Denmark, Japan, Lithuania, and South Korea.

Dr. Ernesto Tapia-Moore has 40 years of professional experience, including 20 years in industry and 20 years in academia. After serving in the U.S. Navy, he worked as international manager for several businesses in France. He shifted from international management to consulting and professional training, and finally to academia. Since 2001, he has been Associate Professor at Kedge Business School in Marseille, France. His research focuses on agency theory, internationalization and turbulence in international markets. His main publications are found in *Journal of International Marketing, Management International, Global Business and Organizational Behavior, Journal of Business*, among others.

Dr. Shlomo Tarba is Professor in Strategy and International Business, at Birmingham Business School. University of Birmingham, the United Kingdom. He is Deputy Editor-in-Chief and an incoming Co-Editor-in-Chief of *British Journal of Management*. He is member of the editorial boards of several top academic journals and served as guest-editor for the special issues at leading journals. Dr. Tarba has published many articles in leading academic journals including *Journal of Management, British Journal of Management, Journal of Organizational Behavior, Human Relations, Academy of Management Perspectives, Journal of World Business, Management International Review, International Business Review, International Journal of Production and Economics* and *International Marketing Review*.

Dr. Ernesto Tavoletti is Associate Professor of Management, International Marketing and International Business Strategy at the University of Macerata, Italy. He received his PhD degree in Economics and Management at the University of Florence, Italy, in 2004. His research interests are in international business, innovation management and higher education management. He has published a book, many book chapters and papers in journals such as *Management Research Review, International Journal of Emerging Markets, International Journal of Operations & Production Management, Transition Studies Review*, among others.

Dr. Julian Teicher is Professor and Deputy Dean of Research at the Central Queensland University, Australia. His PhD degree is from the University of Melbourne, Australia. His research is in workplace and human resources, public management, and governance. With a grant from the Australian Research Council, he undertook a largescale research project: on workforce in Australia. He has published in academic journals as *Industrial and Labor Relations Review, The International Journal of Human Resource Management, South Asia Journal of South Asian Studies*, among others, book chapters and a book.

Dr. George Tesar is Professor Emeritus at Umeå University, Sweden, and the University of Wisconsin-Whitewater, the U.S. He holds a doctorate from the University of Wisconsin-Madison, an MBA degree from Michigan State University, the U.S., and has several years of industry experience as mechanical engineer. He consults on academic and management issues and teaches on visiting assignments at famous universities on international marketing, related issues, as well as on cases and scenarios. Dr. Tesar has advised international corporations, and held corporate and institutional board memberships. He has published books, book chapters, and papers in lead academic journals as *Journal of International Business Studies*, *International Business Review*, among others. He served as Faculty Associate at the Center of Strategic and International Studies in Washington, D.C., marketing specialist at the Department of Energy, as specialist in international trade with the Department of Commerce, and on the Governor's Advisory Committee on International Trade, now the Wisconsin International Trade Council. He is top expert on the internationalization of smaller manufacturing firms.

Angeliki Voskou is Research Scientist at the University of Cyprus, currently participating in a project focusing on corporate social responsibility strategies adopted by multinational firms. Her work has been presented at various conference.

Xiaoying Wang is Senior Lecturer at Shanghai University, Shanghai, China. Her research interests include international business and culture. She has published papers in the following journals *Area Studies and Global Development* and *Contemporary Economy and Management*.

Dr. Thomaz Wood Jr. is Professor of Research Methods at Fundação Getulio Vargas (FGV) São Paulo School of Business Administration, Brazil. His research interests include organizational change and the impacts of management research and knowledge. He has published in international journals, such as *Organization*, *The Academy of Management Executive*, *Management Learning*, *The International Journal of Human Resource Management*, *The Journal of Organizational Change Management* and *Thunderbird International Business Review*. He has worked for 25 years as consultant for large Brazilian firms, managing projects regarding strategic planning, organizational change, restructuring and leadership development.

Julia Zhang is Researcher at the B&R Institute of International Business of Shanghai University, China. She studied at Copenhagen Business School and the University of Southern Denmark, both in Denmark, and Lund University, Sweden. Her research interests are in international business and entrepreneurship and firm internationalization in the context of emerging economies.

Dr. Xiaotian Zhang is SHU Distinguished Professor of International Business and EU Jean Monnet Professor of Entrepreneurship, Associate Vice President of Shanghai University and Director General of SHU Global in Shanghai, China. He sits on the Board of Directors of Sino-European School of Technology of Shanghai and the Advisory Board of Cambridge Innovation Academy in Cambridge, the

United Kingdom. He was Rajawali Fellow at Harvard Kennedy School, Harvard University, the United States, and Visiting Scholar at Saïd Business School of Oxford University, the United Kingdom. He got his PhD degree from the University of Tartu, Estonia. He has published book chapters and papers in scholarly journals as *European Journal of International Management, International Journal of Production Research, Journal of East-West Business, Journal of International Entrepreneurship*, among numerous others.

1 International Business in the COVID-19 Pandemic

Marin A. Marinov and
Svetla T. Marinova

State of the World Economy and COVID-19

A number of experts from various parts of the world have seen the global financial and economic crisis of 2008–2009 as the end of hyper-globalization and have proved partially right. More than a decade later, globalization is in a precarious situation due to critical junctures and changes in national policies across countries that are strongly impacting international trade and investment flows, among many other economic activities. These changes have radically perplexed twentieth century multilateralism that is being currently replaced by unilateralism, nationalism and protectionism. Consequently, we are experiencing ongoing confrontation and competition and a fundamental departure from the globalization paradigm.

The period between 2008 and the outbreak of COVID-19 remained eventful for the whole world economy. The major players of the international institutional structure governing the world economy, i.e., the World Trade Organization (WTO), the International Monetary Fund (IMF), and the World Bank (WB), have stayed intact, although being affected by the changes. So far, they have managed to face the unprecedented COVID-19-related disruptions forcing them to find new mechanisms and adopt measures to deal with the consequences. Nevertheless, such supranational institutions are challenged and calls for their restructuring have become eminent, thus, putting globalization to a test.

By mid-July 2020, the COVID-19 pandemic managed to cause an unexpected, yet dramatic health shock worldwide. It took the lives of hundreds of thousands of people. It instigated one of the worst economic shockwaves humanity had experienced for generations. It contracted the world economy in a completely unexpected manner within just a few months. Looking forward, forecasters predict long-term profound recession, contraction of economic activity, output, trade, investments and job opportunities. Moreover, a decoupling of production, service provision, financial flows and labor are also evident.

According to The Economist (2020) COVID-19 would stay with us for a long time. It will affect almost 90 percent of the world economy and torment economic growth for a long time to come. Such a long-term effect of the pandemic was unimaginable and difficult to foresee as globalization seemed invincible and here to stay.

COVID-19 and International Business

The most important indicators of international business are international trade, measured in value and volume, and investments across borders. They facilitate international activities on all levels – macro, meso, and micro. Data published by the United Nations Conference on Trade and Development (UNCTAD, 2020) in a combined statement with 36 international organizations indicates a 3 percent drop in the value of international trade worldwide only in the first quarter of 2020 with sharp slumps expected in every subsequent quarter. For example, in the second quarter there is a predicted fall of 27 percent.

Foreign direct investment (FDI) has also dropped substantially and is expected to fall further in the future. The most hopeful estimates by the Organization for Economic Cooperation and Development (OECD, 2020) are of a decrease by more than 30 percent in 2020, whereas UNCTAD experts predict at least a 40 percent decline. The reduction in foreign direct investment has been coupled with a trend of FDI divestment adopted by multinational companies (MNCs) (Borga et al., 2020). Divestment decisions are also associated with reshoring and back shoring of global supply and value-adding activities to alter and reconstitute production networks and supply chains. COVID-19 has only accelerated this process.

It has hastened the decoupling of economic activities of developed economy MNCs from the supply chains in China and has forced the removal of strategic production based on FDI from developed economies away from China. In addition, decisions have been made to push out or limit the opportunities for Chinese FDI in economically advanced countries and make some technologies inaccessible for Chinese investors. Such moves are meant to speed up technological decoupling and limit investment flows.

Surprisingly, the expected severe impact of the COVID-19 pandemic on value chains due to their disproportionate exposure to systemic risk has not been supported by existing scarce evidence. Nonetheless, the incoming information indicates such tendencies that might be reinforced in the future by government decisions to withdraw or limit production in China. Consequently, COVID-19 has appeared as a health pandemic, but has been transformed into a critical juncture to initiate a major transformation and re-configuration of political, economic and social forces.

The Book Chapters

COVID-19 is a pandemic, which is unique, although there have been other pandemics and crises throughout history. From a healthcare perspective, sanitary measures have been introduced in different countries at various times depending on the outbreak, scale and scope of the pandemic and the policies adopted by the governments. The lockdown has had multiple impacts on various aspects of life and the economy, in general, and a profound effect on international business, in particular. It is beyond doubt that we have entered a period of colossal unpredictability and insecurity. Impacts are felt in productivity, gross domestic product (GDP), employability, some businesses have amassed incredible losses and many have already declared bankruptcy. Negative consequences have rippled through international trade, FDI flows, global supply and value chains, just to mention a few. How long this situation will continue no one can predict with certainty. Phased release of lockdowns has started in June and July 2020 leading to a significant increase in the number of infected people across the globe, despite measures for containment. There is a genuine threat of virus mutations and new restrictions with no available solution to enforce globally. Thus, this book comes as a reaction to what has happened, how it unfolds and accumulated experiences thus far.

The chapters in this book are in an essay format and present personal points of view of international business scholars based on what has happened in the world by mid-July 2020. While one group of the chapters are reflections on extant experience, others are based on empirical evidence. Expectations on how the COVID-19 pandemic triggered events and follow up policies would impact international business are also included. Therefore, we present an interesting and engaging platform for diversity of viewpoints, interpretations, reflections and critical assessments to enable further discussions. The chapters are grouped into several parts.

Part One offers a general overview and outlook of the effects of the COVID-19 pandemic on international business.

Chapter 2 by Jaqueline Pels analyzes the process of how we think about problems we face, options we have, and solutions we consider. The author focuses on three issues common to COVID-19 and international business. First, our tendency to think in a dichotomous way and, consequently, create axis of tensions. For example, will international trade continue based on the principles of globalization or will it shift to protectionism and rigid borders? Second, what are the differences between Era of Changes, in which the basic logic of how things happen does not change, and Change of Era, during which conventional logic cannot provide solutions. Third, the chapter explores the possibility of Covid-19 to cause radical changes and the subsequent effects on international business.

Chapter 3 by Marin A. Marinov analysis the manifestation of the economic effects of COVID-19 and the ways in which they create challenges for international business in relation to globalization, global supply and value chains, and the changing role of nation state vis-à-vis market forces. The author perceives the pandemic as an objective risk and an augmenter of the already active destabilizers to international business, which have re-installed the importance of the nation state and consequently underlined the need for self-sufficiency in strategic industries. The chapter discusses the emerging firm level and government responses in the form of strategies and concrete actions that provide national economies with augmented internal sovereignty, risk reduction and resilience.

In Chapter 4, Jean-Paul Lemaire claims that the unprecedented crisis, caused by COVID-19, has abruptly blocked most economic and business activities in the world, hitting particularly hard international trade and foreign direct investment (FDI) flows. The crisis also overlaps with and accelerates the recent rifts of bilateral and multilateral relations, e.g., the looming trade war between China and the U.S., Brexit, economic embargoes, tariffs and international trade agreement reconsiderations. In addition, the COVID-19 pandemic causes major environmental changes and widely-spread socio-economic hardships of unemployment, production relocation and protectionism. These enforce changes in countries' and companies' orientations and organization, which refer directly to their survival. COVID-19 has radically shattered international economic integration. The change started with the 2008–2009 global financial and economic crisis, which was later reinforced by the political turnarounds in China, the U.S., the United Kingdom and numerous European countries. This requires a reconsideration of international business in the radically disrupted global environment in order to adjust international management practices. It would encourage the adoption of renewed approaches to organizational and functional decision-making processes in diverse geographies and activities.

Ernesto Tavoletti's Chapter 5 explores the disappointing responses of nation states to COVID-19 from health and economic perspective. The author argues that there has been a consistent set of missing early adequate responses to the pandemic across most nations. These responses have gone through the same stages starting with *denial* based on the presumption – it will not hit us because we are different; followed by *underestimation* – it is just a little more than an ordinary flu; then, it is *really serious*, but we cannot afford shutting down our economy; followed by *sudden panics* and *lockdowns*; moving to *too little too late* health wise and some economic backing to the unemployed and locked down citizens; and eventually moving towards *too early opening ups* of the economy. He maintains that the responses have been particularly disappointing in the European Union where, far from having a united response, the bloc member states shut down their borders and put a temporary end to the common market, blocked trade in medical equipment and competed unfairly among themselves for items of critical importance. In a deflationary context, with the price of oil futures contracts going into negative territory for the first time in history, the European Monetary Union (E.M.U.) delayed a much-needed strong monetary stimulus under concerns of who might benefit of such a stimulus in the condition of a possible stronger intra-E.M.U. competition. The delay of a monetary stimulus and the successive liquidity might well produce a destruction of productive capacity and consequently induce inflationary risk that would propone a prudent fear. Therefore, far from strengthening international cooperation, the external danger has revealed that when it is a matter of life and death people naturally tend to rely mainly on national community as the ultimate repository of a trusted common culture and destiny. Taking a contradictory view, the chapter suggests that a common and worldwide coordinated response is the only plausible option for success compatible with the idea of a sustainable world economy to fight the pandemic and secure health and economic revival post COVID-19.

In Chapter 6, Marian Gorynia proposes that COVID-19 will not kill, or even significantly weaken globalization, rather it would only transform it and the scale of the related modifications compared with its condition before the coronavirus would be moderate because the scale of the changes caused by the pandemic are only temperate. Initially, the author presents a pertinent review of the concept of globalization. Following this, two different scenarios for the future development of globalization are outlined. The first one exemplifies a hypothetical situation assuming the absence of COVID-19 in which case globalization will develop without being challenged. The second scenario progresses reflections on the future of globalization after the COVID-19 pandemic. Based on these scenarios, the conclusion reached by the author is that globalization is here to stay. Any suggestions for its death are premature.

In Chapter 7, Kari Liuhto analyzes the impact of the coronavirus on the global economy. It deals with the overall impact of the COVID-19 pandemic on world development, international trade and logistics, FDI and international tourism. Special attention is dedicated to the consequences of the pandemic for the European Union. The main aim of the chapter is to reveal the immediate impact of COVID-19 on the world economy, in general, and international business, in particular, as well as on the permanent legacy of the pandemic to the established world order and international economic cooperation.

Part Two of the book brings in the industry and business model perspectives related to the impact of the COVID-19 pandemic. The part starts with a discussion about the importance of strategic industries to nation states, followed by chapters exploring specific industries and the business models of international firms.

Chapter 8 by Ahmad Arslan, Zaheer Khan, Minnie Kontkanen and Shlomo Tarba analyzes the impact of COVID-19 on strategic industries, which governments consider important for country competitiveness. Traditionally, reference is made to industries as production of arms and extraction of natural resources. Steel, telecommunications, high-tech manufacturing and more recently robotics have become industries classified as strategic. Since the COVID-19 pandemic struck countries, industries like agro-food, pharmaceutical, retailing, production of personal protective equipment, to name just a few, prior the pandemic internationalized via global value and supply chains, are presently considered strategic by an ever-increasing number of governments. The chapter offers an overview and analysis by incorporating arguments regarding alterations in the classification of strategic industries based on extant literature and, integrating evidence from COVID-19 related changes.

In Chapter 9, William Baber and Arto Ojala deliberate on how COVID-19 impacts firms' business models in the international context. They argue that firms should aim to adopt business models built on network trust, cost reduction and automation to maximize resilience and provide better chances to survive. Innovation of business models also calls for entrepreneurial mindset to find alternative ways of doing business, even changing, expanding, or abandoning the original product/service offerings or entering new markets as COVID-19 eliminates existing and creates new international business opportunities. The authors suggest that international value networks depend strongly on issues such as trust in networks and partners, activities in-house versus those offshored, type of industry and regulations. In some cases, the capability of a firm to backshore international activities in this period might be critical, while value delivery in the international context during the COVID-19 is highly dependent on how much a firm can deliver its services over the Internet or via the use of robots.

In Chapter 10 by Andrei Panibratov, the COVID-19 pandemic is analyzed in terms of healthcare costs (both direct and indirect) that rise suddenly and sharply. Digital health programs and e-platforms based healthcare business models become the area representing not only a solid ground for interdisciplinary research as it combines society, technologies and management, but also a practical tool to mitigate costs and increase the efficiency of medical care in the COVID-19 pandemic. The aim of his chapter is to evaluate the digital healthcare business opportunities at a time of global distress and uncertainty, and discuss the applicability of digital health models during the COVID-19 pandemic at country- and industry-level.

Part Three of the book presents essays on the impact of COVID-19 on international finance and human resource management.

In Chapter 11, Sophie Nivoix and Serge Rey analyze the worldwide economic impact of COVID-19. Considering the impact of the pandemic on international business, the market valuation of the major exporting firms has dropped sharply since the start of the coronavirus outbreak. Drastic falls have been followed by dramatic jumps a few days later, and then again by drops. In order to understand how markets have reacted, the authors investigate stock market returns and volatilities in nine countries located on three continents that have been hugely impacted by the virus, namely, China, France, Germany, Italy, Japan, Spain, South Korea, the United Kingdom, and the U.S. They also explore the values of the French luxury industry being most exposed to the volatility in the Chinese market. Comparison is drawn with other major crises, such as the 9/11 attack in the U.S. and the Fukushima catastrophe in Japan, by considering price changes and the instability of the stock market indexes. The analysis of the amplitude of the shocks and the timespan, suggests that the health, economic, and financial consequences of the Covid-19 pandemic are expected to last for at least several years.

Chapter 12, authored by Winfried Müller, aims to assess how financial measures have been provided in Europe during COVID-19. In addition to corporate crisis management and liquidity support by the banking sector, nation states and central banks are using instruments that are either market conforming or non-market conforming following the paradigm of interventionism. Market conforming actions influence the market conditions in a way in which the law of supply and demand remains intact. In contrast, non-market conforming measures counteract the market mechanisms, but are often applied to reach political aims and avoid unpleasant side effects. While government loans, fiscal support, and investment programs, as well as traditional central bank schemes, are in line with market mechanisms to mitigate the adverse effects of the COVID-19 pandemic, the European Central Bank has already left the ground of market conformity for a number of years. With attempts to push banks to provide loans at relaxed lending rules, first ideas emerge that are following the interventionist paradigm in the banking sector as well. The author expresses the opinion that efficient capital allocation based on sound lending rules and the disciplining element of market forces will help overcome the financial burden of the COVID-19 pandemic better than interventionism that hinders the restructuring of public debt and ultimately endanger the wealth of the European citizens.

Chapter 13 by Marina Latukha argues that when companies struggle with new uncontrolled global challenges such as COVID-19, managerial practices should be reconsidered and redesigned to ensure continuous organizational development. The chapter discusses how talent management (TM) may use opportunities created by the pandemic to build a new competitive advantage. Specifically, two perspectives are highlighted. One is to develop an inclusive TM strategy that allows management to move from scattered activities to systematic approaches in talent training and development to nurture educational advantage. The other is to extend the talent pool by searching for potential new talents, e.g., returnees whom the COVID-19 pandemic pushes back to their country of origin. The chapter provides insights on particular areas that should be included in management's agenda to benefit from the crisis by developing a systemic view of TM.

In Chapter 14, Ahmad Arslan, Ismail Gölgeci and Jorma Larimo explore the importance of expatriates and their role in multinational enterprises (MNEs). The authors highlight that MNEs can use expatriates to establish original subsidiaries in new host countries, train local employees, engage in knowledge transfer and undertake international project assignments. Meanwhile, subsidiary management, which has been generally researched from the perspective of control versus autonomy, is closely intertwined with expatriates playing the role of foreign managers when MNEs seek more control over subsidiaries. Even when applying non-equity international operation modes, expatriate managers are mostly used by MNEs to control the operations as well as deliver the promised final product or service timely. The COVID-19 pandemic has resulted in numerous restrictions of international and local travel. At the same time, there is a visible increase in distance working in MNEs. The chapter offers insights on the pros and cons of distance working during and post-COVID-19 in relation to the role of expatriates in subsidiary management.

Part Four includes contributions exploring the impact of COVID-19 global supply and value chains.

Chapter 15 is by Paolo Barbieri, Albachiara Boffelli, Stefano Elia, Luciano Fratocchi, and Matteo Kalchschmidt. The authors discuss the long-term effect of COVID-19 on the reconfiguration of Global Value Chains (GVCs). In particular, the pandemic is showing how an excessive number of interconnected and distant countries might become a critical issue for global production networks. This is mostly the case when they are very dissimilar on a single key manufacturing hub, e.g. in China, and in case all nodes are asynchronously subject to an emergency, e.g., COVID-19. It could prevent them from undertaking production activities and block the entire GVC for a long time. As a consequence, one of the possible outcomes of this worldwide health and economic emergency might cause a radical reconfiguration of GVCs. This may involve partial relocations and/or a re-concentration of the activities in fewer and/or closer countries that represent less risk and/or that can ensure a faster and more coordinated recovery of the production activities and, hence, of the entire value chain. The authors argue that the reconfiguration of GVCs arises from COVID-19 that accelerates already existing trends, including the decoupling of GVC ties and the relocation of activities across countries, which have been recently fostered by other phenomena such as the spread of digital technologies, the trade war between China and the U.S., the rise of nationalism and protectionism. Together, they call for more resilient, de-globalized, and more sustainable supply chains.

Chapter 16 by Jonas Strømfeldt Eduardsen is dedicated to COVID-19 and managing risk in multinational corporations (MNCs) as one of their crucially important strategic purposes. The existing literature focuses on how MNCs manage 'traditional risks', such as foreign exchange or political risks. The COVID-19 pandemic has set new risks with unpredictable and profound side effects seriously impacting international business, which are not difficult to realize and recognize as well as manage using the management approaches to traditional risks. COVID-19 also serves as a reminder of how the increasing global interconnectedness caused by the hyper-globalization makes the COVID-19 risks borderless as shocks from any part of the world economy are rapidly transmitted all over the world. Consequently, the author seeks to draw relevant lessons from the COVID-19 pandemic by referring to the concept of global systemic risk comprising, firstly, identification of the characteristics of the new emergent forms of risk; secondly, discuss their potential impact on international business; and thirdly, explore how the new emergent forms of risk present their challenges to the conventional approaches to risk management in MNCs. The chapter concludes with reflections on key issues arising from COVID-19 that deserve the close attention of international business scholars relating to the risk debate.

Chapter 17 by Laurent Lacroix and Eric Milliot analyzes supply chains. The authors view commodities as necessary for the economic development of nations, which have continuously fed a system creating markets for products consuming additional natural resources. The extracting industry, which has had a profound impact on the environment over the past several centuries, is now seriously undermined by COVID-19. Indeed, the market networks in commodity exchange are currently disrupted as they are viewed as vectors of contamination. It is now a viral risk, in the epidemiological sense of the term, forcing company management to rethink supply chains and the quality of supplies. The authors propose that firms have to increase resilience and flexibility in a quest for an appropriate and resilient supply chain model.

In Chapter 18, Sardana Islam Khan and Julian Teicher propose a sustainable global supply chain management model in the post-COVID-19 environment. The authors review the existing directions and policy retaliations of advanced economies and identify a range of possible global sourcing scenarios. They explore the possibility of integrating the closed loop supply chain (CLSC) model with some traditional supply management (SM) practices, e.g., reduction, selection, integration and development of suppliers, to propose a more sustainable and flexible global supply chain management regime. The adaptation of the CLSC model and SM practices should be in line with industry's operational context and SM practices should help empower the supply chain partners to improve the coordination and information flow between stakeholders and ensure sustainability of supply chains.

Chapter 19 by Anikó Magasházi reflects upon the emergence of global supply chains, global value chains, and production networks that were facilitated by the upsurge of cross-border foreign direct investments in the era of hyper-globalization. The author suggests that the positive effects of the new international division of labor, supply chain disruptions could spread swiftly across globally dispersed industries and actors, as shown by the impact of other crises, such as SARS in 2003, the floods in Thailand and the earthquake in Japan. The two years of the U.S.-China trade war have led to geographical reconfiguration of global supply chains to a relatively limited extent, while the COVID-19 pandemic is accelerating this process enormously due to its scale and scope. In this situation, national governments and other institutions have expanded their interaction with MNCs that are moving towards contingency planning and greater risk-awareness in strategic planning. The chapter unfolds recent developments in South-East Asia and Singapore amidst the COVID-19 pandemic from the perspective of protecting strategic sectors embedded in the existing global value chains as well as from a micro-economic perspective related to the trends in the internationalization of firms.

Part Five draws attention to the ethical perspectives in international business and corporate social responsibility during the COVID-19 pandemic.

Chapter 20 by Leonidas Leonidou, Bilge Aykol, Pantelitsa Eteokleous, and Angeliki Voskou notes the profound impact of COVID-19 on firms operating internationally. Drawing on the Situational Crisis Communication theory, the chapter explains how international firms match their strategies to preserve corporate reputation in a crisis-situation in order to protect their stakeholders from physical, psychological, and other harmful effects. The authors focus particularly on the Corporate Social Responsibility (CSR) strategies adopted by international firms as a means to harness their corporate reputation, and even boost their business performance, under the unique conditions associated with the current pandemic. They distinguish between internal and external CSR-related initiatives adopted by international firms and provide critical analysis supported by real life examples.

Chapter 21, written by Snejina Michailova proposes that irresponsible business is not only immune to the impacts of Covid-19, but as a result of this pandemic it will grow much stronger. Irresponsible business is the business doing wrong to the community, society, and business practices. Vulnerable 'workers' in exploitative supply chains will feel the repercussions of the coronavirus long after it is (hopefully) overcome. The inverted commas here relate to the dangerous, unbearable, often inhumane working conditions, meagre, if any, wages, lacking protection, if at all existing, contracts are not elements of what constitutes 'work' as these comprise modern slavery. The impacts of the COVID-19 pandemic are and will be multiple: health-related, economic, social and environmental, to mention but a few. Corruption, creative tax avoidance, nepotism have been present in the business scene around the world for time immemorial. But none of these can compare with modern slavery in terms of how ugly those crimes are. Slavery operates mostly across borders in a hidden form within the complex supply chains of producers, labor contractors and global retailers. Modern slavery has become an inseparable part of the business life not only in developing countries but also in very well-developed, advanced economies that pride themselves for their well-organized enforced institutions and sound ethical business practices. Moreover, modern slavery thrives not only in labor-intensive industries like agriculture, farming and construction; it is very much part of high fashion, information technology and electronics, as well as in many other industries. The pressure piles up as one travels down the supply chain, eventuating in an employer, or multiple, not only exploit but in reality enslave their workers. Globalization has always been in the driver's seat when it comes to enslaving people. Nevertheless, in international business, there is hardly any research on modern slavery. The chapter claims that there seem to be two key paths post COVID-19. Path one: companies will delay or cancel orders with their suppliers and subcontractors – divesting is typically under consideration when a severe crisis strikes. Path two: companies will continue doing business as usual, profiting from slavery on a larger scale than before COVID-19. The overarching worry is, no matter which path multinational firms will choose, the losing party will always be the enslaved people.

Part Six brings together contributions on the impact of COVID-19 on small and medium-sized firms and the role of social enteprises.

Chapter 22 by George Tesar addresses the socio-economic impact of the COVID-19 pandemic, which is unprecedented. Because of it, theories and operations of international business experienced their greatest interruptions in modern times. The entire system of international business operations needs to be reconsidered in the context of the pandemic. Large international enterprises have advantageous positions over smaller manufacturing enterprises, mostly in terms of stronger financial and human resources. During the pandemic, smaller manufacturing enterprises operating in international markets are faced with serious survival issues due to lack of financial resources and adequate management styles, and have international communications deficiencies. Smaller manufacturing enterprises are not homogeneous exporters. They consider export operations on different levels with perceived intensities of contributions to sales. Although the research and theories that provide the foundations for export operations are generally sound, limited knowledge accounts for concerns of their abilities to identify and assess the forces that comprise the external business environment in which they function. COVID-19 has forced managers and decision makers of smaller manufacturing enterprises to rethink export operations and to understand the external business environments. They need to understand that each export market creates its own unique environmental forces, including economic, social, technological, and lifestyle. Their contemporary theoretical and operational understanding of export operations must be expanded to include an understanding of how environmental forces in each international business environment power and will direct their export operations in the future.

In Chapter 23, Ernesto Tapia-Moore explores the pre-internationalization decisions of French small and medium-sized enterprises (SME) and their post-internationalization performance. The author found out that companies having the best post-internationalization performance are those whose pre-internationalization performance was worse in comparison to that of their counterparts, especially in the case of early internationalization. Considering the fact that the research referred to was conducted in an entirely globalized economy with highly predictable characteristics, it can be argued with reasonable doubt that the findings would be relevant and applicable under the COVID-19 market conditions and during the pandemics aftermath. The objective of the chapter is to make reserved predictions based on extant research, yet integrating the extremely turbulent conditions resulting from the COVID-19 pandemic in a highly volatile environment and excessive information overload in the internationalization-related decisions of French SMEs.

In Chapter 24, Andrei Kuznetsov and Olga Kuznetsova argue that COVID-19 has disrupted the network and supply chains of MNC in foreign markets. The authors suggest that MNCs may turn this challenge into an opportunity by looking for partners among businesses that are rarely mentioned in the international business literature, namely, the cooperatives. In many countries, the unprecedented social disruptions caused by COVID-19 have highlighted the prominence of organizations originating in the cooperative sector or prioritizing social solidarity and community-focused commitments as they have been able to provide a particularly prompt response to the economic and social calamities of the COVID-19 pandemic. They have proven to be especially efficient in terms of the mobilization and creation of community assets to boost the resilience of local economies. Cooperatives play a major role in the economy of many countries, including Italy, Spain and New Zealand, yet the international business literature has hardly studied them in the context of the growth of multinational business. Cooperatives are prominent in agriculture, food processing, banking and financial services, insurance, retail, utilities, health and social care, information technologies and crafts. The rate of growth of the cooperative sector is ascending steadily and its share in the world economy has reached 15 percent. The resilience shown by cooperatives during the coronavirus crisis cannot be ignored. The focus of this chapter is on revealing and analyzing the largely ignored potential of cooperatives and other social solidarity organizations to make a contribution to the post COVID-19 crisis recovery at national and local level and how this potential may benefit the post-crisis recovery of MNCs.

Part Seven is a selection of geographical perspectives on the impact of COVID-19 on international business, incorporating countries and regions.

Chapter 25 by Shuquan He, Maria Elo, Xiaotian Zhang, and Julia Zhang argues that China has been triple hit by the pandemic, concerning its role in international business. Firstly, there were huge domestic supply disruptions due to business shutdowns lowering or discontinuing the supply to international markets and canceling international orders. Secondly, international demand for Chinese products declined sharply due to business shutdown in the rest of the world. When Chinese businesses resumed their normal production, rather few international orders were available. Thirdly, Chinese businesses face a completely new international business environment as developed countries have modified their laws and regulations on foreign direct investment, mostly targeting Chinese companies. The Chinese example demonstrates that COVID-19 has brought about fundamental changes in the international business environment that have precarious effects on international transactions.

Shuquan He and Xiaoying Wang in Chapter 26 reveal that the COVID-19 pandemic has disturbed international business activities of firms. The calls for relocation of various activities in global supply chains out of China have been led by the U.S. and echoed by other countries. Despite political pressure, it will be a serious challenge to find a viable alternative to China's big production base and sizeable domestic consumer market that is rapidly innovating. China has launched a series of national, regional and big city efforts to boost economic recovery and improve the domestic business environment. While COVID-19 will certainly change the ways in which people engage with business, it has led to innovations in business models by enhancing products and services and offering new solutions. Chinese companies are fast rebuilding, restructuring their commercial and innovation potential, and preparing to launch innovative service and delivery solutions internationally in response to the changing environment by leveraging emerging technologies.

In Chapter 27, Dmitrij Slepniov sets out to explore how Danish companies operating in China have experienced the impact of COVID-19 and the lessons they learnt from their experiences for the post-COVID-19 world. For this purpose, in the period February–May 2020, 15 semi-structured interviews were conducted with top executives of Danish companies in China. The insights from the interviews have been complemented by a survey carried out in May 2020 among the members of the Danish Chamber of Commerce in China. The research findings have provided insights into the specific challenges of COVID-19 for Danish companies operating in China and the efforts these companies implemented to counteract the negative impacts of the coronavirus in order to build a foundation for a robust and stable business operation in the post-pandemic world.

Chapter 28 by Arnold Schuh discusses the effects of the COVID-19 pandemic on the economies of Central and Eastern Europe (CEE) and on their attractiveness for Western investors. The chapter starts with a comparison of the characteristics of the 2008–2009 financial and economic crisis with the features of COVID-19 pandemic, outlining the major economic effects and discusses the impact on selected challenges that foreign multinational companies faced in 2019. A recent economic boom, a shrinking labor pool, and rising labor costs, deteriorating institutions, antagonistic attitudes of host governments towards foreign investors, and the entry of new competitors, particularly Chinese ones, have shaped the business environment in the recent years. Along these lines, the author outlines the possible developments for foreign direct investors that they would face in the CEE region in coming years. For many of the CEE countries, the projected decline in economic output will be significantly severer than the ones in 2008–2009 period whereas the patterns of recovery and the ways in which their international firms will change are completely unpredictable.

Chapter 29 by Thomaz Wood Jr., Jorge Carneiro and Maria Tereza Leme Fleury presents the new mindsets of firms in a country hit particularly hard by the COVID-19 pandemic, Brazil. Executives of large firms operating in Brazil, both domestic and international, as well as from public administration bodies believe that the adaptations that many organizations made to deal with the COVID-19 crisis will most probably have long-lasting effects on numerous dimensions of business management. While the informants have acknowledged the utmost severity of the COVID-19 caused crisis, they have presented an overall positive outlook for the post-crisis prospects. The authors address the following dimensions: customer service and relations, labor relations, supply chain change, and redesigning of organizational culture. Agility, transparency, resilience, operational risk management, as well as evidence-based management, have been the buzz words coming to mind. New perspectives, attitudes and behaviors to running businesses should prove useful during and post the COVID-19 pandemic. At macro level, it is very likely that de-globalization may set in as governments and companies take radical safety measures to reduce hugely their dependency on foreign supplies and links.

Chapter 30 by Svetla T. Marinova concludes the book. The author proposes that the COVID-19 pandemic could be regarded as a critical juncture setting an abrupt process of change the consequences of which are still to unfold, but which is redefining the world in terms of political, economic, technological, sociological, and moral perceptions. The chapter makes a case for a better understanding of the new role of nation-state, international firms and strategic sectors, as well as access to resource and institutional capital in view of the upcoming regionalism around powerful pivots. The changes epitomized in the chapter would most probably have long-lasting effects on the global political and economic conjuncture and on international business as theory and practice. COVID-19 has shown the need for placing the life of people in the centre of international business with a thoughtful redefinition of its economic, psychological, sociological and environmental effects on individual, organization, ecosystem and societal levels.

Concluding Remarks

Due to the colossal unpredictability and enormous insecurity the world is currently experiencing, it is impossible to predict the impending consequences of the government policies adopted in relation to COVID-19 on every aspect of human life. The present variabilities in the economic structures of different countries, as well differences in size of population and economy, level of involvement in the worldwide production networks, and their place and role in trade networks, will inevitably lead to disparate challenges and consequences that will differ across nations. For example, countries with disproportionately high contribution of tourism to their gross domestic product (GDP) will suffer significant immediate and longer-term losses. Each country will have to find plausible ways to restructure its economy. Firms in global value chains (GVCs) will also be affected somewhat differently. Those that are orchestrators of GVCs will seek new suppliers and customers, while those that are locked in and appear to be in an unfavorable supplier country may lose their business. Countries with an economy over-relying on participation in GVCs are already being hurt and will further experience the consequences of re-shoring and back shoring. They will need to find substituting economic activities to secure economic viability. The huge task faced by national governments is to find relevant strategic responses not only on national, but also on industry and firm level. Developed economies, such as Australia, are not immune to the grave consequences of COVID-19, as the country has been seriously hit by a substantial decrease in revenues from numerous international business activities like international tourism as well as sales of commodities and foodstuff. While global cooperation for overcoming the economic consequences of the COVID-19 pandemic may be much desired, it is nation-states and de-globalization that are overriding the world scene.

References

Borga, M., Ibarlucea Flores, P., Sztajerowska, M., 2020. *Drivers of divestment decisions of multinational enterprises - A cross-country firm-level perspective*, OECD Working Papers on International Investment, OECD Publishing. https://doi.org/10.1787/5a376df4-en (accessed 30.06.20.).

OECD, 2020. Foreign direct investment flows in the time of COVID-19, May 4, 2020, https://www.oecd.org/coronavirus/policy-responses/foreign-direct-investment-flows-in-the-time-of-covid-19-a2fa20c4/ (accessed 02.06.20.).

The Economist, 2020. Covid-19 is here to stay. People will have to adapt, July 4, 2020. https://www.economist.com/leaders/2020/07/04/covid-19-is-here-to-stay-people-will-have-to-adapt?fsrc=newsletter&utm_campaign=the-economist-today&utm_medium=newsletter&utm_source=salesforce-marketing-cloud&utm_term=2020-07-03&utm_content=article-link-1 (accessed 04.07.20.).

UNCTAD, 2020. COVID-19 triggers marked decline in global trade, new data shows, May 13, 2020. https://unctad.org/en/pages/newsdetails.aspx?OriginalVersionID=2369 (accessed 04.07.20.).

Part I

General Outlook of COVID-19 and Its Overall Effects on International Business

2 Change of Era or Era of Changes

Jaqueline Pels

The COVID-19 pandemic has set on all alarms, globally. The world, as we knew it, was put on a hold. In April 2020, Fortune online report (Sherman, 2020) stated that "94 percent of the Fortune 1000 are seeing supply chain disruptions"; while one of McKinsey's most read articles by Tonby and Woetzel (2020) highlighted that one of the main changes is a move "from globalization to regionalization" and that "the pandemic has exposed the world's risky dependence on vulnerable nodes in global supply chains [...] We could see a massive restructuring as production and sourcing move closer to end users and companies localize or regionalize their supply chains".

In this chapter, I will reflect on the way we think, face the problem, analyze options and provide solutions. I will also discuss three COVID-19 and international business related issues. Firstly, our tendency to think in a dichotomous way and, consequently, create axis of tensions. Secondly, to clarify the differences between an Era of Changes and a Change of Era. Finally, explore if COVID-19 is the cause of a set of radical changes in international business operations.

The Role of Axis of Tensions in the Evolution of Humanity

After the pandemic, will trade continue on the road to globalization or will it shift to protectionism, regionalism and protected frontiers? If we do not take care of the health of the population, can there be an economy? If we do not take care of the economy, can there be healthy population? The manner in which we present the options to address the pandemic caused by COVID-19 shows that we have an inclination to exacerbate dichotomies and tensions. *Why do we tend to think in terms of opposite pairs and confrontations?*

To answer this question, let me give an example from another field. Many years ago, I coached a sports team in the junior category. Like To answer this question, let every team, we aimed to win, but, in Argentina, after the game was over, both contesting teams met, shared cocoa and developed camaraderie. At that moment, differences were put aside, the result of the match no longer mattered; love of sports and close association arose. We, trainers, knew that the spirit of this after-game get together was as (if not more) important as the game itself. So, why have an adversary instead of a friendly match? One conceivable answer is that confrontation made the sport, as a whole, better. It improved because everyone aimed at doing their best and it was an encouragement to create new moves; finally, a good match was, above all, beautiful, harmonious, and surprising. In short, in any human activity, tensions play the role of driving innovation and creativity with the objective to improve performance. However, there are also frustrating matches, when the teams aim to overrun the opponent at any rate and the effect is devastating. If we extrapolate this metaphor to the current COVID-19 context, it seems that we are in this trap: globalization or protectionism? Health or economy? *So, the question I would like to explore is, why have we exacerbated tensions in recent years?*

Before answering, it would be interesting to see whether there have always been tensions. It seems that tensions have been with us for a long time. In the twentieth century, between communism and capitalism; further back in time; in the sixteenth century – between Protestants and Catholics; further back still, in the twelveth century – between Guelph and Ghibellines; and the list goes on and on. So, if tensions have always accompanied us, it is worth asking if, in essence, they are all one and the same and have so much in common.

Again, the answer seems to be affirmative. To understand their similarity, it is necessary to shift focus from the specific topic and look at the structure of tensions. When we take this approach, tensions can be seen as socially constructed dichotomies manifesting the opposite ends of a continuum. It is easy to visualize the tension between communism and capitalism as extremes of an axis that represents alternative types of political and economic models: planned or free market. Similarly, the tension between Protestants and Catholics can be seen as opposing extremes of an axis that represents contrasting ways of seeing the dialogue with God as direct or mediated by the Pope. In our third example, the tension between Guelph and Ghibellines represents extremes of the axis of power – divine (represented by the pontiff) versus earthly (represented by the emperor of the Holy Roman Empire).

Why is this axis-thinking exercise helpful? Thinking in terms of axis (rather than the specific topic) implies adopting a higher level of abstraction and it enables us to look at the process. From this perspective, ultimately we will be able to analyze the current COVID-19 triggered tensions employing a different rationale. The examples will allow seeing that when the tension occurs within an axis, 'it is good'. It is functional to generate debate, dialogue and acts as a stimulus to development and change. Returning to the metaphor used at the beginning, it improves the match. Without this kind of tension, possibly, there would have been not much progress and we would still be 'living in caves'. More importantly, seeing tensions in terms of pairs of dialectical extremes on a given axis could help us understand the fact that when we have explored all possibilities offered by a certain axis (all the moves within a specific game), we need radical change, and this has been labeled as a Change of Era. These are moments or critical junctures when a new axis needs to emerge.

Our historical examples help illustrate this point. The debate within the Guelph-Ghibellines axis discussed who held power (pontiff or emperor) but it did not question the idea that power was centralized. It was the new Protestantism-Catholicism axis that introduced the idea of decentralization! Similarly, the Protestantism-Catholicism axis did not question the existence of God or the divine word (Bible was the revealed truth). It was modernity and the rise of scientific truth that introduced the possibility of Man as the source of knowledge! If we look at COVID-19 related questions, we know that protectionism restricts economic growth and, now, we have seen the limitations of unrestricted globalizations restricting national harmonious development. Trying to identify the right combination of both extremes does not seem to be the solution either. Our axis has been exhausted, we (humans) need to search for a change of axis; in other words, a Change of Era.

Change of Era or Era of Changes?

This sub-title seems a play of words, but it uncovers a profound distinction. We cannot address our COVID-19 concerns and question whether we understand or not the magnitude of the change and the different types of change. A good way to comprehend these differences is looking at history once again.

If we told a feudal lord that kings would not be the most important political figures, that his servants would have the right to vote (just like him), that agriculture would not be the pivot of the economy, that cities would house the majority of the population, that the horses would not be the means of transportation, that pigeons would no longer be the means of communications – surely, he would have laughed assuming we were jesters in his court. Today we are experiencing a Change of Era of similar significance. These are exceptional moments; humanity has gone through just a few of them. Living it is a privilege but, also, a mystery. So, what distinguishes an Era of Changes from a Change of Era? Drawing on Raskin et al. (2002), as well as long decades studying history and more specifically Eras of Changes, four common patterns emerge.

In an Era of Changes, first, transformations accelerate but they do not change the intrinsic logic of the time. Thus, throughout the twentieth century, cars have become technologically more sophisticated, but the means of transport did not change. Second, it is relatively easy to predict the impact of change; the introduction of Skype directly affected the incumbent business of long distance calls. Third, changes are compartmentalized, what happens in one field does not affect others. For instance, the rise of dotcoms affected industries but did not change the political, legal or economic system. Finally, due to its intense rhythm, we can see, in the course of a person's lifetime – his birth, development and maturity, for example, the emergence and development of television.

Alternatively, in a Change of Era, these four characteristics no longer hold. First, changes are radical. As we saw in the example of the medieval king and modernity, the nature of transportation was revolutionized, i.e., from horses to automobiles. Second, it is easy to 'see what no longer is', but, we do not know, what it shall be. Does it make sense to compare current changes with the industrial revolution of the nineteenth century? Is it necessary to change the education system (not just the delivery, but the content as well)? If we tried to define it, surely we would be right for a short period, but wrong about the final result. Let us return to the example of telecommunications – solutions that seemed new, such as Skype, were quickly replaced by others like WhatsApp and Zoom. Today, we *know* that there will be further developments in interpersonal communications. Third, processes are transversal. As all Eras of Change, the twentieth century can be characterized as focused on specialization. This has led to lose sight of the set of forces that are presented in interrelated mode, where a single change impacts and amplifies others. In the twenty-first century changes have been transcending technological innovations (e.g., the internet of things, artificial intelligence, blockchain), they involve changes in communication (e.g., social networks, fake news), in economics (e.g., the future of work, blockchain/bitcoin), in geopolitics (e.g., Brexit, the rise of China, the fall of the U.S.-Russia axis), in philosophy (e.g., post-modernity, the post-scientific truth), in the collective objectives (e.g., United Nations' sustainable development goals), in art (e.g., digital art), in education (e.g., continuous training), among numerous others. Finally, timespan is long; changes are measured in centuries. Though Raskin's report shows that periods have shortened and we have gone from cycles from 100,000 years to 10,000 years and to 1,000 years, and to approximately 100 years, they all exceed human lifetime. If we take the case of the French Revolution of 1789; usually, we place it as the end of totalitarian monarchies and as the historical fact that lays the foundations of modern democracy. However, in the 80 years following the French Revolution, France went through seven political regimes: three constitutional monarchies, two ephemeral republics and two empires (including the Napoleonic).

We can say that a Parisian surely felt confused: he knew that they had beheaded King Louis XVI, but were they moving forward ... backwards or perhaps sideways?

As a result of the nature of a Change of Era, we need to befriend ourselves with four situations we are, usually, uncomfortable with. We need to accept that a new overall logic will emerge. Recognize that we are in a state of 'being' that is a result of interrelationships, and trying to predict its final form is *just* an exercise. We need to beware that it is risky to think that 'we have arrived' because it creates false certainties. Given that processes are transversal, one should be aware that partial readings will probably be wrong. Moreover, from this perspective, technological advances, while very important, are only a symptom. Changes will occur at the legal, political, economic, social, and individual level. It is, then, important to take a holistic and systemic approach. Finally, the twentieth century taught us how to live with changes; now, we must learn to live with uncertainty and volatility; we have to develop patience.

Is COVID-19 the Cause of this Change of Era? Can We Predict the Effect It Will Have on International Business?

Let us, now, return to our original question. *Why in these last few years, and with the COVID-19 it becomes more evident, tensions are being exacerbated?* At this point, the answer is self-evident, we are witnessing the birth of a new axis. We can position the beginning of this process (though history will surely find another date/fact) with the fall of the Berlin Wall and Fukuyama's (1989) article the *End of History*, where he argues that with the dissolution of the Soviet Union, democracy and capitalism have won the Cold War. At the time, Fukuyama did not see that both extremes were interrelated; that they held a dialectical tension. A first signal of the changes in act, from an economic perspective, was the collapse of Lehman Brothers, in September 2008, and the subsequent rescue of the financial sector by governments. In the same year, also indicating winds of change, Nakamoto coined the bitcoin and more recently came Facebook's Libra announcement (Libra Association, 2020). It is interesting to note that these 'currencies' are not within the decision range of the central banks. From a political point of view, Brexit, as well as the elections in G20 countries of presidents who did not hold long-standing political carriers was also a signal that conventional political parties were reaching saturation point. Post modernism and the central role of discourse (over Truth) and in society the ecological versus growth movements can also be considered as part of the interrelated systemic trend. Zygmunt Bauman (2013) brilliantly synthesized all these trends into the expression of liquid modernity. For example, he signals, ephemeral social relationships (in antithesis of stable ones), the rise of narratives (above data), the speed at which companies change and/or disappear (the average life of a company in the twentieth century was 60 years; today it is 18 years – less than a third), decentralization (which involves loss of control), new forms of management such as lean management, fail fast, canvas (versus long-term planning or corporate structures), among others. Bauman, being a twentieth century philosopher sees 'what it no longer is'. Alternatively, we can see these characteristics as the characteristics of a transitional stage.

From this historic perspective, COVID-19 and its effects can be seen as a catalyzer, i.e., an accelerator of a process that has already been in motion; it is not a coincidence that Harari's books became best sellers. Without doubt, COVID-19 is making visible all the unaddressed tensions globalization/protectionism, human intelligence/artificial intelligence, governments/companies, virtual/real, ecology/growth and the like. As stated, we are in a process of 'being' so it is impossible to make predictions, however, it is very likely that the current situation will become the tipping point. The Cold War, twentieth century axis has reached its saturation in *all* its dimensions. A stage of experimentation is opening in front of us; which will be the new axis?

At this stage, we can address the last question, *how international business will be impacted by the Change of Era, in general, and COVID-19, in particular?* We argued that our rationale is still intrinsically tied to the past, that we are in the process of 'being' and that there is a risk in believing that partial solutions will become institutionalized. With this warning, we can explore a few questions:

- Modernity introduced the notion of nation-states and in the future will governments still define economic frontiers? What industries can exchange across geographies?
- The digital world taught us it is difficult to tax companies that do not have to be physically anchored. Will this expand to non-digital exchanges?
- The twentieth century defined international business in terms of globalization-protectionism. Could international business go beyond these options and, e.g., through 3D technology, allow in-situ production of supplies?
- Specifically, for Latin America, traditionally exporter of commodities and with several economies based on tourism- will communities, internationally, go back to growing their own food? Will experience (e.g., tourism) go virtual?
- Concern with ecology is growing and it seems in conflict with a growth model based on consumption; will ecology be a component in the nascent axis?
- Competition has been the mantra for innovation, growth and profit. Will cooperation, community focus, co-creation, collaborative intelligence, connectivity become the new mantras?

- International supply chains were designed to achieve optimization, minimize costs, reduce inventories, and drive up asset utilization, but they have removed buffers and flexibility to absorb disruptions. Will digital supply networks overcome these limitations?

In short, a Change of Era is not only finding a new axis, but it is a period between two peaks. For example, we described the characteristics of the heyday of the Middle Ages. The height of the Modern Age was characterized, among other things, by the dominance of science over religion, technological changes, and the emergence of nation states. The transit between one and the other was not easy; neither will it be for the current Change of Era.

It is natural to feel uncertainty and disorientation. However, if we are tied to the tensions represented by the axis of the past (globalization versus protectionism), we will not allow the future 'to become'. The challenge lies in innovation, in new moves, in games and patterns that have not been tried before. Why? Simply because the previous ones did not lead us to a world that is either just or harmonious. We may have to accept the exercise of exhausting the current axes, these labor pains, before we can enjoy a period of international prosperity.

References

Bauman, Z., 2013. *Liquid Modernity*. John Wiley & Sons, New York, NY.

Fukuyama, F., 1989. The end of history? *Natl Interest*. 6, 3–18.

Harari, Y.N., 2014. *Sapiens: A Brief History of Humankind*. Random House, New York, NY.

Harari, Y.N., 2016. *Homo Deus: A Brief History of Tomorrow*. Random House, New York, NY.

Libra Association, 2020. *White Paper v2.0*, https://libra.org/en-US/white-paper (accessed 20.04.20.).

Nakamoto, S., 2008. *Bitcoin: A Peer-to-Peer Cash System*, https://bitcoin.org/bitcoin.pdf, (accessed 20.04.20.).

Raskin, P., Banuri, T., Gallopín, G., Gutman, P., Hammond, A., Kates, R., Swart, R., 2002. *Great Transition: The Promise and Lure of the Times Ahead*. Global Scenario Group, Stockholm Environment Institute, Boston, pp. 1–111.

Sherman, E., 2020. *94% of the Fortune 1000 are seeing Coronavirus supply chain disruptions: report*. February 21, 2020, https://fortune.com/2020/02/21/fortune-1000-coronavirus-china-supply-chain-impact/ (accessed 20.03.20.).

Tonby, O., Woetzel, J., 2020. *Could the Next Normal Emerge from Asia?* McKinsey & Company, April 8, 2020, https://www.mckinsey.com/featured-insights/asia-pacific/could-the-next-normal-emerge-from-asia (accessed 22.04.20.).

3 COVID-19

Challenges to International Business

Marin A. Marinov

COVID-19 and Its Specifics Concerning International Business

In recent years, international business has been haunted by numerous processes including spreading trade protectionism, trade clashes between established trading nations, volatile prices of energy sources and commodities, severe economic uncertainties coming from the policy of the U.S. administration and the departure of the United Kingdom from the European Union, among numerous others. In isolation, every of these contests has been a challenging test for the world economy. The combined impact of them all have had altering effects on international business as performed by leading and other economies.

Appearing in an economic environment marred unconducive to further hyper-globalization, COVID-19 may well become a constantly increasing in its importance accelerator of the changes already in place and produce a crucial impact on the already stagnating international business. Consequently, COVID-19 pandemic represents an objective risk and an augmenter of already active destabilizers to international business. Thus, we have already witnessed a momentous influence on the way in which international business is executed decoupling global supply due to the responses of governments worldwide to this global pandemic. Yet, the overall impact of COVID-19 on international business is still to unfold. Meanwhile, international firms will have to put up with the risks of political, economic, social, and health related nature. In a number of cases, initially, the disturbance began in the supply side of the economy and within a short period of time it caused a huge fall of demand, which in effect represened a reversal of the usually demand-driven crunches (Guerrieri et al. 2020).

There are entire economic sectors and national economies that are at high risk due to the pandemic, *per se*, both the demand and supply have been already strongly affected by the coronavirus. Hence, as a result of the highly depressed activity, foreign direct investment flows could fall drastically.

Multinational firms originating from developed economies have vastly invested in robotics in the last 25 years or so. COVID-19 is intensifying this process, which has been boosted by a trend of encouraging and facilitating the reshoring and nearshoring of production from emerging economies, such as China, to advanced economies like Japan or the U.S.

COVID-19, Globalization, and Global Supply and Value Chains

The major consideration in organizing production across national borders has been efficiency driven and thus strongly based on the use of global value chains (GVCs) developed by relocation of production activities to low cost countries concerning production inputs and labor. Accordingly, the early 1990s marked the beginning of hyper-globalization. The efficiency driven location of factor inputs was supplemented by emerging disintegration and opening-up processes. Thus, the 1990s were marred by the disintegration of several integrative countries, i.e., the Soviet Union, Yugoslavia and Czechoslovakia and numerous wars in various geographic locations all over the world, namely in Africa (the first and second Congo wars), the Middle East (the Gulf war), the ex-Soviet Union (the first and second wars in Chechnya, the Tajikistan civil war), the Kargil war, the numerous Yugoslav wars, including the Kosovo war, the Ethiopian civil war, and many more national and regional military conflicts and genocides. Blemished by these, globalization nevertheless accelerated following a number of encouraging events, such as the fall of the Berlin Wall in 1989, China's entry in the World Trade Organization (WTO) in 2001, and the radical change in transportation of goods worldwide via mass containerization that led to enormous upsurge of GVCs. Consequently, in just seven years between year 2000 and the start of the last Global Crisis, world trade grew by more than 60 percent (Timmer et al. 2016). This period between 1990 and 2008 became known as the era of hyper-globalization.

With the Global Crisis of 2008–2009, the process of hyper-globalization was interrupted and the expansion of GVCs was bunged up. The reason why internationalized firms started comparing the cost savings from global supply chains with risk exposure from their implementation is that they found themselves exposed to more risk during and after this crisis as it caused an amassed shock. The current situation with COVID-19 is similar, but far more significant than the one following 2008–2009, as during the pandemic the global supply chains have appeared to be a lot more costly than previously thought as the risk of their failure has increased immensely. In a number of cases, the non-performing GVCs were additionally affected by higher tariffs due to trade disputes, an example of which are those caused by the bitter China-

U.S. trade war. Meanwhile, the situation triggered by COVID-19 has prompted the implementation of robots in production (Kilic and Marin, 2020), making it less expensive in developed economies. This was further promoted by the sharp decrease of interest rates to counteract high labor costs. Consequently, numerous international companies originating from developed economies have been re-shoring production back to their home country or near-shoring in less risky destinations, while simultaneously investing in mass application of robotics in production and logistics.

Meanwhile, many emerging economies have created their economic strategy up to 2008 by predominantly relying on participation in lower value added activities in GVCs. Consequently, countries and regions such as China, Turkey, as well as Central and Eastern European states were very successful in enticing supply chains to their economies. While some of these, such as China and Turkey, Hungary, Poland and the Czech Republic managed to increase their absorptive capacity, to learn and leverage resources and boost their manufacturing and innovation capacity, others such as Romania and Bulgaria have not succeeded in enhancing their innovation potential and thus remained mostly in the lower-value added activities of GVCs.

Major Challenges Set by COVID-19
to International Business

Throughout the COVID-19 crisis, reduced production and consumption have weakened the prospects to speedy recovery. Meanwhile, the exacerbating geopolitical crack between the U.S. and China, as well as numerous other rifts, have prompted self-perpetuating upsurges of deglobalization coupled with adverse supply shockwaves. Consequently, if these disturbances are not counteracted, production and distribution costs would increase and prices would go up. This in effect would cause growth to stagnate even further, whereas markets would shrink as consumption and personal income would fall.

The central banks, such as the Federal Bank in the U.S. or the European Central Bank (ECB) in the European Union as well as giant banking institutions as J.P. Morgan and Goldman Sachs, that were initial proponents of the optimistic V-shaped recovery, have now moved away from their predictions and joined the group arguing for a post-COVID-19 U-shaped recovery.

COVID-19 has caused a mammoth disruption of the economic structures worldwide damaging innumerable existing interconnections and interrelations on various levels, namely between employers and employees, international firms and their foreign suppliers, business debtors and creditors, sellers and buyers, to state just a few.

Employability rates have become highly volatile thus far. There have been transitory layoffs in March and April 2020 with some employees already returning to work in May and June 2020 on a limited scale to at least some sectors of the economy. Nevertheless, partial salary payment provided by governments worldwide, known under different names, e.g., furlough scheme, 60/40, etc., that have managed to ease the unemployment blow to individuals and firms, have been recognized as unsustainable in the long run.

Nevertheless, a huge number of people have become redundant as companies and economic sectors collapsed. For example, in the U.S. there are tens of millions of jobless people as there are a lot fewer working places available than those that existed in the country in February 2020 despite the US$500 billion in federal aid to small businesses who would retain employees under the Paycheck Protection Program.

In the past, globalization tendencies were disrupted by events in the human history subverting the processes of worldwide economic and financial integration on numerous occasions. Such critical events were the Great Depression, pandemics and the World Wars (James, 2001; King, 2017). They played a decisive role in disrupting globalization. This time, the COVID-19 pandemic has accelerated the fundamental departure from globalization (Altman, 2020) that has been trumpeted in the last few years. The point is that the coronavirus pandemic has hastened a process that started quite some time ago. They were caused by conclusive shifts in the government policies of world leading nations. For example, a radical shift in the U.S. policy was ignited by the election of Donald Trump as President of the U.S. in 2016 and it was followed by numerous actions significantly affecting the environment for international business in comparison to that before his election. By accelerating such processes, already in the making, COVID-19 would most likely exercise colossal long-term impact on many aspects of international business – such as trade and foreign direct investments, host country legitimation, location access to national strategic industries, to state just a few.

Even the largest advanced and emerging economies, such as the U.S. and China, are not immune to the impact of COVID-19. Smaller advanced economies, as well as emerging countries of medium or large economic significance, would find it extremely difficult to generate the necessary critical mass needed across key economic sectors. In many cases, the lack of natural resources would impede their attempts to deal with the harsh challenges of accelerating deglobalization. It seems that the time when the idea that a well-run small export oriented economy can flourish helped by globalization is over, as globalization is departing from international business with a speeding up velocity.

The Present and Future of International Business in Relation to COVID-19

COVID-19 has created a critical need for a change of mind in relation to the approaches to and effects of globalization and international business that created the continuous surge of the world economic growth, especially in Asia. Due to the reign of hyper-globalization, the economy as a whole thrived and expanded most of the time in recent years. A crucial critical juncture disrupting the process was in 2008 when decoupling of financial flows started. COVID-19 is the current critical juncture that accelerates the decoupling of people, while simultaneously undermining the bargaining power of multinational corporations (MNCs) vis-à-vis state institutions and limiting the so much desired by MNCs almost 'free' access to location resources worldwide. These processes have effectively strengthened the role of the nation state and consequently, increased the importance of self-sufficiency in strategic areas such as medical and food supplies.

Dealing successfully with the challenges caused by COVID-19 is associated with the creation of relevant firm-level and government strategies providing national economies with augmented internal sovereignty, risk reduction and resilience. These tasks have posed new critical requirements to the competence and capabilities of national institutions and challenged the mobilizing organizational aptitude of national governments.

It is convincingly likely that COVID-19 would last long and will have an everlasting aftermath. The economy of every country in the world, regardless of its size, level of advancement and significance, would continue to be dependent on health conditions in other countries as well as the policies of the national governments in relation to the pandemic. Thus, the coronavirus has to be fully overcome worldwide because until important international business country boundaries continue to be shut and threat stays real for new infection waves coming from abroad, international business will be negatively impacted. COVID-19 has already created serious unprecedented problems for advanced and emerging economies alike. Nations have been hit hard with an unprecedented impact on their economies, which makes recovery difficult to construct, even in the long term. There is high likelihood that demand would continuously diminish and poverty in the low-income economies might make it exceedingly challenging to sustain consumer market transactions at a level even distantly close to the one prior to COVID-19. Numerous countries have found it perplexingly difficult to resort to relevant fiscal and monetary responses that could allow them to lessen trade and industry impairment. This could be due to a number of unfavorable conditions such as, e.g., an extreme country debt that is in some cases bigger than the size of the whole economy, i.e. the case of the United Kingdom in 2020 (BBC, 2020); decoupling supply and value chains, a perfect example of which is China. Meanwhile, many countries have experienced continuously diminishing and unpredictable post-COVID-19 exports (WTO, 2020); national currency risks, and overdependence on excessive borrowing, to mention a few. Once again relevant government strategies and appropriate use of domestic resources and opportunities will prove crucial through the COVID-19 crisis and its aftershocks for presenting probable positive prospects in the post-pandemic recovery. There are success stories of how national governments have dealt with COVID-19 on the health and economic front, for instance, in South Korea and Japan, Singapore and China, Denmark and Finland. Even emerging economies such as India, Turkey and Russia have surprised with massive testing and hundreds of thousands of identified cases of COVID-19 and yet, managing to show an effective response to the health crisis with comparatively low mortality rates. Nevertheless, there have been some not so positive cases such as the one of the United Kingdom (The Economist, 2020b) or Sweden. The Swedish government has chosen a response to COVID-19 without the introduction of lockdown and social protection expecting to rip significant benefits from such a policy for the country's economy, but such an outcome has been questionable, to say the least (Milne, 2020).

There is a real danger that COVID-19 might cause economic and financial disasters in numerous countries across the world, consequently having an overall adverse effect on the world economy. Provided that such a course of events is avoided, it is certain that the recovery process for the world economy would require substantive effort and a longer than initially anticipated period of time.

It is beyond any doubt that the COVID-19 pandemic has seriously questioned globalization (The Economist, 2020a). The policies of protectionist governments, combined with the COVID-19 crisis, would create additional obstacles to the conduct of international business as it used to be in the era of hyper-globalization. The enduring effect of these obstacles and the accompanying transitionary costs are supposedly impossible to assess at present. Due to the deepening rifts between the leading world economies of the U.S. and China, as well as various tensions of different scale and scope all over the world, the desirable international cooperation, which might safeguard globalization, at least to some extent, is very unlikely, not to say completely imaginary. Moreover, the COVID-19 and post-COVID-19 world economy will be progressively more and more battered, with reduced size and greater instability, all of which will contribute to a deeper split between the efforts of various countries rather than the so much needed joint effort for overcoming the damages caused by the COVID-19 pandemic.

Analyzing carefully the divisions brought about by COVID-19 on every level of analysis, be it personal, racial, and nation-state, it is obvious that unfavorable divisions prior the pandemic have deteriorated and deepened throughout its progression. Thus, on a personal level a new gap has been forming between the people who were made redundant and those who preserved their jobs. The existing racial rift has amplified and demonstrated via the Black Lives Matter movement and the related historically embedded slavery issues. Originating in the U.S., triggered by the death of George Floyd, this movement has quickly spread worldwide as a reaction to social inequality and economic divisions. The splits between countries have augmented, for instance the trade war between China and the U.S. has worsened significantly during the COVID-19 pandemic, and the decision by Japan to re-shore and near-shore Japanese global supply and value chains, presently located in China, are only some of numerous other examples. The existing global supply and value chains flourishing during the period of hyper-globalization have started already crumbling due to nonperformance and distorted trust, increased uncertainty and risk, which have hard-pressed the process of de-globalization as never before.

The COVID-19 pandemic has increased the importance of the nation-state and accentuated its interests in defining foreign policies and its engagement as the key rule-setting institution for international business activities of domestic and foreign firms. National policies have come to the fore as the nation-state has claimed back its right to install international business rules for protecting national interests based on transactional bilateralism. This has continuously lessened the role and significance of international integrations of any nature and their corresponding institutions. The unfolding events stemming from COVID-19 have brought out the juxtaposing of state vs market and the role of the state and market mechanisms in defining the principles of international business transaction and the consequent firm-level decisions on investment, divestment, location (offshoring, reshoring, backshoring), knowledge transfer and sharing, and resource acquisition and usage. Before COVID-19, MNCs operated on a global field of their own with a much greater degree of freedom defined by market forces and bargaining power, albeit having to deal with legitimation and liability of foreignness. The latter was much more of a challenge for MNCs from emerging economies or those with liability of country-of-origin. The current crisis is forcing companies operating internationally to abide by state strategies enforcing new limitations. This is changing the defining mechanisms for firm strategy formulation as nation-state policies become more decisive than market mechanisms.

COVID-19 has initiated a huge debate about its impacts on the continuous changes and future reorganizing of the structure of global value and supply chains. A view point supported by numerous economic and international business specialists is that the pandemic would lead to re-nationalization via back-shoring of overseas located activities in existing global supply chains with the aim to secure increased resilience and risk reduction of firm operations minimizing their global exposure. Starting from such a perspective, international firms have to restructure radically their sourcing. To secure that such processes would take place on country level, it would be vital that national governments re-evaluate the definition, role and significance of their strategic industries, goods and services, as well as their international firms' exposure to foreign supplies, and facilitate the creation of new sourcing opportunities for local firms altogether. In the competition for new sourcing opportunities, there seem to be countries that will have to deal with substantial challenges. A coming up example is China as it has been a key big market and a prime destination target for efficiency seeking foreign direct investments by MNCs from developed economies. Another example is Turkey that de-spite its much smaller market and economy size is proactively seeking to partially replace China and in this effort, it has been strongly supported by the European Bank for Reconstruction and Development (Daily Sabah, 2020) for its future role as an important sourcing hub, especially for European MNCs.

During and post the coronavirus pandemic, international firms and their home governments need to figure out the best approach to ensure risk reduction and resilience that can guarantee pliability in the newly emerging conditions for international business. Concerning the strate-gies of international firms, there will be a need to reconsider the changing structures of businesses worldwide whereas national gov-ernments are forced to re-think their trade and investment policies that can best support the resilience of nation-states and international firms in the future.

References

Altman, S. A., 2020. Will Covid-19 have a lasting impact on globalization? *Harvard Business Review*, https://hbr.org/2020/05/will-covid-19-have-a-lasting-impact-on-globalization (accessed 02.06.20.).

BBC, 2020. UK debt now larger than size of whole economy. June 19, 2020. https://www.bbc.com/news/business-53104734 (accessed 23.06.20.).

Daily Sabah, 2020. Turkey among countries likely to benefit most from supply chain shift amid pandemic. June 18, 2020. https://www.dailysabah.com/business/economy/turkey-among-countries-likely-to-benefit-most-from-supply-chain-shift-amid-pandemic (accessed 22.06.20.).

Guerrieri, V., Lorenzoni, G., Straub, L., Werning, I., 2020. Macroeconomic implications of COVID-19: can negative supply shocks cause demand shortages? https://economics.mit.edu/files/19351 (accessed 10.05.20.).

James, H., 2001. *The End of Globalization: Lessons from the Great Depression.* Harvard University Press, Cambridge, MA and London.

Kilic, K., Marin, D., 2020. *A New Era of World Trade: Global Value Chains and Robots.* School of Management, Technische Universität München, Mimeo.

King, S. D., 2017. *Grave New World: The End of Globalization, the Return of History*. Yale University Press, New Haven, CT.

Milne, R., 2020. Sweden unlikely to feel economic benefit of no-lockdown approach. *Financial Times*, May 10, 2020, https://www.ft.com/content/93105160-dcb4–4721-9e58-a7b262cd4b6e (accessed 25.05.20.).

The Economist, 2020a. Has Covid-19 killed globalisation?. https://www.economist.com/leaders/2020/05/14/has-covid-19-killed-globalisation (accessed 31.05.20.).

The Economist, 2020b. The British state shows how not to respond to a pandemic. June 18, 2020. https://www.economist.com/britain/2020/06/18/the-british-state-shows-how-not-to-respond-to-a-pandemic?utm_campaign=coronavirus-special-edition&utm_medium=newsletter&utm_source=salesforce-marketing-cloud&utm_term=2020-06-20&utm_content=article-link-1 (accessed 22.06.20.).

Timmer, M. P., Los, B., Stehrer, R., de Vries, G. J., 2016. *An anatomy of the global trade slowdown based on the WIOD 2016*. No GD-162. GGDC Research Memorandum from Groningen Growth and Development Centre, University of Groningen.

WTO, 2020. *Trade set to plunge as COVID-19 pandemic upends global economy.* https://www.wto.org/english/news_e/pres20_e/pr855_e.htm (accessed 23.06.20.).

4 Digesting a Bitter Cherry on an Overbaked Cake

Renewing the Approach to Corporate Strategy in a Global Turmoil

Jean Paul Lemaire

Introduction

The health crisis, which has dramatically hit almost all countries since the end of 2019, triggered a series of consequences that have already profoundly affected economic growth and, more generally, socioeconomic activities (Nicola et al., 2020), as well as international trade and investment flows (Baker et al., 2020). The first projections made by the OECD, WTO[1] or the World Bank (Fernandes, 2020) point to far reaching immediate and long-term effects that are still difficult to grasp at both geopolitical and environmental levels, as well as for governments, companies, NGOs, and people (Baldwin and di Mauro, 2020a, 2020b), in the current profoundly shaken political, regulatory, socioeconomic and technological context.

It is difficult to consider the pandemic as an isolated phenomenon and to ignore other major incidents that have occurred over the past five years, e.g., Brexit (Tetlow and Stojanovic, 2018), sanctions and embargoes (Nuenkirch and Neumeier, 2015), the China–U.S. trade war (Bolt et al., 2019), the widespread rise of protectionism around the world (Bucifal, 2009), and the growing awareness of environmental degradation, whose interactions and cumulative effects cannot be ignored (Ghesquiere and Mahul, 2016).

The analyses that apply to COVID-19 as a 'disruptive' global phenomenon, insofar as almost all countries are concerned, refer to the financial crisis of 2008–2009 and beyond that, as many authors propose with even more hindsight, to the 1929 crisis (Coibion et al., 2020). This has given rise to comparisons and inspiring evolutionary scenarios (McKibbin et al., 2020), most often of a macroeconomic nature, without always placing them in the current corporate context, marked by series of upheavals, and without specifying their impact on sectors and organizations (Park et al., 2020).

The first effects of this health crisis already observed in organizations (companies, public actors, NGOs, etc.) operating across borders (Curran and

Eckhardt, 2018) show significant differences between them. Effects depend on organization size, mode of governance, sector of activity – with some sectors being hit hard (del Rio et al, 2020), while others being able to take temporary or permanent advantage of the circumstances (Okyere, 2020). Significant differences appear according to the geographical area in which they operate – some areas have appeared to be more 'resilient' than others (Hale et al., 2020; World Health Organization WHO, 2019), at least in terms of the victims of the virus. In fact, in the face of such a phenomenon from a more operational point of view, it is the internationalization process employed by organizations of different types – be they large or small, private or public, profit-making or not, yet operating abroad in a given sector in one or more geographical areas – that is at stake and is called into question.

In a short-, medium- and long-term perspective, given the extent of this questioning triggered by the health crisis, it is a matter for each organization to integrate this unforeseen – if not unpredictable – phenomenon and to consider it either as a temporary turbulence or as a paradigm shift (Gruszczynski, 2020).

Beyond that, each organization will have to consider recent events and processes, which have contributed to questioning the general dynamics of the evolution of trade and investment flows, as well as their impact on the organization's international sector/activity and corporate dynamics. Thus, organizations will have to engage in a thorough analysis of own decision-making, encompassing its design and implementation (Peng, 2004).

It is in this perspective that a 'funnel' approach can be followed at macro-, meso- and micro-level by applying the PREST model (Lemaire, 2000, 2013),[2] which is dynamic, sequential and three-dimensional, including political/regulatory, economic/social and technological aspects (see Figure 4.1).

The analysis should identify various *external pressures* (Hyatt and Berente, 2017) affecting the geographical-sectoral scope targeted by each organization under consideration (its 'area of reference'), taking into account the diversity and renewal of the contextual elements that determine their nature and intensity and which will have to be assessed positively or negatively. Next, the impact on the company activities should be assessed in the 'area of reference' that it is targeting or in which it is developing its business (Bechter et al., 2012), in order to translate them from external pressures into *geo-sectoral challenges* faced in response to the pressures emerging from the previous level of contextual analysis. This would allow an organization to determine the *strategic levers* through a targeted search of key success factors that can become a source of competitive advantage (Palmié et al., 2014). Consequently, these can be used to develop organizational priorities and strategic objectives in the short, medium and long term to guide organizational and functional implementation, according to the more or less severe contextual changes and issues highlighted at the two previous levels.

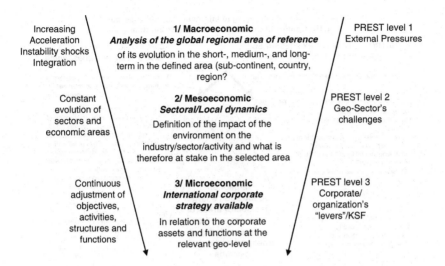

Figure 4.1 The 'Funnel' Approach: The Three Successive Steps of the PREST Model – Political-Regulatory; Economic and Social; Technological – A Three Layers Approach.

Source: The Author.

Step 1: New External Pressures

The new constraints imposed by COVID-19 have multiplied the pressure experienced by organizations participating in international trade and investment across various sectors and target countries, which have been impacted politically in terms of regulations (Ozili et al., 2020), as well as economically, socially and technologically (see Figure 4.2).

There are major contextual elements interacting with each other and affecting firms in all geographical areas, albeit with a specific local nuances.

A. At the Political-Regulatory Level

The Anglo-American-inspired liberal policies, initiated by Margaret Thatcher and Ronald Reagan at the end of the 1970s (Simmons et al., 2006) and adopted by a number of countries, albeit not really converging (Drezner, 2001), have been questioned regularly and especially during the 2008–2009 financial crisis. The liberal orientation with which many governments and companies in various countries and regions seemed to have reconnected with, or at least temporarily embraced, by 2014–2015 came under the pressure of geopolitical upheavals and were further terminated by the COVID-19 health crisis.

This neoliberal trend has been reflected in the progressive liberalization of trade through Preferential Trade agreements (Dür et al., 2014), both in

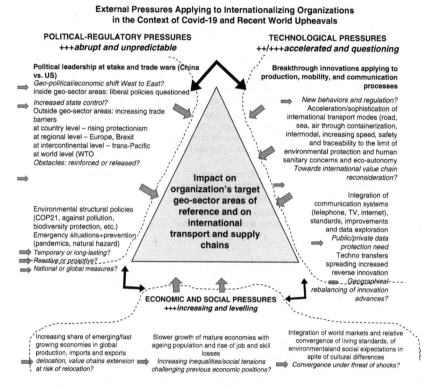

Figure 4.2 PREST Level 1.
Source: The Author.

terms of integration of regional economic zones (trans-Pacific agreements, for example) and of multiplication of trade agreements between zones (as between Canada and the European Union), or via the rapid integration of economic zones that had previously remained dormant, such as ASEAN, and via the reopening – at least briefly – of international trade in 'sensitive' zones, such as Iran (Ianchovichina et al., 2016). However, this trend has been called into question in Europe – by the Brexit vote in the United Kingdom (Sampson, 2017), and in the world – by the new embargo policy on Iran (Albarasneh et al., 2019) imposed by the U.S. on all Iranian economic partners, and even by the proliferation of trade barriers emanating from the American administration as a result – among others – of the economic war between China and the U.S. (Allison, 2017) or the stand-off between the U.S. and Russia. Similarly, American retaliatory measures have been launched against the European Union in a context of growing protectionism, often combined with populism (Inglehart and Norris, 2016).

The changes in the global geopolitical situation can largely explain this turnaround, e.g., China's aspirations for a new world leadership based on its spectacular rise in economic power that has not been interrupted for several decades (Pomeranz, 2009; Jacques, 2012); Russia's return to the forefront through targeted diplomatic and military moves supporting a multi-polar world (Larrabee, 2010); the difficulties – or even regression – of European construction (Milio et al., 2014; and the unpredictability of the decisions taken by the Trump's administration.

Following the Paris agreements on climate change (COP21) (Hourcade and Shukla, 2015), although they have been directly challenged by a number of major players, first and foremost by the U.S. (Zhang et al., 2017) and Brazil (Diele-Viegas and Rocha, 2019), and to a lesser extent by all the countries that have undertaken commitments (Roberts, 2016), but failed to deliver on them, the environmental constraints have also put pressure on trade and investment flows. From global warming to protection of biodiversity, they are gradually imposing, *volens nolens,* new constraints on organizations, thus impacting many activities and modes of logistics and transportation, in particular through CO_2 emission standards.

By largely paralyzing economic activities, such as international transportation, and decoupling international supply chains at an unprecedented speed and for an unprecedented period of time (Ivanov, 2020), the health crisis is intensifying these tensions. Growing steadily, tensions are growing at a variable level of intensity across sectors and countries. New directive government policies would appear, then, necessary, imposing more constraints for people and companies in order to cope with the likely consequences of the pandemics and prevent contamination. These directives are changing working conditions and productivity by putting in place new implicit or explicit imperatives to maintain employment, relocation, and reduction of external dependences (Fornaro et al., 2020).

B. At the Economic and Social levels

The economic and social external pressures have been also significant as the uncertainty caused by the health crisis has suddenly created major economic implications and shocks in most economies. These have affected international trade and investment flows, and transformed the global economic balance.

The emerging economies have shown great dynamism since the early 1990s. Their continuous progress, albeit interrupted by the COVID-19 pandemics, has managed to reduce poverty and ensure economic development (Sumner et al., 2020). Among them, there are countries that are fast growing, e.g., the BRICS (O'Neill, 2001); others that are 'followers', e.g., Middle Income Countries (such as Mexico, ASEAN countries and Nigeria). These are with a high growth rate, a relatively high level of industrialization and export of industrial products, openness to the outside world, a rising middle class and an expanding domestic market driven by demographic growth and lower poverty (Chan, 2018).

Conversely, mature economies are still relying on solid infrastructures, both tangible (transport, utilities, banking and financial system) and intangible (education system, legal framework, etc.). They are characterized by much lower growth rates. They experience ageing population and growing competition from emerging economies in terms of relocation of production and jobs, and loss of skills. These create economic downgrading and social tensions encouraging the rise of populism, which is particularly noticeable among the middle and working classes (Inglehart and Norris, 2016).

In all countries, the improved living standards and the development of communications have created higher expectation for better quality of life and higher consumption (De Mooij and Hofstede, 2002). Nevertheless, the sensitivities and differences of the populations in emerging and mature countries, despite cultural differences, still remain significant in terms of consumption, environmental (pollution) and social (child labor, for example). The latter have given rise to NGOs whose international initiatives are more and more acknowledged (Teegen et al., 2004).

Finally, the multi-governmental framework – at the global, regional (particularly European) and national levels (i.e., Central Banks) – has been strongly strengthened to limit the effects of the 2008–2009 financial crisis and to guarantee the relative stability of international relations. It is this framework that is now suffering from the repercussions of the U.S. administration's policy of withdrawal from international institutions and will be further affected by the consequences of Brexit (Goodell, 2020).

During the current period, COVID-19 has unraveled and exacerbated existing divisions. It has not led to a rapid harmonization of emergency policies (Hale et al., 2020), albeit certain convergence in pandemic rules and exchange of experience (Walt et al., 2004) has happened.

C. At the Technological Level

The pressures due to the production upheavals resulting from the multiplication of 'breakthrough innovations' (Miranda-Silva et al., 2016) to the accelerated processes of mobility and communication have considerably increased in many sectors, gradually eliciting reactions from various public and private stakeholders in terms of behavior and regulation. The acceleration and sophistication of transportation modes, processes and infrastructures – road, air and maritime (e.g., intermodal and containerization; Bontekoning et al., 2010), 2004) – have greatly facilitated the development of trade in volume and efficiency for goods (speed, safety and traceability). These have encouraged the international redeployment of supply chains and facilitated the global relocation of many industrial sectors. However, environmental protection (i.e., CO_2 emission standards and safety concerns (as abruptly generated by COVID-19) requires a reconsideration of these processes (Rondinella and Berryb, 2000) in terms of energy shifts (from hydrocarbon to electrical power), diffusion of new limitations (i.e., political and regulatory pressures) and of new consumer expectations (i.e., economic and social pressures). Similarly, the integration of communication systems (telephone, television and internet) and increase in the speed and volume of data flows and transmission frameworks have greatly contributed to the dissemination and massive exploitation of data. These have generated measures limiting or even prohibiting the activities of global firms as masters of such transformations (Schmieg, 2019; Caglio and Guillou, 2018). The spectacular advances in transportation and communication modes have considerably facilitated the spread of innovation through numerous technology transfer agreements (Di Benedetto et al., 2003). This happened in an attempt to approach promising markets in fast-growing economies and to move the bulk of production in many industrial sectors to low labor-cost economies in order to serve demand all over the world (Liu, 2008). Meanwhile, technology transfers have favored a spectacular emergence of newcomer companies based on innovation and R&D adoption (Kojima, 2000). Consequently, we have witnessed a spectacular upturn in most economic sectors that were previously dominated by Western firms only (Wang, 2007) and an emergence of new global leaders from Japan, South Korea, China, India, Russia, and Brazil.

The financial crisis of 2008 already demonstrated the importance of these technological changes in transmitting such phenomena and spreading their impact in most economic areas. COVID-19 has accelerated these changes creating an acute awareness of these transformations in governance, politics, economics and social processes that have touched the life of people, more directly in the health services sector (Park et al., 2020) with the example of available equipment (respirators) and consumables (masks, hydro-alcoholic gel), and indirectly, through the unbundling and disruptions of global supply chains exposing their vulnerabilities.

The awareness of a growing industrial and technological dependence also seems to have made the concern for self-sufficiency more acute. It is reflected across many economic sectors by calls for preservation of jobs and environmental protection. These calls would certainly lead to 'dislocations' of activities in global value chains (Rincón-Aznar, 2020), as considered below.

Step 2: Geo-Sectoral Challenges to Organizations

As a result of the technological, political, regulatory, economic and so-cial pressures, organizations must consider the geo-sectoral issues they are confronted with, which can profoundly transform them. These are first, in terms of the necessary geo-sectoral redeployment of their activ-ities; second, in terms of the adaptation of their products and production processes – if not of their business model; and, third, in terms of ad-justment to the competitive environment in which they operate from their country-of-origin toward their area(s) (i.e., countries and regions) of expansion abroad (see Figure 4.3).

Due to COVID-19, but also because of the various other types of factors and phenomena that have affected trade and investment flows in recent years, the geo-sectoral challenges, including redeployment, adaptation and competition, differ significantly from the ones experi-enced in previous periods. The current external pressures apply to and affect each area of organizational activities.

The Geo-Sectoral Challenges Applying to Internationalizing Organizations in the Context of Covid-19 and Recent World Upheavals (2015-2020)

3. *INTERNATIONAL COMPETITION CHALLENGES*
- -Identifying the appropriate competitive advantages to master in order to cope with the external pressures
- Assessing all actors' respective competitive advantages evolution in the areas of reference's context
- Positioning of various actors/group of actors on the basis of their assets and liabilities with respect to each other.

POLITICAL-REGULATORY PRESSURES

Organization's geo-sector area of reference

TECHNOLOGICAL PRESSURES

1. *GEO-SECTOR DEVELOPMENT CHALLENGES*
- -Reconsidering the organization's geographic spread related to security issues, local/national regulations or external dependence reduction
- Adaptive or comprehensive local/delocated activity portfolio review
- Adjusting of existing local structures (acquisition or disposal of local assets, legal status change, taking into account new opportunities and threats

1. *OFFER ADAPTATION CHALLENGE*
- -Systemic scanning of weak and strong signals coming from the environment to inspire reactive/proactive corporate measures
- Assessing the existing offer related to local needs to consider possible product range extension/reduction
- Involving in the offer the community in related functional issues in a CSR perspective (sourcing, recruitment, sponsoring).

ECONOMIC AND SOCIAL PRESSURES

Figure 4.3 PREST Level 2.
Source: The Author.

A. The Challenge of Geographic and Sectoral Redeployment

First of all, this challenge relates to any organization and its competitors operating in a given geographic area or economic sector and affects their strategic location choices for sales and/or production, as well as for various parts of their international supply chains. This challenge takes on particular importance when changes in the environment are particularly brutal and the resulting pressures are more intense.

Geographic redeployment may consist of a pure and simple withdrawal from a particular geographical or business area, e.g., European companies' withdrawal from Iran as a consequence of the Iranian embargo adopted under American pressure. It may also be a reorganization of the geographic deployment of a network of subsidiaries related to labor costs considerations (Fish and Zschoche, 2012), or anticipating or following a major political shift such as Brexit, for example (Sampson, 2017), or a change in the status of the establishments (to comply with new regulatory requirements). More broadly, by enlarging the strategic perspective beyond the reference area under consideration, it may involve restructuring the supply and production chain across different locations and calling into question previously favored and implemented relocations (Doh, 2005, Buckley and Ghauri, 2004).

Sectoral redeployment may call into question the nature of the activities located there by considering necessary diversification (Kumar et al., 2012) to balance risks associated with the uncertainties in the local market. For example, this may happen by a radical change of activity that follows a decision to withdraw from a market for economic or regulatory reasons (Sali and Tallman, 2011). Another example is the possibility of restructuring through the acquisition of new assets or the disposal of existing non-priority or overexposed assets.

In the context of COVID-19, a variety of issues have already been discussed and a number of scenarios (McKibbin et al., 2020) include the possibility of restructuring internationalized supply and production chains, precisely in sectors that are considered strategic and with a view of limiting or eliminating external dependence (Doh, 2005). Moreover, the dramatic deterioration of employment in many countries, as well as the renewed need for national autonomy, raises questions about the need to relocate all or part of activities along the supply and production chains. The question of relocating R&D to the country of origin – in the event that it had previously moved across borders – has been also raised (Ivanov, 2020).

B. The Challenge of Adapting the Organization's Offer

This challenge leads to the question of what the organization is likely either to standardize or adapt in its market positioning, geographic markets, environment and processes (Theodosiou and Leonidou, 2003). Here, organizations have to take into account the external pressures and needs of stakeholders such as consumers, corporate customers, domestic and foreign suppliers, local authorities, NGOs, local communities, and the society, at large.

The adaptation challenge concerns the products, services and corporate functions that are involved in the area of reference under consideration, including marketing (Ryans et al., 2003), human resources (Dickmann and Müller-Camen, 2006) or finance, supply, recruitment and, more generally, corporate social responsibility (He et al., 2020). This will make organizations adapt their offer mostly in a reactive manner, particularly under the conditions of disruptive events such as a health crisis or a natural disaster. The experience of COVID-19 shows, however, that it can also encourage more proactive responses where new offers or initiatives are introduced accounting for environmental, market and sector specificity.

In fact, two approaches to decisions can be identified, based on the analysis of the evolution of external pressures:

- One from strong signals indicating more or less sudden and unexpected rupture phenomena (Hubbard, 2020), calling for greater reactivity – appearance of major health risks (Ezzati et al., 2004), sudden changes in regulations or economic difficulties, etc. – the COVID-19 pandemic being an extreme case due to its ruthlessness and unpredictability;

- The other, based on weaker signals (Kaivo-oja, 2012), calling for pro-activity and relying on clusters of clues, or on a historical analysis of past incidents, or on systematically updated data, to anticipate recurring but occasional risks or arising new risks, e.g., from the deterioration of the physical or social environment of an organization in its geo-sectoral area.

The health crisis, but, even more so, the financial crisis and the various challenges to trade and investment flows over the last five years, underline the importance of taking into account and anticipating the need for fundamental structural, and process adjustments.

C. *The Competition Challenge*

This challenge questions the positioning shifts of the organization by determining how it can take into account the new threats and consequent risks, as well as opportunities that emerge (Rapaccini et al., 2020). This leads to identifying how each organization sees its position strengthened or weakened by the evolving external pressures (Liu, 2013) and their national or foreign embeddedness. Following this, traditional or renewed competitive advantages can be identified, according to each organization's resources and skills that should be compared with those of its competitors and applicable in the new context (Schlegelmilch, 2020).

COVID-19 has hit whole sectors, particularly hard hit are those directly exposed to the conditions of lockdown imposed across countries, such as tourism, entertainment, hotels and restaurants, retailers, as well as the automotive industry, aeronautics, etc. Many of them are of a small size and with limited financial resources. Most big organizations, except for the airlines, seem to be more resilient (Bonadio et al., 2020). The situation reminds of the financial crisis of 2008–2009 when organizations that had the least need to resort to banking institution were only affected for a short while (Kildienė et al., 2011). Some organizations and whole sectors have benefited from the pandemics and from the measures that accompanied it, e.g., the health sector or, to a lesser extent, the agri-food sector by benefiting from increased demand.

However, organizations operating in sectors that have benefited from the COVID-19 or that are financially stronger than their competitors have had to search for new assets or new 'levers' in order to overcome the newly emerged handicaps and the uncertainties that have accompanied the pandemics.

Step 3: Searching for Appropriate Competitive 'Levers'

Facing the challenges created by the succession of crises and rising barriers to international trade and investment, each organization, notwithstanding its economic model and the unique character of its domestic and international development potential, must, therefore, reconsider all or part of its internationalization strategy and its implementation (Rapaccini et al., 2020; see Figure 4.4).

Organizations have to mobilize various 'levers' (Palmié et al., 2014) or converging sets of key success factors complying with the prospects created by the previous steps in this three-step-approach. It would make it possible to cope with (or take advantage of) the dynamics of the new context. To do this, – if well identified, exploited and combined – the three levers to be considered – innovation, organization and profitability – can provide each organization with distinctive competitive advantages to cope with emergencies such as the current COVID-19 pandemics (Craven et al., 2020).

A. Innovation Lever

The innovation lever opens up the widest possible field to explore as it concerns products and/or services (Lehrer and Behnam, 2009), as well as their production, distribution and dissemination (Franko, 1989;

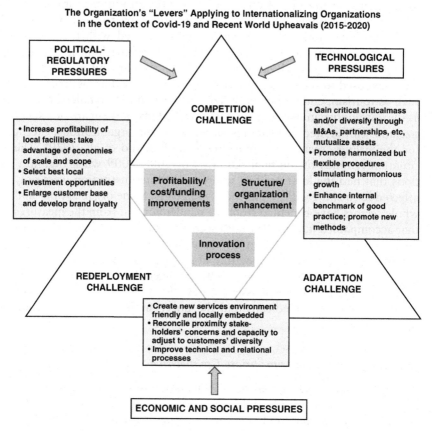

Figure 4.4 PREST Level 3.
Source: The Author.

Patel et al., 2013). It can lead to a total or partial renewal of the product/ service offer or to a change in the business model, especially if there is a radical change in the sector and markets. This has become evident in the past by certain major companies confronted by disruptive crises, innovations and/or major strategic errors, as it has happened in the mobile phone sector (Zaidi et al., 2019).

In this respect, technological changes can provide rapid responses to new challenges. Examples are innovations in the use of the internet and new collective communication solutions, as the ones in higher education during COVID-19 lockdowns (Schlegelmilch, 2020) that have offered traditional services in an innovative way. In the production and/or distribution of goods and services, innovations can also provide answers to the geo-sectoral challenges worsened by crises. For example, innovations can broaden the scope for distribution of products or services through creation of new distribution methods that go beyond the existing geographic domestic or foreign markets (Knowles et al., 2020). Innovation could also help organizations to address urgent global social and environmental challenges (He et al., 2020).

In this way, innovation can be combined with the other levers, i.e., organization and profitability, to improve the organization's corporate performance (Miranda-Silva et al., 2016).

B. *Organizational Lever*

This lever covers a wide range of solutions in response to challenges (Haas, 1990) generated by crises and obstacles to international trade and investment flows:

– Firstly, the organization lever can include major strategic structural moves (mergers and acquisitions, partnerships, changes in governance arrangements, etc.), in order to increase an organization's critical mass, improve its financial strength, optimize its supply chain (Steinle and Schiele, 2008), diversify its portfolio of activities and/or better balance its geographical market exposure;

– Secondly, it can also focus on the methods for implementing strategic decisions and respectively adjusting the organizational architecture (Palmié et al., 2014) by providing flexibility and agility. The latter are needed so that an organization can quickly adapt to a sudden and/or a more evolutionary disruption in the context (Volberda and Lewin, 2003) – by reconsidering its internal structure (e.g., through decentralization) and by more effectively organizing and implementing each of its functions – in order to better mobilize teams, especially if they are geographically dispersed (Lee and Wu, 2010), or CSR, to better interact with other organizations.

C. *Profitability Lever*

This lever includes optimization of both costs and revenues, although in Europe, the support measures of national and supra-national authorities tend to limit the negative consequences of crises on employment and business failures (Pomerleano, 2007), especially since the financial crisis of 2008–2009.

On the cost side, these include measures to discover productivity reserves (Castellani et al., 2016). These include, but are not limited to, finding a better balance between face-to-face and remote work (teleworking) that aims at improving employees' safety and reducing costs of travel and distribution. Such responses to the constraints resulting from a crisis such as COVID-19 have seemed to be fruitful, although it is not possible yet to assess their quality over the long term (Belzunegui-Eraso et al., 2020).

On the revenue side, the use of automated and secure payment methods, centralized cash management and the search for added-value linked to each product/service offer (Lu and Beamish, 2017) can improve profitability and provide an organization with the necessary resources to deal with the uncertainties generated by the crisis and secure the future development of the organization.

Conclusion

COVID-19 has confronted organization with disruptive changes in the global environment within their specific 'area(s) of reference' and these changes require changes in the strategic approaches used in domestic and foreign markets in terms of scope, scale and product/service offers.

Such changes are only possible if organizations engage in analysis of environmental transformations comprising strong and weak signals that herald phenomena of unequalled amplitude and that happen in a world where the time it takes for their effects to spread is hardly noticeable. The proposed approach tends to identify the political, regulatory, economic, social and technological 'pressures' that are exerted on various economic sectors and the organizations constituting them, in a single or multiple geographical area(s).

The identification of external pressures, then, allows organizational leaders to deduce the major 'challenges', i.e., redeployment, adaptation and competition, confronted by each organization is in the targeted geo-sectoral area(s) in order to better define the nature and scope of the questions it has to answer, and more accurately adjust its strategic orientations and their implementation.

This progressive methodological process, beyond the 'pressures' and 'challenges', enables organizations to select appropriate 'levers', i.e., innovation, organization and profitability, and any specific combination of these. The redefinition of the organization's international strategic orientations, as well as their implementation will logically stem from the choice of levers and the balance between re-active and pro-active responses to ensure effective and efficient ways to cope with the changes caused by crises and minimize risks.

Such an approach is only worthwhile, considering the scale of globalized trade and investment flows, if it is regularly and rigorously monitored and seeking to combine and integrate the diversity of signals emanating from the environment, in order to transfer them from analysis to decisions and actions.

The lessons of the COVID-19 pandemic, which are still far from being understood in all their implications by political, economic and social actors, call for recognizing the fast speed and extent of change and the need for assessing and pro-actively mitigating the new risks that emerge by exercising vigilance, developing an intelligence system and adequate response scenarios.

The 2008–2009 financial crisis and the newly emerging obstacles to trade and investment, created by countries that have long been promoters of an assertive liberalism, have not only triggered but also magnified the instability and uncertainty in the global world. COVID-19 has just accelerated the speed of change, its scope and extent as to call for a new approach to national, regional, global and organizational responses.

Notes

1 WTO, "Services Trade Barometer", 19 May 2020: « The volume of world merchandise trade is likely to fall precipitously in the first half of 2020 as the COVID-19 pandemic disrupts the global economy, according to the WTO Goods Trade Barometer released on 20 May. The index currently stands at 87.6, far below the baseline value of 100, suggesting a sharp contraction in world trade extending into the second quarter. This is the lowest value on record since the indicator was launched in July 2016 ». https://www.wto.org/english/news_e/news20_e/wtoi_19may20_e.htm.
2 Sketched for the banking sector in the book co-authored by the author and P.B. Ruffini, "*Vers l'Europe Bancaire*" (Dunod, Paris, 1993), then in his doctoral thesis, "*Stratégies bancaires internationales*", Paris 1 Panthéon Sorbonne, 1995, generalized to all sectors for the 2000 IMP conference, and improved in successive editions of his textbook *Stratégies d'internationalisation: Nouveaux enjeux d'ouverture des organisations, des activités et des territoires*, Management sup, Paris, Dunod, 3rd ed, 2013.

References

Allison, G., 2017. *Destined for War, Can America and China escape the Thucydides's Trap?* Houghton Mifflin Harcourt, New York, NY.

Fernandez, I. A., Garcia, F. P., Tortosa-Ausina, E., 2007. *Measuring International Integration, Theory and Evidence of Globalization.* Fundacion BBVA, https://www.fbbva.es/wp-content/uploads/2017/05/dat/DT_2007_24.pdf. (Accessed on May 26, 2020).

Baker, S. R., Bloom, N., Davis, S. J., Terry, S. J., 2020. COVID-induced economic uncertainty, *NBER Working Paper* No. 26983, April, NBER Program (s): Economic Fluctuations and Growth.

Baldwin, R., di Mauro, B. W., (Eds.), 2020a. *Economics in the Time of COVID-19.* CEPR Press, London.

Baldwin, R., di Mauro, B. W., (Eds.), 2020b. *Mitigating the COVID Economic Crisis: Act Fast and Do Whatever It Takes.* CEPR Press, London.

Bechter, B., Brandl, B., Meardi, G., 2012. Sectors or countries? Typologies and levels of analysis in comparative industrial relations. *Eur. J. Ind. Relat., 18*(3), htts://doi.org/10.1177/0959680112452691. (Accessed on June 20, 2020).

Belzunegui-Eraso, A., Erro-Garcés, A., 2020. Teleworking in the context of the Covid-19 crisis. *Sustainability* 12(9), 36–62.

Bolt, W., Mavromatis, K., van Wijnbergen, S., 2019. *The global macroeconomics of a trade war: The Eagle Model on the US-China trade conflict. CEPR Discussion Paper* No. DP13495. January. https://ssrn.com/abstract= 3328506. (Accessed on May 23, 2020).

Bonadio, B., Huo, Z., Levchenko, A.A., Pandalai-Nayar, N., 2020. *Global supply chains in the pandemic. NBER Working Paper* No. 27224, May https://www.nber.org/papers/w27224 (Accessed on June 15, 2020).

Bontekoning, Y. M., Macharis, C., Trip, J. J., 2004. Is a new applied transportation research field emerging?–A review of intermodal rail-truck freight transport literature. *Transportation Research Part A Policy and Practice* 34(1), 1–34.

Bucifal, S., 2009. *Challenges to the Multilateral Trading System: The Rising Trade Protectionism amid the Global Economic Recession.* October. https://ssrn.com/ abstract=1494805 or http://dx.doi.org/10.2139/ssrn.1494805 (Accessed on May 24, 2020).

Buckley, P. J., Ghauri, P., 2004. Globalization, economic geography, and the strategy of multinational enterprises. *J. Int. Bus. Stud.* 35(2), 81–98.

Caglio, C., Guillou, S., 2018. L'Europe numérique. *Entre singularités, faiblesses et promesses, Rev. de. l'OFCE 4*, 11–36.

Castellani, D., Piva, M., Schubert, T., Vivarelli, M., 2016. The *Productivity Impact of R&D Investment: A Comparison between the EU and the US. IZA Discussion Paper* No. 9937. https://ssrn.com/abstract=2786021 (Accessed on May 26, 2020).

Chan, S., 2018. *East Asian Dynamism, Growth, Order and Security in the Pacific Region.* Second ed. Routledge, New York, NY.

Coibion, O., Gorodnichenko, Y., Weber, M., 2020. Labor markets during the COVID-19 crisis: A preliminary view. *NBER Working Paper* No. 27017, April.

Craven, M., Liu, L., Mysore, M., Wilson, M., 2020. *Risk practice COVID-19: Implications for business.* McKinsey, March.

Curran, L., Eckhardt, J., 2018. Strategic responses of trade-dependent firms to rising trade protectionism. In Akcaoglu, E., Bolsinger, H.J. and Wehner, R. (Eds.) *Managing International Political Risk: Arising Challenges for Multinationals in a Changing World. Würzburg International Business Forum, International Business Conference proceedings.*

De Mooij, M., Hofstede, G., 2002. Convergence and divergence in consumer behavior: implications for international retailing. *J. Retail.* 78(1), 61–69.

Del Rio-Chanona, R. M., Mealy, P., Pichler, A., Lafond, F., Farmer, D., 2020. *Supply and demand shocks in the COVID-19 pandemic: An industry and occupation perspective, arXiv. Cornell University,* 14 April, 1–38.

Di Benedetto, C. A., Calantone, R. J., Zhang, C., 2003. International technology transfer: Model and exploratory study in the People's Republic of China. *Int. Mark. Rev.* 20(4), 446–462.

Dickmann, M., Müller-Camen, M., 2006. A typology of international human resource management strategies and processes, *The. Int. J. Hum. Resour. Manag.* 17(4), 580–601.

Diele-Viegas, L. M., Rocha, C. F. D., 2019. Climate change and Brazil's political perspectives are threatening the Amazon. *Science*, June 14, https://science.sciencemag.org/content/climate-change-and-brazil's-political-perspectives-are-threatening-amazon (Accessed on May 22, 2020).

Doh, J. P., 2005. Offshore outsourcing: implications for international business and strategic management theory and practice. *J. Manag. Stud.* 42(3), 695–704.

Drezner, D. W., 2001. Globalization and policy convergence. *Int. Stud. Rev.* 3(1), 53–78.

Dür, A., Baccini, L., Elsig, M., 2014. The design of international trade agreements: introducing a new dataset. *Rev. Int. Organanizations 9*, 353–375.

Ezzati, M., Lopez, A.D., Rodgers, A., Murray, C.J.L., (Eds). 2004. *Comparative Quantification of Health Risks, Global and Regional Burden of Disease Attributable to Selected Major Risk Factors*, Vol. 1. World Health Organization, Geneva.

Fernandes, N., 2020. *Economic Effects of Coronavirus Outbreak (COVID-19) on the World Economy*, March 22, http://dx.doi.org/10.2139/ssrn.3557504 (Accesed on May 22, 2020).

Fish, J. H., Zschoche, M., 2012. The effect of operational flexibility on decisions to withdraw from foreign production locations. *Int. Bus. Rev.* 21(5), 806–816.

Fornaro, L., Wolf, M., 2020. Covid-19 Coronavirus and Macroeconomic Policy, *CEPR Discussion Paper* No. DP14529.

Franko, L., 1989. Global corporate competition: Who's winning, who's losing, and the R&D factor as one reason why. *Strategic Manag. J.* 10(5), 449–474.

Gersbach, H., Schmutzler, A., 2011. Foreign direct investment and R&D-offshoring. *Oxf. Econ. Pap.* 63(1), 134–157.

Ghesquiere, F., Mahul, O. 2016. *Financial Protection of the State Against Natural Disasters: A Primer, Working Paper No. 5429, World Bank Policy Research*, 20 Apr.

Goodell, J. W., Jul. 2020. COVID-19 and finance: agendas for future research *Finance Res. Lett.*, 35. p. 101512.

Guerrieri, V., Lorenzoni, G., Straub, L., Werning, I., 2020. Macroeconomic Implications of COVID-19: Can Negative Supply Shocks Cause Demand Shortages? *NBER Working Paper* No. 26918, April.

Gruszczynski, L., 2020. The COVID-19 pandemic and international trade: temporary turbulence or paradigm shift?. *Eur. J. Risk Regul. 11*(Special Issue 2), 337–342.

Haas, E.B., 1990. *When Knowledge is Power: Three Models of Change in International Organizations*. University of California Press, Berkeley, Los Angeles, Oxford.

Hale, T., Angrist, N., Kira, B., Petherick, A., Phillips, T., Webster, S. 2020. Variation in government responses to COVID-19 *Blavatnik School of Government Working Paper*. May 25. www.bsg.ox.ac.uk/covidtracker (Accessed on June 10, 2020).

He, H., Harris, L., 2020. The impact of Covid-19 pandemic on corporate social responsibility and marketing philosophy. *J. Bus. Res. 116*(August), 176–182.

Hourcade, J., Shukla, P., 2015. Cancun's paradigm shift and COP21: to go beyond rhetoric. *Int. Environ. Agreem. 15*(November), 343–351.

Hubbard, D. W., 2020. *The Failure of Risk Management, Why It's Broken and How to Fix It* (2nd ed.). John Wiley & Sons, New York, NY.

Hyatt, D. G., Berente, N., 2017. Substantive or symbolic environmental strategies? Effects of external and internal normative stakeholder pressures. *Business, Strategy Environ.* 26(8), 1212–1234.

Ianchovichina, E., Devarajan, S., Lakatos, C. 2016. Lifting economic sanctions on iran: global effects and strategic responses, *World Bank Policy Research Working Papers.* February. https://doi.org/10.1596/1813-9450-7549 (Accessed on May 15, 2020.)

Inglehart, R. F., Norris, P., 2016. Trump, Brexit, and the rise of populism: economic have-nots and cultural backlash, *HKS Working Paper* No. RWP16-026.

Ivanov, D., Apr. 2020. Predicting the impacts of epidemic outbreaks on global supply chains: A simulation-based analysis on the coronavirus outbreak (COVID-19/SARS-CoV-2), case . *Transp. Res. Part E Logist. Transp. Rev.* 136, 101922. https://doi.org/10.1016/j.tre.2020.101922.

Jacques, M., 2012. *When China Rules the World: The End of the Western World and the Birth of a New Global Order.* Penguin Books, London.

Kaivo-oja, J., 2012. Weak signals analysis, knowledge management theory and systemic socio-cultural transitions. *Futures* 44(3), 206–217.

Kildienė, S., Kaklauskas, A., Zavadskas, E. K., 2011. COPRAS based comparative analysis of the European country management capabilities within the construction sector in the time of crisis. *J. Bus. Econ. Manag.* 12(2), 417–434.

Kojima, K., 2000. The "flying geese" model of Asian economic development: origin, theoretical extensions, and regional policy implications. *J. Asian Econ.* 11(4), 375–401.

Kumar, V., Gaur, A. S., Pattnaik, C., 2012. Product diversification and international expansion of business groups. Evidence from India. *Manag. Int. Rev.* 52(2), 175–192.

Knowles, J., Ettenson, R., Lynch, P., and Dollens, J., 2020. Growth oppurtunities for bands during the COVID-19 crisis. *MIT Sloan Manag. Rev.* 61(4), 2–6.

Larrabee, F. S., 2010. Russia, Ukraine and Central Europe: The return of Geopolitics. *J. Int. Aff.* 63(2), Spring/Summer:, 33–52.

Lee, C. Y., Wu, F.C., 2010. Factors affecting knowledge transfer and absorptive capacity in multinational corporations. *J. Int. Manag. Stud.* 5(2), 119–126.

Lehrer, M., Behnam, M., 2009. Modularity vs programmability in design of international products: beyond the standardization–adaptation tradeoff? *Eur. Manag. J.* 27(4), 281–292.

Lemaire, J. P., 2000. From an international and sector approach to a corporate decision formulation: The PREST model, *16th IMP conference.* Bath, UK.

Lemaire, J. P., 2013. *Stratégies d'internationalisation, Nouveaux enjeux d'ouverture des organisations, des activités et des territoires.* Third edition. Dunod, Paris.

Liu, Y., 2013. Sustainable competitive advantage in turbulent business environments. *Int. J. Prod. Res.* 51(10), 2821–2841.

Liu, Z., 2008. Foreign direct investment and technology spillovers: theory and evidence. *J. Dev. Econ.* 85(1–2), 176–193.

Lu, J. W., Beamish, P.W., 2017. International diversification and firm performance: the S-curve hypothesis. *Acad. Manag. J. 47*(4), 598–609.

McKibbin, W. J., Fernando, R. 2020. The global macroeconomic impacts of COVID-19: Seven scenarios, *CAMA Working Paper* No. 19/2020.

Milio, S., Durazzi, N., Garnizova, E., Janowski, P., Olechnicka, A., Wojtowicz, D., 2014. Impact of the economic crisis on social, economic and territorial cohesion of the European Union, *Regional Development Study* (Vol. 2). European Parliament, Brussels, Belgium.

Miranda-Silva, G., Styles, C., Lages, L.F., 2016. Breakthrough innovation in international business: The impact of tech-innovation and market-innovation on performance. *Int. Bus. Rev. 26*(2), 391–404.

Nicola, M., Alsafi, Z., Sohrabi, C., Kerwan, A., Al-Jabir, A., Iosifidis, C., Agha, M., Agha, R., Jun. 2020. The socio economic implications of the coronavirus pandemic (COVID-19): a review. *Int. J. Surg. 78*, 185–193.

Nuenkirch, M., Neumeier, F., 2015. The impact of UN and US economic sanctions on GDP growth. *Eur. J. Polit. Econ. 40*(Part A), 110–125.

Okyere, A. M., Forson, R., Essel-Gaisey, F. Apr. 2020. *Positive externalities of an epidemic: the case of the coronavirus (COVID-19) in China, Journal of Medical Virology*, 92, 1376–1379, https://doi.org/10.1002/jmv.25830 (Accessed on June 10, 2020.)

O'Neill, J. 2001. Building better global economic BRICs. *Global Economics Paper* No: 66, goldmansachs.com. (Accessed on June 10, 2020).

Ozili, P., Arun, T. K. 2020. Spillover of COVID-19: Impact on the global economy. *MPRA Paper* No. 99850, April 26, https://mpra.ub.uni-muenchen.de/99850/ (Accessed on June 28, 2020).

Palmié, M., Keupp, M. M., Gassmann, O., 2014. Pull the right levers: Creating internationally "useful" subsidiary competence by organizational architecture. *Long. Range Plan. 47*(1–2), 32–48.

Patel, P. C., Fernhaber, S. A., McDougall-Covin, P. P., van der Have, R. P., 2013. Beating competitors to international markets: the value of geographically balanced networks for innovation. *Strategic Manag. J. 35*(5), 691–711.

Park, C. Y., Kim, K., Roth, S., Beck, S., Kang, J. W., Tayag, M. C., Griffin, M. 2020. Global shortage of personal protective equipment amid COVID-19: Supply chains, bottlenecks, and policy implications, *ADB Briefs*, No. 130, April, https://www.adb.org/publications/shortage-ppe-covid-19-supply-chains-bottlenecks-policy (Accessed on June 28, 2020).

Peng, M. W., 2004. Identifying the big question in international business research. *J. Int. Bus. Stud. 35*(2), 99–108.

Pomeranz, K., 2009. *The Great Divergence: China, Europe, and the Making of the Modern World Economy*. Princeton University Press, Princeton, Oxford.

Pomerleano, M. 2007. Corporate financial restructuring in Asia: Implications for financial stability. *BIS Quarterly Review*, September. SSRN: https://ssrn.com/abstract=1599612 (Accessed on June 27, 2020).

Porter, D., Craig, D., 2004. The third way and the third world: Poverty reduction and social inclusion in the rise of 'inclusive' liberalism. *Rev. Int. Political Economy 11*(2), 387–423.

Rapaccini, M., Saccani, N., Kowalkowski, C., Paiola, M., Adrodegari, F., Jul. 2020. Navigating disruptive crises through service-led growth: The impact of COVID-19 on Italian manufacturing firms. *Ind. Mark. Manag. 88*, 225–237.

Rincón-Aznar, A., Mao, X., Tong, M., May 2020. Global value chains and economic dislocations: Introduction. *Natl Inst. Econ. Rev. 252*, R1–R3.

Roberts, D., May/Jun. 2016. A global roadmap for climate change action: from COP17 in Durban to COP21 in Paris. *South. Afr. J. Sci. 112*, 5–6.

Rondinella, D., Berryb, M., 2000. Multimodal transportation, logistics, and the environment: Managing interactions in a global economy. *Eur. Manag. J. 18*(4), 398–410.

Ryans, J. K., Griffith, D. A., White, S. D., 2003. Standardization/adaptation of international marketing strategy: Necessary conditions for the advancement of knowledge. *Int. Mark. Rev. 20*(6), 588–603.

Albarasneh, A. S., Khatib, D. K., 2019. The US policy of containing Iran – from Obama to Trump 2009–2018. *Glob. Aff. 5*(4–5), 369–387.

Sali, L., Tallman, S., 2011. Research notes and commentaries: MNC strategies, exogeneous shocks and performance outcomes. *Strategic Manag. J. 32*(10), 1119–1127.

Sampson, T., 2017. Brexit: The economics of international disintegration. *J. Econ. Perspect. 31*(4), 163–184.

Schlegelmilch, B. B., 2020. Why business schools need radical innovations: drivers and development trajectories. *J. Marketing Educ.*, 1–15, https://journals.sagepub.com/doi/full/10.1177/0273475320922285 (Accessed on June 10, 2020).

Schmieg, C., 2019. The US-China trade war, the Huawei battle, and its effects on the world. *Diplomacy, Sustainable Development and Global Economics*, Oct. 14, https://journal.euclid.int/the-us-china-trade-war-the-huawei-battle-and-its-effects-on-the-world/ (Accessed on May 15, 2020).

Simmons, B. A., Dobbin, F., Garett, G., 2006. Introduction: the international diffusion of liberalism. *Int. Organ. 60*(4), 781–810.

Steinle, C., Schiele, H., 2008. Limits to global sourcing: strategic consequences of dependency on international suppliers: cluster theory, resource-based view and case studies. *J. Purchasing Supply Manag. 14*(1), 3–14.

Sumner, A., Hoy, C., Ortiz-Juarez, E., 2020. Estimates of the impact of COVID-19 on global poverty. *United Nations University UNU-WIDER working paper* 2020/43, April.

Teegen, H., Doh, J. P., Vachani, S., 2004. The importance of nongovernmental organizations (NGOs) in global governance and value creation: an international business research agenda. *J. Int. Bus. Stud. 25*(6), 463–483.

Tetlow, G., Stojanovic, A., 2018. *Understanding the Economic Impact of Brexit.* Institute for Government, London.

Theodosiou, M., Leonidou, L. C., 2003. Standardization versus adaptation of international marketing strategy: an integrative assessment of the empirical research. *Int. Bus. Rev. 12*(2), 141–171.

Volberda, J., Lewin, A. Y., 2003. Co-evolutionary dynamics within and between firms: From evolution to co-evolution. *J. Manag. Stud. 40*(8), 2111–2136.

Walt, G., Lush, L., Ogden, J., 2004. International organizations in transfer of infectious diseases: iterative loops of adoption, adaptation, and marketing. *Governance 17*(2), 189–210.

Wang, J. H., 2007. From technological catch-up to innovation-based economic growth: South Korea and Taiwan compared. *J. Dev. Stud. 43*(6), 1084–1104.

World Health Organization (WHO), 2019. *A World at Risk, Annual report on global preparedness for health emergencies.* Global-Preparedness-Monitoring-Board, Geneva.

Zaidi, N., Tyagi, P., Singh, A., 2019. Nokia's comeback—Is it revival of an iconic brand? *Asian Case Res. J. 23*(2), 415–426.

Zhang, Y.-X., Chao, Q.-C., Zheng, Q.-H., Huang, L., 2017. The withdrawal of the U.S. from the Paris Agreement and its impact on global climate change governance. *Adv. Clim. Change. Res. 8*(4), 213–219.

5 We Are Different

Cross-national Similarities in the Non-response to COVID-19 Pandemic and the Need for Global Cooperation

Ernesto Tavoletti

Introduction

The state of our knowledge in relation to the origins of the 2019–2020 coronavirus pandemic (COVID-19) is that on December 31, 2019 the World Health Organization (WHO) was informed of cases of pneumonia of unknown cause in the Chinese city of Wuhan. On January 7, 2020 the Chinese authorities identified a novel coronavirus as the cause and temporarily named it '2019-nCoV' (WHO, 2020a).

Still on April 20, 2020 the official website reported, *"WHO does not recommend any restriction of travel or trade. Standard recommendations to prevent infection spread for travelers in or from affected areas include regular hand washing, covering mouth and nose when coughing and sneezing, and avoiding close contact with anyone showing symptoms of respiratory illness"* (WHO, 2020a). On that same day, the Coronavirus Research Center at Johns Hopkins University reported over 2.4 million cases and over 166,000 deaths across 185 countries (JHU, 2020).

On April 14, the International Air Transport Association (IATA) reported that worldwide flights were down almost 80 percent by early April, with industry virtually grounded outside the U.S. and Asian domestic markets (IATA, 2020).

On April 8, the WTO issued its Annual Trade Outlook and as Director-General Roberto Azevêdo said, the "numbers are ugly": world merchandise trade is set to plummet by between 13 and 32 percent in 2020 due to the COVID-19 pandemic (WTO, 2020).

On 18 April, the United Nations' estimated that full or partial lockdown measures were affecting almost 2.7 billion workers, representing around 81 percent of the world's workforce (UN, 2020). Therefore, amidst the worst pandemic in a century that kills a few hundred thousand people in 185 nations and which has grounded almost all international flights, disrupted all the global supply chains and locked down 80 percent of the world population, the *"WHO does not recommend any restriction of travel"* but *"standard recommendations"* such as *"regular hand washing"* and *"covering mouth and nose when coughing and sneezing"*. The WHO was late in studying the outbreak in China, late in launching the alarm and late in providing recommendations in relation to medical protocols, resources and equipment. It was a high organizational failure. Far from protecting world health, the WHO re-assured public opinion in order to protect the world economy. In doing so, it has failed to protect both the world health and the world economy.

The disappointing response extended also to nation states and hence, my thesis is that there has been a consistent path of missing early responses across most nations in relation to the COVID-19 pandemic. The missing early responses have all gone through the same stages, i.e:

1. denial (it is not going to hit us as we are different);
2. underestimation (it is little more than an ordinary flu);
3. it is serious but we cannot afford shutting down the economy;
4. sudden panic and lock down;
5. too little and too late health and economic assistance to locked down citizens, and
6. too early opening up as a consequence.

The response has been even more disappointing in the European Union where, far from having a united response, countries have shut down borders and put a temporary end to the Common Market, blocked the trade of medical equipment and competed unfairly for some critical items. In a deflationary context, with the price of oil futures contracts going into negative territory for the first time in history (Huang and Stevens, 2020), the European Monetary Union (EMU) has delayed a much-needed strong monetary stimulus under concerns about who might take advantage of such a stimulus in a climate of even stronger intra EMU competition if possible. The delay of a monetary stimulus and the illiquidity might well produce a destruction of productive capacity and consequently, induce that inflationary risk that the proponents of a prudent approach fear. Therefore, far for strengthening international co-operation, the external danger has revealed that when it is a matter of life and death people tend to rely mainly on the national community as the ultimate repository of a trusted common culture and destiny. On the opposite, the chapter suggests that a common and coordinated global response is the only option that is compatible with the idea of a sustainable, global and open economy. Cooperation should start from a fair and reliable collection of data about the pandemic and even that is far from being achieved.

The Fog of Pandemic in the Data

One of the most shocking revelation of the COVID-19 pandemic is the unreliability of data for cross-national comparisons and the ineffectiveness of the WHO in fixing standards for data collection. COVID-19 has mostly been killing elderly people with previous chronical diseases, but there is no common standard, not even inside the European Union in relation to the recording of those deaths as COVID-19 or other pre-existing diseases, as each national and sub-national regional government has its own local standards. The lack of testing on suspected deaths in some countries, due to the lack of readily available test equipment and laboratories, generated a situation of complete unreliability to a point that the only reliable cross-national comparison seemed to be the number of deaths in 2020 as compared to deaths in 2019. By April 28, 2020, in some selected European countries, there were the following excesses of mortality in 2020 in respect to 2019 (official COVID-19 deaths in brackets): Spain 27,484 (20,749); Italy 20,875 (15,328); United Kingdom 16,850 (8,781); France 12,560 (8,881); The Netherlands 6,242 (2,713); Sweden 1,347 (1,008); Switzerland 1,152 (854) (Villa, 2020). Therefore, everywhere the excess of mortality in 2020 in respect to 2019 is far larger than the official COVID-19 reported deaths and this is a clear clue of an underestimation of officially reported deaths from COVID-19. If we look at the aggregate, in those seven European countries we have 86,510 additional deaths in 2020 by comparison to the corresponding period in 2019, but only 58,314 deaths from COVID-19: that suggests that on average one deaths out of three might not have been recorded as a COVID-19 death. If we normalize to one the absolute number above for every single nation, we have two clusters: Spain, Italy, France, Sweden and Switzerland that miss just one death every four; the United Kingdom and the Netherlands that miss one death every two and reveal a severe underestimation (Villa, 2020). That underestimation might signal a spread of the contagious disease in those two nations that is far larger than the one reported by their respective national authorities. Underestimation of deaths produces an underestimation of the danger and a delay in action that jeopardized the containment policies at the European level.

Using the same criteria, we can infer a significant level of under-estimation of deaths from COVID-19 in Germany, too. In fact, according to the German Federal Statistical Office in 2020 – week 15 – there were 2,150; in week 16 – 12 percent more deaths, compared with the four-year average. Higher mortality rates have been observed since week 13: "The current development is striking because death figures tend to decline continuously from week to week at the end of March and the beginning of April as the influenza epidemic recedes" (Destatis, 2020).

Therefore, official data about COVID-19 deaths do not look reliable. If we look at COVID-19 deaths per million as of May 16, 2020, the most affected country is Belgium (773), followed by Spain (590), Italy (523), UK (501), France (422), and The Netherlands (329), but it is a con-tinuously changing and evolving situation, depending on the stage of the pandemic. If we look at COVID-19 cases per million people at the same date, the most affected country is Spain (4,923), followed by Belgium (4,715), the U.S. (4,361), Italy (3,703) and the UK (3,487) (Our World in Data, 2020). It is clear that while the number of deaths may depend by the response capacity of the national health system, number of intensive treatment beds per capita, number of doctors per capita, national strategy of containment, social behavior, climate and the environment, the number of detected cases is highly dependent on the number of tests. In that regard the higher number of tests per thousand people was in Italy (49), followed by Belgium (47), Spain (41), Australia (40), Germany (38), Canada (34), USA (33), UK (26), The Netherlands (17) (Our World in Data, 2020). Hence, there has not only been lack of consistent and unified data, but decisions on action were made based on that basis.

Policy Response

The most striking aspect of the COVID-19 pandemic is how little countries have been learning from each other. The WHO was probably late in declaring the pandemic on March 11, as according to *Nature* the spread of coronavirus had already reached the necessary epidemiological criteria for it to be declared such on February 27 (Callaway, 2020). However, it has been even slower with its recommendations. In fact, still on April 20, 2020 the official website reported that *"WHO does not recommend any restriction of travel or trade"* (WHO, 2020a), despite the fact that on that same day, the Coronavirus Research Center at Johns Hopkins University reported over 2.4 million cases and over 166 thousands deaths across 185 countries (JHU, 2020). The response of nation states has been even more inadequate. Almost everywhere, it has followed a regular path in six stages:

1. denial (it is not going to hit us as circumstances in our nation are different);
2. underestimation (it is little more than an ordinary flu);
3. it is serious but we cannot afford shutting down the economy;
4. sudden panic and lockdown down;
5. too little and too late health and economic assistance to locked down citizens, and
6. too early opening up as a consequence.

Some nation states have been doing better than others have, and some others distinguished themselves for their late response, underestimation, lack of planning, and lack of economic assistance to citizens, Italy being one of them.

The first response of Italian authorities on February 1, 2020, was a ban of flights from China, but the very negative consequence was that all Chinese travelers went through an intermediary airport and were subsequently admitted with no control whatsoever as the intermediary destination was not infected by the coronavirus (Keating, 2020). The relevance of economic ties with China is so strategic for an open economy like Italy that benefits from a positive current account and a positive net contribution to the balance of payments of around €20 billion a year from tourism (Banca d'Italia, 2020), that the first concern was protecting the economy. Consequently, in February the fear of coronavirus has been fought with a propaganda campaign that included the visit of the Italian President to a Chinese school (Balmer, 2020). Political and opinion leaders were taking pictures in Chinese restaurants, the Prime Minister and Ministry of Health reassured Italians that there was no risk for Italy and its citizens due to its advanced national health system, and scientists close to the government were making reassuring statements addressing the population on TV (Horowitz et al. 2020).

That ostentatious underestimation, lack of prophylactic measures, lack of planning and lack of contingency measures (such as early storage of masks and medical equipment), had a very severe impact when the reality of COVID-19 hit with Italy becoming for a few weeks the world epicenter of the pandemic and thus was forced into severe nationwide lockdown (Remuzzi and Remuzzi, 2020). Numbers of infections and deaths were soon to become disastrous from a health point of view in Lombardia and Emilia – the most industrial Italian regions with strong international relations. Some cities in them experienced a sharp increase in deaths in the first three months of 2020 compared to the same period in 2019, e.g.: +568 percent in Bergamo, +391 percent in Cremona, +371 percent in Lodi, +291 percent in Brescia (Istat, 2020). The national health system was locally overwhelmed and accusations were exchanged between regional and national governments.

One of the main differences between the lockdown in China and the one in Italy is that the Chinese one was limited to a single province, albeit it was a large and important one, with the rest of the nation supporting the affected province, while the Italian lockdown was a nationwide one. Therefore, there were no other parts of the nation left to support the affected areas. The images of nine large Russian military planes landing in Rome or the Russian military trucks travelling from Rome to Bergamo sent a strong and visible signal and "have exposed the European Union's failure to provide swift help to a member in crisis and handed President Vladimir Putin a publicity coup at home and abroad" (Emmott and Osborn, 2020). That was combined with fast aids from China (Ferraresi, 2020) and unfair practice of medical export blockage by other members of EU Common Market—"When Italy asked for urgent medical supplies under a special European crisis mechanism, no EU country responded. Fearful of its own shortages, Germany initially banned the export of medical masks and other protective gear. 3M, a producer, said the German restrictions had made it impossible to supply the Italian market"

(Hall et al. 2020). All this left a long lasting euroscepticism in Italy whose geo-political consequences are yet to be seen.

The Italian economic response, under the European Union monetary and fiscal framework, was even more disappointing than the medical response. There has been extensive consensus that in face of a shock on both the demand and supply side, a quick and coordinated expansionary fiscal policy was needed as a partial monetization of debt (Blanchard and Pisani-Ferry, 2020; Galì 2020; Gürkaynak and Lucas, 2020). Nonetheless, extensive disagreements and debates at the European level and mutual distrust among member nations have delayed a coordinated stimulus decision and increased economic divergence due to the asymmetrical impact of COVID-19. Italy was already the country with the slowest growth inside the European Monetary Union and IMF forecasts suggested a higher negative growth in Italy than the rest of EMU.

Underestimating the danger of the pandemic in the early stages in order to reassure citizens and keep the economy running, did not work well in Italy, the United Kingdom and the U.S., as they all moved very fast from reassurance to lockdown, with a high toll of COVID-19 registered deaths: 90,353 in the U.S., 34,796 in the United Kingdom, 32,007 in Italy by May 19, 2020 (Our World in Data, 2020). They also moved fast to re-opening and the effects of which are still to be seen. Sweden followed a very different approach with very limited restrictions and tests (21 per thousand people), reaching a toll of 3,698 COVID-19 registered deaths (364 per million people) by May 19. This latter strategy has been supported by the Swedish population under a questionable sense of exceptional social behavior in comparison to neighbors, but the international implications for a small open economy have been overlooked. Once the national lockdowns in Europe are lifted, "Swedes might find themselves in a particularly difficult position. Without having been under a lockdown or undergone a testing regimen like other European states, and with many of those infected not showing any symptoms, some will regard Swedes as having a higher chance of bringing in the disease" (Kim, 2020). Other nations, and especially Nordic neighbors, who imposed much more restrictive measures than Sweden and whose capitals are a few kilometers away from Sweden, such as Oslo and Copenhagen, and have back and forth commuting across borders, might single out Swedes within EU. Sweden is an additional example that international coordination, both on the health and economic side, is necessary in a pandemic and this is even more so in a common market.

Conclusion

According to Lancet (Chen et al. 2020) since December 8, 2019 several cases of pneumonia have been registered in Wuhan, Hubei province, and on January 7, a novel coronavirus was identified, named COVID-19 by WHO. Chinese media reported the emergence of a new virus from Wuhan at the end of December. On December 31, the Taiwanese government informed the WHO of a human-to-human transmission, but the WHO organization did not share the information and on January 14 tweeted that "Preliminary investigations conducted by the Chinese authorities have found no clear evidence of human-to-human transmission of the novel coronavirus". As an ultimate example of its inadequate response even on April 20, 2020, in the middle of a global lockdown, the WHO official website reported that *"WHO does not recommend any restriction of travel or trade"*.

On May 18, 2020, the U.S. Government took a strong public stance against the WHO reporting in detail the supposed chain of delays, shortcomings and lack of transparency, freezing the funding and threatening to reconsider its membership to the WHO. While many of the accusations might be a matter of debate and part of a power struggle between China and the U.S., there is a wide international consensus about a lack of transparency of the Chinese government in the early stages of the pandemic. It is clear that the WHO was hostage of economic and political considerations that made the organization poorly effective in the face of big economic interests and an intimidating national power. A renewed word order would require an independent WHO, on the model of independent authorities and central banks, that puts world health before international economic and political interests.

The second take away of the COVID-19 pandemic is that every single nation thought to be different from the early or most affected nations, each for a different reason: the presence of a public national health system the nation was proud of (UK, France and Italy), different (or superior?) social behavior in relation to distancing or washing (Sweden, Turkey), better material conditions in relation to the density of population (the U.S.), a more resilient economy and a world-leading health system (Germany), a stronger institutional frame (Russia), just to quote some of the most covered issues in the international press. Unfortunately, the unfolding of the disruption and the connection between the economies due to free trade agreements, a common market, or intensity of trade and movements of people, proved many of them wrong. While being on different points of the pandemic curve, no nation was especially spared from the impact of COVID 19 or different and safe without the cooperation and safety of others.

The geo-political competition among nation states for regional or global hegemony is every day practice, but the idea that national states compete as firms do is a theoretically wrong idea that has been infecting the political debate. The 'winners and losers' approach or the emphasis on the opportunities coming out from the misfortunes of competitors, that are so typical in the management and international business discourse, were dangerous and misleading metaphors in the international politics and economics of a pandemic. Nations do not compete like firms, nor do they go out of business (at least in a post-imperialistic world). Nations are there to stay and they benefit from the increased productivity of other nations, both on the supply and demand side. Their welfare depends mainly on their own internal growth in productivity and they do not benefit from the misfortune of other nations, as it is especially the case of the very open and interconnected economies of Europe. Approaching the international economics and politics of nations with the strategy analysis framework of business would be not just theoretically wrong and dysfunctional, but dangerous (Krugman, 1994).

On the opposite, the international relations in Europe have been following a competitive-driven approach among national states, who saw as their responsibility to help domestic firms in severe distress so that they could win the competition with foreign firms. While this approach is dangerous in general, it might have an explosive effect in a common market and monetary union that includes large nations and very tiny ones with uneven fiscal space for subsidies to both large corporations and SMEs. Divergence among national European Union states has been growing and this pandemic crisis is a candidate for the worst to come as the periphery has been hit much more severely than the core (Gräbner et al. 2020). It has yet to be seen if nations, and European nations in particular, will find the political capital to move away from the damaging competitiveness rhetoric in order to set an agenda based on the international and mutually beneficial cooperation that they need for a fast recovery.

References

Balmer, C., 2020. Italian president visits Chinese schoolchildren to allay coronavirus fears. *Reuters*. February 6, 2020. https://www.reuters.com/article/us-china-health-italy/italian-president-visits-chinese-schoolchildren-to-allay-coronavirus-fears-idUSKBN2001ZN (accessed 18.05.20).

Banca, d'Italia 2020. *Bilancia dei pagamenti e posizione patrimoniale sull'estero al 20 aprile 2020F*. https://www.bancaditalia.it/pubblicazioni/bilancia-pagamenti/2020-bilancia-pagamenti/statistiche_BDP_20200420.pdf. (accessed 18.05.20).

Blanchard, O., Pisani-Ferry, J., 2020. Monetisation: do not panic. *Vox CEPR Policy Portal*. April 10, 2020. https://voxeu.org/article/monetisation-do-not-panic_ng-information-warfare/ (accessed 18.05.20).

Callaway, E., 2020. Time to use the p-word? Coronavirus enter dangerous new phase. *Nature* 579(277), 12.

Chen, N., Zhou, M., Dong, X., Qu, J., Gong, F., Han, Y., Yu, T., 2020. Epidemiological and clinical characteristics of 99 cases of 2019 novel coronavirus pneumonia in Wuhan, China: a descriptive study. *Lancet* 395(10223), 507–513.

Destasis, 2020. *Mortality figures above previous years' average also in Week 16.* Press release No. 177/May 15, 2020. https://www.destatis.de/EN/Press/2020/05/

PE20_177_12621.html;jsessionid=C1420CE75085F7F6E4091ECB8DA34A07. internet8732 (accessed 17.05.20).

Emmott, R., Osborn, A., 2020. Russian aid to Italy leaves EU exposed. *Reuters*. March 26, 2020. https://www.reuters.com/article/us-health-coronavirus-russia-eu/russian-aid-to-italy-leaves-eu-exposed-idUSKBN21D28K (accessed 18.05.20).

Ferraresi, M., 2020. China isn't helping Italy. It's waging information warfare. *Foreign Policy*. March 31, 2020. https://foreignpolicy.com/2020/03/31/china-isnt-helping-italy-its-waging-information-warfare/ (accessed 18.05.20.)

Galì, J., 2020. Helicopter money: the time is now. *Vox CEPR Policy Portal*. March 17, 2020. https://voxeu.org/article/helicopter-money-time-now (accessed 18.05.20).

Gräbner, C., Heimberger, P., Kapeller, J., Schütz, B., 2020. Is the Eurozone disintegrating? Macroeconomic divergence, structural polarisation, trade and fragility. *Camb. J. Econ.* 44(3), 647–669.

Gürkaynak, R., Lucas, D., 2020. Funding pandemic relief: monetise now. *Vox CEPR Policy Portal*. May 14, 2020. https://voxeu.org/article/funding-pandemic-relief-monetise-now (accessed 18.05.20).

Hall, B., Johnson, M., Arnold, M., 2020. Italy wonders where Europe's solidarity is as coronavirus strains show. *Financial Times*. March 13, 2020. https://www.ft.com/content/d3bc25ea-652c-11ea-b3f3-fe4680ea68b5 (accessed 18.05.20).

Horowitz, J., Bubola, E., Povoledo, E., 2020. Italy, pandemic's new epicenter, has lessons for the world. *New York Times*. March 21, 2020. https://nyti.ms/3bcTDCz (accessed 18.05.20).

Huang, E., Stevens, P., 2020. *An oil futures contract expiring Tuesday went negative in bizarre move showing a demand collapse.* https://www.cnbc.com/2020/04/20/oil-markets-us-crude-futures-in-focus-as-coronavirus-dents-demand.html?fbclid=IwAR3UwcfXru-7FprJIwr32EnihceATjMGnY-OADUkQv4o-Sm9DDMRDB8mUpE (accessed 20.04.20.).

Kim, T. H., 2020. Sweden's coronavirus exceptionalism will not be remembered favourably by Europe. *Euronews*. April 29, 2020. https://www.euronews.com/2020/04/27/sweden-s-covid-19-exceptionalism-will-not-be-remembered-favourably-by-europe-view (accessed 20.05.20).

Krugman, P., 1994. Competitiveness: a dangerous obsession. *Foreign Aff.* 73(2), 28–44.

International Air Transport Association, 2020. *COVID-19 Updated impact assessment*. April 14, 2020. https://www.iata.org/en/iata-repository/publications/economic-reports/covid-fourth-impact-assessment/ (accessed 20.04.20).

Istat, 2020. *Impatto dell'epidemia covid-19 sulla mortalità totale della popolazione residente primo trimestre 2020.* May 4, 2020. https://www.istat.it/it/files//2020/05/Rapporto_Istat_ISS.pdf (accessed 18.05.20).

John Hopkins University, 2020. *COVID-19 detail in the making.* https://coronavirus.jhu.edu/map.html (accessed 20.04.20).

Keating, D., 2020. Italy banned flights from China before America - It didn't work. *Forbes*. 12, March 2020. https://www.forbes.com/sites/davekeating/2020/03/12/italy-banned-flights-from-china-before-americait-didnt-work/#3ce67091481b (accessed 18.05.20).

Our World in Data, 2020. *Coronavirus pandemic.* https://ourworldindata.org/coronavirus (accessed 16.05.20).

Remuzzi, A., Remuzzi, G., 2020. COVID-19 and Italy: what next? *Lancet* *395*(10231), 1225–1228.

United Nations, 2020. *UN calls for measures to cushion COVID-19 shocks to labour market.* https://www.un.org/en/un-coronavirus-communications-team/un-calls-measures-cushion-covid-19-shocks-labour-market (accessed 20.04.20).

Villa, M., 2020. *Fase 2: morti sommerse, "eccesso" di zelo?*, Istituto per gli studi di Politica Internazionale. April, 28. https://www.ispionline.it/it/pubblicazione/fase-2-morti-sommerse-eccesso-di-zelo-25878 (accessed 16.05.20).

World Health Organization, 2020a. *Coronavirus Disease (COVID-19) Outbreak* http://www.euro.who.int/en/health-topics/health-emergencies/coronavirus-covid-19/novel-coronavirus-2019-ncov (accessed 20.04.20).

World Trade Organization, 2020. *Annual Trade Outlook*, https://www.wto.org/english/tratop_e/covid19_e/faqcovid19_e.htm (accessed 20.04.20).

6 Will COVID-19 Kill Globalization?[1]

Marian Gorynia

My answer to the question above leaves no room for doubt: COVID-19 will not kill or even significantly weaken globalization, but it will definitely modify this phenomenon. Still, the scope of these modifications will not be drastic compared to pre-coronavirus conditions: I would advise against overestimating the extent of these pandemic-induced changes.

Above all, this text is a diagnosis: I describe what I see and provide my understanding of the surrounding world. I do not intend to say that my description overlaps with my values and evaluations, its nature is purely diagnostic. The world we live in may differ from the world we desire or dream of. I do not mean to express my approval of what I see; I only seek to describe it. The mere fact of publishing a text on globalization does not mean that the author displays an uncritical fascination with the phenomenon. This message is worth considering before you begin to read the essay.

The Nature of Globalization

Globalization has many dimensions: virtually everybody sees the one that is closest to them due to professional or other reasons. However, we must be aware of this multidimensionality and also be mindful of what is fundamental and essential and what is secondary. We could provide a long list of the abovementioned dimensions: economic, financial, political, sociological, cultural, religious, educational, communicative, technological and infrastructural (Al-Rodhan and Stoudmann, 2006; Kowalski, 2013; Gorynia, 2019). Indeed, there is no area of life unaffected by globalization.

As an economist, I discuss the economic aspect of globalization, as it seems to provide a foundation for the whole phenomenon, along with technological changes. The causative mechanism of globalization connects to the essence of market economy. In simple terms, the core of this mechanism amounts to the overcriticized *homo oeconomicus* stereotype. In line with this stereotype, companies (entrepreneurs, employers, 'beneficiaries') seek to maximize their profits, and the people (consumers) seek to maximize utility resulting from consumption. I oppose fetishizing the meaning of this stereotype; however, despite of its many weaknesses, it largely explains people's behavior as entrepreneurs, employees, investors, and consumers.

This mechanism is the main driving force behind the development of market economy – or capitalism – a system that has an exceptional ability to effectively and efficiently meet people's needs, unlike its predecessors, such as feudalism or slavery. A comparison of capitalism with the pre-1990 socialist economy also seems to be in favor of the former. However, it is not a perfect system: such systems do not exist. Moreover, capitalism has many forms and is subject to continuous evolution.

The capitalist market economy is not free from weaknesses, the greatest of which is the pursuit of profit (companies) and utility (consumers) based solely on market forces, which can become dangerous. Such pursuit may exclude a large part of the population from reaping the fruits of management processes and, above all, from developing the prosperity of production processes. For various reasons, some individuals are unable to cope with market economy conditions. Among other reasons, this inability may be due to their health, education and communication access issues. These are certain forms of exclusion. Exclusion designates unequal participation in the whole society's welfare. If a part of society cannot participate in management processes, the community itself becomes dysfunctional, which can go as far as to challenge the system's stability. To prevent such scenarios, a vital element of each socioeconomic system is the state, which contributes to mitigating the weaknesses of market economy through such measures as taxation, social security systems, or public services. We cannot overlook the fact that – apart from state measures – philanthropy and charitable activities, socially responsible businesses, volunteering and similar non-*homo oeconomicus* behaviors have an increasing role in the redistribution of the benefits of economic growth. Although we cannot overlook these behaviours, we should not overestimate them. They remain a mere periphery, a supplement to the market economy or, rather, its less significant component. Indeed, they keep growing, but they are still not its dominant attribute. Thus, the perception of such inequalities fuels programs of political parties.

This same mechanism is the main driving force behind the development of market economy on a global scale, but also in individual regions, continents, economic communities and states. Therefore, from an international perspective, we see that the nature of this mechanism remains the same. In simple and clear terms: the rich seek to become even richer, and the poor try to escape poverty. On an international scale, we observe a great diversity – even an abundance – of institutional solutions governing the organization of economic activity and the role of the state. State actions that seek to adjust the market mechanism's operation are organized differently in different countries; their scope also varies. The same is true of the second corrective mechanism, that is, charity work in the broad sense. However, the result remains the same: in charity work, as in individual states, we observe inequalities, which are signs of exclusion. The impact of entire groups of factors noticeably diversify the achievements of individual state economies in building prosperity and welfare. However, this was always the case, even when globalization was not as strong. Therefore, it seems justified to assert that globalization as such is not the primary cause of inequality and the uneven distribution of the fruits of prosperity, which is sometimes raised as its main weakness. All these processes arise from capitalism itself.

Therefore, we may treat globalization as the next step in the evolution of the market economy, a step in line with its elementary principles. At the same time, it is a stage when existing forms of interference in the operation of pure market mechanisms fail. The essence of globalization boils down to the following phenomenon: in pursuit of achieving selfish individual and group interests, the main economic actors – companies and people – locate their operations in such a way that production occurs in places that ensure the minimization of production costs, which is to maximize profit margins. Producers seek cheap production to achieve a higher profit margin; consumers seek to maximize utility; that is, at a given budget, they want to buy products at the cheapest possible price (*ceteris paribus*). Let us note the technological changes that currently occur in the process of globalization giving new foundations and additional impetus to the exploitation of these fundamental – and not at all new – aspects of business development. I refer to production and service technologies, but this way of acting applies equally well to transportation, communication technologies, and data processing. However, it appears that an excessive pursuit of low production costs may lead producers to locate their operations in places with different environmental standards (environmental dumping) or different standards concerning employment conditions, occupational safety and social security (social dumping). The above examples of globalization-related malpractices demonstrate the necessity to coordinate specific rules of operation on an international level in order to avoid such spillover effects from the application of market economy principles. Among other things, such coordination is missing in the current stage of globalization development. Thus, globalization is not an ideal system devoid of serious drawbacks.

The economic sciences adopt varying approaches to globalization. We should note the significant discrepancies in the understanding of globalization, especially the possible perceptions of globalization in terms of its effects and the opportunities and threats that it presents. From this viewpoint, we can distinguish four basic approaches in the extensive subject literature:

- enthusiasm slightly cooled by reason, which we may describe as a pro-globalization attitude approving of globalization (albeit not blindly): "globalization is good but not good enough" (Bhagwati, 2004);
- concerned reflection and a balanced understanding of the nature of globalization (Streeten, 2001);
- a highly suspicious and critical approach, although not overwhelming (Stiglitz, 2002);
- an approach that relies on questioning the meaning of globalization, which manifests itself in ideas and policies described as new protectionism and new nationalism, as seen in the actions of Trump's administration and other political leaders (Rodrik 2017).

Globalization Development Scenarios

A Pandemic-Free Globalization

We may object to the discussion on what the world economy would look like without the appearance of COVID-19, considering it a useless exercise. However, it appears that at least several such remarks can help to identify potential post-pandemic scenarios better. A good summary of the effects of globalization was McKinsey's 2007 study, which found that multinational corporations based in the U.S. were responsible for at least 19 percent of private-sector jobs, 25 percent of salaries, 48 percent of exports and 74 percent of research and development expenditures (Economist, 2017). The 2008–2011 global financial crisis was a particular milestone in the development of globalization processes. If we assume that international trade volumes, the location of foreign direct investments, and the relation of trade and investment to the gross domestic product are good simplified measures of globalization levels, the data indicate that globalization slowed down during the crisis and never returned to the pre-crisis levels afterwards. Other measures of global integration, as globalization is sometimes called, also confirm this thesis (Economist, 2019). Therefore, the years 1990–2010 – or rather 1990–2007 – are considered the 'golden age' of globalization. Besides the abovementioned distortions, other effects of globalization have also become apparent. Inequalities in international wealth levels and environmental risks have increased. The decline in transportation costs – previously a factor in the growth of international trade – came to a halt. The rates of return on foreign direct investments began to decrease, subject to an increasingly intense competition from the target market's local companies. Moreover, the relocation of production to sites with lower labor costs – to less developed countries – led to lay-offs in developed countries. A good example are the U.S., where the appeal to economic patriotism led to the election of Donald Trump. In other countries, populist and nationalist political movements also gained significance, questioning the alleged excessive intensity of globalization, which they call a hyper-globalization. As a result, the real threat of trade wars emerged. These circumstances are primarily responsible for inhibiting the development of globalization and its deceleration. It appeared that the slowdown in the growth of the trade in goods might be compensated by growth in services; but this prediction proved incorrect. However, we saw the emergence of a tendency to shorten supply chains and regionalize trade; an increase in the importance of regional supply. We observe similar phenomena in foreign direct investments: there is an increase in the importance of regional (continental) investments. However, the revival of regional economic cooperation does not seem able to compensate for the slowdown in global integration.

Thus, even in a COVID-19-free world, we would see a clear halt or deceleration in global integration. In 2015, the Dutch writer and trend watcher Adiedj Bakas called this phenomenon 'slowbalization' (slow globalization). However, the general belief was that the slowdown would be temporary, and the forces of globalization would return with an even greater force in the long run. Such a way of thinking was based on the assumption that the main development mechanism described above would also apply to less developed countries. We should realize that aspirations for prosperity in these countries can be realized in two main ways: local work and development, which favors foreign direct investments and export, or workforce migration to more prosperous countries. Many assumed that the former would prevail, which would result in a return to the acceleration of global integration.

For instance, the American economist Dani Rodrik (2017) believes that there could be three subscenarios of world development in a world with slower globalization. He considers them dependent on the relationship between globalization and nationalist and populist themes in the economic policy of key international political actors. The first scenario is the 1930s-like collapse of global economic cooperation and the rise of extreme right- or left-wing regimes. Rodrik deems the second scenario 'ugly': creeping populism and protectionism lead to a gradual erosion of both liberal democracy and open world economy. The third scenario he called 'good': a democratic rebalancing that would retreat from hyper-globalization and restore greater autonomy to state economies.

In conclusion, we would find it difficult to disagree with the following statement from *The Economist* (2019): "Viewed in the very long run, over centuries, the march of globalisation is inevitable, barring an unforeseen catastrophe. Technology advances, lowering the cost of trade in every corner of the world, while the human impulse to learn, copy and profit from strangers is irrepressible. Yet there can be long periods of slowbalisation, when integration stagnates or declines. The golden age of globalisation created huge benefits but also costs and a political backlash. The new pattern of commerce that replaces it will be no less fraught with opportunity and danger".

Pre- and Post-Pandemic Globalization

First, both during and after the pandemic period, the forces that decelerated globalization before the emergence of COVID-19 will not cease to operate. These forces will continue, although they will temporarily become less important, 'overshadowed' by the coronavirus.

Second, the sudden and unexpected impact of COVID-19, especially on the so-called Western civilization, led many to believe that the post-pandemic world will never return to its pre-pandemic state. The pandemic itself translates into a sudden reduction, inhibition, or even a complete halt of production and trade processes – that is, sales and purchases – which simultaneously affects any economy's traditional sides: supply and demand. National and international supply chains have been disrupted. Global economic activity has declined, including the movement of goods, services, capital, and finance. A common sense approach is enough to understand that a post-COVID-19 – most probably temporary – reduction in global integration will be necessary to ensure supply security, among other things. That is, local production would increase the security of supply. The trauma of disrupted supply chains will surely trouble managers for some time. Nevertheless, we should remember that production close to the market outlet frequently raises production costs. Keeping larger stocks has similar consequences: it also generates costs. Such decisions will probably be taken at the company level. These operations will possibly precede a lower propensity to use financial leverage in an ordinary, post-pandemic economic situation; at least temporarily. At the national level, there are already calls for stronger economic patriotism. Such calls will be a lighter version of strong appeals for economic nationalism and protectionism. Nationalist and protectionist measures concern jobs, restrictions on imports through tariff and non-tariff measures, and reduction in the free movement of capital, particularly foreign direct investments.

Third, the reactions to COVID-19 of governments, politicians, scientists and intellectuals show highly divergent opinions on the role of the state and the market, the importance of international cooperation, and the virtues and vices of open economies. Nationalist rhetoric and such politics will not necessarily be isolated cases in the future. Thus, maybe the constructivist visions of repairing the world are unjustified and unrealistic? Dani Rodrik (2019) goes so far as to suggest that the crisis may not be as large a breakthrough in world politics and economy as many claim, or as we thought at the very beginning, when we found it very difficult to predict its scope. Instead of setting an entirely new path, COVID-19 may intensify and consolidate pre-existing trends. These trends have subsided and become less important due to current short-term events, but they will reemerge once the crisis is over. Briefly speaking, Rodrik claims that COVID-19 may well not change, let alone reverse, the pre-crisis trends. Neoliberalism will continue its slow death. Populist autocrats will become even more authoritarian. Hyper-globalization will remain on the defensive as states regain room for own policies. China and the U.S. will continue on their collision course. Individual countries will witness the intensification of the battle among oligarchs, authoritarian populists, and liberal internationalists.

Fourth, the pandemic demonstrates the importance of international cooperation. The world became a system of communicating vessels and will remain one. In a diagnostic sense, we see the ill effects of the lack of good interstate cooperation, as tellingly and rather pessimistically demonstrated the restrictions that the states imposed on trade in medical goods after the COVID-19 outbreak. However, in the normative sense we can see how much remains to be achieved in the area. The need for international cooperation to combat COVID-19 is obvious, but an even greater task for humanity is to improve global governance.

Fifth, international cooperation in all spheres of civilization is important yet insufficient. It is a long-term proposal. Another, short-term proposal concerns coordinated aid to countries most affected by the crisis and the less developed countries. Further initiatives in this matter exist, arise and develop. This sphere demonstrates the importance of solidarity, co-operation and global democracy. Numerous renowned economists stress that less developed countries cannot cope with COVID-19 on their own.

Sixth, we should consider the outcome of the present crisis: a map of potential winners and losers. We may discuss this matter in many possible planes or cross-sections of reflections on the global economy as a whole, economic blocs, integration communities, individual states, regions within individual states, branches of the world economy, national economies and individual companies. What may also prove valuable are analyzes of small and medium-sized enterprises compared to large companies in terms of exporters versus importers, or foreign direct outgoing and incoming investors. A discussion on this subject could become the object of a separate study.

Seventh, the indicated trends are likely to emerge, but their scope and duration will undoubtedly depend on the impact of COVID-19 on global GDP. The extent of changes – counted as GDP increase and decrease – will depend on the duration and end time of the pandemic, its geo-graphical and sectoral scope and the profoundness of changes in individual sectors.

To summarize my answer to the question of how the post-pandemic global economy will look, we should note three particular aspects. First, we should distinguish what this economy is likely to become from what it should be or what we would like it to be. Between these two categories, we will most probably observe a significant gap, which has accompanied humanity for millennia; the real and desired worlds have always differed. Second, COVID-19 is unlikely to radically undermine or change the trends observed in the pre-pandemic global economy. In simple terms, these trends contributed to the slowdown of the 'golden age' of globalization (1990–2010) with all its positive and negative effects. This 'hyper-globalization' is giving way to 'slowbalization'. The latter process will continue its course. Third, COVID-19 will have a likely short-term impact on the intensity of globalization's slowdown, which will nevertheless subside in the medium and long run. Fourth – which best summarizes the whole text – globalization is alive and well, and will continue in this vein. The reports on the death of globalization are greatly exaggerated and premature. Globalization is good, but it is not as good as it could be. Let us do everything we can to make it better.

Note

1 The chapter has been prepared within a grant of the National Science Centre in Poland, grant No UMO-2016/21/B/HS4/03030 - Innovation performance of a foreign subsidiary and its position in the network of a multinational enterprise - the perspective of foreign subsidiaries established in Poland.

References

Al-Rodhan, N. R. F., Stoudmann, G., 2006. *Definitions of Globalization: A Comprehencive Overview and a Proposed Definition.* Geneva Center for Security Policy, Geneva.

Bhagwati, J., 2004. *In Defence of Globalization.* Oxford University Press, Oxford.

Economist 2017. *Multinationals: The Retreat of the Global Economy.* 28 January, 12–24

Economist 2019. *Globalisation has Faltered: It Is Now Being Reshaped.* 24 January, 9–11

Gorynia, M., 2019. Competition and globalisation in economic sciences. Selected aspects. *Econ. Bus. Rev.* 5((19) (3)), 118–133.

Kowalski, T., 2013. *Globalization and Transformation in Central European Countries: The Case of Poland.* Poznań University of Economics Press, Poznań.

Rodrik, D. 2017. *Populism and the Economics of Globalization.* Paper presented at the AIB Conference, Dubai.

Rodrik, D. 2020. *Will COVID-19 Remake the World?* Project Syndicate, 6 April. https://www.project-syndicate.org/commentary/will-covid-19-remake-the world-by-dani-rodrik-2020-04?barrier=accesspaylog.

Stiglitz, J. E., 2002. *Globalization and its Discontents* (Vol. 500). W.W. Norton Company, Washington.

Streeten, P., 2001. *Globalisation: Threat or Opportunity?* Copenhagen Business School Press, Copenhagen.

7 The Impact of the Great Lockdown on the Future of the World Economy and International Business

Kari Liuhto

Pan(dem)ic 2019+

In my chapter, I set to analyze the impact of the coronavirus COVID-19 on the world economy and international business with special emphasis on its consequences for the European Union (EU). At its end, I present my views of what will be the legacy of COVID-19, or what kind of permanent changes the pandemic will leave behind for the world economy and international business.

However, it is anything but easy to predict holistically the immediate effects of the pandemic, let alone its long-term legacy, since even experts of any area of epidemiology disagree on when the pandemic began, where it originated from and even how the virus ended up in a human carrier. We also lack reliable information on the contagiousness of the coronavirus, the mutability and life cycle of the virus and the development of immunity to COVID-19.

Our information on former virus outbreaks does not help us much in predicting the economic impact of COVID-19, since the SARS epidemic that began in China almost two decades ago or the MERS virus, detected in the Middle East less than 10 years ago, did not cause a pandemic. The swine flu, also ten years ago, spread extensively but definitely cannot be compared to COVID-19 in terms of contagiousness and lethality. Still, the swine flu should have served as a wake-up call, since the disease had certain similarities with the Spanish flu. A century ago about 500 million people, or one-third of the world's population at the time, became infected with the Spanish flu, and the death toll came to several tens of millions. We must not forget either that the Spanish flu killed people around the world in several waves (CDC, 2020).

Even though the Spanish flu evidently caused a whole lot more deaths than COVID-19 probably would, we should remember that 100 years ago, the world was not as interdependent as it is today. Secondly, in today's world, people, goods as well as information travel much faster than they did a century ago. It should also be borne in mind that despite the changes in the world economy, no change has happened in how susceptible people are to viral diseases.

While I am completing this essay at the end of May 2020, the number of registered coronavirus cases stands at approximately six million or below 0.1 percent of the whole population of our planet, i.e., the world is very far from the possible herd immunity rate of 60 percent. According to official statistics, by end of May 2020, COVID-19 killed less than 400,000 people. Three-quarters of the virus deaths have been verified in the most advanced parts of the world, Europe and North America. In the U.S. alone, a total of over 100,000 people have died of complications caused by the virus, i.e., a quarter of the COVID-19 deaths globally can be found in the U.S. alone. Correspondingly, according to official statistics, in India, with four times larger population than the U.S., COVID-19 has registered to have killed only around 5,000 people (HS, 2020).

COVID-19 is currently particularly deadly among the elderly population. Despite this, the state with the oldest demographic structure in the world – Japan – has managed, at least at the time when this chapter is written, to save itself from a large number of fatalities. At the end of May 2020, there had been less than 1,000 deaths in Japan. It is very difficult to believe that, despite their young population structure, India, Africa and the rest of the developing world would be able to escape the pandemic with such low mortality rates (Johns Hopkins University, 2020).

As an economist, I am not the best person to predict the spread, lethality or life cycle of the virus, but, in the light of the official information published so far, it seems that by closing borders and imposing internal restrictions on movement, we can only slow down the spread of the virus, but these measures will not be enough to eradicate it, because we must open the borders and lift the travel restrictions sooner or later. Slowing down the spread of the virus, or playing time, is of course vital, because it helps us prevent the overburdening of the health care system and, thereby, prevent countless unnecessary deaths. Although playing time is a necessary step, unfortunately, it is not a sufficient step.

Since we cannot put the whole planet in quarantine for a month at the same time, we cannot totally prevent the spread of the rampant virus because, like a rubber ball, the virus keeps on bouncing from one continent to another, from one country to another, and even from one part of a country to another, as soon as travel restrictions are alleviated.

In practice, all we can do is to gradually expose the whole world population to the virus while trying to preclude preventable deaths. In addition to the controlled exposure of the population to the virus, we must continue the active efforts to develop a vaccine against the virus. Once a reliable and functional vaccine would be created, it must be produced and distributed to a very large part of the world population of over seven billion people.

Given the long time it takes to develop, produce and distribute such a vaccine, we should be prepared for the fact that the coronavirus will continue to torment us for much longer than the optimistic experts hope. In this context, it should not be forgotten that the spread of the virus may have started with one individual and, as long as there is even one person who spreads the virus, I do not believe that we can rule out the possibility of new waves of the COVID-19 pandemic. Nor can we rule out the possibility of the virus mutating. If the mutation causes a reduction of the lethality of the disease, the whole world would breathe a sigh of relief. If, on the other hand, the mutated virus begins to spread more aggressively or becomes more lethal than it now is, the human race would go from a pandemic to an uncontrolled panic.

To control the COVID-19 virus, the whole humanity must change their behaviors. Changes in human behavior would also be accompanied by radical changes in our economic activities especially the cross border ones. Some of the changes would most likely be temporary, while others would everlastingly change the way we behave. Some of the changes would have local consequences, while others would have worldwide significance.

The Impact of COVID-19 on the World Economy and the EU

Impact on the World Economy

Over the last half a century, the humanity has perpetually experienced one major economic crisis per decade. Thus, oil crises slowed down the world economic growth in the 1970s and 1980s. In the late 1990s, the Asian financial crisis shook the regional economies with worldwide effects. The global financial crisis stopped the economic growth at the end of the first decade of this millennium. The coronavirus pandemic arrived abruptly to torment us at the very end of the last decade, as unconfirmed data indicate that the virus began to spread in Central China as early as the fall of 2019.

Although, at the time when this essay is written, it is still unclear what kind of economic havoc the COVID-19 pandemic will ultimately bring about, it is already quite clear that this crisis, called also the Great Lockout, will be more devastating than any world economic crisis since the Great Depression of the 1930s.

The Great Depression dropped the overall real gross domestic product (GDP) of the advanced economies by more than 15 percent between 1930 and 1932. In other words, the global economy fell at an average rate of over 5 percent per year during those darkest years of the Great Depression (Crafts and Fearon, 2010).

The decline in the world economy caused by COVID-19 pandemic in 2020 will also be historically steep. The real GDP of advanced countries

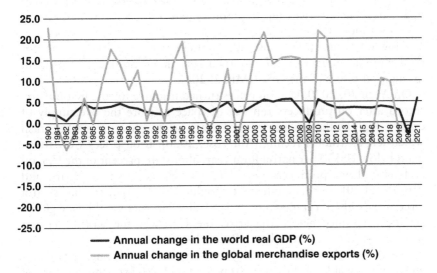

Figure 7.1 The Development of the World Economy and the Global Exports in 1980–2021.

Sources: The Author, based on IMF (2020b); WTO (2020a).

is forecast to fall by more than 6 percent within a single year (IMF, 2020a). In this context, it should not be forgotten either that the above-stated IMF report assumes the recovery of the global economy to begin already in fall 2020. According to the IMF, the global economy would take a turn toward an unforeseen rise of almost 6 percent already in 2021. The world economy has not experienced such a rapid growth for four decades, if such a growth will take place after all. In practice, this means that the IMF is forecasting a V-shaped recovery curve, as shown in Figure 7.1.

I dare predict that the world economy would experience several waves of the COVID-19 pandemic, like what was the case with the Spanish flu. This is why I believe that the development would be W-shaped rather than V-shaped. In other words, because the pandemic is progressing at different rates in various parts of the world, and new epidemic waves are really likely to occur, in 2021, the world economy would probably grow at a variable and slower rate than what the IMF forecasts.

As Western economies shrink, it is interesting to see that, despite COVID-19, the IMF believes the Chinese economy will grow even in 2020. However, if other COVID-19 waves were to strike China and the world, the IMF growth estimate would prove unrealistic even in reference to China.

No matter how deep the plunge in world GDP would be as a result of COVID-19, it is expected that a decline in economic activities would lead to a drop in raw material prices. In fact, in the period January-March 2020, base metal prices fell by approximately 15 percent, natural gas price by almost 40 percent and crude oil price by more than 60 percent. The low oil futures prices until 2023 anticipate in fact difficult times for the economies reliant on oil exports and shale oil producers dependent on high oil prices in the U.S. (IMF, 2020a).

On April 20, 2020, U.S. oil prices turned negative for the first time on record after oil producers ran out of space to store the oversupply of crude oil left by the coronavirus crisis, activating a historic market crash which left oil traders reeling (Ambrose, 2020). If oil prices were to re-main below US$30 per barrel for a year, almost 40 percent of the U.S. oil and natural gas producers would face insolvency (Adams-Heard and Saraiva, 2020). In this context, it should not be forgotten that such a large wave of bankruptcies among U.S. oil companies would have global significance, since before the crisis the U.S. was the world's largest producer of oil and natural gas (BP, 2019).

The IMF predicts that the total decrease in world trade, including goods and services, will be slightly over 10 percent in 2020. Even though a global financial crisis was different from the COVID-19 pandemic, I would per-sonally be prepared for an even greater drop than the IMF estimates, because in 2009, the world trade plummeted by more than 20 percent. In this connection, it should be borne in mind that in 2009 only the growth of the world economy stopped, while the global real GDP fell by only 0.1 percent. According to the IMF, the world economy will fall by 3 per cent in 2020. Here we should keep in mind that the global export orders dropped by nearly 20 percent only in March 2020 (WTO, 2020b).

When the world economic growth stopped as a result of the global financial crisis, the global foreign direct investment (FDI) flows fell by between 20 and 30 percent to reach the pre-crisis level within a few years (UNCTAD, 2020). The present pandemic might cause a much deeper drop of the FDI flows than what happened during the global financial crisis of 2007–2009, and it is evident that the recovery from the decline would be slower. It is also possible that the pandemic would enhance the focus on the security of supply, which would result in the shortening of global supply chains. This, consquently, would mean that production would move closer to consumption.

Beata Javorcik, Chief Economist at the European Bank for Reconstruction and Development, summarizes the impact of the COVID-19 pandemic on the global value chains as follows (Javorcik, 2020: 20): "The combination of the US-China trade war and COVID-19 may have created a perfect storm. Each of the shocks by itself would not be enough to spark rethinking of global value chains, but their combination may just do so. The trade war created uncertainty about future trade policy. Firms can no longer take it for granted that current tariff commitments enshrined in the WTO rules will prevent sudden protectionist surges. The WTO dispute mechanism has stopped functioning. At the same time, COVID-19 has exposed what many may consider an excessive reliance of suppliers located in China."

COVID-19 has closed borders, stopped international tourism, and in most countries, reduced drastically domestic travel. The paralysis of tourism is a major blow to the world economy, as travel and tourism as a whole, including domestic tourism, accounted for one-tenth of the world economy in 2019. Correspondingly, the share of international tourism of the world's total travel and tourism revenue was almost 30 percent. The halt in international tourism does punish equally developing and advanced economies. We should not forget that the advanced economies account for most of the world tourism revenue. However, in the same context, we should remember that the importance of revenue from international tourism in relation to GDP is greater among the poorer countries of the world than in the richer ones (see Table 7.1).

According to WTTC (2020), the coronavirus pandemic has endangered 75 million jobs in travel and tourism. The World Travel and Tourism Council estimates the impact of COVID-19 to be five times bigger compared to the one caused by the global financial crisis. It seems regrettably likely that it would take some years for the revenue streams of international tourism to return to their pre-pandemic level.

The EU Economy

The sudden stop in travel and tourism including its international component in Europe has had strong impact on Germany, Italy, the United Kingdom, France and Spain. In total, travel and tourism generated

Table 7.1 Travel and Tourism in the Global GDP in 2019

	Contribution of travel and tourism to regional GDP ($ billion)	Share of travel and tourism in regional GDP (%)
North America	2,100	8.8
North-East Asia	2,100	9.8
Europe	2,000	9.1
South-East Asia	380	12.1
Latin America	299	8.8
Middle East	245	8.6
South Asia	234	6.6
Oceania	197	11.7
Africa	168	7.1
Caribbean	59	13.9
Others	1,118	n.a.

Source: The Author, based on WTTC (2020).

almost US$1,300 billion in these economies in 2019. In Europe, however, the halt in travel and tourism would hit most severely Spain, where international tourism accounted for more than half of all travel and tourism revenue in 2019. In the other four countries, the average share of international tourism was slightly over 20 percent (WTTC, 2020).

The IMF (2020a) has predicted that the Spanish unemployment rate would rise by 5 percentage points in 2020, increasing the country's official total unemployment to above 20 percent. Because of hidden unemployment, the actual unemployment rate would rise even higher. In this context, it is also worth remembering that even before the coronavirus epidemic, the official youth unemployment rate in Spain, Greece and Italy was already around 30 percent (Eurostat, 2020).

High unemployment rates, especially among socially mobile young people, combined with the mental malaise caused by the COVID-19 pandemic would inevitably build social pressures, increase the support of extremist movements and might consequently cause riots. It may also increase the violence against minorities and immigrants or spur discontent of various nature. The recent history of Europe shows that social unrest spreads rapidly from country to country.

According to the IMF, the real GDP of the Euro Zone would fall by 7.5 percent in 2020. In Italy, GDP would drop even more, by a whopping 9 percent. Since the banking sector in several Mediterranean EU member countries was in trouble before COVID-19 pandemic, the deep plunge in GDP caused by it, combined with the spiraling bankruptcy of businesses and rapid rise in unemployment, would create significant pressure on economic and social sustainability, particularly in the southern part of the EU (see Table 7.2).

Although the EU is now much better prepared for tackling a financial crisis than it was in connection with the Greek economic crisis ten years ago, the failures of the Italian and Spanish financial systems would be a threat to the whole of the EU.

The Legacy of COVID-19 Pandemic

The End of the Beginning

"Now this is not the end. It is not even the beginning of the end, but it is, perhaps, the end of the beginning", said Sir Winston Churchill in November 1942, when a frail ray of light began to seep into the darkness of World War II (Churchill, 1942). Even though COVID-19 might probably kill numerous more people in the period from when this article was written to when it would be published, let us hope that the number of deaths per day would decline. In March, according the official statistics, COVID-19 killed on average less than 1,300 people per day worldwide. In April, the daily death figure was over 6,300, but

Table 7.2 Key Economic Indicators for the EU 27 Member Countries

EU27	Real GDP change 2020	Foreign trade/ GDP 2018 (%)	Inward FDI stock/GDP 2018 (%)	International tourism income/total exports 2018 (%)
Austria	−7.0	83	46	10
Belgium	−6.9	170	96	2
Bulgaria	−4.0	108	74	12
Croatia	−9.0	75	54	39
Cyprus	−6.5	64	898	19
Czech Republic	−6.5	158	63	4
Denmark	−6.5	60	32	5
Estonia	−7.5	118	79	10
Finland	−6.0	56	24	5
France	−7.2	45	30	8
Germany	−7.0	72	24	3
Greece	−10.0	47	15	26
Hungary	−3.1	157	56	7
Ireland	−6.8	71	238	3
Italy	−9.1	50	21	8
Latvia	−8.6	104	50	5
Lithuania	−8.1	131	33	3
Luxembourg	−4.9	57	232	4
Malta	−2.8	64	1,421	9
Netherlands	−7.5	150	183	3
Poland	−4.6	91	40	5
Portugal	−8.0	65	56	23

(Continued)

Table 7.2 (Continued)

EU27	Real GDP change 2020	Foreign trade/ GDP 2018 (%)	Inward FDI stock/GDP 2018 (%)	International tourism income/total exports 2018 (%)
Romania	−5.0	74	39	3
Slovakia	−6.2	176	54	3
Slovenia	−8.0	160	31	7
Spain	−8.0	52	46	16
Sweden	−6.8	61	58	6
Other countries				
China (mainland)	+1.2	34	12	2
Russia	−5.5	42	25	4
UK	−6.5	41	66	6
USA	−5.9	21	36	10

Sources: The Author, based on IMF (2020a); UNCTAD (2020); World Bank (2020).

in May, it had fallen to approximately 4,500 (HS, 2020). Let us hope for the better.

Although it is likely that new COVID-19 waves would occur when countries begin lifting their mobility and travel restrictions, there is some hope in sight for a better future that the vaccine against the coronavirus is getting closer every day. Hopefully, a worthwhile vaccine would be found soon, and it can be produced in sufficient quantities to meet the needs worldwide.

Permanent Legacy of the Pandemic

Predicting the permanent legacy of the pandemic is in fact difficult because of the enormous uncertainty. One example is the U.S. presidential election in November 2020. The outcome of this election may either accelerate the crumbling of the globalization as we know it, or, the Great Lockdown experience might make Americans realize that great does not always mean good.

Henry Kissinger, former U.S. Secretary of State and National Security Adviser, wrote in April 2020 (Kissinger, 2020): "*The reality is the world will never be the same after the coronavirus. … Leaders are dealing with the crisis on a largely national basis, but the virus's society-dissolving effects do not recognize borders. While the assault on human health will—hopefully—be temporary, the political and economic upheaval it has unleashed could last for generations. … Now, we live an epochal period. The historic challenge for leaders is to manage the crisis while building the future. Failure could set the world on fire.*"

In Table 7.3, I present a summary of my views on what the permanent impacts of COVID-19 would be. In this respect, it should be pointed out that not all permanent impacts arise immediately. The pandemic triggers some global processes that can lead slowly, but almost inevitably, to the outcomes presented in the table, unless the great powers change their attitude towards international cooperation.

Order Out of Chaos

Hopefully, the COVID-19 pandemic would help us understand that all countries are interdependent on each other and that no nation can base its operations on its own goals only. We are all interconnected. For our own sake, we must ensure other countries are also doing well. Without understanding the concept of responsibility in its broadest sense, we would inevitably advance toward future crises, which might be called Great Crushes. Now the most powerful politicians should realize their responsibility, address opportunities to affect things, become active, and start creating order out of chaos, *ordo ab chao*, for the common good.

Table 7.3 Permanent Impacts of the Pandemic

- The weakening of international institutions, such as the UN, WHO and WTO, will continue even though the development should go in the opposite direction if we are to successfully combat global threats and crises in the future.

- Xenophobia and populist nationalism will raise their heads around the world, which will increase the likelihood of conflicts between states and even within states. The geopolitical situation will become more strained. The opposition to immigration will also increase, which will provide a source of additional support for populist and nationalist parties.

- The selfish first reactions of EU Member States in the fight against the virus, the slowness of the European Commission, the weakness of the economic structures in the southern parts of the EU and nationalist populism are disintegrating the foundations of the EU. Even before this decade is over, the EU will be completely different from what we have become used to.

- The global supply chains will shorten, and security of supply thinking will increase, in other words, production will move closer to consumption. Globalisation will be replaced by a continent-based world order.

- The free world trade will be at risk. Governments will use the pandemic as an excuse for their protectionist actions. In the world trade, a trade system between economic blocs will emerge. The world trade will increasingly shift towards e-commerce, meaning that there will be more direct supply chains from producers to customers.

- FDIs will decline significantly and, like in the previous crises, investments will begin to withdraw from peripheral regions and cluster in the centres of global economy. After the pandemic, however, the global production model will not be fully restored.

- International business travel will go through a significant transformation as electronic meeting practices reduce business travel. The corona pandemic will also have a serious long-term impact on tourism-supporting industries, such as airplane, cruise ship and hotel construction.

Source: The Author.

References

Adams-Heard, R., Saraiva, C., 2020. Oil companies warn Kansas City Fed of widespread insolvencies, *Bloomberg*, April 7, 2020, https://www.bloomberg.com/news/articles/2020-04-07/oil-companies-warn-kansas-city-fed-of-widespread-insolvencies, (Accessed on April 22, 2020).

Ambrose, J., 2020. Oil prices dip below zero as producers forced to pay to dispose of excess, *The Guardian*, April 20, 2020, https://www.theguardian. com/world/2020/apr/20/oil-prices-sink-to-20-year-low-as-un-sounds-alarm-on-to-covid-19-relief-fund, (Accessed on April 21, 2020).

BP, 2019. *BP statistical review of world energy*, 68th Edition, https://www.bp. com/content/dam/bp/business-sites/en/global/corporate/pdfs/energy-economics/ statistical-review/bp-stats-review-2019-full-report.pdf, (Accessed on April 22, 2020).

CDC, 2020. *1918 Pandemic (H1N1 virus)*, Centers for Disease Control and Prevention, https://www.cdc.gov/flu/pandemic-resources/1918-pandemic-h1n1. html, (Accessed on April 26, 2020).

Churchill, W., 1942. *The end of the beginning, Speech,* The Lord Mayor's Luncheon, Mansion House, November 10, 1942, http://www.churchill-society-london.org.uk/EndoBegn.html, (Accessed on April 14, 2020).

Crafts, N., Fearon, P., 2010. Lessons from the 1930s Great Depression. *Oxf. Rev. Econ. Policy 26/3*, 285–317.

Eurostat, 2020. *Youth Unemployment*, https://ec.europa.eu/eurostat/statistics-explained/index.php/Unemployment_statistics#Youth_unemployment, (Accessed on April 26, 2020).

HS, 2020. Suomessa kaksi uutta koronaviruskuolemaa, sairaalassa nyt 71, *Helsingin Sanomat*, https://www.hs.fi/kotimaa/art-2000006497114.html, (Accessed on May 31, 2020).

IMF, 2020a. *World Economic Outlook, April 2020*, International Monetary Fund, https://www.imf.org/en/Publications/WEO/Issues/2020/04/14/weo-april-2020, (Accessed on April 15, 2020).

IMF, 2020b. *World Economic Outlook Database*, Download WEO Data: April 2020 Edition, International Monetary Fund, https://www.imf.org/external/ pubs/ft/weo/2020/01/weodata/index.aspx, (Accessed on April 15, 2020).

Javorcik, B., 2020. COVID-19 will revolutionise global supply chains, *Baltic Rim Economies 2/2020, 20*, https://sites.utu.fi/bre/, (Accessed on May 29, 2020).

Johns Hopkins University, 2020. *COVID-19 dashboard by the Center for Systems Science and Engineering (CSSE) at Johns Hopkins*, https:// coronavirus.jhu.edu/map.html, (Accessed on May 31, 2020).

Kissinger, H. A., 2020. The coronavirus pandemic will forever alter the world order, *The Wall Street Journal*, April 3, 2020, https://www.wsj.com/articles/ the-coronavirus-pandemic-will-forever-alter-the-world-order-11585953005, (Accessed on April 21, 2020).

UNCTAD, 2020. *UNCTADstat*, United Nations Conference on Trade and Development, https://unctadstat.unctad.org/EN/, (Accessed on April 15, 2020).

World Bank, 2020. *International tourism receipts (% of total exports)*, https://data. worldbank.org/indicator/ST.INT.RCPT.XP.ZS, (Accessed on April 14, 2020).

WTO, 2020a. *WTO data portal.* World Trade Organization. https://timeseries. wto.org/, (Accessed on April 15, 2020).

WTO, 2020b. *WTO goods barometer flashes red as COVID-19 disrupts world trade,* https://www.wto.org/english/news_e/news20_e/wtoi_19may20_e.pdf, (Accessed on April 23, 2020).

WTTC, 2020. *Economic impact report*, https://wttc.org/en-gb/Research/ Economic-Impact, (Accessed on April 20, 2020).

Part II

COVID-19: Industry Perspectives and Business Models

8 COVID-19 and the Changing Perception of Strategic Industries

Implications for International Business

Ahmad Arslan, Zaheer Khan,
Minnie Kontkanen, and Shlomo Tarba

Introduction

The COVID-19 pandemic has been referred to as one of the most significant health related crises in recent memory, which has also had significant economic and societal implications (WHO, 2020a). As of May 2020, COVID-19 has spread to almost every country on the planet, and in most cases, national and local governments have resorted to strategies like social distancing and lockdowns to control its spread (ECDC, 2020; WHO, 2020). At the same time, COVID-19 has raised challenges and renowned calls to curtail globalization in the form we know it as it has forced countries (nation-states) to think about their own citizens and focus on securing the basic supply of goods and services. Moreover, the economic consequences of this pandemic are expected to be really significant based on estimates of experts (see e.g., Atkeson, 2020). Therefore, it is quite logical that many experts claim that the post-COVID-19 world would be less open and more inward looking, where operations of non-native firms may face significant hindrances and screening from rising nationalist elements (Garver, 2020; Miller, 2020). Already, numerous countries have put restrictions on acquisitions during the COVID-19 pandemic, as well as restricting foreign direct investments into certain sectors (*Japan Times*, 2020; Singh, 2020). At the same time, the term *strategic industries* has become a key part of the mainstream discourse gaining local political capital. Recently, some industries have become strategic not due to their strategic value to the local economic development but due to the political interests of powerful stakeholders. Traditionally, industries like military, high-tech manufacturing, banking, as well as infrastructure have been referred to as strategic by policy makers and scholars. Along with these industries, agriculture has been viewed as important and strategic historically due to its importance in fulfilling the most important human need for food (McNeely and Scherr, 2003). However, since the dawn of globalization, agricultural (and processed food) products have increasingly globalized depending upon long and complex networks of supply chains spanning many countries (Blank, 2014). COVID-19 has brought agro-food sector back in focus as a strategic industry along with industries like pharmaceuticals, ventilator, personal protective equipment (PPE) manufacturing, finance, credit, insurance and 5G technology in the case of Italy, and biotechnology in the case of France. We have witnessed some examples of countries stopping the export shipments of pre-paid orders of PPE or ventilators (FT, 2020; Tong, 2020) in the recent months, as well as stopping domestic firms from exporting basic medicines including even painkillers (Tripathy, 2020). Other measures include, for instance, export bans on medical equipment and in some cases requiring mandatory local production of certain items.

All of these recent events form the core of this chapter, where it aims to offer a conceptual overview of strategic industries and then link the discussion to the changing perceptions of such industries in the times of crises, as the COVID-19 pandemic. An effort has been made to substantiate the conceptual discussion by presenting a number of relevant practical examples in this chapter. By focusing on the changing perceptions of strategic industries due to COVID-19; we contribute to the extant international business (IB) literature in two-ways. Firstly, this is one of the first studies to specifically highlight changing perception of strategic industries from an IB perspective, thereby setting bases for further theorization on this specific topic. Secondly, this chapter is one of the first studies to also link the changing perceptions of strategic industries to the respective implications for the multinational enterprises (MNEs), which have been the key driving force behind globalization. The chapter further highlights that such changing perceptions of strategic industries will have a far-reaching impact on the future collaboration and co-ordination of global value chains activities across developed and emerging economies. Many countries have cut down (or restricted) important supplies, including food exports, which will have significant consequences for the ways in which global value chains are governed and controlled. In the same vein, the reinvigoration of the debate around strategic industries has created long-term consequences for sustainable international trade and foreign direct investment across different locations and sectors, so the locational advantages of countries and the widespread global value chains are expected to come under a greater scrutiny.

The rest of the chapter is organized as follows. The next section offers a conceptual discussion on strategic industries and the changing perception of such strategic industries at the time of crises, where we offer historical examples. After that, the COVID-19 crisis and its influences on strategic industries as well as for related international business dynamics are discussed in-depth. The last section of the chapter presents conclusions, limitations and directions for future research.

Strategic Industries and Crises: An Overview

Scholars suggest that defining strategic industries is rather difficult due to the fluidity of the criteria, which can be used to define them, as it tends to change (Stevens, 1991; Los, 2004). One of the broadest criteria used to classify such industries is the long-term access or availability of products/services in a particular sector, which is considered to be vital for a country's economic interest and local development (cf. Soete, 1991; Stevens, 1991). Being crucial to a country's economy can be further perceived in a variety of ways, ranging from fulfilling specific needs to employment dependence, to long-term economic competitiveness and security aspects (e.g., Rabe and Gippner, 2017). Another criterion for defining strategic industries emphasizes the interdependence of activities in the industry through forward and backward linkages within the national economy. Industry, which acts as supporting infrastructure to other related industries and thus creates positive external economies of scale can also be regarded as a strategic one (Teece, 1991; Narula, 2014). Di Tommaso et al. (2017) state that economics literature argues that strategic industries or sectors *promote economic growth*, mostly calling for the sectors to be competitive over time. Thus, high-tech industries, with high value added and capabilities of developing economies of scale, achieving highest profits and having good export performance have been considered strategic by many scholars (Narula, 2014; Di Tommaso et al. 2017). Sector's weight in the national economy economy such as its share in employment and implications on economic growth, is an additional criterion often linked to strategic sectors. Another distinct area of literature, in the meantime, emphasizes the *benefits, which the sector brings to the society as a whole,* as a key determinant for that industry being strategic. From this perspective, implications of those industries for national security and social well-being are important, and this view goes beyond the narrow focus on only economic importance and growth. Prior literature has referred to health, agriculture, education and cultural sectors as being examples of such industries (Di Tommaso et al., 2017; Dodgson, 2018). Moreover, the service sector, telecommunications, information technology, banking and infrastructure provision have also been viewed as strategic (Golub, 2009; Dodgson, 2018).

It is clear from the above discussion that the criteria used to define strategic industries can vary significantly from country to country (see the earlier example of Italy and France). Still most scholars argue that governments are able to identify which industries they perceive strategic in their specific country contexts (Stevens, 1991; Los, 2004). Hence, differences in the perceptions of strategic industries exist across countries. For instance, in some developed economies, strategic industries tend to be mostly high-tech, advanced manufacturing and defense. In developing or emerging economies, which generally have infrastructure problems; strategic industries encompass infrastructure such as power, transportation and telecommunications in the case of Nigeria (Chete et al., 2016). Similarly, logistics has been referred to as a strategic industry in case of Cambodia because of its connectivity, socio-economic development and poverty reduction consequences (Cheang, 2017:268). Thus, the development level of a country is linked to what is considered a strategic sector in a country context (Narula, 2014; Dodgson, 2018). Yoshitomi (1991) argues that there are industries, which are considered strategic by all governments when they have dynamic potential for future growth and technological change. This aspect of industry categorization becomes visible during crises when certain products and services may become in high demand worldwide. Crises generally result in strong domestic sentiments due to fear and uncertainty. Hence, gaining political capital in the home market becomes important for many decision makers. Such changes have been witnessed as immediate consequences against the backdrop of COVID-19. Judged by the attitudes and actions of national governments and regional integrations such as the European Union (EU), the prioritizing of what constitutes strategic industries has changed towards a strong emphasis on industries with critical inputs to health and food sector as well as those having impacts on the national security. Such changes had taken place in the global economy during previous crises.

During the twentieth century, the most significant crises, having taken place globally, were World War I (WWI) and World War II (WWII) (both human created), as well as multiple influenza pandemics (health crises), of which the Spanish flu (1918–1920) being the most severe one (Reiter, 1996; Killingray and Phillips, 2003). The period before WWI has been referred to as the first era of globalization, where global trade in agricultural as well as industrial products became very visible (Clark, 1997). Britain, which was the largest trading nation in the world before 1914, depended on imports for 80 percent of its food consumption. As a consequence of WWI, the trade routes were cut, resulting in huge demand for food and escalating to near starvation across Britain and Germany (e.g. Simmonds, 2013). The challenges experienced during the war itself, promoted agriculture to become strategic industry after the war. This change in perception was seen in almost every country when domestic agriculture was protected through different protectionist activities such as tariffs and subsidies. (Strikwerda, 2016).

In addition to the influence of wars, previous studies have found that even mild pandemics had significant consequences for the global economic output (McKibbin and Sidorenko, 2006). Besides the severe economic consequences, pandemics represent also direct threats to national security (Atkeson, 2020; Jonung and Roeger, 2006; Price-Smith, 2009; Atkeson, 2020), and thus also have implications on the perceptions of strategic industries. Such situations are very relevant to the crisis caused by COVID-19, whose influences on the strategic industries as related to international business dynamics are discussed in the next section of this chapter.

COVID-19, Strategic Industries and International Business Dynamics

The COVID-19 pandemic has brought a renewed focus on strategic sectors, which can have far reaching implications for international business. During the recent decades, food production and consumption have been driven by globalization (Blank, 2014). As an outcome, the majority of countries have depended on imported food (Southy, 2020) and food exporting. According to Kinnunen et al. (2020), the local food crop production can satisfy the demand of less than one-third of the population. An extreme example of the dependence on food imports is Singapore, which imports 90 percent of its food supplies form 170 countries worldwide (Neo, 2020c). The Food and Agriculture Organization (FAO) has raised the concern of disruption in food supply chain and the increased threat of hunger and poverty because of reduced access to markets and deteriorating purchasing power as a direct consequence of COVID-19 (Muhammad-Bande, 2020). Due to its obvious role as an industry with critical inputs and thus, a sector having implications for national security; food industry has been emerging as an industry of increasing strategic importance as a consequence of COVID-19. The food sector has been emphasized as a critical sector in developed economies such as Japan (Neo 2020d) and regions such as the EU (EU 2020b) in response to the COVID-19 crisis. However, this sector's importance as a strategic industry is emphasized even more in emerging economies (such as Malaysia) and countries with high dependence on imports like Singapore (Neo 2020c). The rising cost of food and shortage of food due to several countries halting food exports have resulted in the

United Nation's (UN) warning of extreme shortage of food supplies in certain parts of the world.

The most visible danger for national security and social well-being caused by the COVID-19 pandemic has been the lack of access to vitally important medical products, for which global demand has increased exponentially. As an outcome, WTO (2020a) reports that an increasing number of export prohibitions and restrictions (by 80 countries and custom territories) to mitigate the shortages at national level. The products covered by these new export prohibitions and restrictions vary considerably; most have focused on medical supplies (e.g., facemasks and shields), pharmaceuticals and medical equipment (e.g., ventilators). As a huge number of countries, report additional restrictions on exporting or foreign direct investment (FDI) procedures, the emphasis on health technology related sectors, such as medical supplies, pharmaceuticals and biotechnology, as strategic sectors has emerged worldwide. This is visible across developed economies as the EU, the U.S., and in emerging economies such as India and China (BDI 2020a).

Strategic industries are generally promoted by governments (Teece, 1991; Selen, 2020), making their importance very high for the global operations of multinational corporations (MNCs), as well as their impact on local economic development. Michalski (1991) identified the following four types of support policies in strategic industries: 1) Trade-related measures (e.g. tariffs, export restrictions across different sectors such as automotive, defense and energy); 2) Investment-related policies (e.g., selective acceptance of FDIs; domestic content requirement and foreign equity restrictions); 3) Industrial and technology policies (e.g. strategic support to crucial foreign acquisitions); 4) Fiscal and financial market policies (e.g. favorable tax treatment); and 5) Competition policies. From MNCs' points of view, these policies create either opportunities or threats for their operations in those countries especially in relation to controlling rights over their operations and repatriation of profits back to their headquarters. International business-related measures linked to COVID-19 pandemic are visible in the strategic industries of food, PPE, pharmaceutical and IT sectors. Different governments have introduced a range of measures to restrict exports of critical products. In some country contexts, such as India, import tariffs have been announced on food and agricultural products in order to further local trade (Singh, 2020). These policies on the one hand influence negatively the possibilities of both domestic and foreign firms to export their products manufactured locally, and on the other hand, weaken the competitive position of importing firms. In general, the disruptions in food supply chains have caused serious problems for food manufacturing from firms because of the lack of raw materials, requiring from firms to make adjustments to their production processes (Neo, 2020d). Large MNCs operating in the food sector, such as Nestlé and Unilever, have experienced challenges in their production and supply chains (IE 2020; Sarkar 2020). Numerous countries, such as Indonesia, emphasized the importance of continued exports due to their importance for the local economy and employability (Rahman, 2020).

It should also be noted that restrictive investment policies have been set up by many governments to minimize the risk of attempts to acquire local firms operating in the critical sectors of production of medical or protective equipment or related industries (EU, 2020b; Investment Policy Monitor, 2020b). These policies can potentially have negative implications for the MNC's opportunities to acquire and share knowledge and ultimately to innovate across their network of subsidiaries. A the same time, support measures for FDI have also been introduced in some cases, which resulted in speeding up of investment approval procedures (Investment Policy Monitor, 2020b). National investment promotion agencies, like Invest India, APEX Brazil and Germany Trade & Invest, have put strong emphasis on attracting companies and facilitating foreign investors (Investment Policy Monitor, 2020a) in strategic sectors. Meanwhile, the global needs for developing COVID-19 vaccines as well as developing digital solutions like contact tracking COVID-19 infected persons present opportunities to MNCs (Aaltonen, 2020; Bremmer, 2020) originating from developed and emerging economies to develop digital business models and related capabilities. IBM, for instance, has been involved in several projects globally to use their technology and expertise through supercomputers and machine learning to speed up the process of discovery and development of treatments for a cure of deadly complications of COVID-19 (Gill 2020; Martineau 2020). Microsoft, on the other hand, has enabled through their Start-up Accelerator Programs new innovations in bio-IT, such as a cloud-based genome analysis computing platform accelerating the development of COVID-19 vaccine (Microsoft Asia News Center, 2020). It has further been argued that the COVID-19 pandemic can trigger a competition between countries for attracting investments in critical sectors of biotechnology and pharmaceutical research (Bennhold and Sanger, 2020; Investment Policy Monitor, 2020a).

Despite all restrictive policies, discussed above, it is a well-known fact based on the outcomes of prior crises (Davis and Pelc, 2017; Gawande et al., 2015) that in order to limit the negative outcomes of the pandemic, international cooperation and collaborations are fundamental among private sector firm, including MNCs, global institutions and policy makers (ASEAN, 2020; Glauber et al., 2020;

Muhammad-Bande, 2020; WHO, 2020a, c; WTO, 2020a). Thus, even though restrictions may cause some challenges in knowledge transfer in the form of acquisitions and other entry modes, it is expected that such cooperation via alliances will lead to the development of innovative products and services, especially in health technology (GSK, 2020a). Corporate social responsibility (CSR) would also be important in such endeavors, especially when collaboration to address the challenges by COVID-19 is between entities representing private, public and non-government organization (NGO) sectors (GSK, 2020b; Opiyo, 2020). Based on this discussion, it is logical to expect that in the post COVID-19 world, CSR would play a more important role in MNCs and their global operations, especially in the strategic industries of food, PPE, pharmaceuticals, and high-tech.

Conclusions, Limitations and Directions for Future Research

A key conclusion drawn from the current chapter is about the increased importance of industries like agriculture, food production, healthcare equipment manufacturing and pharmaceuticals, for IB research. In the past, these industries have not received enough attention from IB scholars, but keeping in mind their importance, specific research into operations, dynamics and strategies in these industries, to include FDI and the organization of their global and regional value chains, is needed from IB perspectives. It is further important to mention that significant prior IB research has focused on FDI strategies at aggregate level, where specificities of industries, especially strategic industries, are not always visible. The IB literature would also benefit from researching FDI strategies, entry modes and divestment of firms originating from strategic industries, as well as FDI into strategic industries across developed and emerging economies. In some cases, host governments might restrict FDI into strategic industries whereas others might seek more FDI to facilitate local economic development. Thus, it is important to enrich our understanding of issues such as how entry mode choice or mergers and acquisition strategies differ in strategic versus non-strategic industries in a particular country. Another conclusion is related to MNCs' operations in an increasingly restrictive and changing global world, which is dominated by inward -looking nationalistic sentiments. This consideration can have a far reaching impact on the outsourcing, offshoring and reshoring or near shoring strategies adopted by MNCs across different sectors. There are important implications for MNCs from different sectors as to how MNCs would navigate the rising private power brokers and domestic political interests in order to create value for a range of stakeholders to guarantee the long-term sustainability of MNCs.

The chapter has certain limitations. Firstly, it is only a descriptive piece of work, thereby lacking empirical data analysis. This can make generalization based on its content difficult. However, the purpose of the chapter has not been to present specific findings, which can be generalized, but rather to offer an overall evaluation of the importance of strategic industries during COVID-19. Moreover, as we have attempted to conceptualize the impacts of COVID-19, we are aware that certain aspects being discussed in this chapter may have changed over time. However, despite this limitation, our chapter brings into focus strategic industries and their changing perceptions due to the COVID-19 induced crisis, which is highly relevant for IB. We believe that this chapter lays the foundation for future studies into the specificities of strategic industries in relation to different IB strategies of both MNCs and small and medium-sized enterprises, including the nature and scope of future collaborations and alliances between MNCs and local firms.

Further research is needed on how virus outbreaks and global pandemics will alter the location strategies of MNCs across strategic and non-strategic industries. Recently, countries have used trade sanctions as policies to protect their national interests, thus future studies could examine how such sanctions would change the structure, patterns and behavior of firms and their global value chains.

Lastly, the nationalistic and protectionist policies pursued by numerous countries need to be examined in the context of strategic industries and the changing geography of MNCs' value chains activities.

References

Aaltonen, R., 2020. Suomen rokotemarkkina on keskittynyt muutaman suuren toimijan käsiin, ja nyt ne kaikki valmistelevat koronavirusrokotetta – "Saatavilla aikaisintaan vuoden 2021 lopulla". https://www.talouselama.fi/uutiset/te/aafbba7b-c3ab-4692-a451-fabd9998e003? (accessed 05.05.20).

ASEAN, 2020. Statement of ASEAN ministers on agriculture and forestry in response to the outbreak of the coronavirus disease (COVID-19) to ensure food security, food safety and nutrition in ASEAN. https://asean.org/storage/2020/04/STATEMENT-OF-ASEAN-MINISTERS-ON-AGRICULTURE-AND-FORESTRY-ON-COVID-19-FINAL-00000002.pdf (accessed 04.05.20.).

Atkeson, A., 2020. *What will be the economic impact of COVID-19 in the US? Rough estimates of disease scenarios.* National Bureau of Economic Research (No. w26867). https://www.nber.org/papers/w26867.pdf (accessed 14.05.20.).

Bennhold, K., Sanger, D.E., 2020. *U.S. Offered 'Large Sum' to German Company for Access to Coronavirus Vaccine Research, German Officials Say.)* https://www.nytimes.com/2020/03/15/world/europe/cornonavirus-vaccine-us-germany.html (accessed 14.05.20).

BDI, 2020a. Position, foreign trade policy, COVID-19. Export controls and export bans over the course of the Covid-19 pandemic export restrictions impair ability to respond to the crisis. https://www.wto.org/english/tratop_e/covid19_e/bdi_covid19_e.pdf (accessed 29.04. 20).

Blank, S.C., 2014. *The Economics of American Agriculture: Evolution and Global Development: Evolution and Global Development.* Routledge, Oxon.

Bremmer, I., 2020. Top geopolitical risks in 2020: coronavirus update. https://www.eurasiagroup.net/live-post/top-geopolitical-risks-2020-coronavirus-update (accessed 02.05.20.).

Chete, L.N., Adeoti, J.O., Adeyinka, F.M., Ogundele, O., 2016. Industrial development and growth in Nigeria: lessons and challenges. Learning to compete. Working paper No.8. Brookings. https://www.brookings.edu/wp-content/uploads/2016/07/L2C_WP8_Chete-et-al-1.pdf (accessed 14.05.20.).

Cheang, V., 2017. FDI, services liberalization and logistics development in Cambodia. In: Tham, S.Y., Sanchita, B.D. (Eds.), *Services liberalization in ASEAN: Foreign direct investment in logistics.* Wiley, Hoboken, NJ, pp. 268–297.

Clark, I., 1997. *Globalization and Fragmentation: International Relations in the Twentieth Century.* Oxford University Press, Oxford.

Das, S.B., Widjaja, E.P.O., 2017. Services sector liberalization in Singapore: Case of the logistics sector. In: Tham, S.Y., Sanchita, B.D. (Eds.), *Services Liberalization in ASEAN: Foreign Direct Investment in Logistics.* Wiley, Hoboken, NJ, pp. 148–180.

Davis, C.L., Pelc, K.J., 2017. Cooperation in hard times: self-restraint of trade protection, *J. Confl. Resolut.* 61(2), 398–429.

Di Tommaso, M, Tassinari, M., Bonnini, S., Marozzi, M., 2017. Industrial policy and manufacturing targeting in the US: new methodological tools for strategic policy-making. *Int. Rev. Appl. Econ.* 31(5), 681–703.

Dodgson, M., 2018. *Technological Collaboration in Industry: Strategy, Policy and Internationalization in Innovation* (Vol. 11). Routledge, Oxon.

ECDC, 2020. COVID-19 situation update worldwide, as of 14 May. https://www.ecdc.europa.eu/en/geographical-distribution-2019-ncov-cases (accessed 14.05.20.).

EU, 2020a. Regulation (EU) 2019/452 of the European Parliament and of the Council of 19 March 2019 establishing a framework for the screening of foreign direct investments into the Union PE/72/2018/REV/1. https://eur-lex.europa.eu/eli/reg/2019/452/oj (accessed 14.05.20.).

EU, 2020b. Guidance to the Member States concerning foreign direct investment and free movement of capital from third countries, and the protection of Europe's strategic assets, ahead of the application of Regulation (EU) 2019/452 (FDI Screening Regulation). https://trade.ec.europa.eu/doclib/docs/2020/march/tradoc_158676.pdf (accessed 25.03.20.).

FT, 2020. Export bans blocked signed contracts to buy PPE, MPs told. Available from: https://www.ft.com/content/8c0a29fc-a523-4901-a190-fe5a2dcc8faa (accessed 14.05.20.).

Garver, R., 2020. Will COVID-19 kill globalization?. https://www.voanews.com/covid-19-pandemic/will-covid-19-kill-globalization (accessed 14.05.20.).

Gawande, K., Hoekman, B., Cui, Y., 2015. Global supply chains and trade policy responses to the 2008 crisis. *World Bank. Economic Rev.* 29(1), 102–128.

Gill, D., 2020. IBM helps bring supercomputers into the global fight against COVID-19. https://newsroom.ibm.com/IBM-helps-bring-supercomputers-into-the-global-fight-against-COVID-19 (accessed 16.06.20.).

Glauber, J., Laborde, D., Martin, W., Vos, R., 2020. COVID-19: Trade restrictions are worst possible response to safeguard food security. https://www.ifpri.org/blog/covid-19-trade-restrictions-are-worst-possible-response-safeguard-food-security (accessed 02.05.20.).

Golub, S.S., 2009. Openness to foreign direct investment in services: an international comparative analysis. *World Economy* 32(8), 1245–1268.

GSK, 2020a. Sanofi and GSK join forces to fight COVID-19. https://www.gsk.com/en-gb/media/resource-centre/our-contribution-to-the-fight-against-2019-ncov/sanofi-and-gsk-join-forces-to-fight-covid-19/ (accessed 14.04.20.).

GSK, 2020b. GSK actions to support the global response to COVID-19. https://www.gsk.com/en-gb/media/resource-centre/our-contribution-to-the-fight-against-2019-ncov/ (accessed 14.04.20.).

IE, 2020. Nestlé boss admits Covid-19 is creating production problems. *IE Food & Beverage.* https://industryeurope.com/sectors/food-beverage/nestle-boss-admits-covid-19-is-creating-production-problems/ (accessed 16.06.20.).

Investment policy monitor, 2020a. Issue 23, April, UNCTAD.https://unctad.org/en/PublicationsLibrary/diaepcbinf2020d1_en.pdf (accessed 14.04.20.).

Investment policy monitor, 2020b. Investment policy responses to the COVID-19 pandemic. Special Issue 4, May, UNCTAD. https://unctad.org/en/pages/newsdetails.aspx?OriginalVersionID=2353 (accessed 14.05.20.).

Japan Times, 2020. Japan moves to limit foreign investment in half of listed firms. https://www.japantimes.co.jp/news/2020/05/11/business/economy-business/japan-limit-foreign-investment-listed-firms/ (accessed 14.05.20.).

Jonung, L., Roeger, W., 2006. The macroeconomic effects of a pandemic in Europe. A model-based assessment. DG ECFIN, European Commission. https://ec.europa.eu/economy_finance/publications/pages/publication708_en.pdf (accessed 14.05.20.).

Killingray, D., Phillips, H., 2003. *The Spanish Influenza Pandemic of 1918-1919: New Perspectives.* Routledge, Oxon.

Kinnunen, P., Guillaume, J.H.A., Taka, M., 2020. Local food crop production can fulfil demand for less than one-third of the population. *Nat. Food 1,* 229–237.

Los, B., 2004. Identification of strategic industries: a dynamic perspective. *Pap. Regional Sci.* 83(4), 669–698.

Martineau, K., 2020. Marshaling artificial intelligence in the fight against Covid-19. *MIT Quest for Intelligence,* May, 19. http://news.mit.edu/2020/mit-marshaling-artificial-intelligence-fight-against-covid-19–0519 (accessed 16.06.20.).

McKibbin, W., Sidorenko, A., 2006. Global macroeconomic consequences of pandemic influenza analysis. Lowy Institute for International policy & Brookings Institute. https://www.brookings.edu/wp-content/uploads/2016/06/200602.pdf (accessed 14.05.20.).

McNeely, J.A., Scherr, S.J., 2003. *Ecoagriculture: Strategies to Feed the World and Save Wild Biodiversity.* Island Press, London.

Michalski, W., 1991. Support policies for strategic industries. An introduction to the main issues. In OECD, *Strategic Industries in a Global Economy: Policy Issues for the 1990s*. OECD, Paris, pp. 51–80.

Microsoft Asia News Center, 2020. Cloud-based genome analysis could help speed up development of a COVID-19 vaccine.19.5.2020. https://news.microsoft.com/apac/2020/05/19/cloud-based-genome-analysis-could-help-speed-up-development-of-a-covid-19-vaccine/ (accessed 16.06.20.).

Miller, C., 2020. Will COVID-19 Sink Globalization? https://www.fpri.org/article/2020/04/will-covid-19-sink-globalization/ (Accessed on May14, 2020).

Muhammad-Bande, M., 2020. Preventing a pandemic-induced food emergency. https://www.un.org/en/coronavirus/preventing-pandemic-induced-food-emergency (Accessed on May1, 2020).

Narula, R., 2014. *Globalization and Technology: Interdependence, Innovation Systems and Industrial Policy*. John Wiley & Sons, Hoboken, NJ.

Neo, P., 2020a. Boosting 'Make in India' food strategy hitting nation's hopes of regional free trade agreements. https://www.foodnavigator-asia.com/Article/2020/04/07/Boosting-Make-in-India-food-strategy-hitting-nation-s-hopes-of-regional-free-trade-agreements (accessed 14.04.20.).

Neo, P., 2020b. COVID-19 in China: food supply and lax regulations cause for concern as government touts 'return to normalcy'. https://www.foodnavigator-asia.com/Article/2020/04/08/COVID-19-in-China-Food-supply-and-lax-regulations-cause-for-concern-as-government-touts-return-to-normalcy (accessed 08.04.20.).

Neo, P., 2020c. COVID-19 in ASEAN: protectionist measures threaten global supply chain as lockdowns persist. https://www.foodnavigator-asia.com/Article/2020/04/14/COVID-19-in-ASEAN-Protectionist-measures-threaten-global-supply-chains-as-lockdowns-persist (accessed 14.04.20.).

Neo, P., 2020d. 'No crackdowns for now': Japan temporarily loosens food labelling rules to help firms deal with COVID-19. https://www.foodnavigator-asia.com/Article/2020/04/23/No-crackdowns-for-now-Japan-temporarily-loosens-food-labelling-rules-to-help-firms-deal-with-COVID-19 (accessed 13.04.20.).

OECD, 2009. Agricultural policies in emerging economies: monitoring and evaluation 2009. https://www.oecd.org/countries/ukraine/42347206.pdf (accessed 14.05.20).

Opiyo, E., 2020. Q&A: COVID-19 is fuelling innovation, R&D in Africa. https://www.scidev.net/sub-saharan-africa/coronavirus/opinion/covid-19-is-fuelling-innovation-in-africa.html (accessed 07.05.20.).

Price-Smith, A.T., 2009. *Contagion and Chaos: Disease, Ecology, and National Security in the Era of Globalization*. MIT Press, Cambridge, MA.

Rabe, W., Gippner, O., 2017. Perceptions of China's outward foreign direct investment in European critical infrastructure and strategic industries. *International Politics 54*(4), 468–486.

Rahman, D.F., 2020. Exports of agricultural commodities continue despite logistical disruptions. https://www.thejakartapost.com/news/2020/05/04/exports-of-agricultural-commodities-continue-despite-logistical-disruptions.html (accessed 04.05.20.).

Reiter, D., 1996. *Crucible of Beliefs: Learning, Alliances, and World Wars*. Cornell University Press, Ithaca, NY.

Sarkar, C., 2020. Responding to the COVID-19 challenge –an interview with Hanneke Faber, Unilever. *The Marketing Journal*, 5.4.2020. https://www. marketingjournal.org/responding-to-the-covid-19-challenge-an-interview-with-hanneke-faber-unilever/ (accessed 16.06.20).

Selen, U., 2020. Why do countries use temporary trade barriers? *Appl. Econ. Lett.* 27(6), 437–440.

Simmonds, A.G., 2013. *Britain and World War One*. Routledge, Oxon.

Singh, M., 2020. To avoid hostile takeovers amid COVID-19, India mandates approvals on Chinese investments. https://techcrunch.com/2020/04/18/to-avoid-hostile-takeovers-amid-covid-19-india-mandates-approvals-on-chinese-investments/ (accessed 14.05.20.).

Soete, L., 1991. National Support Policies for Strategic Industries: The International Implications, *Strategic Industries in a Global Economy: Policy Issues for the 1990s*. OECD, Paris, pp. 81–97.

Southy, F., 2020. COVID-19 and self-sufficiency: Is local food production capable of meeting demand? https://www.foodnavigator.com/Article/2020/04/22/COVID-19-and-self-sufficiency-Is-local-food-production-capable-of-meeting-demand (accessed 22.04.20.).

Stevens, B., 1991. Support policies for strategic industries: An assessment and some policy recommendations, *Strategic Industries in a Global Economy: Policy Issues for the 1990s*. OECD, Paris, pp. 97–104.

Strikwerda, C., 2016. World War I in the History of Globalization. *Historical Reflect.* 42(3), 112–132.

Stringer, C., Michailova, S., 2018. Why modern slavery thrives in multinational corporations' global value chains. *Multinatl. Bus. Rev.* 26(3), 194–206.

Teece, 1991 Support policies for strategic industries: Impact on home economies, *Strategic Industries in a Global Economy: Policy Issues for the 1990s*. OECD, Paris, pp. 35–50.

Tong, S., 2020. Countries race to limit, ban exports of masks, ventilators, other gear. https://www.marketplace.org/2020/03/30/countries-race-to-limit-ban-exports-of-masks-ventilators-other-gear/ (accessed 14.04.20.).

Tripathy, S., 2020. The World Needs to Change How It Trades Drugs. https://foreignpolicy.com/2020/04/21/trading-drugs-during-coronavirus-pandemic/ (accessed 14.05.20.).

WHO, 2020a. Coronavirus disease 2019 (COVID-19): situation report, 72. https://apps.who.int/iris/bitstream/handle/10665/331685/nCoVsitrep 01Apr2020-eng.pdf (accessed 14.05.20.).

WHO, 2020b. Commitment and call to action: Global collaboration to accelerate new COVID-19 health technologies. https://www.who.int/news-room/detail/24-04-2020-commitment-and-call-to-action-global-collaboration-to-accelerate-new-covid-19-health-technologies (accessed 24.04.20.).

WHO, 2020c. Global leaders unite to ensure everyone everywhere can access new vaccines, tests and treatments for COVID-19. https://www.who.int/news-room/detail/24-04-2020-global-leaders-unite-to-ensure-everyone-everywhere-can-access-new-vaccines-tests-and-treatments-for-covid-19 (accessed 24.04.20.).

WTO, 2020a. Export prohibitions and restrictions. Information note. https://www.wto.org/english/tratop_e/covid19_e/medical_products_report_e.pdf (accessed 23.04.20.).

WTO, 2020b. The treatment of medical products in regional trade agreements. Information note. https://www.wto.org/english/tratop_e/covid19_e/medical_products_report_e.pdf (accessed 27.04.20.).

Yoshitomi, M., 1991. New trends of oligopolistic competition in the globalization of high-tech industries: Interactions among, trade, investment and government, *Strategic Industries in a Global Economy: Policy Issues for the 1990s*. OECD, Paris, pp. 15–34.

9 Change of International Business Models during COVID-19

William W. Baber and Arto Ojala

COVID-19 and International Business Models

The tremendous impact the novel Corona Virus of 2019, known as COVID-19, has had on the international business environment is incontrovertible. When writing this chapter, the nature of those impacts however has not yet become fully clear. Moreover, we cannot know whether the world will return to a 'pre-pandemic normal', or some sort of a different 'post-pandemic normal'. Indeed, if there is no affordable effective and safe vaccine or cure available and affordable worldwide, we may live in a permanently pandemic world. Thus, the nature of international business and how it might change in the near future are unavoidably undistinguishable. International business practitioners and academics must get prepared for radical as well as subtle shifts in business models of large multinational firms, small technology companies, and governmental or not for profit organizations that are expected to impact the execution of production, profit, policy, strategy of such organizations just to mention a few. Nonetheless, we should search for informed estimates and responses to probable changes supporting them with examples from firms that have taken actions to reduce the impact of the pandemic on their international business operations.

The term *business model* refers to a narrative, often in a graphic form, that explains and depicts how a business functions (Baden-Fuller and Morgan, 2010; Osterwalder et al., 2010; Wirtz, 2019). The depiction can refer to an industry, a single firm, or a business activity within a certain company (Wirtz, 2019). Business models comprise several elements including products and services, value proposition, activities, structure of organization, value network, value delivery, costs-revenues, information, decision making and decision making structure, environment, strategy, partner network, and so on (Al-Debei and Avison, 2010; Osterwalder et al., 2005; Teece, 2010; Timmers, 1998; Voelpel et al., 2004; Zott and Amit, 2010). In this chapter, we apply five business model elements adapted from the business model literature focusing on recent developments in the digitalized world (Baber et al., 2019a, 2019b, 2020;

Ojala, 2016) to better understand business models in the current pandemic world. We also believe that these elements matter most to international business itself in the COVID-19 period because its impact will cause ever perpetuating changes (Kindström and Kowalkowski, 2014) as they become inevitable. The elements are: 1) Product/Service, 2) Value Constellation, 3) Finance Structure, 4) Information Flow, and 5) Decision Making Structure.

Changes in Business Model Elements

To survive through the hard times of COVID-19 pandemic, and in a new post-COVID-19 environment, firms need to look for innovative solutions and be ready to make radical changes to their business models. Transformations may occur in physical, digital, and cultural spaces. Our hope is that this discussion will help firms survive these changes and help theoreticians to link better various interactions among business model elements. The following sections propose credible emerging changes for each business model element and identify their impacts on the other elements.

Products/Services

The Product/Service element refers to innovation that firms bring to markets and the related business logic (Baber et al., 2019a). Innovating new business models require entrepreneurial mindsets to find alternative ways of doing business, such as changing, expanding, or abandoning the original Product/Service offerings or entering new markets as COVID-19 pandemic simultaneously destroys and creates opportunities for international business. Because of COVID-19, firms may be under pressure to make changes to the Product/Service element of their business models, or even provide totally new types of Products/Service offerings to redefined international markets.

There are numerous examples where the pandemic has forced changes in a firm's Product/Service element, such as distilleries making hand sanitizers or Mercedes F1 designed ventilators. For instance, Kyrö Distillery Company in Finland was planning to lay off in the first instance a significant number of their employees as the international demand for their alcohol drinks had decreased dramatically. This was due to the fact that restaurants and bars in the importing countries closed down because of COVID-19. At the same time, there was a strong demand for hand sanitizers in the same country market. At Kyrö, they invented a process for manufacturing sanitizers using their existing equipment and, in this way, responded to the huge demand for sanitizers in their international markets. By adding a new product portfolio to their offering, Kyrö was able to avoid any lay off of their employees and cover the accumulated losses from the lost sales of their alcohol products. Such quick responses can benefit company brand image as well as secure revenues. Firms in other industries can implement more conventional Product/Service shifts such as from fixed wing to rotary wing aircraft or different package sizes.

Changes in the Product/Service element may cause changes within other elements of the business model. For instance, Finance Structure may change as costs might increase and become a challenge because new or adjusted products could require significant investment. Changes of the Product/Service element may be really difficult to implement, as they may require significant digital transformation: For example, regular manufacturing giving way to 3D printing or remote implementation through digital tools. Firms exporting physical products, may need to comply with new standards and regulations requiring certification of product and process regarding hygiene of materials, packaging, and workers. New compatibility issues in terms of matching regulatory and cultural expectations might become significant barriers to the adoption of such products.

Value Constellation

The Value Constellation refers to the key actors, supply chains, and value exchange among partners, shareholders, customers, etc. within an ecosystem (Autio et al., 2017; Normann and Ramirez, 1993; Ojala, 2016). The impact of COVID-19 on Value Constellation depends on a variety of issues such as trust in the network, members of the network, and which activities are in-house versus offshore or outsourced. If a component provider or a partner providing critical services has difficulties, such as slow delivery or work stoppages, due to the pandemic, these may have direct impact on a firm's ability to survive.

The Value Constellation creates the value proposition of a business model through interaction, bringing together strategic partners as well as major and minor suppliers. In the past decade or so, the emphasis has shifted from networks of tightly connected firms optimized for cost and speed efficiency in the Just-in-Time (JIT) relationships to broader but more robust and expensive networks (Christopher and Peck, 2004). These new networks will be more trusted after removal of partners that failed to maintain quality or reliability under the overall impact of the pandemic. An increase in trust has been previously connected to the creation and intensification of sole supplier relationships (Chandra and Kumar, 2000). However, the pressure to create parallel supply chains, which are less efficient than sole supplier relationships (Slack et al., 2013) increases in a world that is less driven by efficiency and more by resilience (Christopher and Peck, 2004). Networks may insist on trust in order to be activated, especially in urgent situations (Gelles, 2020). Need for resilience among members of the value Constellation is underlined by disasters such as the 2011 earthquake in Japan, the COVID-19 pandemic and political reactions against globalization.

Nonetheless, international businesses may find it sensible to move from making and delivering goods to designing them and sending the order specifications to local makers. Apple's 'Designed in California, Made in China…shipped everywhere' business model is copied by numerous international businesses exploiting offshore manufacturing. The model could, for example, transform to 'Designed in home country, Made everywhere…shipped locally'. In this model, the batch size is far smaller, delivered only locally, and the manufacturer depends on a suite of tools assembled by the distant parent firm rather than relying on giant factory sites in, e.g., China. In the innovated business model, specifications, manufacturing processes, and orders would all move digitally. As the current COVID-19 pandemic has shown, if a firm is dependent on one manufacturer of spare parts and the manufacturer closes the factory because of COVID-19, there is very little to do more than wait until the factory reopens. The suggested model would save on shipping costs, but increase manufacturing costs while sharply decreasing political and disaster risk. Thus, much would depend on the technical competence of local partners (Zhu et al., 2006) and the ability of manufacturers to provide foolproof, turnkey manufacturing tool suites and systems.

Value Constellation in international contexts during COVID-19 may become highly dependent on how much a firm can deliver its services over the Internet or robotically. Delivery of value can be shifted from physical to virtual through the Internet. Converting from physical products to online products may not be possible for all product categories. Once production is local rather than foreign, delivery can be done by trusted means within that country. Multinational corporations seeking to keep control over local delivery might develop robotic services from point of entry to destination. In order to demonstrate complete control over sanitation, they might consider also robotic delivery from factory door to point of embarkation. If regulatory agencies or customers demand, international businesses can create and protect value by collecting video of the product as it moves through automated lines and packaging to show disinfection and other key activities. Thus, the confirmation of safety during delivery of value can become a value proposition that is created during production and shipping. Geely Auto Group, in China, already delivers the keys to new cars by robotic drones to ensure hygienic, no-touch handover. Similarly, the international hotel chain Motel One now identifies hygiene practices including certification by a respected hygienic institute. These challenges can be met by additional sensors, drones, and data capacity, especially as 5G and Internet of Things (IoT) applications mature.

Finance Structure

The third element, Financial Structure, referred to also as the revenue model (e.g., Ojala, 2016), includes the processes and actions through which a firm makes money in the market. These include lending, subsidies, leasing, investments and so on. Changes in other business model elements may cause reconsideration and adjustment of the international Finance Structure. Examples might include a radical cut of costs around expatriate staffing and travel due to the pandemic which necessitate expensive third-party services such as auditing and certifying that are needed when trusted home country nationals become absent.

The standard model of buying supplies (cost), transforming them (cost) and selling them (cost) for money (revenue) is expected to survive. However, newer finance models such as leasing, servitization, subscription ownership, etc. may become more common in the COVID-19 and post-COVID-19. For example, if disaster risk is evaluated to have grown, shorter terms of ownership and lower immediate costs may give way to higher lifetime revenues per customer. Customers may have to pay more to allow themselves freedom to end payments; businesses may gain more total income but risk sudden drops in revenue as end users cancel in reaction to economic, political, natural and other disasters. This part of business models may become more volatile and more dependent on borrowed capital at the start of projects. In the face of long and uncertain repayment cycles, finance partners may insist on local partners, causing change in the Value Constellation. Electronic payment already allows direct international transfer of payments and this is unlikely to change. This conventional approach however may be eclipsed by fintech upstarts such as Wirecard and Revolut or by tokenized payments because blockchain solutions allow payment as contract conditions are fulfilled. Crypto exchanges such as Gemini, Quoine, and others are well positioned to handle such work. In a post-COVID-19 world, the advantage of these payments is speed and disintermediation of clumsy international clearing systems allowing direct transactions with suppliers and even end users. Such digital and locally managed systems may also decrease the political risk of blocked profit repatriation. Tokenized payments could mean incidental changes to Information Flows, but adjustments to the element covering finance, cost, and revenue do not absolutely necessitate changes in other business model elements.

Information Flow

The fourth element, Information Flow, refers to the information exchange among the partners, customers, and other stakeholders within the business model (Timmers, 1998). This information is used to create value or to reassess the business model (Amit and Zott, 2001; Timmers,

1998). In the global pandemic, international Information Flow relies all the more on existing digital communications tools like Zoom, Microsoft Teams, Skype, Slack and other communication and collaboration systems. At the same time, certain types and sources of information might become unnecessary or unreliable, especially those relying on direct interaction through physical platforms such as trade shows, conferences and co-located offices.

Much information, especially tacit knowledge (Polanyi, 1966), which is by nature intangible and non-digitized, moves person to person. The social distancing requirements of the COVID-19 pandemic have made such knowledge transfer and management much more difficult. If social distancing continues, changes to physical interaction will have to happen. One example would be the ubiquitous installation of high-resolution screens that allow individuals to hear and see the actions of co-workers, mentors and teammates. These electronic windows that would approximate side-by-side work atmospheres. Not only would these allow teammates in the same building to safely work together transferring tacit knowledge, such screens would allow teammates in distant cities to remain in close touch registering body language, even facial expressions and instant reactions to the news and events. This would cause a shortening of the information pipeline in business models and thus accelerate information dissemination within an organization and its network.

Fewer expatriate workers may mean less information about foreign market opportunities and changes transferring from branches to international headquarters. Thus, international businesses may need to adjust the Value Constellation, spending more on consultants and verifiers to scan the horizon and to confirm actualities on the ground. Increasing automation of data production and its management through IoT technologies means an opportunity for centralized analysis and understanding of trends. These functions are developing currently in international businesses. As costs decrease and ability increases, the analysis may decentralize from HQ into local markets. The pandemic is likely to accelerate implementation of IoT which, as skills and systems improve, will speed the dissemination of data and analyzes through the network.

Decision Making Structure

Changes may also occur to the structure of Decision Making Structure including decision making in the business model. Currently, it is typical for decisions with local, not global, impact to be made locally. However, if trusted expatriate staff are removed due to health or political concerns, more decision making or authorizing of power may migrate from branches to headquarters offices. Governance networks with (high trust) and without (low trust) trusted expatriates are shown in Figures 9.1 and 9.2 respectively below.

In Figure 9.1, local and regional problems are resolved at the local and regional levels; the headquarters becomes involved only with regard to global problems. This process is comfortable to headquarters because trusted expatriates are collocated with teams outside of headquarters.

In Figure 9.2, the headquarters has far fewer or no trusted staff in remote locations. The result is that fewer decisions are made in those locations and more decisions are made at the headquarters. Unless there are enriched information flows to the headquarters, the decisions are likely to be of lower quality than in the state described by Figure 9.1. Since the expatriates themselves are the source and filter of local insights and information, the system must replace the information flows or suffer

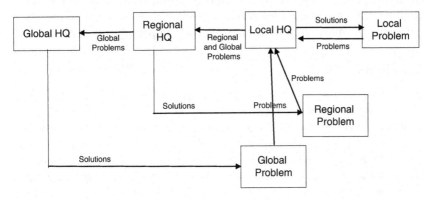

Figure 9.1 High Trust due to Collocation of Expatriates.
Source: The Authors.

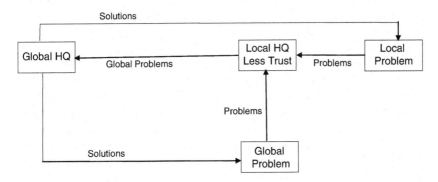

Figure 9.2 Low Trust Due to Lack of Expatriates.
Source: The Authors.

with poor information. One solution for multinational firms is to pay new Value Constellation members, i.e. consultants, for local information. Another is to develop novel flows of information, perhaps through human capital or through digital sensors. Another is to place more trust in local staff.

Change centered on the Decision Making Structure element is likely to cause other elements to change. Partners in the Value Constellation may be added or removed as expatriates and decision making move away from local branches and new parties are hired to adjust, replace and improve Information Flow. Finance Structure may adjust by becoming local, or becoming more centralized. The Product/Service element may change as decision making is abandoned at one level or another. While the Decision Making Structure has direct impact on at least three other elements, the other elements do not necessarily impact Decision Making Structure. Thus, business planners should consider altering the Decision Making Structure carefully, perhaps using it to cause change in other elements, or minimizing its change to avoid impact on other elements.

Conclusion

It can be concluded that there are intrinsic radical changes to business models of international business taking place. These changes though challenging are possible to manage. Many of them would be driven by new cost structures, adoption of technology by partners, or the claiming of advantages created. The business model elements may well interact dynamically, for example a change in Decision Making Structure may save costs and at the same time allow more local decision making in finance. Changes in Decision Making Structure as a result of withdrawing expatriates and changing the Finance Structure will impact other business model elements. Changes following those changes may in turn cause or make possible additional adjustments to other elements of a business model. Dynamic cycles of adjustments to business model elements may mean that the process of change lasts longer than a single cycle of action and reaction. It is likely that changes will interact dynamically as adjustments in any one business model element cause change in others, and those changes cause new changes to the first element.

Figure 9.3 depicts the relative power of change that business model elements are likely to have on each other. While Product/Service element is inextricably linked to the Value Constellation, they are less closely linked to finances and information flows, though the latter would change if digital transformation was in play. Value Constellation changes would most likely impact Finance Structure and Information Flow as parties entered or exited the network. Nonetheless, impact on other elements is not strictly necessary. While other elements seem likely to change the Information Flow, changing the flow of information may not directly or

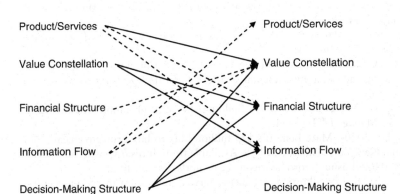

Product/Services — Product/Services
Value Constellation — Value Constellation
Financial Structure — Financial Structure
Information Flow — Information Flow
Decision-Making Structure — Decision-Making Structure

Figure 9.3 Likely Impacts Caused by COVID-19 by Means of Business Model Elements on Business Model Elements.
Source: The Authors.

immediately impact the other elements. In the end, it is place and process of making decisions that is likely to impact other elements.

Beyond considerations about business models, the nature of changes depends on the course of the pandemic. The longer the pandemic lasts and the poorer the medical solutions, the more radical the innovations will be. The root cause may be the COVID-19 virus, but the triggers will be regulation, demands of customers and suppliers and risk management. These triggers of change will cause dynamic interactions and change among business elements.

References

Al-Debei, M. M., Avison, D., 2010. Developing A Unified Framework Of The Business Model Concept. *Eur. J. Inf. Syst. 19*(3), 359–376.

Amit, R., Zott, C., 2001. Value creation in E-business. *Strategic Manag. J. 22*(6/7), 493–520.

Autio, E., Nambisan, S., Thomas, L.D.W., Wright, M., 2017. Digital affordances, spatial affordances, and the genesis of entrepreneurial ecosystems. *Strategic Entrepreneurship J. 12*(1), 72–95.

Baber, W., Ojala, A., Martinez, R., 2020. Digitalization and evolution of business model pathways among Japanese software SMEs. In: Khare, A., Ishikura, H., Baber, W.W. (Eds.), *Transforming of Japanese Business: Rising to the Digital Challenge.* Springer, pp. 154–165.

Baber, W., Ojala, A., Martinez, R., 2019a. Effectuation logic in digital business model transformation: Insights from Japanese high-tech innovators. *J. Small Bus. Enterp. Dev. 26*(6/7), 811–830.

Baber, W., Ojala, A., Martinez, R., 2019b. Transition to digital distribution platforms and business model evolution. Proceedings of *52nd Hawaii*

International Conference on System Science (HICSS 2019), Maui, Hawaii, January 8–11, 2019.

Baden-Fuller, C., Morgan, M. S., 2010. Business models as models. *Long. Range Plan.* 43(2/3), 156–171.

Chandra, C., Kumar, S., 2000. Supply chain management in theory and practice: A passing fad or a fundamental change? *Ind. Manag. Data Syst.* 100(3), 100–113.

Christopher, M., Peck, H., 2004. Building the resilient supply chain. *Int. J. Logist. Manag.* 15(2), 1–13.

Gelles, D. (2020). Marc Benioff's $25 million blitz to buy protective gear from China. New York Times. April 28. Available from: https://www.nytimes.com/2020/04/28/business/coronavirus-marc-benioffsalesforce.html.

Kindström, D., Kowalkowski, C., 2014. Service innovation in product-centric firms: A multidimensional business model perspective. *J. Bus. Ind. Mark.* 29(2), 96–111.

Normann, R., Ramirez, R., 1993. From value chain to value constellation: Designing interactive strategy. *Harv. Bus. Rev.* 71(4), 65–77.

Ojala, A., 2016. Business models and opportunity creation: How IT entrepreneurs create and develop business models under uncertainty. *Inf. Syst. J.* 26(5), 451–476.

Osterwalder, A., Pigneur, Y., and Clark, T. (2010). *Business Model Generation: A Handbook for Visionaries, Game Changers, and Challengers.* Wiley. Available from :https://books.google.co.jp/books?id=ACWGX8pK8kQC.

Osterwalder, A., Pigneur, Y., Tucci, C. L., 2005. Clarifying business models: origins, present, and future of the concept. *Commun. Assoc. Inf. Syst.* 15(1), 1–43.

Polanyi, M., 1966. *The Tacit Dimension.* Peter Smith, Gloucester, MA.

Slack, N., Brandon-Jones, A., Johnston, R., 2013. *Operations Management,* seventh ed. Pearson Education, Harlow, UK.

Teece, D.J., 2010. Business models, business strategy and innovation. *Long. Range Plan.* 43(2/3), 172–194.

Timmers, P., 1998. Business models for electronic markets. *Electron. Mark.* 8(2), 3–8.

Voelpel, S. C., Leibold, M., Tekie, E. B., 2004. The wheel of business model reinvention: How to reshape your business model to leapfrog competitors. *J. Change Manag.* 4(3), 259–276.

Wirtz, B. W., 2019. *Digital Business Models.* Springer International Publishing, Cham.

Zhu, K., Dong, S., Xu, S. X., Kraemer, K. L., 2006. Innovation diffusion in global contexts: Determinants of post-adoption digital transformation of European companies. *Eur. J. Inf. Syst.* 15(6), 601–616.

Zott, C., Amit, R., 2010. Business model design: An activity system perspective. *Long. Range Plan.* 43(2/3), 216–226.

10 Digital Health Business Models during and Post-COVID-19

Andrei Panibratov

Introduction

Information technologies (IT) have resulted in significant transformations in different organizational fields including many social services, whereas health care turned out to be resistant to radical change (Barnett et al., 2011; Wallin and Fuglsang, 2017). Nevertheless, the COVID-19 pandemic will further entail technological advances in the national and global health care sector.

The previous predictions seem to have worked well for the current pandemic. For example, Lahiri (2013) and Chetley et al. (2007) argue that IT can influence the health care sector in three different ways: firstly, improve the delivery of health care ensuring better and faster diagnosis and disease surveillance; secondly, improve the functioning of the health care system through amended logistics and management; and thirdly, improve the communication about health among all stakeholders. All three types of improvement are of critical importance for all infected and ill patients across the world.

In the rapidly changing health- and medicine-related environment, medical organizations have to reengineer themselves. Such reengineering potentially allows them and their suppliers to address better the competing needs for fast reaction and dynamic health care provision via their operational processes and strategies (Khuntia et al., 2014). Consequently, a general implication of the COVID-19 is that it has triggered the development of new entrepreneurial business models as well as intrapreneurial (within the organization) efforts. In the first case, the goal is to differentiate a firm's product or service in a market, which is valid under 'normal' conditions, while in the second case, it is about reducing costs and creating value added services for clients, which is an implication for the 'new normal', with (post-) COVID-19 in mind.

The business model concept in the context of the pandemic might help in addressing a unique set of questions regarding value creation, which cannot be explained by traditional approaches. In this context, Digital Health (DH) business has several characteristics such as critical importance of health issues for people and sensitivity of the health care sector regulation, which make it a unique field for research in the 'new normal' time.

Admitting the fact that DH is an emerging area of scholarly attention, we strive to identify theoretical tenets explaining this phenomenon and to suggest research avenues that will contribute to management studies.

DH Sector: Paradoxes and COVID-19 Implications

Telemedicine has been recognized as one of the fast-growing segments of the DH sector (Broderick et al., 2017). The telemedicine industry was estimated at US$26 billion in 2018 and projected to be US$41 billion by 2021 (Digital Heatlh Market Insight, 2019). Given the exponential growth and money-generating capacity of this sector, there is a lot of investment and many competitors, including newcomers, finding niches in this field.

Apart from all high-tech aspects that have to be further enhanced in the future in order to keep up with the rising demand for digitalized services and advancements in DH, multiple constraints to this sector, such as poor administration or government regulations, remain and require urgent attention. The local context in the provision of telemedicine has to be taken into account as health care is location bound and, hence, involving local academic institutions, internet companies, health administration and professionals (World Health Organization, 2010). Surprisingly, the so-called paradoxes in the DH phenomenon are becoming extremely topical to reflect upon and reconsider when there is a pandemic.

The first paradox is that despite the obvious for the public advantages of DH (Schwamm et al., 2009), it is still not considered as part of the mainstream health sector provision. In this regard, studying and better understanding business models could contribute to clarifying the paradox. More specifically, the e-business models seem to fit the idea of the general application of distance-based appointments, diagnoses and probably treatment. After the pandemic is over, this might remain the 'normal' way of health care practices.

The second paradox refers to the barriers impeding the successful implementation of IT advances in the health sector. Among these barriers, we can include institutional reluctance and inertia, unwillingness of professional health care bodies and organizations to adopt DH, the resistance of the majority of health professionals and patients to digital instead of face-to-face contact between medical practitioners and patients, patient privacy and data protection issues, poor knowledge management and lack of supportive frameworks, policies and funding. What we witness today is the fast transformation of institutions, overcoming the inertia and mitigating the resistance of organizations, doctors and patients alike.

The third paradox is the limitations of extant research on DH. Authors argue that DH studies lack rigor and do not provide enough evidence (Norris et al., 2009; Kumar et al., 2014). The implication is that research should formulate appropriate and relevant research questions and elaborate on the most appropriate research designs and methodologies for DH studies in the future, most probably in the post-pandemic times.

DH Business Models: Pre- and Post-Pandemic Thinking

The traditional perspective on the environment implies that it is a complex of elements outside the firm's boundaries, which is central for strategic decision making. Demil et al. (2018) argue that in the traditional view on the environment there are certain essential issues:

- the analysis of the environment should come first in its importance and effects on the strategy process;
- industry should become a focal level of analysis, because it largely defines firm performance; and
- firm performance can be improved by increasing its fit to the environment.

The business model approach suggests that entrepreneurs can select an existing or construct a new ecosystem and embed their activities in the relevant for their business environment (Lecocq and Demil, 2006). In the COVID-19 pandemic environmental conditions, firms have to co-ordinate the creation of a totally new business model in an ecosystem across diverse industries (medicine, IT, pharmaceuticals, electronics, construction, etc.) and authorities (from federal state to local municipalities). This can in effect operationalize the business model across sectors, industries and administrative levels, which could limit the boundary constraining effect of aggregates such as industries or markets.

Business model thinking makes several assumptions. Firstly, the business model represents a sum of interacting components that create and deliver value to customers and, consequently, allow firms to capture value. However, scholars have different perspectives on the nature of these components (Zott et al., 2011). Secondly, business model is about interaction between firm's value proposition and the way in which value is created – being produced with and for its stakeholders. Thirdly, value capture, often used as synonym to performance, is evaluated not unilaterally depending on the type of business. For example, for social entrepreneurs, it is different compared to traditional for-profit firms. Finally, more often firms choose their environment than the environment chooses them (Lecocq and Demil, 2006).

The value proposed by the DH-based business model is rather specific. The four essential questions here are: what makes the value for consumers;

who produces it; how it is produced, and how it is delivered. Answering these questions in the context of the pandemic would not be easy. Experience with COVID-19 shows that not only treatment and recovery, but also protection and coordination of regular daily life activities can create value for consumers. In a traditional situation, medical organizations create value for patients. During the pandemic, it is also transportation, pharmaceutical, appliances and IT firms, and even the police who contribute to the final product and service bundle, which combines prevention and treatment in their broad sense. This product and service bundle is produced with the involvement of and coordination among various organizations, including even foreign government aid and firms. The same applies to the delivery of the bundle: supply emergency calls for new forms and channels combining physical and online, government and private, organizational and individual aspects in the delivery process.

While reviewing the literature, Clauss (2017) identified 120 business model components which can be allocated in three major groups: value creation, value proposition and value capture. The value creation component answers the question 'what does the customer value?', whereas the value capture component addresses 'how do we make money in this business'? (Magretta, 2002). The value creation component captures key processes and resources, system governance (Casadesus-Masanell and Ricart, 2010), organizational structure, resources and components (Demil and Lecocq, 2010), each of which will warrant detailed and careful analysis by companies and academics alike in the post-COVID-19 world.

As business models represent a company's core business framework and relationships, they determine a company's economic success to a large extent. Maglio and Spohrer (2013) argue that extant business model frameworks (e.g., Osterwalder et al., 2005, Wirtz et al., 2015) fall short in their ability to analyze, describe and classify business models of DH services.

Peters et al. (2015) proposed four dimensions of a business model framework to analyze telemedicine services. These dimensions are the value proposition; the mode of value co-creation; the method of value communication and transfer; and value capture. They also identified three patterns in the telemedicine business models. The first one is enablement that integrates professional partners and takes place in the B2B domain. The second pattern is support and it refers to services from providers of technologies to be used by health care professionals and which ensure that the contact between provider and patient is indirect. The third type is empowerment and it takes place in the B2C sector where patients benefit from DH care services directly. In practice, those patterns may have different significance for the COVID-19 pandemic and any other critical events of a similar nature and magnitude. The role of enablement will be defined by the existing partners' integration in the value chains; demand for support will depend on the extant state of social infrastructure. The need for empowerment will be influenced by the sophistication and simplicity of digital services.

Garbuio and Lin (2019) argue that today entrepreneurs offer solutions that can drastically change the health care system in terms of the way we diagnose, prevent or support heath conditions. Scholars propose two notable focuses of value creation in health care startups – patients and health care providers. Value creation for patients includes health care accessibility and lifestyle management; clinical effectiveness and patient satisfaction; and patient safety. Value creation for health care providers includes operational effectiveness and efficiency, and financial and administrative performance. Both focuses have been articulated in different countries fighting the COVID-19 pandemic. For instance, in the Nordic countries and Russia, with their advantage of having free health care systems and relatively low socialization lifestyle, the focus would switch to the operational efficiency. For Southern Europe or the U.S.A., with their relatively high density of population and intensive socialization in daily life (at least in the large cities), the focus would become the organization of more accessible and free-of-charge medical treatment to all patients, at least during the pandemic.

In summary, the (business model) BM thinking approach aims to advance the understanding of value-creation and value-proposition mechanisms in DH services. Depending on these mechanisms, scholars attempt to classify DH businesses. Despite this, there is still no unified concept for a 'universal' business model that fits best the reality and responds to the extraordinary challenges faced by millions of people across the world during the pandemic.

Theoretical Extension for Further DH Studies

Effectiveness and efficiency are critical in DH care (Aday, 2004). Many aspects, such as patient complexities, service costs, efficiency and technological ability to support and deliver across service platforms, should be addressed by DH creators (Ostrom et al., 2010). In this regard, one can argue that DH services aim to facilitate interactions by reducing transaction costs and by enabling externalized innovation.

The network perspective is clearly relevant for understanding wealth (value) creation in e-business because of the importance of networks of firms, suppliers, customers and other partners in the virtual market space (Prahalad and Ramaswamy, 2000). However, it may not fully capture the value creation potential of e-businesses that enable transactions in new and unique ways. None of the theoretical approaches can fully identify sources of value-creation in online business.

Amit and Zott (2001) suggested four sources of value creation in online business, namely, efficiency, complementarities, lock-in and novelty. In line with transaction cost theory, efficiency is one of the important drivers of online business. Greater efficiency cuts costs and hence increases value. In e-business, some costs can be decreased, including search costs and selection range costs in order to increase speed and scale economies.

Network theory confirms the importance of complementarity among the participants in networks (Gulati, 1999). 'Lock-in' supposes that customers and clients do not migrate to competitors, because they participate in value co-creation, which means that customers are motivated to be involved in repeat transactions and partners aim to launch and improve their associations. Novelty refers to innovativeness. Online businesses innovate in a way they do business, as well as they create new products and/or services. Novelty is also linked to complementarities, which allow combining different resources and capabilities that could result in innovations (Amit and Zott, 2001).

The dynamic capabilities perspective suggests that a company's competitive advantage refers to its ability to create, extend and modify key competences and resources over time (Helfat and Raubitschek, 2018). Analyzing firms exposed to technological and market change, Teece (2007) suggested a framework that can be used to explore how these firms adapt their resources and organizational competences to such a dynamically changing environment. This framework includes three stages: 1) sensing business opportunities; 2) seizing business opportunities and 3) reconfiguring organizational resources to sustain firm's competitiveness. These stages configure the micro-foundations of the dynamic capabilities contributing to company's competitive advantage.

Dynamic capabilities have been studied both at the firm and individual levels. At individual level, they enable managers to conform to the external environment and to recognize emerging opportunities (Panibratov and Klishevich, 2020; Mostafiz et al., 2019). The capabilities' development depends on individuals and the firm, but are also influenced by external pressures and environmental changes such as global diseases and epidemics, when the role of dynamic capabilities dramatically increases. With respect to platform business, dynamic capabilities lenses can be applied to the process of the technological and institutional change and the DH ecosystem governance as it involves a diverse range of actors interacting with each other.

Discussion and Future Research Directions

Health care has always been a public sector under the jurisdiction of the state, and it has been existing in an established institutional framework. In an extraordinary period of time such as the current COVID-19 pandemic and subsequent social turbulence, digitalization allows for both faster and more efficient response to arising problems and for greater coordination, adaptation, and integration among different, often complementary, actors within a firm's ecosystem (Parker et al., 2017). Digitalization of health care made it possible for new actors, such as technological providers or IT professionals, to enter this sector and play an important role in it.

New actors and technologies (biologists and clinical doctors, food delivery and health diagnostic services, driverless transportation and quarantine scheduling) can change the institutional environment and challenge established rules of many traditional sectors based on the evidence and experience from COVID-19 and these may well lead to respective social, economic and political changes. Surprisingly only few studies covered this issue by investigating DH actors and their institutional entrepreneurship (Mountford, 2019). Nevertheless, we still do not fully understand how the institutional boundaries of the health care sector are changing and what actions new players will have to undertake in order to change those boundaries. We also do not know the reverse influence of modified institutional boundaries on new forms of business development in the health care sector. Moreover, we know little how traditional medical institutions react to a changing environment and what intra-preneurial efforts they will undertake in order to adjust to the digital world in the post-pandemic times.

The DH business model research is limited not only in terms of quantity but also in relation to context. We used to consider developed countries as more advanced in digital business; however, there are examples of very complex DH business models in emerging economies, such as China, Brazil and Russia. On the one hand, DH is global by its nature because business processes are universal, on the other hand, health care is very much context specific as there are different regulations, medical traditions, doctors' training approaches and language issues in the world. We lack understanding of the impact that national context will have on the development and survival of DH business models. Furthermore, firms from emerging economies (particularly in the post-Soviet countries) might possess surprisingly strong dynamic capabilities (Panibratov and Klishevich, 2020), which would result in more sophisticated forms of the DH ecosystems' development and respective responses to the COVID-19 and other global critical events and disasters. This research area remains underexplored by scholars.

References

Aday, L. A., 2004. *Evaluating the Healthcare System: Effectiveness, Efficiency, and Equity*. Health Administration Press, Chicago, IL.

Amit, R., Zott, C., 2001. Value creation in e-business. *Strategic Manag. J.* 22(6), 493–520.

Baden-Fuller, C., Morgan, M. S., 2010. Business models as models. *Long. Range Plan.* 43(2), 56–171.

Bardhan, I. R., Demirkan, H., Kannan, P. K., Kauffman, R. J., Sougstad, R., 2010. An interdisciplinary perspective on IT services management and service. *J. Manag. Inf. Syst. 26*(4), 13–64.

Barnett, J., Vasileiou, K., Djemil, F., Brooks, L., Young, T., 2011. Understanding innovators' experiences of barriers and facilitators in implementation and diffusion of healthcare service innovations: a qualitative study. *BMC Health Serv. Res. 11*(342), 1–12.

Broderick, A., Lindeman, D., Dinesen, B. I., Kidholm, K., Spindler, H., Catz, S. L., Baik, G., 2017. Telehealth innovation: Current directions and future opportunities. *Transatlantic Telehealth Research Network (TTRN)*.

Casadesus-Masanell, R., Ricart, J. E., 2010. From strategy to business models and onto tactics. *Long. Range Plan. 43*(2), 195–215.

Chetley, A., Davies, J., Trude, B., McConnel Hl., Ramirez, R., Shields, T., Drury, P., Kumekawa. J., Louw, J., Fereday, G., and Nyamai-Kisia, C., 2007. Improving health, connecting people: The role of ICTs in the health sector of developing countries - A Framework Paper, Working Paper 1, by consortium of Healthlink Worldwide (www.healthlink.org.uk), AfriAfya (www.afriafya. org) and the Institute for Sustainable Health Education and Development (ISHED – www.ished.org).

Clauss, T., 2017. Measuring business model innovation: conceptualization, scale development, and proof of performance. *RD Manag. 47*(3), 385–403.

Demil, B., Lecocq, X., Warnirer, V., 2018. Business model thinking, business ecosystems and platforms: the new perspective on the environment of the organization. *Management 21*(4), 1213–1228.

Demil, B., Lecocq, X., 2010. Business model evolution: in search of dynamic consistency. *Long. Range Plan. 43*(2), 227–246.

Digital Heatlh Market Insight 2019. Available from https://rockhealth.com/reports/in-2019-digital-health-celebrated-six-ipos-as-venture-investment-edged-off-record-highs/ (Accessed on May 20, 2020).

Garbuio, M., Lin, N., 2019. Artificial intelligence as a growth engine for health care startups: emerging business models. *Calif. Manag. Rev. 61*(2), 59–83.

Gulati, R., 1999. Network location and learning: The influence of network resources and firm capabilities on alliance formation. *Strategic Manag. J. 20*(5), 397–420.

Helfat, C. E., Raubitschek, R. S., 2018. Dynamic and integrative capabilities for profiting from innovation in digital platform-based ecosystems. *Res. Policy 47*(8), 1391–1399.

Khuntia, J., Karimi, J., Tanniru, M., Meyers, A., 2014. The University of Colorado digital health consortium initiative: a collaborative model of education, research and service. *J. Commercial Biotechnol. 20*(3), 31–37.

Kumar, S., Nilsen, W. J., Abernethy, A., 2014. Mobile e-health technology evaluation: the mHealth evidence workshop. *Am. J. Preventive Med. 45*(2), 228–236.

Lahiri, K., 2013. Telemedicine, e-health and health related IT enabled services: the Indian situation. *Galen. Med. J. VII*(1&2), 1–16.

Lecocq, X., Demil, B., 2006. Strategizing industry structure: the case of open systems in a low-tech industry. *Strategic Manag. J. 2*(9), 891–898.

Lecocq, X., Mangematin, V., Maucuer, R., and Ronteau, S. 2018. Du modèle d'affaires à l'écosystème: Comprendre les transformations en cours. *Finance Contrôle Stratégie*, NS-1, Advance online publication, http://journals. openedition.org/fcs/2072; DOI: 10.4000/fcs.2072 (Accessed on May 25, 2020).

Maglio, P. P., Spohrer, J., 2013. A service science perspective on business model innovation. *Ind. Mark. Manag. 42*(5), 665–670.

Magretta, J., 2002. Why business models matter. *Harv. Bus. Rev. 80*(5), 86–92.

Mostafiz, M., Sambasivan, M., Goh, S., 2019. Impacts of dynamic managerial capability and international opportunity identification on firm performance. *Multinatl. Bus. Rev. 27*(4), 339–363.

Mountford, N., 2019. Managing by proxy: organizational networks as institutional levers in evolving public good markets. *J. Bus. Res. 98*, 92–104.

Norris, A. C., Stockdale, R. S., Sharma, S., 2009. A strategic approach to m-health. *Health Inform. J. 15*(3), 244–253.

Osterwalder, A., Pigneur, Y., Tucci, C. L., 2005. Clarifying business models: Origins, present, and future of the concept. *Commun. Assoc. Inf. Syst. 15*(1), 1–26.

Ostrom, A. L., Bitner, M. J., Brown, S., Burkhard, K. A., Goul, M., Smith-Daniels, V., Demirkan, H., Rabinovich, E., 2010. Moving forward and making a difference: research priorities for the science of service. *J. Serv. Res. 13*(1), 4–36.

Panibratov, A., Klishevich, D. 2020. *Dynamic capabilities during the internationalization of MNCs from post-socialist emerging markets. Multinational Business Review*, DOI: 10.1108/MBR-06-2019-0052.

Parker, G., van Alstyne, M., Jiang, X., 2017. Platform ecosystems: How developers invert the firm. *MIS Q. 41*(1), 255–266.

Peters, C., Blohm, I., Leimeister, J.-M., 2015. Anatomy of successful business models for complex services: Insights from the telemedicine field. *J. Manag. Inf. Syst. 32*(3), 75–104.

Prahalad, C. K., Ramaswamy, V., 2000. Co-opting customer competence. *Harv. Bus. Rev. 78*(1), 79–87.

Schwamm, L. H., Holloway, R. G., Amarenco, P., 2009. A review of the evidence for the use of telemedicine within stroke systems of care: a scientific statement from the American Heart Association/American Stroke Association. *Stroke 40*(7), 2616–2634.

Teece, D. J., 2007. Explicating dynamic capabilities: the nature and microfoundations of (sustainable) enterprise performance. *Strategic Manag. J. 28*(13), 1319–1350.

Wallin, A., Fuglsang, L., 2017. Service innovations breaking institutionalized rules of health care. *J. Serv. Manag. 28*(5), 972–997.

Wirtz, B. W., Pistoia, A., Ullrich, S., Göttel, V., 2015. Business models: origin, development and future research perspectives. *Long. Range Plan. 49*, 36–54.

World Health Organization 2010. Telemedicine. Opportunities and developments in member states. Global Observatory for eHealth series, 2. https://www.who.int/goe/publications/goe_telemedicine_2010.pdf (Accessed on May 30, 2020).

Zott, C., Amit, R., Massa, L., 2011. The business model: Recent developments and future research. *J. Manag. 37*(4), 1019–1042.

Part III

Impacts of COVID-19 on International Finance and Human Resource Management

11 COVID-19

Stock Market Responses

Sophie Nivoix and Serge Rey

Pandemics have always existed in history (see, e.g., Martin, 2008, Jones, 2020). COVID-19 is a pandemic that occurred worldwide, regardless of the level of their economic development, their health care system or medical expertise. The fast spread of the disease is a major characteristic of this virus, and the 90 percent reduction of air transportation, the lockdown of half of humanity and the economic slowdown among others create unique and dreadful threats for both sanitary and economic state of affairs in all countries. *"Since the World Health Organization declared COVID-19 as a global pandemic on 11 March 2020, nearly 80 per cent of global population has come under stay-home orders, lockdowns and quarantines, inflicting increasingly severe direct and indirect economic impacts"* (United Nations, 2020). This fact has resulted in an unprecedented drop in activities excluding wartime periods.

The reactions of the financial markets are essential as they play crucial roles in the financing of companies, they are also the unavoidable financing means of many states, which will have increased financing needs during this period. This chapter analyzes the response of the world's main financial markets to this crisis, with a focus on the stocks of the French luxury industry, which is highly exposed to Asian markets.

The remainder of this chapter is organized as follows. First, it presents the characteristics of the global COVID-19 crisis, followed by methodology, then results are set out, finalized by conclusions.

An Unprecedented Worldwide Situation

The modern period of human existence has undergone numerous significant crises due to various causes, such as natural disasters including pandemics, wars, political turmoil, terrorist attacks, industrial disasters or financial crashes. The COVID-19 crisis stands out from all others as it led the national governments in many countries across the world to adopt measures protecting their population from the pandemic in the meantime disrupting or even discontinuing the economic activity of really important economic sectors.

The Specificities of COVID-19

A crisis is generally characterized by several parameters, which help to assess the implications of the event. The first group of concerns is related to the threat, which may be political or social (e.g., wars, strikes, social disturbances such as the Arab Spring or attacks as the 9/11 in New York); environmental (e.g., fires, earthquakes, tsunamis like the one in December 2004), industrial (e.g., technical defaults, accidents, pollutions like the nuclear one in the Chernobyl region in 1986 or the Fukushima region in 2011), sanitary (pollutions, infections like the SARS in 2003, the Spanish flu in 1917, the Asian flu in 1957 or the COVID-19), economic (market crash as during the Great Depression starting in 1929, credit crunches similar to the one in 2008 initiated with the crash of the U.S. property market in 2007, currency crisis like in 1997 in Asia, mass unemployment), or organizational (data hacking, computer viruses and loss of competences).

The second set of factors is related to the origin of the crisis. It may be caused by a natural, technical or human problem. This origin may be accidental, intentional, mixed, and thus under or out of control to a certain extent. Considering the length of the crisis, it is sometimes fairly short and followed by a squat recovery period as in a stock market bubble burst, or it may last for years or decades, like a long-term ban on a nuclear radiation contaminated region.

The third set of issues helps us to understand the consequences of the crisis. Its spatial extent may be limited to a specific area (geographic region, country or industry sector) or else impact a whole country or economic area, or be spread worldwide. The likelihood to undergo such a crisis is generally difficult to assess because the pointers are problematic to indicate ahead of time (e.g., a stock market crash or an earthquake) or previously unknown because the crisis is a completely new one such as an unidentified virus. Once a crisis has happened, it is often tricky to evaluate if and when the same type of event may reoccur (e.g., introduction of new financial rules after a credit crisis, a vaccine against a newly spread virus).

As for the COVID-19 crisis, the threats are obviously first and foremost sanitary immediately after the realization of its seriousness and then economic, which have a continued life span. It can be assumed that the origin of the crisis is natural, even so serious concerns have emerged about human responsibility for the crisis. Whatever the origin, the consequences of this crisis have become global as despite the first contamination in the Hubei region of China, the widely spread intercontinental travels of people and the advanced globalization created an almost instantaneous economic impact on many sub-tractors of lots of companies worldwide engaged in international business. Thus, advanced and emerging economies and mostly their international firms have been affected in a variety of ways. Considering the forecast for a second wave of virus and the timespan of the current wave, it is too early to give a precise answer what the real overall impact of COVID-19 is going to be.

Once risk analysis is done, it is possible to identify the patterns of the impacts and evaluate their consequences. If risk is considered, the study of the persistence of risk and the perception of shocks by the financial market is a major issue. It is all the more interesting that viruses like COVID-19 may continue to spread frequently in the future, and thus have an increasing probability to create huge damages.

Thus, the shocks in the financial market are investigated in the empirical part of this chapter, with a focus on the return and volatility of stock markets, as they are an important financing means for firms engaged in international business.

The Health and Economic Context

Table 11.1 provides an overview of the health and economic situation of the world's major economies as a result of the COVID-19 pandemic. First, there is a clear disparity in mortality between Asia and the rest of the world. Although some figures should be considered with caution, Western Europe, with the exception of Germany, is by far the most seriously affected area in terms of health by COVID-19. Secondly, when we compare mortality figures with the reaction of the financial markets since the beginning of 2020, we can see that the countries that have suffered the worst health crisis experienced the largest market falls.

Again, there are two clear exceptions. On the one hand, Germany has experienced a significant fall in the stock market of minus 19 percent, although it is less affected by the health crisis than many of the other European countries. This can be explained by measures to reduce activity within Germany but also by the containment measures taken by its main European economic partners, France in particular. Export markets, especially for car, shrunk dramatically or closed down rapidly. On the other hand, the initial decline in the U.S. equity market has been limited. There are numerous reasons for this fact. Firstly, the U.S. has taken containment measures in parts of the country and the health crisis affects different states in various ways. Secondly, there has been a time lag in the health crisis caused by COVID-19, which spread later in the U.S. than in Asia and Europe. Thus, it can be assumed that if the number of deaths continues to rise and the lockdowns are prolonged, the impact on the financial market and economy could become more significant. Finally, while in recent years, unemployment has been declining across many developed countries, it is beginning to rise again all over the world, particularly in the U.S.

Table 11.1 State of Affairs for the First Five Months of 2020

	Total deaths per million by 05/08/2020[‡]	Stock return 01/02/2020-05/08/2020	Unemployment rate[‡]	
			December 2019	March 2020
China	3.2	−6.15%	5.2% (*)	5.9%
South Korea	5	−10.54%	3.8%(**)	3.8%
Japan	4.4	−13.04%	2.2%	2.5%
France	398.1	−24.73%	8.4%	8.4%
Germany	86.8	−18.82%	3.2%	3.5%
Italy	495.5	−27.08%	9.6%	12.4%
Spain	561.5	−30.13%	13.7%	14.5%
United Kingdom	451	−21.89%	3.8%	4%
U.S.	228.6	−10.07%	3.5%	14.7%

Sources: Author created based on https://ourworldindata.org/coronavirus, https://countryeconomy.com/unemployment; Italy and U.S. (April 2020).
(*) The urban surveyed unemployment rate for China; http://www.stats.gov.cn/english/Statisticaldata/.
(**) Source: http://kostat.go.kr/portal/eng/index.action.

In order to have an international reach of our study, we analyze the stock markets as they are a key factor to finance international firms in advanced economies.

Methodology

We have analyzed nine market indexes (SSE for China, CAC40 for France, DAX30 for Germany, FTSE MIB for Italy, NIKKEI225 for Japan, KOSPI composite for South Korea, IBEX for Spain, FTSE100 for the UK and S&P500 for the U.S.) for countries in locked down in three continents. Our daily data come from the Factset database, for the period January 2, 2000–May 8, 2020.

We addressed the following key question: 'Has this unprecedented crisis had a greater impact on the markets than previous crises?' Researchers have different views on addressing it, depending on the investigated period. We have chosen the period 2000–2020, which will enable us to compare the current situation with other very important crises such as the subprime crisis, the bursting of the dot-com bubble in the early 2000s, the 2001 attacks, and, for Japan, the Fukushima disaster.

The behavior of the financial markets will be analyzed on the basis of stock price volatility, which is a measure of risk and reflects the uncertainty faced by economic agents.

To compute volatility, we use daily returns R_t. It is defined with $R_t = 100. \ln(P_t/P_{t-1})$, where P_t represents the stock price at date t. Volatility is measured with a GARCH[1] (1,1) model, which is justified when ARCH effects are observed in the residuals ε_t of the stock return model $(R_t = \mu + \varepsilon_t)$.[2] This econometric model is currently standard (Engle, 1982) and we will not go into detail here. Volatility σ can be computed with the standard deviation of daily returns in the GARCH model, defined by $\sigma = \sqrt{h}$, where h is the conditional variance derived from GARCH(1,1) (see Nivoix and Rey, 2017).

Results

As most of the present stock indexes did not exist in 1917 or in 1957, we cannot make a direct comparison with another virus crisis, but to some extent, other events are comparable to the present situation.

Considering the 9/11 attacks, this local event created quickly a shock on world financial markets and on the air transportation sector. This lasted for several months, even if the 2000 internet bubble burst was an economic event in itself. Considering the Fukushima catastrophe in 2011, the TEPCO Company was highly impaired and its stock experienced a volatility regime change for the long run (Nivoix and Rey, 2018b). Moreover, the whole electric power sector risk-return equilibrium was impacted, and the accident also unveiled some structural weaknesses of this industry in Japan (Nivoix and Rey, 2018a). In the same way, the COVID-19 crisis pointed out some sanitary or industrial weaknesses in many countries, considering intensive care units, masks or economic dependences.

Volatility of Financial Markets

Figure 11.1 shows the markets' volatility over the period 2000–2020 as estimated with a GARCH model. Over the entire period, the shock that had so far the greatest impact on the markets was the subprime crisis, in particular the bankruptcy of Lehman Brothers. COVID-19 had a similar impact, but with contrasted effects depending on the country. The Asian countries, Japan and China experienced relatively limited disruption compared with the effects of the other shocks over the past 20 years. The impact was stronger on the South Korean market but till the time of research remained below what was observed during the crisis in 2008–2009. Moreover, for all other countries in Europe and the U.S., the effects were comparable to those of the subprime crisis, and even greater for Italy, Spain and the U.S.

However, given the unprecedented reactions of the authorities during peacetime, and given the uncertainty about the evolution of the pandemic, it is still too early to say whether these disruptions will continue in the long run on such an international scale. Moreover, the effects of the containment measures on economic activity, GDP, unemployment, international trade, etc., are still limited (in June 2020, there was an estimated loss of less than 10 percent of the world GDP), but if they were to worsen, the volatility of the financial markets could persist or even increase.

Previous crises, such as the burst of the dot-com bubble in 2000 or the subprime mortgage crisis, have shown that not all industrial sectors were affected to the same degree. We will now try to examine what the situation is in France by comparing values in the luxury industry with values in the traditional economy.

The Case of French Luxury Industry

The French industry of luxury goods is world leading with LVMH, Kering, Hermès and L'Oréal representing a quarter of the world sales in these product categories. We have chosen to focus on LVMH, Kering and Hermès that have huge overseas sales with wide penetration into the Asian markets. The Japanese market is the world's second largest market for luxury goods, after that of the U.S. one followed by the Chinese. For Hermès, the Japanese market represents 14 percent of its sales, and for Kering, owner of Gucci or Saint-Laurent, around 10 percent and for LVMH (Louis Vuitton, Céline or Sephora) more than 7 percent (Denis,

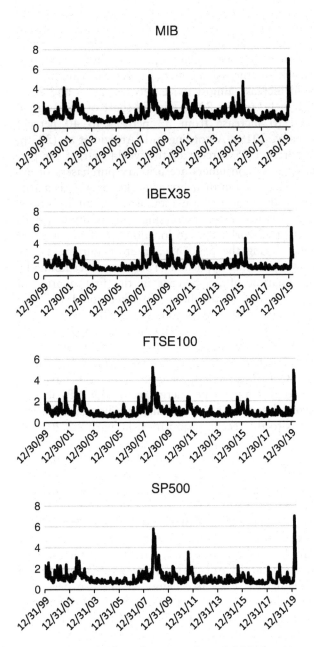

Figure 11.1 Volatility of Various Financial Markets.
Source: The Authors.

2017). Apart from Japan, the rest of the Asian region accounts 30 percent of LVMH's total sales, 32 percent for Kering's and 36 percent for Hermès (Asfouri, 2020). Indeed, the Chinese market and more specifically the Chinese consumers have a determining role in the evolution of the luxury goods market in the Asian region. Expectations are that the Chinese market would increase almost twice between 2017 and 2025 from 770 billion RMB to 1.2 trillion RMB. China's share of luxury good purchases is expected to increase from 32 percent to 40 percent (McKinsey and Company, 2019). According to D'Arpizio et al. (2020), Chinese consumers represent 35 percent of the world market for personal luxury goods. Chinese consumers are primary purchasers of extravagant branded products sold in their home market as well as across Asia where luxury brand producers use established retail networks. Chinese consumers account for an ever increasing share of luxury goods purchases in the rest of the world. Due to lockdown and restricted or stopped tourist travels during the pandemic, in store purchases may become really problematic if at all applicable. Therefore, after falling by a preliminary approximation of 25 percent in the first quarter of 2020, the overall contraction of the luxury market could be from 20 percent to 35 percent in 2020 (D'Arpizio et al., 2020).

Under these conditions, since the COVID-19 crisis originated in China, expectations are that the stocks in China are particularly impacted. In order to check whether there is a specificity of luxury values in the response to the COVID-19 crisis, we compared the behavior of these stocks with those of Total in the energy sector, BNP Paribas in the banking and financial sector and Michelin in traditional industry. We limited our analysis to the recent period from January 02, 2020 to May 8, 2020.

The results are presented in Table 11.2 and show that in 2020, the luxury sector is not more affected than any other sectors, and even less so compared to impacts suffered by Total or BNP Paribas. Two stocks of LVMH and especially Hermès are more resistant than those of other firms regarding the shock caused by COVID-19. Kering's performance is fairly comparable to that of the CAC40 in terms of yield. On the other hand, the Kering share has been more volatile than that of the market.

If we look now at the volatility of equities over two decades, we can see that in the past, the luxury sector (see Figure 11.2) has experienced similar or even greater disruptions, e.g., after the 9/11 2001 terrorist attacks for LVMH and Hermès. It can also be noted that with the exception of the episode of acquisition rumors that affected Hermès at the end of 2010, the Kering share is the one with the highest volatility over the last ten years.

For the rest of the economy (see Figure 11.3), it can be seen that this crisis has had the greatest impact on the Total Group's share over the past 20 years. COVID-19 caused volatility in the BNP Paribas share

Table 11.2 French Stock Returns over the Period January 2–May 8, 2020

	Stock return	Average daily stock return	Daily volatility
LVMH	-15.96%	-0.19%	2.94
Hermès	1.55%	0.01%	2.56
Kering	-28.35%	-0.32%	3.44
Total	-41.13%	-0.70%	4.48
BNP	-61.81%	-0.47%	4.28
Michelin	-19.43%	-0.22%	3.23
CAC40	-24.73%	-0.32%	2.84

Source: The Authors.

Note
The average daily stock return or rate of growth of the stock prices (*gm*) is calculated according to the formula $gm = |(a_n/a_0)^{1/n} - 1| \times 100$, where a_n and a_0 are the end-of-period and start-of-period stock prices. Daily volatility is calculated as the daily standard deviation of the stock returns.

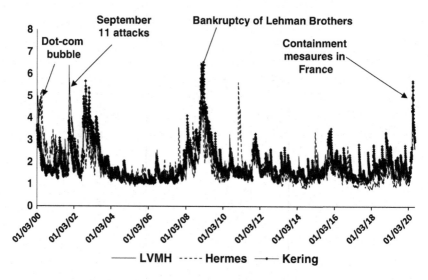

Figure 11.2 Volatility of French Luxury Stocks.
Source: The Authors.

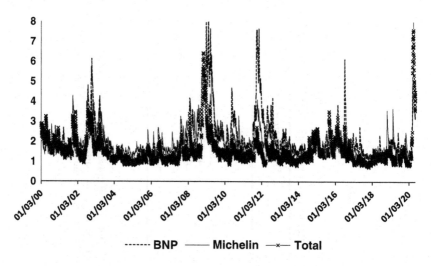

Figure 11.3 Volatility of French Traditional Sectors Stocks.
Source: The Authors.

which has also been high, but less than in some past episodes. In the end, therefore, it appears that this COVID-19 crisis has had no specific impact on French equities compared to previous events in the long run. Similarly, while we might have expected a sharp deterioration in luxury

Table 11.3 Correlation between Daily Stock Returns 01/03/2000–05/08/2020

	R_BNP	R_Hermès	R_Kering	R_LVMH	R_Michelin	R_Total
R_BNP	1,0000					
R_Hermès		0,3013				
R_Kering		1,0000	0,4923			
R_LVMH			0,4080	0,5508		
R_Michelin			1,0000	0,5009	0,5317	
R_Total				0,6624	0,3230	0,5576
				1,0000	0,5103	0,3280
					0,5139	0,4910
					1,0000	0,5441
						0,4560
						1,0000

Source: The Authors.

Table 11.4 Correlation between Daily Stock Returns 01/02/2020–05/08/2020

	R_BNP	R_Hermès	R_Kering	R_LVMH	R_Michelin	R_Total
R_BNP	1,0000	0,6771	0,6993	0,7513	0,6960	0,7396
R_Hermès		1,0000	0,8321	0,8149	0,5708	0,6734
R_Kering			1,0000	0,8870	0,7342	0,7049
R_LVMH				1,0000	0,7274	0,7604
R_Michelin					1,0000	0,6676
R_Total						1,0000

Source: The Authors.

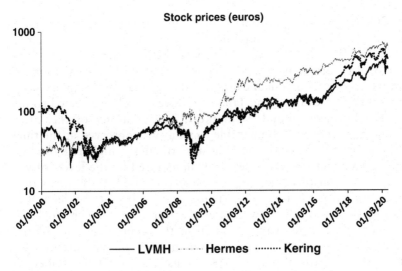

Figure 11.4 Dynamics of the Prices of the Luxury Sector Stocks.
Source: The Authors.

goods stocks, the impact is important but not greater than what was experienced during the subprime crisis, or for LVMH and Hermès after the 9/11 attacks.

Finally, when diversifying a portfolio to reduce risk, the correlations between asset returns are important. Tables 11.3 and 11.4 show the correlation matrix for the six stocks studied, over the entire period and for the recent period, January 2020–May 2020. As R_BNP indicates the return of the BNP Paribas stock, so this goes for the other stocks.

Figure 11.4 presents the evolutions of the prices (in logarithm) of the three stocks of the luxury sector. It should be noted that between 2002 and 2018, the prices of LVMH and Kering shares follow very similar dynamics and strongest correlation.

Conversely, the Hermès stock return exhibits the lowest correlation with other securities, as this company is smaller and less diversified than the other two.

Considering the studied period in 2020 period, Table 11.4 leads to different conclusions. All correlation coefficients are higher. The correlation coefficients for the three luxury values are the highest, ranging from 0.81 to 0.88. The lowest coefficients are the ones for Total and BNP Paribas stocks, which experienced the strongest falls in their prices.

Therefore, in terms of portfolio management, it is not recommendable for an investor to include all companies of the luxury sector in his portfolio, but rather to diversify with stocks from other sectors. Thus, such a strategy remains the same with or without the crisis.

Conclusion

The COVID-19 crisis led to a sudden downturn in the economies of many major advanced economies of a magnitude not seen since World War II. The financial markets were heavily impacted, resulting in both price drops as well as great volatility and unpredictability. However, while the pandemic originated in China, the Asian markets, particularly the Chinese and Japanese, have been less affected so far than the European and U.S. markets. The volatility of the latter markets appears to be comparable to what was observed at the time of the subprime crisis, indicating a particularly high risk for investors. This fact has been clearly demonstrated by the levels of volatility of the various stock markets. The presented study shows that French stocks of the luxury companies with substantial sales in the Asian markets did not show greater volatility than French stocks in other sectors. In this way, to diminish the unpredictability of the volatility in the value of stocks, diversification of the portfolio investment internationally and across industries should be applied to mitigate risks at least to a certain extent.

Notes

1 Generalized Autoregressive Conditional Heteroskedasticity.
2 To save space these detailed results are not presented here.

References

D'Arpizio, C., Levato, F., Fenili, S., Colacchio, F., and Prete, F., 2020. Luxury after COVID-19: Changed for (the) good? Bain & Company, https://www.bain.com/insights/luxury-after-coronavirus/. (Accessed on May 9, 2020.)

Asfouri, N., 2020. Coronavirus: Le confinement des Chinois va peser sur l'industrie mondiale du luxe. *Challenges, Economie*, AFP, https://www.challenges.fr/economie/coronavirus-le-confinement-des-chinois-va-peser-sur-l-industrie-mondiale-du-luxe_697836. (Accessed on May 5, 2020.)

Denis, P., 2017. Le luxe français cajole le stratégique marché japonais, *Challenges, Finance et marchés*. Reuters, https://www.challenges.fr/finance-et-marche/le-luxe-francais-cajole-le-strategique-marche-japonais_502907. (Accessed on April 12, 2020.)

Engle, R. F., 1982. Autoregressive conditional heteroskedasticity with estimates of the variance of United Kingdom inflation. *Econometrica 50*, 987–1007.

Jones, D. S., 2020. History in a crisis: lessons for Covid-19. *N. Engl. J. Medecine 382*, 1681–1683. 10.1056/NEJMp20043611. (Accessed on May 2, 2020.)

McKinsey & Company, 2019. *China Luxury Report 2019*, April. https://www.mckinsey.com. (Accessed on March 15, 2020.)

Martin, P., 2008. History of sciences Epidemics: Lessons from the past and current patterns of response. *C. R. Geosci. 340*, 670–678.

Nivoix, S., Rey, S., 2017. TEPCO's (Tokyo Electric Power Co Holdings) stock behaviour in the long run. *J. Transit. Stud. Rev. 24*(2), 45–62.

Nivoix, S., Rey, S., 2018a. The Great East Japan Earthquake's effects on electric power companies' financial situation. In: Andreosso, B., O'Callaghan, Jaussaud, J., Zolin, B. (Eds.), *Asian Nations and Multinationals: Overcoming the Limits to Growth*. Palgrave Macmillan, London, pp. 121–138.

Nivoix, S., Rey, S., 2018b. Dynamics of Tokyo Electric Power company and the Nikkei: 1985 to 2016 including the Fukushima disaster. *J. Econ. Integr. 33*(1), 979–1010.

United Nations, 2020. The pandemic crisis will worsen global inequality. *World Economic Situation and Prospects*: May 2020 Briefing, No. 137.

12 Market Conforming and Non-market Conforming Financial Support Measures in Europe during COVID-19

Winfried Müller

The Economic Nature of the COVID-19 Pandemic

When in mid-March the COVID-19 virus emerged as a mass phenomenon in Europe, public life and business came to a halt. Notwithstanding the medical challenges, very soon it became obvious that the economic impact of the high, and not yet well-foreseeable, cost of the pandemic will be severe and probably lasting for some years (Boumans et al., 2020).

The COVID-19 pandemic is different to other economic crises from the resent past in terms of timing, cause, geographic scope and social implications. While during other crises, counter measures were discussed and decided upon physically in teams, the nature of the current pandemic and the subsequent need for distancing made the crisis management process, at least initially, a self-centered experience. Despite some geographical time lags, the crisis took over countries by surprise and developed as a global phenomenon within a very short timeframe. Consequently, the pandemic brought the world to a halt all of a sudden with economic shocks simultaneously exerted on both the supply and demand side (Boumans et al., 2020).

In contrast to the financial crisis of 2007–2009, no economic deterioration over time took place before the pandemic struck; instead, a sudden health threat of a long-forgotten global proportion endangered human life and survival. Following the all-time high major stock indices on February 23, 2020, the pandemic stalled their upward flight like a falling guillotine as 40 percent of market valuation was lost.

Need for Business Crisis Management

Such an unprecedented health crisis brought business to a standstill posing enormous challenges to the economy as a whole and to each individual business. Together with efforts for human survival, the fight for the financial survival of companies and individuals was paramount and calling for proactive action and speedy effect.

Corporate crisis management under the conditions of a crisis aims to maintain the capacity of firms to act by transforming and moving any organization intact from the stage of uncertainty and the edge of chaos into a crisis mode where functional management in a calm and collected manner takes over. The first financial priority is to ensure short-term liquidity by preserving cash positions and committed open credit lines followed by durable cash planning for surviving the 'hibernating' phase (Backhaus, 2020). However, quite frequently, the crisis is exceeding the monetary capabilities of companies and individuals, and support is then needed to be secured from other sources, mainly, from the banking sector and public institutions.

The Role of Banks in the COVID-19 Crisis

Traditionally, the banking sector provides liquidity supply to businesses and individuals based on their business model. Banks are companies with a dedicated economic task exceeding the pure business model - dealing with one single good: money. At a time of crises, banks are stuck in the middle between the systemic task towards the economy and some specific managerial considerations. This means that on the one hand they have to perform the economic task of supporting customers even in difficult times, and on the other hand, they need to avoid financing 'dead horses' with subsequent breaches of insolvency laws and raising bad loans and credit losses (Koestens, 2020).

To avoid a 'credit crunch' reluctance of lending and to mitigate adverse effects, governments, regulators and central banks have quickly imposed various instruments during the COVID-19 pandemic, e.g., loan schemes, interest rate subventions or special state guarantees, to support banks in fresh lending. The latter has become the dominant backbone of fiscal measures in Europe (Chinn et al., 2020). Moreover, the temporary loosening of regulatory equity and liquidity rules has aimed to support banks' ability and willingness to provide fresh funds (ECB, 2020).

The Public Side: Measures of Governments and Central Banks in COVID-19 Support

Governments and Central Banks have acted from the beginning of the COVID-19 pandemic fast and bold. Substantive generous support to individuals and business has been extended to avoid more substantive economic and social harm as the human pain of the pandemic itself has been huge.

While public measures are understandable and necessary, given the potential consequences of the pandemic, the imposed measures have been characterized with a significant peculiarity. The basis of the distinction here is the underlying paradigm (Guba, 1990) that emerged following the last financial crisis, i.e., the paradigm of interventionism. Reckless banking has made interventions necessary, however since 2008 European politicians and financial markets increasingly got addicted to the deep pockets of government spending and central bank money creation in the form of printing more money and channeling them in the economy.

Generally, government interventions, whether from a fiscal or from a central bank side, can be distinctively divided into actions that are market conforming and non-market conforming. Market conforming actions influence the conditions on the market and thus the supply-demand relationship in a way in which the law of supply and demand remains intact.

In contrast, non-market conforming measures are designed to counteract, manipulate and weaken the market mechanisms ultimately leading towards a state-directed or command economy. Non-market conforming actions frequently 'taste sweet' as they are often aimed at avoiding an unpleasant and politically undesired short-term malaise, but they are creating long term pain and unavoidable disturbances due to their costly nature.

When comparing and assessing public COVID-19 support measures in the banks' lending business with pandemic actions on capital markets initiated by central banks, fundamental differences concerning market conformity are easy to observe. The COVID-19 pandemic hit a financial world that had already been in a particularly vulnerable situation for some years (Lichtenstein, 2020). Already before the COVID-19 crisis emerged, all conventional central bank instruments had been utilized to an unparalleled extent whenever risks of market turbulence had occurred. Central banks worldwide, but especially in the Euro-zone and the European Central Bank (ECB) had fully exhausted the potential for providing liquidity, lowering interest rates down to zero and below, as well as cleaning up the market of government debts in an unprecedented manner, on the eve of the crisis.

While traditional central bank interventions like short-term borrowing schemes and liquidity support via selective short-term purchase programs stay within market-conformity, programs of virtually unlimited size have been including doubtful counterparts and collaterals, which have exceeded the boundaries of market conformity. ECB, not subject to economic considerations within their interventions, has become the biggest actor, accounting for the majority of demand in some formerly liquid market segments and crowding out other participants, thus drying out the market and setting interest rates quasi autonomous.

Supported by regulatory rules issued during the last decade, banks and other institutional investors have been pushed into government bonds in a manner of financial repression (Monnet et al., 2019), putting not only interest rates but also credit spreads of European government debts to record lows.

Thus, it is not surprising that immediately after the virus hit Europe, governments abandoned the Euro stability criteria (Mussler, 2020) and announced substantial national and supranational rescue packages (German Federal Ministry of Finance, 2020; European Parliament 2020). Then, a new 'whatever it takes moment' occurred. Furthermore, within the Pandemic Emergency Purchase Program (PEPP), the ECB has announced to push additional liquidity up to a total of €1,350 billion into the market (ECB, 2020a) to monetize subsequently the new COVID-19 public debts and to flatten all potentially occurring market turbulences.

Intended to relieve the refinance cost of the overarching debt burden of the Southern European countries, this interventional action resulted in a sharp liquidity driven upward re-bounce of stock markets after their short but strong decline – thus, at least on the equity market the 'V'-recovery shape seemed to materialize.

To be clear: supporting with unconventional financial actions is the task of central banks during crises. What is alarming is the intensity of such measures during the last decade, their diminishing effectiveness and thus, the subsequent ever-increasing extent of interventionism.

Such a significant level of non-market conformity and direct inter-ventionist actions were not observed in the lending business of banks so far. During the hectic COVID-19 legal sprint, most support measures such as COVID-19 loans, tax cuts, subventions, government investment programs – even though generous and with potential free-rider and loss spreading effects (Freitag et al., 2020), can be seen as market con-forming, given the short timeframe for decisions. Deferral of payments has allowed corporate and private borrowers to 'take a deep breath' and to safeguard themselves from the grim consequences. At the same time, the ability to pay is temporarily covered under a veil making any credit assessment for further lending difficult.

One can argue that state guaranteed bridging finance contains the risk of moral hazard, where formerly weak businesses take the opportunity to take shelter under the umbrella of public protection, while their well-managed peers would use own funds during the crisis. On the other hand, the obligation to repay and a remaining share of risk on the books of banks reduces the misguiding in comparison to free monetary support. Bridging finance facilities are market-conforming instruments for ad-hoc support in order to create cash, thus, helping to close gaps from rapid liquidity outflow where suddenly lost income meets a cost base that cannot be reduced at once.

Non-market conforming mechanisms are recent ideas for a more generous lending practice at a time when people and businesses have faced a critical event such as the COVID-19 pandemic. In a desperate moment, the German Minister of Finance called the banks to ease their credit approval standards and adopt a more laissez-faire approach ('fuenf grade sein lassen') (Freitag et al, 2020; N.A., 2020). What was meant with it was the imagination of a need to act against a seemingly petty-minded and overstated cautiousness of banks during a crisis not behaving entirely in line with the expectations of the interventionist paradigm.

Nevertheless, even though all efforts for overcoming the pandemic are worth considering, relaxed lending rules are not measures to help the economy and citizens during a pandemic. Even in borderline situations of national crises banks must not forget the fundamentals of risk culture and business rules (Freitag et al., 2020). This is absolutely important for the sake of customers, the public, banks and the economy as a whole. This is the key fundamental lesson drawn from the wrong developments in American consumer and real estate financing during the first decade of the twenty-first century that imminently led to the financial crisis of 2008 (Financial Crisis Inquiry Commission, 2011).

Providing funds without critical credit assessment is not a means for borrowers to help themselves, but an irresponsible misallocation of capital and a violation of fair lending principles. Only those borrowers who have a realistic possibility of repayment capacity should be financed. Otherwise, more individual harm is created than without lending at all.

To the public, the obligation of personal and financial preparedness for taking debts and thus the understanding of scarcity and value of capital (maybe an outdated view given the implications of negative interest rates) would be undermined. As a result, social wealth imbalances would rather dramatically increase.

For banks, obviously relaxed standards during a crisis could rarely be reversed during boisterous boom times and would lead to the occurrence of a significantly higher level of non-performing loans over time. Once lending rules are released on demand of the state, moral hazard and principal agent problems would occur as bank failures could be exculpated by the role of executors of the public will only.

From an economic point of view, the acceleration mechanism of such funds will be limited, if any. In contrast, the impact will manifest in a rise of either individual debt or government deficit with a further substantial societal burden in the future. Wrong incentives would be set, supporting a mindset where stabilization is more valued than development and dynamics. Within the current paradigm of interventionism, the disruption of capital allocation and the 'zombification' of more and more actors would continue where survival is subject to the continuation of subventions, ultra-low-zero- or negative interest rates (Banerjee and Hofmann, 2018; El-Erian, 2020).

Outlook

At the time when this text goes to the editors, the future is still impossible to predict as we are still amid a crisis from which it is likely that national economies and businesses will be recovering for years to come, even though the interventionist paradigm of a stability-oriented economic approach has drawn in political majority and become mainstream. Thirty years after the fall of the Iron Curtain, non-market conforming central bank actions have been assumed for political reasons to unimaginable extent.

Post-crises times rarely result in a process of reduced state interventions (Peacock and Wiseman, 1961) and this is likely to be the case after COVID-19. It remains unclear for how long the breaking points within the financial system can be obliterated and how the adjustment mechanisms can still be handled without endangering the economy, the wealth of European citizen and – ultimately – our free democratic basic order.

In order to mitigate the financial burden of the crisis within a foreseeable time span, interventionist measures will not provide the intended results. On the contrary, interventionism will result in just the ultimate financial, social and human misery it was initially intending to prevent by increasing debts and monetarization.

One key aspect is that capital needs to be located in a market-conforming manner where it can be used in the most efficient way manifested in the risk-return based free lending policy of banks. That lending supply works without intervention is manifested by a recent healthy €184 billion new lending volume generated during March and April 2020 in the Euro-Zone (Kuehnlenz, 2020).

Instead, what is needed in order to ignite the recovery process are economic measures to create a positive economic outlook, strengthen demand of business and private persons to support new dynamics in business activities and consumer demand, and thus, stimulate acceleration mechanisms. Thus, structural reforms on the level of national states of the Euro-Zone in order to regain track on internal and international competitiveness, e.g., reduction of administrative hurdles, 'cost of doing business' supporting individual entrepreneurship, are overdue for a long time. For such a fundamental task, and in contrast to many doomed prophets, the current crisis would even set the best possible scene – and probably the last chance – for a controlled solution.

On the way, market forces as disciplining and sometimes painful actors ought to play a new role. The ECB has to allow the re-occurrence of market activities and the subsequent frictions. Credit spreads of government bonds, today manipulated downwards, will indicate over time the effectiveness of the change efforts of member states.

Only in case of a re-set of the current paradigm, the future of the monetized public debts could then be assessed in a broader context, including necessary restructuring and waiving scenarios. Political feasibility would require a changed paradigm as a basis for renewed trust in a more reliable fiscal behavior and future central bank politics in Europe that goes beyond permanent non-market conforming actions.

References

Backhaus, D., 2020. Vorbereitet fuer den Worst Case. *Der Treasurer*, 5, 44–46.

Banerjee, R., Hofmann, B., 2018. The rise of zombie firms: causes and consequences. *BIS Quarterly Review*, September. https://www.bis.org/publ/qtrpdf/r_qt1809g.htm (accessed 10.06.20.).

Boumans, D., Link, S., Sauer, S., 2020. Covid-19: The world economy needs a lifeline - but which one? Expert survey on the word-wide effects of the Covid-19 crisis and policy options. *Econmic Policy Policy Brief* 27(4), https://www.econpol.eu/sites/default/files/2020-04/EconPol_Policy_Brief_27_COVID19_Economy_Lifeline.pdf (accessed 24.06.20.).

Chinn, D., Sjatil, P. E., Stern, S., Tesfu, S., Windhagen, E., 2020. Navigating the post-Covid-19 era: a strategic framework for European recovery. https://www.mckinsey.com/industries/public-sector/our-insights/navigating-the-post-covid-19-era-a-strategic-framework-for-european-recovery?cid=other-eml-alt-mip-mck&hlkid=0402609b02c443c195c107ac96f52b19&hctky=1844697&hdpid=af59eed4-81f6-4b4e-92c7-fb317afa7039 (accessed 24.06.20.).

ECB, 2020. Press release: ECB announces measures to support bank liquidity conditions and money market activity. 12 March 2020. https://www.ecb.europa.eu/press/pr/date/2020/html/ecb.pr200312_2~06c32dabd1.en.html (accessed 22.06.20.).

ECB, 2020a. Press release: Monetary policy decisions. 4 June 2020. https://www.ecb.europa.eu/press/pr/date/2020/html/ecb.mp200604~a307d3429c.en.html (accessed 22.06.20.).

El-Erian, Mohamed, 2020. Es droht ein Zombie-Markt. In: *Finanz und Wirtschaft*. FuW, Zurich, p. 17.

European Parliament, 2020. Covid-19: the EU plan for the economic recovery. May 18, 2020. https://www.europarl.europa.eu/news/en/headlines/economy/20200513STO79012/covid-19-the-eu-plan-for-the-economic-recovery (accessed 26.06.20.).

Financial Crisis Inquiry Commission, 2011. *Crisis Inquiry Report: Final Report of the national Commission on the Causes of the Financial and Economic Crisis in the United States*. Official Government Edition, U.S. Government Printing Office. http://fcic.law.stanford.edu/report/ (accessed 26.12.15.)

Freitag, M., Maier, A., Noe, M., Palan, D., Rest, J., Schwazer, U., Slodczyk, K., 2020. *DistanzkampfManager Magazin.*, Mai: 3, 24–41.

German Federal Ministry of Finance, 2020. German cabinet adopts major stimulus package. https://www.bundesfinanzministerium.de/Content/EN/Standardartikel/Topics/Public-Finances/Articles/2020-06-04-fiscal-package.html (accessed 27.06.20.).

Guba, E. C., 1990. *The Paradigm Dialog*. Sage, London, New Delhi.

Koestens, U., 2020. Strategie und Corporate Performance: Wie komme ich an privilegierte Finanzmittel? https://blog.enomyc.com/wie-komme-ich-an-privilegierte-finanzmittel-uwe-koestens-corona-kompakt-gutachten-enomyc (accessed 02.05.20.).

Kuehnlenz, A., 2020. Die Euro-Währungshüter dürften ihre Nothilfen ausweiten. https://www.fuw.ch/article/die-euro-waehrungshueter-duerften-ihre-nothilfen-ausweiten/ (accessed 22.06.20.).

Lichtenstein, M., 2020. Rückbesinnen statt Geld drucken. https://www.fuw.ch/article/rueckbesinnen-statt-geld-drucken/ (accessed 27.06.20.).

Monnet, E., Pagliari, S., Vallee, S., 2019. Beyond financial repression and regulatory capture: the recomposition of European financial ecosystems after the crisis. LSE 'Europe in Question' Discussion Paper Series. No. 147/2019. https://www.ecb. europa.eu/press/pr/date/2020/html/ecb.mp200604~a307d3429c.en.htm (accessed 26.06.20.).

Mussler, W., 2020. Schwerer wirtschaftlicher Einbruch: EU-Länder setzen Schuldenregeln erstmals aus. Frankfurter Allgemeine Zeitung, 23 March 2020. https://www.faz.net/aktuell/wirtschaft/corona-krise-eu-finanzminister-setzen-stabilitaetspakt-aus-16692691.html#:~:text=Die%20EU-Finanzminister %20haben%20sich%20darauf%20geeinigt%2C%20dass%20der,die %20Staatsverschuldung%20waren%20in%20der%20EU%20genau%20vor-geschrieben(accessed 27.06.20.).

N.A., 2020. VIRUS/Scholz: Banken sollten bei Corona-Krediten Fünfe gerade sein lassen. https://www.focus.de/finanzen/boerse/wirtschaftsticker/virus-scholz-banken-sollten-bei-corona-krediten-fuenfe-gerade-sein-lassen_id_11833968.html (accessed 16.06.20.).

N.A., 2020a. The collected words. https://www.tcwords.com/helmut-schmidt-zitate-des-politikers/ (accessed 10.06.20.).

Peacock, A. T., Wiseman, J., 1961. Possible future trends in government expenditure. In: Peacock, A. T., Wiseman, J. (Eds.), *The Growth of Public Expenditure in the United Kingdom*. University Press, Princeton.

Robinson, G., 2006. *Risk Thinkers Guide: The Breakthrough Book on Risk Management*. Brolga Publishing, Melbourne.

13 COVID-19

The Need for New Talent Management Agenda

Marina Latukha

Crises as a Trigger for New Opportunities

Crises have affected businesses, governments and people many times in the past all over the world. A crisis can trigger changes in the macro- and meso-environment that impact organizations by pushing them to find new competitive advantages, opportunities and solutions as a response to the crises-ignited challenges ensuring organizational survival in the short-term and organizational resilience and longevity in the long-term. Thus, organizations facing such new realities should adjust their operational responses and their strategies, which require an adjustment or even a new, fresh perspective on their strategic and operational decisions.

Existing narratives and conversations about the impact of crises are mostly associated with negative predictions and outcomes, and discussing emergency organizational responses to threats. We are constantly reminded and being convinced by different theoretical and empirical investigations about the necessity to be accurate with innovations and risk taking (Barnett and Pratt, 2000), and to analyze the impact of any crises on different levels - individual, group and organizational (Mckinley et al., 2014; Staw et al., 1981). However, a range of studies have also introduced a juxtaposing idea, i.e., that crises induced threats can be useful for businesses and they can embrace them as opportunities to create positive outcomes. The consequences of crises that are, on the one hand a threat or a challenge to organizations, may also, on the other hand, increase companies' motivation to act strategically and look for new opportunities inside and outside a firm in order to compensate for the losses incurred as a result of the crises (March, 1991; Uotila et al., 2009).

We see that discussions about such activities are drawing the attention of some practitioners and researchers and they are not limited to the studies mentioned above. Moreover, many of them discuss organizational crises without properly investigating the impact of global economic problems on business. In the COVID-19 response, the primary objective of firms is understating and clarifying the new business challenges that seemingly 'emerged overnight' (McKinsey Analytics, 2020). The spread of the pandemic in 2020 around the world has drastically changed many aspects of the behavior of people and firms due to quarantine measures, mass insolvency, fast rising unemployment, subsequent economic recession and restrictions on global and domestic mobility. Some experts are already predicting that many economies will be struggling with poverty, decreasing or reconsidering consumer needs and attitudes and restructuring global labor markets. McKinsey has tracked the changes in people's behavior, collecting data on such indicators as consumer sentiment, consumer income, expectations or personal attitudes (McKinsey Analytics, 2020). However, companies need to understand not only how to respond to the challenges set by COVID-19, but they have to also look for and identify opportunities emerging along with limited mobility, global unemployment and economic recession.

What Does Not Kill You – Makes You Stronger

The crisis provoked by COVID-19 suggests that the global pandemic in 2020, and possibly later, will intensify uncertainty mostly related to human capital. The response of global financial and labor markets to the coronavirus pandemic indicates that the global economy is currently moving towards recession, mass unemployment, decrease in salaries, stalling organizational growth and investments in employee professional development. The need for human capital previously involved countries and organizations globally in their 'war for talent' and many highly-skilled talents were attracted to developed countries by economic and career-related pull factors, thus downsizing talent pools and creating brain drain in their country-of-origin. As the COVID-19 crisis has appeared unexpectedly and has threatened business positions and traditions, international trade, and the future of free migration, it has opened up new perspectives for companies related to human capital attraction, development, and retention. We may look at some potential benefits from the restrictions on global migration and provide insights on how talent management (TM) may gain a new head start to create new competitive advantages for organizations at the time of pandemic.

Creating New Pool of Talent

To be able to analyze highly-skilled workforce migration and human capital formation challenges and opportunities created by COVID-19, it is important to explore return migration. Research interest in return migration started in the mid-1960s and became a self-sufficient field in the 1980s when scholarly discussions about the phenomenon of returning labor (i.e., returnees) and their impact on the county-of-origin gathered speed worldwide. Most studies on returnees' willingness to go back to their home countries have been in so far interested in understanding the different reasons (also referred to as determinants or antecedents) for their behavior. These have included determinants such as, for example, home country's 'pull' factors, i.e., government and institutional support, availability of new technologies, and economic stability (Biondo et al., 2012; Kenney et al., 2013; Kautto, 2019). In some cases, the determinants may be associated with dissatisfaction from living in a foreign country often expressed in inability to find employment relevant to returnee's qualifications, or being treated as a less valuable staff member than local employees, getting lower pay or worse job progression prospects compared to locals who have equivalent or lower skills; and psychological problems – feeling of exclusion or incompatibility of values (Wong, 2014). Scholars emphasize that returnees are an essential talent pool because they have international experience, knowledge of foreign markets, innovative capabilities and cross-cultural intelligence, which are highly needed for increasing business productivity and innovativeness. Such competences can constitute important strategic resources for companies in home countries and be valuable for their organizational renewal, provided that companies are ready to absorb these resources (Guo and Al Ariss, 2015; Zikic, 2015).

The new realities with the coronavirus crisis in 2020 have added a new dimension to migration. They have served as an accelerator or a push factor for immigrants who had left their country-of-origin driven by various motives. When international economic migration is under severe restrictions imposed through lockdowns, social distancing requirements, and closure of international borders, many countries have left borders open exclusively for their nationals and residents. Having accumulated social and human capital – including knowledge-based ties and social networks, behavioral competences, and experiential learning (Adler and Kwon, 2002; Davidsson and Honig, 2003), returnees have become a primary target of TM organizational systems as a new talent group. Many migrants, and particular the highly skilled ones, are returning to their country-of-origin motivated by the effects of the pandemic. Some go home either because of a well-organized and/or free access healthcare system; others because their families have been left behind in the home country; some are simply drawn back to their Motherland identified as a foundation of self-identity and roots; some as a consequence of economic losses – loss of or threat to their employment and income in the host country, and many due to any combination of these aforementioned reasons. After coming back to their home country, returnees have a potential to realize themselves in local firms as they bring new knowledge and capabilities acquired abroad that allow them to bring unique and difficult to imitate resources to firms in order to improve their performance, innovation and absorptive capacity (Fu et al., 2017; Ma et al., 2019; Zhang, 2018).

Companies may benefit from returnee inflows by acquiring and utilizing highly valued human capital creating opportunities to overcome global and domestic challenges (Frenkel, 2017; Li, 2020). Governments and firms have launched different activities to encourage migrants to return (Wahba, 2015), realizing the opportunities COVID-19 has unraveled. These may lead to restructuring of the human capital accumulation model and create opportunities especially for emerging economies that lost many of their talents in the pre-pandemic times. During the crisis, organizations should initiate and implement an agenda on creating a talent pool in order to accelerate human capital development that can integrate returnee talent from nearby and afar a country-of-origin. Such a new talent pool of returnees may strengthen organizational human capital and develop firm's competitive advantage. This can only be achieved by continuing the discussion about the value of returnees in a talent pool and answering some questions. These include, but are not limited to: how further migration perspectives may shape talent demand and supply in home countries; how home countries may benefit from returnee human capital; and how to integrate returnees effectively so that companies can gain from returnee presence and employment.

Turning to Inclusive TM

The COVID-19 crisis may contribute to furthering the TM system based on an inclusive TM strategy. TM functions as a set of practices focus on talented employees whose human capital is essential for organizational performance and competitive advantage, and are aimed at leveraging the knowledge and competences talents have (Collings and Mellahi, 2009; Gallardo-Gallardo et al., 2019). Researchers in the area of TM discuss the importance of alignment of TM strategy with organizational purposes and conditions (De Vos and Dries, 2013; Zhao and Du, 2011). In particular, there is an assumption that inclusive TM strategy is more appropriate and suitable as employees play a crucial role in building organizational reputation oriented towards achieving enhanced performance and competitive advantage (Gallardo-Gallardo et al., 2013). Research in TM highlights the existence of two distinct approaches – exclusive and inclusive, depending on who in an organization is perceived as talent and should be engaged in enhancing organizational performance (Iles et al., 2010; Meyers et al., 2019).

An inclusive TM approach has emerged which, corresponds to such a system in which all employees of an organization are considered talents and may have access to training and development in order to find their place and role within that organization. The reason for such a view lies in the unique knowledge, experience, and skills of each employee, which may be of great importance for a firm's strategic goals, if managed (e.g. developed) properly (Gallardo-Gallardo et al., 2013). Therefore, an inclusive approach aims at reaching the best performance of the entire workforce of a firm rather than of a fraction of the best and the brightest.

We see that during the ongoing COVID-19 pandemic, a global shift to online education has occurred. The important condition for the talents of all employees to be realized is sufficient training and opportunities, in other words talent should be nurtured (Swailes et al., 2014; Tansley, 2011). Inclusive TM actively promotes learning and development practices (Meyers et al., 2019) which promote firm performance as part of a talent development system, but at the same time such training intensity can be managed to benefit an organization mostly through inclusive TM. In particular, as a the share of employees to be identified and trained as talents is substantial, inclusive TM strategy allows leveraging such positive effects of talent identification and development as increased job satisfaction, commitment, work effort, motivation and individual performance (De Boeck et al., 2018; Gelens et al., 2014). Moreover, besides providing learning and development opportunities to employees, inclusive TM can promote social integration and communication, exchange of ideas among all employees through social capital (Crane and Hartwell, 2018), which will facilitate the distribution of information and knowledge transfer within a firm. One of the challenges in the inclusive approach is the concept of fit – the need to fit each employee into positions where their talent can be fully expressed (Swailes et al., 2014). Practices that can be used to enhance learning for as many employees as possible, thus gaining more insights from inclusive TM, are important and contribute to firm's results. While COVID-19 has pushed companies to decrease investment in training and development programs, it has also revealed incredible perspectives and opportunities as many courses, development programs, and educational platforms – on a single company, group of companies, regional, national and global level, have become free and available for almost all those who are interested in personal and professional development. Online learning has become part of talent development unraveling new opportunities for employees and companies solidifying the inclusive approach position and taking it to a more prominent level of application and recognition.

Knowledge and its effective management have become a key success factor in today's global environment characterized by high dynamism, volatility, and knowledge-intensity (Khan et al., 2019). Global shift to online learning in the pandemic has reinforced opportunities to knowledge assimilation and transformation, and maximized the value of human capital for companies, whereas inclusive TM allows using an opportunity to acquire and allocate talents to make an organization more resilient. Moreover, turning to talent pool development, possibilities emerged for companies to consolidate their positions on local, regional and global markets via integrating and utilizing returnee talent. An organization providing opportunities to its talents can increase organizational cumulative expertise and support human capital growth. Moreover, by engaging employees into R&D and other innovation activities, firms can contribute to developing new products and solutions in order to gain long-term competitive advantage. Finally, it is important to consider that TM systems and their configuration during a crisis may secure renewal of organizational business processes and enhance organizational performance.

References

Adler, P., Kwon, S. W., 2002. Social capital: prospects for a new concept. *Acad. Manag. Rev.* 27, 17–40.

Barnett, C.K., Pratt, M.G., 2000. From threat-rigidity to flexibility: toward a learning model of autogenic crisis in organizations. *J. Organ. Change Manag.* 13, 74–88.

Biondo, A. E., Monteleone, S., Skonieczny, G., Torrisi, B., 2012. The propensity to return: theory and evidence for the Italian brain drain. *Econ. Lett.* 115, 359–362.

Collings, D. G., Mellahi, K., 2009. Strategic talent-management: A review and research agenda. *Hum. Resour. Manag. Rev.* 19, 304–313.

Crane, B., Hartwell, C., 2018. Global talent management: A life cycle view of the interaction between human and social capital. *J. World Bus.* 54(2), 82–92.

Davidsson, P., Honig, B., 2003. The role of social and human capital among nascent entrepreneurs. *J. Bus. Venturing* 18, 301–331.

De Boeck, G., Meyers, M. C., Dries, N., 2018. Employee reactions to talent management: assumptions versus evidence. *J. Organ. Behav.* 39(2), 199–213.

De Vos, A., Dries, N., 2013. Applying a talent management lens to career management: the role of human capital composition and continuity. *Int. J. Hum. Resour. Manag.* 24(9), 1816–1831.

Dustmann, C., Weiss, Y., 2007. Return migration: Theory and empirical evidence from the UK. *Br. J. Ind. Relat.* 45(2), 236–256.

Frenkel, M., 2017. Is migration good for an Economy? A survey of the main economic effects. *J. Mark. Ethics* 5(1), 13–22.

Fu, X., Hou, J., Sanfilippo, M., 2017. Highly skilled returnees and the internationalization of EMNEs: firm level evidence from China. *Int. Bus. Rev.* 26(3), 579–591.

Gallardo-Gallardo, E., Dries, N., González-Cruz, T., 2013. What is the meaning of 'talent' in the world of work? *Hum. Resour. Manag. Rev.* 23(4), 290–300.

Gallardo-Gallardo, E., Thunnissen, M., Scullion, H., 2019. Talent management: context matters. *Int. J. Hum. Resour. Manag.* 31(4), 457–473.

Gelens, J., Hofmans, J., Dries, N., Pepermans, R., 2014. Talent management and organizational justice: Employee reactions to high potential identification. *Hum. Resour. Manag. J.* 24(2), 159–175.

Glaister, A., Karacay, G., Demirbag, M., Tatoglu, E., 2017. HRM and performance – the role of talent management as a transmission mechanism in an emerging market context. *Hum. Resour. Manag. J.*, 28, 148–166, 10.1111/1748-8583.12170.

Guo, S., Al Ariss, A., 2015. Human resource management of international migrants: current theories and future research. *Int. J. Hum. Resour. Manag.* 26, 1287–1297.

Iles, P., Chuai, X., Preece, D., 2010. Talent management and HRM in multinational companies in Beijing: definitions, differences and drivers. *J. World Bus.* 45(2), 179–189.

Kautto, D., 2019. Social influences in cross-border entrepreneurial migration policy. *J. Int. Bus. Policy* 2, 397–412.

Kenney, M., Breznitz, D., Murphree, M., 2013. Coming back home after the sunrises: returnee entrepreneurs and growth of high tech industries. *Res. Policy* 42, 391–407.

Khan, Z., Lew, Y., Marinova, S., 2019. Exploitative and exploratory innovations in emerging economies: the role of realized absorptive capacity and learning intent. *Int. Bus. Rev.* 28(3), 499–512.

Li, H., 2020. Role of overseas ethnic and non-ethnic ties and firm activity in the home country in the internationalization of returnee entrepreneurial firms. *J. Int. Manag.*, 26(1), 1–15, DOI: 10.1016/j.intman.2019.100706.

Ma, Z., Zhu, J., Meng, Y., Teng, Y., 2019. The impact of overseas human capital and social ties on Chinese returnee entrepreneurs' venture performance. *Int. J. Entrepreneurial Behav. Res.* 25(1), 67–83.

March, J.G., 1991. Exploitation and exploration in organizational research. *Organ. Sci.* 2(1), 71–87.

Meyers, M. C., van Woerkom, M., Paauwe, J., Dries, N., 2019. HR managers' talent philosophies: prevalence and relationships with perceived talent management practices. *Int. J. Hum. Resour. Manag.* 31(4), 562–588.

Mckinley, W., Latham, S., Braun, M., 2014. Organizational decline and innovation: Turnarounds and downward spirals. *Acad. Manag. Rev.*, 39, 88–110, 10.5465/amr.2011.0356.

McKinsey Analytics, 2020. Accelerating analytics to navigate COVID-19 and the next normal. https://www.mckinsey.com/business-functions/mckinsey-analytics/our-insights/accelerating-analytics-to-navigate-covid-19-and-the-next-normal (accessed 14.06.20.).

Osiyevskyy, O., Dewald, J., 2015. Explorative versus exploitative business model change: the cognitive antecedents of firm-level responses to disruptive innovation. *Strategic Entrepreneurship J.* 9(1), 58–78.

Staw, B. M., Sandelands, L. E., Dutton, J. E., 1981. Threat-rigidity effects in organizational behavior: a multilevel analysis. *Adm. Sci. Q.* 26(4), 501–524.

Swailes, S., Downs, Y., Orr, K., 2014. Conceptualizing inclusive talent management: potential, possibilities and practicalities. *Hum. Resour. Dev. Int.* 17(5), 529–544.

Tansley, C., 2011. What do we mean by the term "talent" in talent management? *Ind. Commercial Train.* 43(5), 266–274.

Uotila, J., Maula, M., Keil, T., Zahra, S., 2009. Exploration, exploitation, and financial performance: analysis of S&P 500 corporations. *Strategic Manag. J.* 30, 221–231.

Wahba, J., 2015. Who benefits from return migration to developing countries? https://wol.iza.org/uploads/articles/123/pdfs/who-benefits-from-return-migration-to-developing-countries.pdf (accessed 10.06.20.).

Wei, Y., Liu, X., Lu, J., Yang, J., 2019. Chinese migrants and their impact on homeland development. *World Economy* 40(11), 2354–2377.

Wong, M., 2014. Navigating return: the gendered geographies of skilled return migration to Ghana. *Glob. Netw. 14*(4), 438–457.

Zhang, H., 2018. Review on returnee – the perspective of dual social network, knowledge spillovers and institutional-based view. *Am. J. Ind. Bus. Manag. 8*(12), 2344–2363.

Zhao, S., Du, J., 2011. The application of competency-based talent assessment systems in China. *Hum. Syst. Manag. 30*(1), 23–37.

Zikic, J., 2015. Skilled migrants' career capital as a source of competitive advantage: implications for strategic HRM. *Int. J. Hum. Resour. Manag. 26*, 1360–1381.

14 Expatriates, Rise of Telecommuting and Implications for International Business

Ahmad Arslan, Ismail Gölgeci, and Jorma Larimo

Introduction

International business (IB) travel has long been considered an important aspect of international business management strategies of multinational enterprises (MNEs) (see e.g., Welch et al., 2007; Beaverstock et al., 2009; Derudder and Witlox, 2016). In fact, international travel expenses constitute a visible aspect of the budgets of many MNEs (Latta, 2004). Extant research has focused on IB travel by segmenting it into two categories. The first category consists of short-term IB travelers, including MNE managers, who are permanently based in their home countries but undertake frequent international travels related to their jobs (Schaffer et al., 2012; Dimitrova et al., 2020). Prior studies have referred to a range of reasons associated with frequent IB travels by such managers including searching for new opportunities (e.g., Budd and Vorley, 2013; Derudder and Witlox, 2016), meeting partners and participating in negotiations (e.g., Welch et al., 2007; Mäkelä et al., 2017), project operations (e.g., Köster, 2009; Mäkelä, et al., 2017), foreign subsidiary and operations establishment (e.g., Jaeger, 1983; Beaverstock et al., 2009; Kornacker et al., 2019), training of local employees and knowledge transfer (e.g., Kobrin, 1988; Patel et al., 2018, 2019), and operations monitoring (e.g., Boeh and Beamish, 2012; Derudder and Witlox, 2016). At the same time, literature recognizes other IB travelers who are permanently based in foreign locations, i.e., expatriates who need to travel in some cases rather regularly to other locations and MNE headquarters (HQs) for a range of organizational responsibilities and functions (McNulty and Selmer, 2017; Dimitrova et al., 2020).

Extant literature further recognizes that expatriate managers are an essential cornerstone of MNEs' global strategies. They play a crucial role in the management of subsidiaries (especially the newly established ones) as well as in knowledge transfer of organizational routines and practices (e.g., Scullion and Brewster, 2001; Paik and Sohn, 2004; McNulty and

Selmer, 2017; Patel et al., 2018). As such, they constitute the backbone of MNEs' human capital.

Keeping in view the brief discussion offered above, IB travel is an important component and aspect of MNE management and strategies. However, so far, it has been taken for granted that both short term travelers, as well as long term expatriates, can travel to various locations globally when needed. This specific argument forms the starting point of this chapter where we ponder the potential influences of Covid-19 on IB travel and use of expatriates by MNEs because the current pandemic has severely hampered global travel and perhaps changed it permanently from the way it was known earlier. Since the start of the pandemic, numerous news articles and opinion pieces have been written about the future of the aviation industry and international travel in times of Covid-19 and potentially in the post-Covid-19 world (e.g., Forbes, 2020; New York Times, 2020; WEF, 2020). The majority of these articles have stated that international travel would become difficult, expensive, and with more hurdles, including medical checks on certain flights (e.g., Forbes, 2020; Guardian, 2020). Due to lockdowns placed in most countries across the globe, remote (distance) working has emerged as a viable replacement option in both public and private sector organizations (e.g., Business Insider, 2020; Slack, 2020). Hence, we have witnessed physical meetings being replaced by usage of tools like Zoom or Microsoft Teams, among others (e.g., EY, 2020).

However, can all physical tasks, including the need for travel in general and international travel in particular be undertaken remotely? This is the question which many theorists in multiple disciplines are already pondering upon, and we can expect several studies coming out on this topic in the recent future. This chapter also aims to join this debate and offers a conceptual analysis of COVID-19's influences on IB travel and expatriation as well as a discussion for the pros and cons of remote working. We believe that the chapter would strengthen extant IB literature in three-ways. Firstly, it is one of the pioneering studies to specifically focus on both IB travel and expatriation in the context of the disruptions caused by the Covid-19. Secondly, to our knowledge, it is also one of the first studies to investigate the viability of telecommuting in this context from a critical lens and offer an analysis. Finally, it contributes to the extant literature on disasters and pandemic influences by specifically linking the ongoing pandemic of Covid-19 to an essential aspect of MNE management, i.e., IB travel.

The rest of the chapter is organized as follows. The next section offers an overview of telecommuting and remote working by addressing different aspects associated with them in prior studies. This is followed by the section where we link the rise of telecommuting with IB travel and analyze the potential implications. The last section presents a discussion on the chapter's implications, limitations, and future research directions.

Telecommuting and Remote Working: An Overview

Telecommuting, which has also been referred to as distance working or working from home, has become increasingly visible in many fields during the last decade due to developments in internet speed and other technologies needed for it (e.g., Ansong and Boateng, 2018). At the same time, academic interest in telecommuting has also increased due to its visibility in many spheres of life, including academia (in the form of online or virtual teaching). In an earlier study on this topic, Manochehri and Pinkerton (2003) define telecommuting as a phenomenon where employees of an organization work away from their office, one or more days per week, using a computer with telecommunications facilities. It has further been proposed that the rise of telecommuting is, to an extent, due to the increasingly competitive business landscape where many firms are being forced to cut operational costs while increasing their productivity at the same time (Nicklin et al., 2016).

In the specific context of telecommuting, scholars stress the fact that technological advancements resulting in the employees being able to access all office functions from their homes, has played a big role in its rise (Nicklin et al., 2016). Studies on telecommuting have indicated that the percentage of firms engaging teleworkers is rapidly on the rise year after year. Thus far, researchers have analyzed the dynamics of telecommuting from multiple angles including technology, societal and organizational aspects, being the most important ones. A number of studies have focused on infrastructure and skills that need to be associated with the implementation of telecommuting in different firms (Johnson, 2000; Blount and Gloet, 2017). Some studies have focused on the societal dimension highlighting that increased awareness of carbon emissions, as well as pressure on transport infrastructure, has been a motivation for many firms to move in this direction, especially in large cosmopolitan cities (Kim, 2017).

Moreover, researchers from organizational behavior and human resource management have addressed organizational control, employee evaluation, performance dynamics and teamwork related factors in the context of telecommuting (Leonard, 2011; Peters et al., 2016; Golden and Gajendran, 2019). The findings of these studies suggest that telecommuting can potentially lead to improved work-life balance for many employees as they do not lose much time in commuting away from families, especially in large cities (Kossek et al., 2006; Gajendran and Harrison, 2007; Nicklin et al., 2016). It has further been argued that telecommuting can potentially result in improved time management skills of workers, as well as less pressure and giving an opportunity to homebound workers to work (Crandall and Gao, 2005; Blount and Gloet, 2017).

Despite these positive aspects, extant research has also highlighted many pitfalls associated with telecommuting. It has been argued that telecommuting can result in increased alienation of employees from the organizational culture (context) and it can make getting guidance from supervisors difficult (Gajendran and Harrison, 2007; Lautsch et al., 2009). Some other studies have referred to the social status, belongingness and reputational needs of employees, which can be negatively influenced by telecommuting or distance working (Manochehri and Pinkerton, 2003). Telecommuting has also been linked with increased conflicts both at home and the workplace of employees (e.g., Sarbu, 2018). As the boundary between home and work has been disappearing, family members may perceive an employee as working too much and ignoring them, while disruptions caused by the events at home can delay output from an employees that may lead to conflict with supervisors or team members (e.g., Solís, 2017). Some social scholars have also argued that feelings of alienation or seclusion from working and social environments have long term detrimental influences not only on individual employees, but also on society (Larsen and Urry, 2016).

It is further important to mention that prior literature has highlighted organizational training and incentives as useful tools in overcoming some of the above-mentioned problems (Gajendran and Harrison, 2007; Blount and Gloet, 2017). In recent years, technological developments mean that use of hologram and augmented reality is also increasingly being used for strategic meetings in firms that in the past required travel. At the same time, it has been acknowledged that face-to-face interaction is still needed in certain cases and full change to virtual modes of work and interaction can lead to a range of social, psychological and organizational challenges (Growe, 2019).

Telecommuting has become a mainstream topic due to the Covid-19 pandemic since early 2020 as increasingly office workers in most fields switched to working from home, whenever possible (Bouziri et al., 2020). At the same time, due to lockdown measures being taken in many countries across the world, travel restrictions meant that all kinds of meetings and organizational level or large-scale conferences went online (e.g., Price, 2020). As a result, software like Zoom, Microsoft Teams and others witnessed a significant growth in their demand and usage (EY, 2020). As of end May 2020, the Covid-19 pandemic does not appear to be subsiding whereas some writers are arguing that the way work is done has changed fundamentally forever (e.g., Chainey, 2020). However, it remains to be seen if this is really true.

Covid-19, Rise of Telecommuting and Implications for IB Travel

At the start of this chapter it has been mentioned that IB travel and the use of expatriates have remained an essential aspect of MNE management for long. Even though specific statistics related to IB travel are not possible to access, it is still important to refer to some general business travel statistics before proceeding further. The global business travel spending was estimated to be US$1.33 billion in 2017 (Statista, 2020a). The statistics further reveal that business travel increased significantly during 2010–2018 in developed European and North American countries, as well as in many emerging economies (Statista, 2020b). The industry experts expected business travel spending to grow to US$1.6 billion in 2020 (GBTA, 2020). The use of air traffic for business travel has also become very common in the last couple of decades, as statistics suggest that five percent of European corporate travelers flew more than 20 times per year, while 30 percent traveled at least once a month during the period 2017–2018 (Fly Aelous, 2020). Despite the rise in telecommuting and virtual meeting possibilities, business travel was found to pay off for firms. For example, for every U.S. dollar spent on business tarveling, the firms received an average of US$12.50 in incremental revenue (Oxford Economics USA, 2019). The same report states that 28 percent of business deals would be lost if business travel is suddenly cut. Even though these statistics are in particular for the U.S. market, it is logical to expect similar statistics in other developed and rapidly advancing emerging economies.

Covid-19 has caused a collapse of the airline industry due to travel restrictions, which have been referred to remain in place in one way or another for the foreseeable future (New York Times, 2020; Whitley, 2020). At the same time, due to the slowdown of economic activity as a result of COVID-19, it is logical to expect that firms, including MNEs, will increasingly become thrifty and business travel possibilities will be limited, even when it becomes allowed. Moreover, since telecommuting has become a norm due to Covid-19 in all organizations, including MNEs, it is highly likely that this trend would continue in one form or another in the future (CNBC, 2020).

Based on these factors, we expect IB travel and use of expatriates to be limited by MNEs, where they may prefer to use modern technological tools like virtual reality or hologram meetings to increasingly replace physical presence. It is further likely that due to increased restrictions on air travel, MNEs may adopt a more regional strategy concerning IB travel. In such a scenario, MNEs with subsidiaries in Western Europe may use fast rail connections to send managers on temporary assignments to other countries. This will not be unusual considering that cross-country IB travel via trains is quite common in well-connected countries of Western Europe like the Netherlands, Belgium, Germany, France and Austria as well as in ths Scandinavian countries. At the same time, it is further likely that MNEs that may need to give technical guidance to their subsidiaries with complex assignments in international projects in developing countries, will need to invest more in advanced telecommuting technologies like a hologram for the virtual presence of their engineers or technical experts on those sites. These technologies have already become better, and it is highly likely that further investments by MNEs may hasten the process of their further development.

However, despite all this, it is paramount to mention that human interaction needs in face to face formats are really important and not everything can be shifted to the virtual model of communication. It is further important to highlight that the IB literature stream focusing on negotiations and relationship development has established that personal ties, as well as mutual trust developed through close personal interactions, are critically important, especially in certain collective countries (Ghauri and Usunier, 2003; Usunier, 2019). In such circumstances, it is likely that IB travel to important customers for negotiating business deals would continue in the future in one way or another. At the same time, it is not possible to undertake all international tasks from a distance despite the fact that managers may not be working from home but from well-connected offices. Specifically, aspects of emotional fatigue emanating from continuous online connectivity to workplace during the pandemic have been highlighted as significant health risks by organizational psychologists (e.g., Jack, 2020). Moreover, keeping in mind several other challenges associated with telecommuting mentioned in the previous section can potentially become even tougher due to the ambiguities of cross-cultural interactions which are part of IB management routines. Hence, our overall assessment is that IB travel in a certain form would remain needed in the foreseeable future, although with a reduced frequency.

Conclusions and Future Research Directions

The issue of international travel has become a daunting problem in relation to Covid-19 pandemic. Many MNEs have been overwhelmed by the unprecedented and severe problems they face in regard to the mobility of their workforce. As they have been trying to come to terms with the new reality of the pandemic world. The impact of the Covid-19 pandemic on MNEs and expatriates has not been fully studied yet. In this chapter, we took a look at the potential influence of the Covid-19 pandemic on IB travel and expatriation and we offer a discussion n remote working in view of the new realities during the pandemic and in the post-Covid-19 world. Consequently, we claim that we have made three particular contributions.

First, our chapter is one of the pioneering studies to particularly concentrate on the dynamics of IB travel and expatriation following the severe and unexpected disruptions brought about by Covid-19. While IB travel and expatriation have been evolving over the years with the rise of digitalization and the gig economy (Petriglieri et al., 2019; Sutherland et al., 2020), the Covid-19 pandemic suddenly brought the disruption to a higher level. As such, scholars have been caught off-guard with the unexpected speed of change Covid-19 triggered. Our chapter is an early attempt to contemplate on the potential future implications of such a disruption by offering early insights into how the future of IB travel and expatriation might look like.

Second, our chapter delves into the viability of telecommuting and remote working in this context from a critical lens offering relevant analysis. Our examinations highlight that telecommuting as a flexible work arrangement has several positive aspects and can be a viable option for various types of jobs. Nonetheless, it also comprises caveats that need to be considered. In particular, we suggest that tele-commuting can potentially lead to improved work-life balance for many employees and decrease significantly time and money spent on commuting with positive artefacts for the natural environment (Kossek et al., 2006; Gajendran and Harrison, 2007; Nicklin et al., 2016). However, we have highlighted that, among other pitfalls, such remote working arrangements may blur the boundaries between work and personal lives, agonize employees (Petriglieri et al., 2019), and amplify the potential alienation of employees from their organizational culture (Gajendran and Harrison, 2007; Lautsch et al., 2009).

Finally, the chapter contributes to the extant literature on the influences of disasters and pandemics by specifically linking Covid-19 to an essential aspect of MNE management, i.e., IB travel. We highlight the shock which hit IB travel due to Covid-19 and predict that some knockout effects would be permanent. While the benefits and economic returns of IB travel have been documented, the hurdles created by the pandemic appear to stay with us. This is expected to force firms to reassess the benefits of labor mobility in the age of the increasingly widespread use of digital platforms. While softer aspects of globaliza-tion (i.e., the global flow of ideas and knowledge) would still entail some degree of IB travel, the contraction in the physical aspects of globalization (material flows of goods and products) (Gupta, 2020) may curb some of the travel needed to coordinate business activities.

The fundamental changes in the way the global economy is being run, and firms operate offer profound future research opportunities on labor mobility and IB travel. Future research could study implications on individual and firm-level of the growing presence of virtual rather than physical means of doing work. In fact, the recent digitalization, the growth of the virtual work platforms and the lockdown effect of Covid-19 constitute one of the most fundamental changes to the way people have worked since the beginning of civilization, potentially on par, if not more fundamental, than the changes brought about by the industrial revolution. As such, there is ample room for discovering cognitive, attitudinal and behavioral responses to the digitalization of the workplace at the individual level. At the firm level, the recent developments mean fundamental and potentially disruptive changes to international human resource management strategies. Future research can explore how smaller international firms and MNEs respond to recent developments on work patterns and steer the external changes shaping their human capital. At the macro-level, there would be policy implications of the new ways of working and labor relations. Some jobs would be lost, others transformed, some might be created. Future research can explore the impact of virtual work arrangements and travel restrictions on employment and work regulation as a result of the Covid-19 pandemic.

References

Ansong, E., Boateng, R., 2018. Organisational adoption of telecommuting: evidence from a developing country. *Electron. J. Inf. Syst. Developing Ctries.* *84*(1), 1–15.

Beaverstock, J.V., Derudder, B., Faulconbridge, J.R., Witlox, F., 2009. International business travel: some explorations. *Geografiska Annaler: Ser. B, Hum. Geogr. 91*(3), 193–202.

Blount, Y., Gloet, M., 2017. *Anywhere Working and the New Era of Telecommuting.* IGI Global, Hershey, PA.

Boeh, K.K., Beamish, P.W., 2012. Travel time and the liability of distance in foreign direct investment: location choice and entry mode. *J. Int. Bus. Stud. 43*(5), 525–535.

Bouziri, H., Smith, D.R., Descatha, A., Dab, W., and Jean, K. 2020. Working from home in the time of COVID-19: how to best preserve occupational health?. Occup. Environ. Med. https://oem.bmj.com/content/early/2020/04/30/oemed-2020-106599 (accessed on 10.05.20.).

Business Insider, 2020. The office as we knew it is dead. https://www.businessinsider.com/coronavirus-pandemic-wont-kill-office-but-it-will-change-forever-2020-4?r=US&IR=T (accessed 11.05.20.).

Budd, L., Vorley, T., 2013. Airlines, apps, and business travel: a critical examination. *Res. Transportation Bus. Manag. 9*, 41–49.

Chainey, R., 2020. This is how COVID-19 could change the world of work for good. https://www.weforum.org/agenda/2020/04/here-s-how-coronavirus-has-changed-the-world-of-work-covid19-adam-grant/ (accessed 20.05.20.).

CNBC, 2020. 13 ways the coronavirus pandemic could forever change the way we work. https://www.cnbc.com/2020/04/29/how-the-coronavirus-pandemic-will-impact-the-future-of-work.html (accessed 20.05.20).

Crandall, W., Gao, L., 2005. An update on telecommuting: review and prospects for emerging issues. *SAM. Adv. Manag. J. 70*(3), 30–50.

Derudder, B., Witlox, F., 2016. *International Business Travel in the Global Economy.* Routledge, Oxon.

Dimitrova, M., Chia, S.I., Shaffer, M.A., and Tay-Lee, C. 2020. Forgotten travelers: adjustment and career implications of international business travel for expatriates*J. Int. Manag.* 26(1). Available from: https://reader.elsevier.com/reader/sd/pii/S107542531830437X?token=3B0C7A863E44677FE94B31214D13E5B52BB04BE84F1E54329A518EBDE0266D87837C23F5F8FDD1670EA8AE0A785F9190 (accessed 12.05.20.).

EY, 2020. Why remote working will be the new normal, even after COVID-19. https://www.ey.com/en_be/covid-19/why-remote-working-will-be-the-new-normal-even-after-covid-19 (accessed on 11.05.20.).

Fly Aelous, 2020. The business flight travel survey statistics. https://flyaeolus.com/blog/2017-business-travel-statistics/ (accessed on 20.05.20.).

Forbes, 2020. Future air travel: four-hour process, self check-in, disinfection, immunity passes. https://www.forbes.com/sites/ceciliarodriguez/2020/05/10/future-air-travel-four-hour-process-self-check-in-disinfection-immunity-passes/ (accessed 11.05.20.).

Gajendran, R.S., Harrison, D.A., 2007. The good, the bad, and the unknown about telecommuting: meta-analysis of psychological mediators and individual consequences. *J. Appl. Psychol.* 92(6), 1524–1541.

GBTA, 2020. GBTA forecasts global business travel spend to reach $1.6 trillion by 2020. https://www.travelpulse.com/news/business-travel/gbta-forecasts-global-business-travel-spend-to-reach-16-trillion-by-2020.html (accessed 20.05.20.).

Ghauri, P.N., Usunier, J.C., 2003. *International Business Negotiations.* Emerald Group Publishing, Bingley.

Guardian, 2020. Small planes and no business class: will flying ever be the same again?. https://www.theguardian.com/business/2020/apr/16/small-planes-and-no-business-class-will-flying-ever-be-the-same-again-covid-19 (accessed 11.05.20.).

Golden, T.D., Gajendran, R.S., 2019. Unpacking the role of a telecommuter's job in their performance: examining job complexity, problem solving, interdependence, and social support. *J. Bus. Psychol.* 34(1), 55–69.

Growe, A., 2019. Developing trust in face-to-face interaction of knowledge-intensive business services (KIBS). *Regional Stud.* 53(5), 720–730.

Gupta, A., 2020. After covid: the new normal webinar. https://www.youtube.com/watch?v=uqBqSIl3ItU&app=desktop (accessed 20.05.20.).

Jack, A., 2020. We must harness the power of home working tech, not be slave to it. https://www.ft.com/content/0087e432–9085-11ea-bc44-dbf6756c871a (accessed 22.05.20.).

Jaeger, A.M., 1983. The transfer of organizational culture overseas: an approach to control in the multinational corporation. *J. Int. Bus. Stud.* 14(2), 91–114.

Johnson, N., 2000. *Telecommuting and Virtual Offices: Issues and Opportunities.* IGI Global, Hershey, PA.

Kim, S.N., 2017. Is telecommuting sustainable? An alternative approach to estimating the impact of home-based telecommuting on household travel. *Int. J. Sustain. Transportation* 11(2), 72–85.

Kobrin, S.J., 1988. Expatriate reduction and strategic control in American multinational corporations. *Hum. Resour. Manag.* 27(1), 63–75.

Kornacker, J., Trapp, R., Ander, K., 2019. Rejection, reproduction and reshaping–a field study on global budget control practices in multinational companies. *Qualitative Res. Account. Manag.* 15(2), 24–52.

Kossek, E.E., Lautsch, B.A., Eaton, S.C., 2006. Telecommuting, control, and boundary management: Correlates of policy use and practice, job control, and work-family effectiveness. *J. Vocational Behav. 68*(2), 347–367.

Köster, K., 2009. *International Project Management*. Sage, Thousand Oaks, CA.

Larsen, J., Urry, J., 2016. *Mobilities, Networks, Geographies*. Routledge, Oxon.

Latta, G.W., 2004. Foreign business travel: getting a handle on rising costs. *Compensation Benefits Rev. 36*(3), 53–56.

Lautsch, B. A., Köster, E.E., Eaton, S.C., 2009. Supervisory approaches and paradoxes in managing telecommuting implementation. *Hum. Relat. 62*(6), 795–827.

Leonard, B., 2011. Managing virtual teams-coordinating the work of tele-commuters presents managers with special challenges. *HR Magazine-Alexandria 56*(6), 38–55.

Mäkelä, L., Saarenpää, K., McNulty, Y., 2017. International business travellers, short-term assignees and international commuters. In: McNulty, Y., Selmer, J. (Eds.), *Research Handbook of Expatriates*. Edward Elgar, Cheltenham, pp. 276–294.

McNulty, Y., Selmer, J., 2017. *Research Handbook of Expatriates*. Edward Elgar, Cheltenham.

Manochehri, G., Pinkerton, T., 2003. Managing telecommuters: Opportunities and challenges. *Am. Bus. Rev. 21*(1), 9–16.

Nicklin, J. M., Cerasoli, C. P., Dydyn, K. L., 2016. Telecommuting: What? Why? When? and How? In *The Impact of ICT on Work*. Springer, Singapore, pp. 41–70.

New York Times, 2020.The airline business is terrible. It will probably get even worse. https://www.nytimes.com/2020/05/10/business/airlines-coronavirus-bleak-future.html (accessed 11.05.20.).

Oxford Economics USA, 2019. The return on investment of US business travel. Available from: https://www.oxfordeconomics.com/Media/Default/Industry%20verticals/Tourism/US%20Travel%20Association-%20ROI%20on%20US%20Business%20Travel.pdf (accessed 23.05.20.).

Paik, Y., Sohn, J.D., 2004. Expatriate managers and MNC's ability to control international subsidiaries: the case of Japanese MNCs. *J. World Bus. 39*(1), 61–71.

Patel, P., Sinha, P., Bhanugopan, R., Boyle, B., Bray, M., 2018. The transfer of HRM practices from emerging Indian IT MNEs to their subsidiaries in Australia: the MNE diamond model. *J. Bus. Res. 93*, 268–279.

Patel, P., Boyle, B., Bray, M., Sinha, P., Bhanugopan, R., 2019. Global staffing and control in emerging multinational corporations and their subsidiaries in developed countries. *Pers. Rev. 48*(4), 1022–1044.

Peters, P., Ligthart, P.E., Bardoel, A., Poutsma, E., 2016. 'Fit' for telework'? Cross-cultural variance and task-control explanations in organizations' formal telework practices. *The. Int. J. Hum. Resour. Manag. 27*(21), 2582–2603.

Petriglieri, G., Ashford, S.J., Wrzesniewski, A., 2019. Agony and ecstasy in the gig economy: Cultivating holding environments for precarious and personalized work identities. *Adm. Sci. Q. 64*(1), 124–170.

Price, M. 2020. As COVID-19 forces conferences online, scientists discover upsides of virtual format. https://www.sciencemag.org/careers/2020/04/covid-

19-forces-conferences-online-scientists-discover-upsides-virtual-format (accessed 20.05.20.).

Sarbu, M., 2018. The role of telecommuting for work-family conflict among German employees. *Res. Transportation Econ. 70*, 37–51.

Schaffer, R., Agusti, F., Dhooge, L.J., Earle, B., 2012. *International business law and its environment*. Cengage Learning, Boston, MA.

Scullion, H., Brewster, C., 2001. The management of expatriates: messages from Europe?. *J. World Bus. 36*(4), 346–365.

Slack 2020. Report: Remote work in the age of Covid-19. https://slackhq.com/report-remote-work-during-coronavirus (accessed 11.05.20.).

Solís, M., 2017. Moderators of telework effects on the work-family conflict and on worker performance. *Eur. J. Manag. Bus. Econ. 26*(1), 21–34.

Statista 2020a Global business travel spending. https://www.statista.com/statistics/612244/global-business-travel-spending/ (accessed 20.05.20.).

Statista 2020b Annual growth in business travel spending in selected countries. https://www.statista.com/statistics/275401/compound-annual-growth-in-business-travel-worldwide/ (accessed 20.05.20.).

Sutherland, W., Jarrahi, M.H., Dunn, M., Nelson, S.B., 2020. Work precarity and gig literacies in online freelancing. *Work, Employ. Soc. 34*(3), 457–475.

Usunier, J.C., 2019. Guidelines for effective intercultural business negotiations. *Strategic HR Rev. 18*(5), 199–203.

WEF, 2020. Here's what travelling could be like after COVID-19. https://www.weforum.org/agenda/2020/05/this-is-what-travelling-will-be-like-after-covid-19 (accessed 11.05.20.).

Welch, D.E., Welch, L.S., Worm, V., 2007. The international business traveller: A neglected but strategic human resource. *Int. J. Hum. Resour. Manag. 18*(2), 173–183.

Whitley, A. 2020. How coronavirus will forever change airlines and the way we fly. https://www.bloomberg.com/news/features/2020-04-24/coronavirus-travel-covid-19-will-change-airlines-and-how-we-fly (accessed 20.05.20.).

Part IV

COVID-19

Global Supply and Value Chains

15 COVID-19 and Global Value Chains

Reconfiguration of Activities across Borders

Paolo Barbieri, Albachiara Boffelli,
Stefano Elia, Luciano Fratocchi, and
Matteo Kalchschmidt

Introduction

The notion of global value chains (GVCs) has been used since the 1990s to describe the phenomenon of international fragmentation of the production process (Gereffi and Korzeniewicz, 1994). The strategy pursued by internationalizing firms has materialized by either relocating some activities to foreign markets, e.g., through captive or in-house offshoring or by outsourcing some activities to foreign suppliers, e.g., through outsourcing offshoring. One of the main drivers underlying the creation of GVCs has been cost reduction, which explains why several manufacturing activities have been offshored from advanced to emerging economies, the latter offering low-cost labor and cheaper raw material inputs (Kedia and Mukherjee, 2009; Mudambi, 2008). This is the case of manufacturing activities relocated from the U.S. toward Mexico and other emerging economies and from Western to Eastern Europe (Fratocchi et al., 2015; Kinkel and Maloca, 2009; Schmeisser, 2013). An additional driver of GVC configuration has been the search for high-quality, more-productive and value-added inputs, which typically occurs in advanced economies offering high-skilled labor in upstream (e.g., R&D and Design) and downstream (e.g., marketing and after-sales services) activities of the value chain (Mudambi, 2008).

Nevertheless, the GVC model has started to be challenged since the last decade. Indeed, a new trend of spatial reconfiguration of the supply chains is rising, reflecting companies' willingness to relocate their activities in other countries. Barbieri et al. (2019) have labelled these movements as 'relocation of second degrees' to identify either the return back to firms' home country or the relocation to third countries. The first type of relocation is known as 'back-reshoring', while the second one has been labelled as either 'further-offshoring' when the activity is moved from one far to another far away country, e.g., a European firm relocating from China to Vietnam; or as 'near-shoring' when the activity is relocated from a far away to a closer situated country, e.g., a U.S. firm relocating activity from China to Mexico (Ellram, 2013; Fratocchi et al., 2014). Extensive attention has been given to the drivers underlying back-reshoring, while neglecting the role of other relocations of second degree. In addition, the typical unit of analysis of the vast majority of the literature has been the single firm, while GVCs have been rarely considered as focus of relocations. In the next paragraph, we will take into account the different drivers underlying the relocation of second degree, by paying attention to the GVC level of analysis and by distinguishing among the different types of relocations. We will then investigate the potential role of COVID-19 within this phenomenon, by concluding with a short discussion on the policies for GVC reconfiguration.

From Global to Regional and National Value Chains: Pre-COVID-19 Drivers of Reconfiguration

The drivers underlying the reconfiguration of GVCs are multiple. A primary role is played by macroeconomic changes, such as the rise of new low-cost destinations, the international fluctuations of cost factors and comparative advantages that modify the relative attractiveness of countries (Ellram et al., 2013). This has been the case, for instance, of China, which has clearly switched from being a major cost-saving destination in the early 2000 to becoming one of the main market-seeking recipients in recent years. Another driver of GVCs reconfiguration is a general dissatisfaction over the advantages associated with offshoring (Albertoni et al., 2017), in terms of, e.g., less-than-expected cost reduction or quality drawback. These negative performance effects are typically due to the so-called 'hidden costs' of offshoring (Larsen et al., 2013) arising from excessive coordination, monitoring and transportation costs, from over-complexities and opportunistic behaviors in the relationship, with, for instance, the suppliers. The effects of both the macroeconomic changes and the negative outcomes have been further exacerbated by the world financial crisis of 2008/2009 (Gereffi and Luo, 2014). However, both these forces might result not only in back-reshoring and near-shoring outcomes, but also in further-offshoring decisions, meaning that firms might simply move their activities from a faraway to another country, thus preserving the nature of the GVCs.

More specific drivers fostering back-reshoring, i.e., making the GVCs more national and near-shoring, that is, making the GVCs more regional and/or national can also apply (2018; Srai and Ané, 2016). The first one is the 'made-in' effect, i.e., the possibility to improve the reputation and to capitalize on the use of the country of origin, thus affecting consumers' perceptions and behaviors, e.g., purchase intentions (Roth and Diamantopoulos, 2009).

Another very effective driver underlying the back-reshoring and near-shoring of GVCs is a technological change. More specifically, the emergence of new and integrated digital technologies, having disruptive consequences on manufacturing systems, products and business models, can reduce the need to search for low-cost locations (Ancarani et al., 2019; Dachs et al., 2017; Strange and Zucchella, 2017). The possibilities offered by digital technologies to substitute labor, to consolidate intermediate products and to reduce the production stages are likely to open new production opportunities also in advanced economies (Laplume et al., 2016; Rezk et al., 2016). As a consequence, digital technologies provide firms with an unprecedented possibility to switch from a global and complex to a regional and more integrated value chain that can be concentrated either in one or in few locations, thus making back-reshoring and near-shoring a valuable option.

In recent times, two additional drivers are further reinforcing these trends. The first one is the emergence of nationalism and populism, e.g., the Brexit phenomenon, and the associated rise of protectionism and trade wars, e.g., China the U.S. trade war, which push policy makers to overemphasize the need for domestic productions and national value chains (Rodrik, 2018). This mantra has been supported by both back-reshoring policies implemented by certain countries, e.g., the U.S., the U.K. and France, and policy recommendations proposed at regional level such as the 2016 policy brief 'Renaissance of Industry for a Sustainable European Strategy' of the European Union, which mentioned the back-reshoring to European countries, including also the option of near-shoring, among one of the main strategies to favor the return of manufacturing activities in Europe.

The second and probably more effective driver fostering the back-reshoring and near-shoring phenomena is the increasing attention toward social and environmental sustainability (Orzes and Sarkis, 2019; Fratocchi and Di Stefano, 2019), which is prompting firms to become more sensitive to these issues and, in several cases, to consider even green and social transformation of their business model in an attempt to improve their reputation and thus reinforce their competitive advantage (Pagell and Wu, 2009; Ioannou and Serafeim, 2019). The rising concerns about climate change and ethical issues are pushing firms to opt for shorter and tighter value chains, which allow to reduce emissions and transportation costs and to better manage and supervise supplier's operations and capabilities, by ensuring also a more effective enforcement of environmentally and socially acceptable practices for the whole value chain (Gualandris et al., 2014). Indeed, the shorter the distance, the more firms are able and willing to cooperate with suppliers to develop more sustainable products and processes, up to the adoption of a circular economy organization. Besides, the increasing attention for social issues has convinced firms in specific industries, e.g., in the fashion industry, to back-reshore some activities from those countries where labor and human rights are not respected. Hence, climate change and social sustainability can be considered, at least before the start of COVID-19 pandemic, one of the main drivers underlying GVCs reconfigurations.

COVID-19 as an Activator of Near-Shoring and Back-Reshoring Waves: Expected Modes

The Chief Economist at the European Bank for Reconstruction and Development, Professor Javorcik, has recently stated that the combination of trade policy shocks and COVID-19 has sparked a rethinking of GVCs (Javorcik, 2020). In other words, the COVID-19 pandemic has emerged as a trigger (Benstead et al., 2017) that activates and accelerates the back-reshoring and/or near-shoring decision-making process (Boffelli and Johansson, 2020; Boffelli et al., 2020). The first stage of COVID-19, mainly concentrated in China, and the second one, with the consequent evolution from an epidemic into a pandemic, has started to induce managers and entrepreneurs to carefully re-evaluate their location decisions, independently of the adopted governance mode of out- vs. insourcing. At the same time, several policy makers, especially in Europe, who have experienced their huge dependence on China and, partially, on India for certain products have had to struggle with the situation brought in by COVID-19. Consumables like surgical masks and disinfectants and also high-value products as Active Principle Ingredients (API) for pharmaceuticals have become scarce. The business community and governments understood that the COVID-19 pandemic has not been a 'one-off shock event', which has generated just a 'temporary disturbance', like the 2011 tsunami in Japan (Javorcik, 2020). The tremendous shock of COVID-19 on business activities worldwide has been defined as the most impactful scenario of its time (The Economist Intelligence Unit, 2020).

To investigate such a significant impact, we suggest the adoption of a 5 W approach (Who, What, Why, Where, When) since it has already been adopted, at least partially, to investigate the back-reshoring phenomenon (Barbieri et al., 2018; Fratocchi, 2018). COVID-19 is the trigger of the decision-making process regarding the redesigning of GVCs, thus it is the 'Why'. Based on it, the actor(s) of such a process (Who) should be defined. In this respect, attention should be paid to decisions involving not only individual companies, but also on the broader manufacturing networks. To make the relocation of specific product lines more resilient and effective, it is necessary to relocate either to the home country or to the home region the entire set of business relationships within the product supply chain. Otherwise, the relocation of some production phases would not secure to cope with future pandemics and/or other supply chain disruption events.

The 'Where' dimension refers to the final location of re-shored production activities, namely to the home country (back-reshoring) or the home region (near-shoring). The 'What' dimension refers to the object of

Why	When	Who	Where	
			Home-country (Back-reshoring)	**Home-region** (Near-reshoring)
Covid-19 as a trigger	Short-term vs.medium /long term	Single firm	**(What)** Individual back-reshoring	**(What)** Individual near-shoring
		Manufacturing network	**(What)** Joint back-reshoring	**(What)** Joint near-shoring

Figure 15.1 Proposed Analytical Framework.
Source: The Authors.

the relocation, as the type of products and activities or the industries that are more likely to be involved in the back-reshoring and/or near-shoring process, based on their relevance for the home country/region survival. Finally, the 'When' dimension usually pertains to the time perspective, that can be short vs. medium/long term. In this respect, it seems the timing of either back-reshoring or near-shoring decisions will be mainly related to the type of products (What) and the readiness of the home country/region manufacturing systems (Where), in terms of availability of skilled workforce and/or suppliers. For instance, medium/high tech industries production processes take more time to be set up than low tech ones.

Based on the 5 W adopted perspectives, we propose a theoretical framework to analyze and classify the expected modes that would emerge as a result of the back-reshoring and/or near-shoring decision-making processes triggered by the COVID-19 (see Figure 15.1). Particularly, four alternatives are identified, namely individual back-reshoring, individual near-shoring, joint back-reshoring and joint near-shoring.

Based on the proposed analytical framework, we used secondary data to illustrate the evidence of the four suggested alternatives. Secondary data have already been used both in international business and operations management research (Roth et al., 2008; Yang et al., 2006). Among sources of secondary data, a specific role is played by newspapers and magazines, which have been considered particularly useful when no other sources have been available (Cowton, 1998; Franzosi, 1987; Mazzola and Perrone, 2013). This might be the case of back-reshoring and near-shoring decisions triggered by COVID-19, due to its novelty. With specific reference to international business, Judd et al. (1991) consider written records such as newspapers suitable sources for longitudinal and multi-country studies. Yang et al. (2006) found that 20 empirical articles published in 6 leading international business journals from 1992 to 2003 adopted samples found in newspapers articles.

More specifically, we retrieved news of back-reshoring and near-shoring decisions or at least considerations checking journals, magazines, consulting company reports and similar sources adopting internet research engines through several combinations of different keywords (like 're-shoring', 'relocation', 'COVID-19', 'pandemics', etc.). In this respect, it must be pointed out that our aim was not to have an exhaustive state-of-the-art of COVID-19-caused relocation decisions but rather to populate the 'What' section of the proposed framework with some examples in order to test its usefulness for future research on the impact of COVID-19 on manufacturing location reconsiderations.

As far as the upper left quadrant is concerned, *Individual back-reshoring*, we found two interesting cases. More specifically, the first case relates to the French company, Stil, which relocated to its home country the production of glass-made thermometers after its Chinese suppliers were obliged to interrupt the production due to the local lockdown. Fortunately, the French company had spare capacity at its plant in France and was able to leverage on production competences owned by the oldest employees who manufactured this type of products until 2005 when the production was offshored in China to reduce production costs (www.euroepe1.fr/economie/coronavirus-une-usine-de-thermometre-reloalise-sa-production-en-france-3953430). The second evidence belongs to the Italian firm, Coccato and Mezzetti, which developed a single-use biodegradable surgical mask. In 2005, production was interrupted due to the high cost of this innovative product compared to the low cost of alternative goods that the company could import from China. At the beginning of March 2020, the company restarted local production due to the scarcity of surgical masks on the Italian and European markets and to the usefulness of biodegradable solution when millions of products will be used daily for a long period (Greco, 2020).

When considering the lower left quadrant, *Joint back-reshoring*, an interesting case was proposed by Fondazione Altagamma, an Italian association of 107 brands operating in the high-end markets of fashion, jewellery, design, food, hotels, automotive and wellness industries. In April 2020, the Chairman of the association proposed to develop a systematic relocation of silk manufacture as 80–90 percent of this material is currently imported from China. At the same time, he suggested developing a production-network-based relocation project for technical fabrics, which are rarely manufactured in Europe (Crivelli, 2020). Another interesting example comes from the Chairman of the French Federation of Health Industries and of the French pharmaceutical Group Sanofi. In March 2020, he stated that time had come to review the earlier decision to offshore production of active pharmaceutical ingredients

(APIs) for the production of drugs such as antibiotics, anticancer drugs and vaccines (Fayçal, 2020).

When considering the lower right quadrant, *Joint near-shoring*, useful evidence comes from a UE-financed project called Tex-Med Alliances, presented in February 2020 in Madrid, has assumed a new role due to the COVID-19 pandemic. The project includes textile and fashion industrial districts in the Mediterranean basin (namely, Catalonia in Spain, Prato in Italy, Central Macedonia in Greece, Ben Arous and Tunis in Tunisia, Alessandria in Egypt, and Amman in Jordan All partners will collaborate until 2022 to develop a certified traced supply chain to support back-reshoring and near-shoring strategies based on higher product quality and shorter delivery times compared to imports from Asia.

Shoring decisions implemented by single companies, *Individual near-shoring*. Nevertheless, cases may emerge in the future based on the recent decision of Japanese central government to develop an industrial policy to support the relocation of manufacturing activities offshored in China by Nippon companies either at the home country or in other Asian countries. More specifically, the policy finances the relocation costs to transfer production to home country/region, for example, up to 70 percent for small and medium companies operating in the health-related businesses aimed to relocate to Japan. As a consequence, it is expected that low-cost productions are more likely to be transferred to South-East Asia countries (near-shoring) than to Japan, given the high level of labor and production costs there. Figures 15.2 summarizes collected evidence within the proposed framework.

Concluding Remarks

The proposed analytical framework, based on the 5 W questions, provides opportunities for analysis and classification of the modes adopted

Why	When	Who	Where	
			Home-country (Back-reshoring)	Home-region (Near-reshoring)
Covid-19 as a trigger	Short-term vs. medium /long term	Single firm	Stil (France) Coccato & Mezzetti (Italy)	Expected near-shoring evidence boosted by Japanese policy Individual
		Manufacturing network	Silk &technical fabrics (Italy) APIs (France	EU-financed Tex-Med Alliances

Figure 15.2 Proposed Analytical Framework Filled in with Collected Evidence.
Source: The Authors.

for re-designing GVCs by making them either more regional (near-shoring) or more national (back-reshoring). Preliminary collected evidence shows back-reshoring or near-shoring decisions have already been implemented or are at least under consideration for implementation, both at individual firm and manufacturing network level.

The role of policy makers emerges as key in the case of near-shoring of individual companies. This fact suggests to add a sixth question to the proposed analytical framework, namely 'How', i.e., how post-COVID-19 reshoring decisions may be boosted by new industrial policies. It is noteworthy that already in mid-2020, numerous initiatives have been implemented or discussed to support post-COVID-19 re-designs of GVCs. The first country to implement such a type of policy was Japan in April 2020, offering financial and fiscal assistance to companies aiming to relocate their manufacturing activities from China either to their home country, Japan, or to other Asian countries. This decision is likely to create tension in political relationships between Japan and China (Oxford Analytics, 2020). At the same time, the French government decided to support the relocation of API manufacturing activities to France. The French President, Emanuel Macron has recognized the self-sufficiency of the drug supply chain is more likely to be reached at the European level rather than national level. Thus, the European Commission has planned a roadmap for a new Pharmaceutical Strategy in which the goal is to provide Europe with supplies of safe and affordable medication (Sarantis, 2020).

The French Minister of Finance has requested the automaker Renault, partially state-owned, to back-shore production activities, if they want to receive financial aids from the government to cope with the post-COVID-19 problems (Reuters, 2020). A similar policy is under discussion in Spain, where the Ministry of Industry announced a specific policy to support the relocation of health-related products and attract foreign direct investments for their production in Spain. Evidence collected adopting a 'How' perspective allow us to revise the proposed analytical framework introducing the role of policy makers aiming to support the post-COVID-19 pandemic recovery and make supply chains in strategic industries more resilient and with decreased risk at national or regional levels.

Policy makers should carefully evaluate how to design their industrial policies, since previous experiences of re-shoring had been partially unsuccessfully in some cases. For instance, in 2013, the South Korean government provided tax reductions and subsidies for land, equipment and employment to promote the relocation of manufacturing activities at the home country. Only 44 South Korean manufacturers have back-re-shored and they were generally marginal rather than important firms. Poor relocation results have been mainly due to issues related to country's economic system, mainly, shortage of high quality workforce and high wages, and non-conducive regulation characteristics, e.g., insufficiency of incentives and support for R&D (Choi, 2019). Therefore, policy makers aiming to develop pro-re-shoring initiatives should carefully evaluate how to make their initiatives successful by matching re-shoring policies consistent with others aimed to re-establish manufacturing and and secure appropriate infrastructures.

Finally, at least relevant for Europe, it is recommendable to set up policies under a Pan European regional approach to leverage on wide and heterogeneous resources and capabilities in order to recreate the GVCs existing in Europe.

References

Albertoni, F., Elia, S., Massini, S., Piscitello, L., 2017. The reshoring of business services: Reaction to failure or persistent strategy? *J. World Bus.* 52(3), 417–430.

Ancarani, A., Di Mauro, C., Mascali, F., 2019. Backshoring strategy and the adoption of Industry 4.0: Evidence from Europe. *J. World Bus.* 54(4), 360–371.

Barbieri, P., Ciabuschi, F., Fratocchi, L., Vignoli, M., 2018. What do we know about manufacturing reshoring? *J. Glob. Oper. Strategic Sourc.* 11(1), 79–122.

Barbieri, P., Elia, S., Fratocchi, L., Golini, R., 2019. Relocation of second degree: Moving towards a new place or returning home? *J. Purchasing Supply Manag.* 25, 1–14.

Benstead, A. V., Stevenson, M., Hendry, L.C., 2017. Why do firms reshore? A contingency-based conceptual approach. *Oper. Manag. Res.* 10(3/4), 85–103.

Boffelli, A., Golini, R., Orzes, G., Dotti, S., 2020. Open the box: A behavioural perspective on the reshoring decision-making and implementation process, https://doi.org/10.10161/j.pursup.2020.100623, (Accessed May 6, 2020).

Boffelli, A., Johansson, M., 2020. What do we want to know about reshoring? Towards a comprehensive framework based on a meta-synthesis, *Operations Management Research*. https://doi.org/10.1007/s12063-020-00155-y, (Accessed April 20, 2020).

Choi, H., 2019. Innovation and its Implications for Reshoring. KIEP Opinions, February 13, 2019. http://www.kiep.go.kr/eng/sub/view.do?bbsId=kiepOpi& nttId=202884, (Accessed on May 3, 2020).

Cowton, C.J., 1998. The use of secondary data in business ethics research. *J. Bus. Ethics* 17(4), 423–434.

Crivelli, G. 2020. Il lusso pronto a portare in Italia anche le filiere decentrate in Asia, *il Sole 24 Ore*, April, 4.

Dachs, B., Kinkel, S., Jäger, A., 2017. Bringing it all back home? Backshoring of manufacturing activities and the adoption of Industry 4.0 technologies. *Munich Personal. RePEc Archive Bringing* 83167, 1–32.

Ellram, L.M., 2013. Offshoring, reshoring and the manufacturing location decision. *J. Supply Chain Manag.* 49(2), 3–6.

Ellram, L.M., Tate, W.L., Petersen, K.J., 2013. Offshoring and reshoring: an update on the manufacturing location decision. *J. Supply Chain Manag.* 49(2), 14–22.

Fayçal, B., 2020. Amid outbreak, French economy's dependency on China in the spotlight, https://cnsnews.com/article/international/faycal-benhassain/amid-outbreak-french-economys-dependency-china-spotlight, (Accessed on March 30, 2020).

Franzosi, R., 1987. The press as a source of socio-historical data: issues in the methodology of data collection from newspapers, *Historical. Methods: A J. Quant. Interdiscip. History* 20(1), 5–16.

Fratocchi, L., 2018. Additive manufacturing technologies as a reshoring enabler: a why, where and how approach. *World Rev. Intermodal Transportation Res.* 7(3), 264–293.

Fratocchi, L., Ancarani, A., Barbieri, P., Di Mauro, C., Nassimbeni, G., Sartor, M., Vignoli, M., Zanoni, A., 2015. Manufacturing back-reshoring as a non-linear internationalization process. In: van Tulder, R., Verbeke, A., Drogendijk, R. (Eds.), *The Future of Global Organizing, Progress in International Business Research (PIBR)* Vol. 10. Emerald, pp. 367–405.

Fratocchi, L., Ancarani, A., Barbieri, P., Di Mauro, C., Nassimbeni, G., Sartor, M., Vignoli, M., Zanoni, A., 2014. Motivations of manufacturing back-reshoring: an interpretative framework. *Int. J. Phys. Distrib. Logist. Manag.* 46(2), 98–127.

Fratocchi, L., Di Mauro, C., Barbieri, P., Nassimbeni, G., Zanoni, A., 2016. When manufacturing moves back: concepts and questions. *J. Purchasing Supply Manag.* 20, 54–59.

Fratocchi, L., Di Stefano, C., 2019. Does sustainability matter for reshoring strategies? A literature review. *J. Glob. Oper. Strategic Sourc.* 12, 449–476.

Gereffi, G., Korzeniewicz, M., 1994. *Commodity Chains and Global Capitalism.* ABC- CLIO.

Gereffi, G., Luo, X., 2014. *Risks and Opportunities of Participation in Global Value Chains.* World Bank, New York, NY.

Greco, F. (2020). Promovita, Cina addio "Torniamo in Italia", *il Sole 24 Ore*, 11 Marzo.

Gualandris, J., Golini, R., Kalchschmidt, M., 2014. Do supply management and global sourcing matter for firm sustainability performance? *An.. Int. Study. Supply Chain Management: An Int. J.* 19(3), 258–274.

Ioannou, I., and Serafeim, G. (2019). Yes, Sustainability Can Be a Strategy. *Harvard Business Review*, February 11, 2019, https://hbr.org/2019/02/yes-sustainability-can-be-a-strategy (Accessed on June 7, 2020).

Javorcik, B., 2020. Global supply chains will not be the same in the post-COVID-19 world. In: Baldwin, R.E., Evenett, S.J. (Eds.), *COVID-19 and Trade Policy: Why Turning Inward Won't Work.* CEPR Press..

Judd, C., Smith, E., Kidder, L., 1991. *Research Methods in Social Science.* Holt, Rinehart and Wanston, Fort Worth, TX.

Kedia, B.L., Mukherjee, D., 2009. Understanding offshoring: a research framework based on disintegration, location and externalization advantages. *J. World Bus.* 44(3), 250–261.

Kinkel, S., Maloca, S., 2009. Drivers and antecedents of manufacturing offshoring and backshoring-a German perspective. *J. Purchasing Supply Manag.* 15(3), 154–165.

Laplume, A.O., Petersen, B., Pearce, J.M., 2016. Global value chains from a 3D printing perspective. *J. Int. Bus. Stud.* 47(5), 595–609.

Larsen, M.M., Manning, S., Pedersen, T., 2013. Uncovering the hidden costs of offshoring: the interplay of complexity, organizational design, and experience. *Strategic Manag. J. 34(5),* 533–552.

Mazzola, E., Perrone, G., 2013. A strategic needs perspective on operations outsourcing and other inter-firm relationships. *Int. J. Prod. Econ. 144(1),* 256–267.

Mudambi, R., 2008. Location, control and innovation in knowledge-intensive industries. *J. Economic Geogr. 8(5),* 699–725.

Orzes, G., Sarkis, J., 2019. Reshoring and environmental sustainability: an unexplored relationship? *Resources. Conserv. Recycling 141,* 481–482.

Oxford Analytics, (2020). Japan's reshoring subsidies will antagonise Beijing. April 22nd, https://dailybrief.oxan.com/Analysis/ES252131/Japans-reshoring-subsidies-will-antagonise-Beijing (Accessed May 2, 2020).

Pagell, M., Wu, Z., 2009. Building a more complete theory of sustainable supply chain management using case studies of 10 exemplars. *J. Supply Chain Manag. 45(2),* 37–56.

Reuters, (2020). French automakers must bring production back for aid, minister says. Reuters, May 11, https://www.reuters.com/article/us-health-coronavirus-france-autos/french-carmakers-must-bring-production-back-for-aid-minister-idUSKBN22N0RQ, (Accessed on May12, 2020).

Rezk, R., Singh Srai, J., Williamson, P. J., 2016. The impact of product attributes and emerging technologies on firms' international configuration. *J. Int. Bus. Stud. 47(5),* 610–618.

Rodrik, D., 2018. Populism and the economics of globalization. *J. Int. Bus. Policy 1(1),* 1–22.

Roth, A.V., Schroeder, R.G., Huang, X., Kristal, M.M., 2008. *Handbook of Metrics for Research in Operations Management.* SAGE Publications, Inc, Thousand Oaks, CA.

Roth, K. P., Diamantopoulos, A., 2009. Advancing the country image construct. *J. Bus. Res. 62(7),* 726–740.

Sarantis M., (2020). Commission's new pharmaceutical strategy wants to touch core issues. March 12, https://www.euractiv.com/section/health-consumers/news/commissions-new-pharmaceutical-strategy-wants-to-touch-core-issues/, (Accessed on 14March2020).

Schmeisser, B., 2013. A systematic review of literature on offshoring of value chain activities. *J. Int. Manag. 19(4),* 390–406.

Srai, J. S., Ané, C., 2016. Institutional and strategic operations perspectives on manufacturing reshoring. *Int. J. Prod. Res. 54(23),* 7193–7211.

Strange, R., Zucchella, A., 2017. Industry 4.0, global value chains and international business. *Multinatl. Bus. Rev. 25(3),* 174–184.

The Economist Intelligence Unit, (2020). The great Unwinding. Covid-19 and the regionalisation of global supply chains.

Yang, Z., Wang, X., Su, C., 2006. A review of research methodologies in international business. *Int. Bus. Rev. 15(6),* 601–617.

16 COVID-19, Global Value Chains, Risk, and Resilience

Jonas Strømfeldt Eduardsen

Introduction

On March 11, 2020, the World Health Organization (WHO) announced that the coronavirus – also known as COVID-19 or SARS-CoV-2 – was now considered a pandemic. Just three months prior to this announcement, Chinese authorities first alerted the WHO of pneumonia cases with an unknown cause in Wuhan City. Thus, in just 71 days, a new infectious disease had turned into an epidemic occurring worldwide and affecting numerous people across the world. What started as a small outbreak in China scaled rapidly to disperse over many geographic regions, with the epicenter of the outbreak changing from China to Europe to Latin America.

The coronavirus has not only caused severe human suffering across the globe, it has also snowballed and brought about devastating effects on businesses and economies across the world, including many multinational corporations (MNCs). Global value chains (GVCs) have been put under a spotlight with concerns related to their vulnerabilities coming to the fore (Strange, 2020). The current pandemic is unlikely to be a one-off event, but should instead act as a reminder that global systemic risks, which are often caused by improbable events with unknown causes and consequences, pose significant threats to both countries and organizations (Centeno et al., 2014; Goldin and Mariathasan, 2016; van der Vegt et al., 2015). It is therefore imperative that we learn more about how these emerging risks affect international business (IB) activities and how MNCs can confront and manage such low-probability, high-impact risks. Doing so can help MNCs avoid or cope better with similar situations in the future and thereby reduce the likelihood and severity of value chain disruptions (Blackhurst et al., 2011; Sharma et al., 2020).

The purpose of this chapter is therefore to reflect upon the impact of the pandemic on IB and draw lessons from this experience in terms of how to avoid or manage a similar event in the future. While the purpose of this chapter is not to present a comprehensive review of existing literature, it aims to draw upon the growing literature on GVCs and supply chain risk management to offer suggestions that might help MNCs develop better preparedness for future disruptions, defined as foreseeable or unforeseeable events, which affect the operations and stability of MNCs and GVCs. In particular, the chapter focuses on how MNCs should adjust their strategies with regard to the boundary and location decisions of value chain activities in order to increase GVC resilience.

The structure of the commentary is as follows. First, the impact of COVID-19 on MNCs and GVCs is considered and highlighted. Second, the dilemma that MNCs face in balancing efficiency and risk in relation to GVC configurations is discussed. Third, GVC resilience is introduced before discussing how MNCs might redesign their GVC configurations, in relation to their boundary and location decisions, in order to create an organization that has the capabilities to quickly adapt, evolve and avoid adverse effects to the organization in the face of unfavorable critical events such as COVID-19.

Impact of Coronavirus on Multinationals and GVCs

The coronavirus is first and foremost a human tragedy, which has caused severe human suffering across the globe. However, it has also severely affected many MNCs, particularly those relying on highly complex and globally connected value chains. In response to the spread of COVID-19, governments around the world have been forced to implement policies to contain the disease and fight the pandemic. The policies taken to control the spread, including lockdown measures, export restrictions, limitations on travel and border closures, have created a shock to both aggregate demand and supply (Baldwin and Tomiura, 2020). The lockdown measures have forced many businesses to shut down, preventing them from producing goods and services. This, in turn, has resulted in decreased supply and created a negative supply shock. In addition, the pandemic has forced major economies, such as the U.S. and China, to slow down causing a macroeconomic drop in aggregate demand, while consumers are postponing investments by adopting a precautionary wait-and-see approach (Baldwin and Tomiura, 2020). Consequently, the World Trade Organization (WTO) has announced that it expects global trade to decrease by 13 to 32 percent in 2020 with nearly all regions suffering double-digit declines in trade volumes, as the pandemic continues to spread across the world and disrupt economic activity (World Trade Organization, 2020). Thus, the pandemic has snowballed and brought about devastating effects on businesses across the world, including many MNCs (Caligiuri et al., 2020).

The nature and characteristics of MNCs has changed dramatically over the past four decades. As explained by Liesch and Welch (2019, p. 44), the MNC of today "has evolved from the highly internalized form of the post-WWII period to the focal firm of today orchestrating its constellation of suppliers". Today, MNCs are increasingly fragmenting their value chains by outsourcing value chain activities to contract manufacturers and specialist suppliers and locating these activities where it is most efficient. This has been made possible by recent changes in the net benefits of internalization, which has made MNCs rethink their boundary and location strategies (Buckley and Strange, 2015). Previously, MNCs often internalized business activities because of market imperfections, which caused internalization benefits to exceed its costs. However, over the past four decades, the market imperfections of the past have been significantly reduced due to the gradual liberalization and deregulation of international trade and investment, the rapid development and penetration of information and communication technologies, and the growth of contract manufacturers and specialist suppliers. These changes have led to a situation where the internalization costs exceed the benefits, changing MNEs from highly internalized and vertically integrated organizations to orchestrators of GVCs, defined as "the full range of activities that firms and workers perform to bring a product from its conception to end use and beyond" (Gereffi and Fernandez-Stark, 2011, p. 4). MNCs are, therefore, becoming much more like differentiated networks, creating an era of network competition, where the winners are those organizations that are superior in structuring, coordinating and managing relationships with their value chain partners (Christopher and Towill, 2000).

There are several reasons for MNCs to increasingly rely on GVCs, including cost advantages, diversification benefits and the ability of MNCs to focus on their core competencies. However, relying on GVCs also comes at a cost, including an increase in complexity and exposure points, which magnifies the vulnerabilities in MNCs (Stecke and Kumar, 2009). COVID-19 is a great example of how the reliance on highly complex and globally connected value chains is superior in normal times, but vulnerable to disruptions. It has posed an unprecedented challenge to GVCs, by striking several GVC hub regions, which has led to severe implication for many value chains. Some of the most severely affected countries include China, Korea, Italy, Japan, U.S. and Germany, which together account for more than half of world supply and demand, world manufacturing and world manufacturing exports (Baldwin and Tomiura, 2020). In addition, these countries are central actors in GVCs, with each of them being an important supplier of industrial inputs to each other and to other countries. A supply shock in any of these nations is therefore likely to cause disruptions of GVCs and create supply shocks in many other countries, including those that are less affected by the pandemic (Baldwin and Tomiura, 2020).

There are several examples of how COVID-19 has affected MNCs by disrupting the GVCs that they rely upon. For example, following the initial outbreak of the virus in China, Apple has reported in their Q2

FY2020 10-Q filings how it experienced disruptions to its manufacturing, supply chain and logistics services provided by outsourcing partners, which resulted in temporary iPhone supply shortage contracting sales worldwide. One reason for this disruption was due to certain components being sourced from single or limited suppliers. This is particularly true in relation to new products that utilize custom components available from only one source. This has given rise to speculations that Apple may be forced to postpone the launch of their new iPhone 12, which would mark the first time in more than a decade, where Apple has gone a full calendar year without introducing a new flagship smartphone. Another example of a sector, which has been hit hard by the COVID-19 pandemic due to its high reliance on complex and globally connected value chains, is the automobile industry. Wuhan, which is considered the breeding ground for COVID-19, is the home to the manufacturing plants of several car manufacturers, including General Motors, Honda, Nissan, Peugeot Group and Renault. Because of COVID-19, many of the car plants had to close down, which not only affected China's domestic car production, but also had severe impact on global car manufacturing, as almost all major global car manufacturer rely on parts produced in China (He and Huang, 2020). This supply shortage has forced car manufacturers such as Kia and Hyundai to stop several assembly lines in Korea and Nissan to suspend their production in Japan (Dolan, 2020; Lee and Hyunjoo, 2020). In addition, several other car manufacturers have since announced that the continued spread of COVID-19 forced them to close plants in both the U.S. and Europe (Tajitsu, 2020). However, Apple and car manufacturers, such as Kia, Volkswagen, Nissan and Honda, are not the only large MNCs suffering disruption to their operations and GVCs. In fact, 94 percent of the Fortune 1000 companies have experienced value chain disruptions due to COVID-19, with three-fourths having experienced negative or strongly negative impacts on their business (Sherman, 2020). Consequently, the current pandemic has dramatically affected GVCs highlighting the vulnerabilities of the modern MNC and its heavy reliance on globally dispersed, efficiency driven and fragile GVCs.

Balancing Efficiency and Risk Management in Global Strategy

More than three decades ago, Ghoshal (1987) noted that one of the main strategic objectives of MNCs is to achieve efficiency in its activities, while managing the risks that it assumes in carrying out those activities. MNCs should aim to achieve efficiency in its activities to enhance efficiency rents from the use of their resources. This involves maximizing the ratio of the value of its inputs to the costs of all its inputs, while also enhancing the efficacy of internal processes via economies of scale and/or more efficient production processes. However, while achieving efficiency in operations is important, it must also effectively manage the risks that it assumes in carrying out its operations by identifying risks and alleviating the level of vulnerability of the firm (van der Vegt et al., 2015). However, Ghoshal (1987) notes that this is difficult to achieve, as these two objectives are often mutually contradictory and difficult to prioritize. For example, pursuing a strategy that seeks to maximize the efficiency of the MNC's operations by carefully separating and locating value chain activities where the activity can be carried out at the lowest costs is likely to increase risk by multiplying the MNCs' exposure points where it is exposed to disruptions (Stecke and Kumar, 2009). In contrast, an excessive focus on reducing the exposure to disruption points will likely cause the efficiency to decrease. Thus, there is an apparent trade-off between efficiency and risk and MNCs must focus on finding the right balance between the two when designing and structuring their GVCs.

Built for efficiency, today's GVCs are often unnecessarily fragile and cannot easily cope with the consequences of low-probability, high-impact events like a global pandemic (Stecke and Kumar, 2009). The boundary and location decisions in MNCs are typically driven by efficiency considerations aiming to maximize efficiency rents and profits (Liesch and Welch, 2019). Consequently, many MNCs have organized their GVCs and logistics to make themselves leaner and more efficient, e.g., by reducing inventory levels. In addition, MNCs are also prone to restrict themselves to work with few, larger and more specialized suppliers that operate in few strategic locations around the world (Hernández and Pedersen, 2017). While this can help MNCs reduce costs and overcome domestic complexity factors such as political, socio-economic, technological and macroeconomic factors, it has also increased risk and left little room for unexpected disruptions (Goldin and Mariathasan, 2016; Ivanov et al., 2014). One problem with lean and efficient value chains is that they are designed to have less buffer capacity for disturbances, thereby making them more fragile in the face of unexpected critical events creating disruptions. Consequently, even small, localized events, such as fires, earthquakes or strikes, can have magnified implications in an international scale, as also highlighted by porevious events such as the Fukushima earthquake and tsunami or the Chao Phraya river floods in Thailand, which also caused GVC disruptions and resulted in significant losses for companies relying on these (Goldin and Mariathasan, 2016). Thus, while globalization and digitalization have made GVCs more efficient, they have simultaneously left MNCs and the GVCs they rely upon unnecessarily vulnerable to even minor disturbances.

Resilience and GVCs

COVID-19 reminds MNCs that it is too simplistic to base boundary and location decisions solely on efficiency and the desire to optimize their operations and minimize costs. While some predict that the pandemic will cause MNCs to re-shore some of their value chain activities and returning the companies to highly internalized and vertically integrated organizations, a more realistic prediction is that MNCs will rethink their boundary and location strategies by balancing efficiency considerations with the need to effectively manage all types of risk. Consequently, once the pandemic is over, MNCs should move away from managing and configuring their GVCs as in the past, with a one-sided focus on efficiency and cost-reduction. However, if done correctly, global value networks can enable MNCs to respond more effectively to external shocks, such as a pandemic (Pedersen et al., 2020). Thus, MNCs will increasingly need to reassess and redesign their GVC configurations in order to be better positioned to respond and recover if something similar will happen in the future.

MNCs must learn from the current pandemic and be better prepared for future unexpected critical events such as terrorism, natural disasters and cyber-attacks, which may have severe consequences for organizations. The main challenge in developing a better preparedness is that traditional risk assessment cannot deal with such unforeseeable events (Gunasekaran et al., 2015). The traditional way of coping with adverse effects is for MNCs to develop approaches and systems to identify risks, using historical data to analyze the past and predict future adverse events (van der Vegt et al., 2015). While such an approach will most likely help MNCs identify and prepare for certain adverse events, it falls short in terms of identifying risks where the lack of a priori evidence would render them predictable to any degree. In fact, the very organizational structures and processes used to control other risks may desensitize MNCs to unpredictable and unknowable risks, because of the heavy reliance on risk identification (Centeno et al., 2014). Thus, MNCs should adopt new management models that take into account the increasing diversity and complexity of risks.

It has been suggested that in a context where anticipating the future is difficult, organizational focus should shift from identifying and mitigating risk toward increasing resilience. The idea is that if an organization cannot predict or foresee the future, it must instead focus on developing its capacity to more quickly respond, adapt and learn from consequential rare events and disturbances. As such, resilience becomes an important organizational capability during disruptions such as the COVID-19 pandemic (Sharma et al., 2020). Broadly speaking, resilience, which originates from the latin word *resilire* (which means to leap or jump back) refers to a characteristic of a system (e.g., economies, societies, organizations) and its ability to maintain functionality, recover and learn from severe disruptions or unfavorable critical events, which may be either known or unknown (Ponomarov and Holcomb, 2009). In the context of GVCs, resilience refers to an "adaptive capability of the supply chain to prepare for unexpected events, respond to disruptions, and recover from them by maintaining continuity of operations at the desired level of connectedness and control over structure and function" (Ponomarov and Holcomb, 2009, p. 131). The ultimate goal of organizational resilience is to create an organization that is in possession of the necessary absorptive, adaptive and restorative capacities to quickly and efficiently respond to and recover from unpredictable and disruptive events (Hamel and Välikangas, 2003). Resilience offers an alternative or a supplement to traditional probabilistic risk assessment approaches, which are limited in their ability to analyze complex systems characterized by large uncertainties (Aven, 2019). Rather than trying to foresee the type of events, hazards and threats that can occur and their probabilities, as in traditional risk assessment, resilience reduces consequences of anticipated and unanticipated events by improving organizations' ability to maintain functionality and recover in the face of disruptions (van der Vegt et al., 2015). Thus, resilience can be seen as a distinctive organizational capability and is an important element in preparing organizations – especially those with IB activities – to cope with low-probability, high-impact risks (Smith and Fischbacher, 2009).

Creating Resilient MNCs and GVCs to Deal with Disruptions

COVID-19 reminds MNCs that are dependent on GVCs in bringing products from conception to end use and beyond that it is necessary to invest in creating resilient value chains to reduce the likelihood and severity of future disruptions while maintaining effective GVCs. To become more resilient, MNCs must consider engraining resilience in the design and structure of GVCs and increasing responsiveness capabilities through redundancy and flexibility (Carvalho et al., 2012). Flexibility and redundancy are resilience enhancers, defined as attributes that increase a firm's ability to quickly and effectively respond to and recover from disruptions. These GVC characteristics both provide MNCs with options that can allow them to offset the losses in a part of a GVC by gains from available alternatives (Stecke and Kumar, 2009). Redundancy refers to "an additional capacity that can be used to replace the loss of capacity caused by a disturbance" (Carvalho et al., 2012, p. 331), with the most common form being keeping some resources in reserve to be used in case of disruption (Sheffi and Rice, 2005). Redundancy duplicates capacity, e.g., by having multiple suppliers, safety stock, overcapacity and backup suppliers, thus, allowing MNCs to use this operational slack during disruptions and thereby lowering the likelihood of negative impact of GVC disruptions. However, redundancy also comes at a costs, as it may introduce inefficiency and increased transaction costs because of capacity duplication, which in situations with no disruptions cause an underutilization of resources and creates inefficiencies (Adobor and McMullen, 2018). Thus, the incremental costs of redundancy (e.g., safety stock, additional suppliers or backup sites) can ultimately be considered an insurance premium (Sheffi and Rice, 2005). In contrast, flexibility entails restructuring previously existing capacity and allows companies to adapt faster to significant changes in GVCs (Gunasekaran et al., 2015). This can be achieved by having flexible transportation systems, production facilities, supply base, capacity and labor arrangements (Kamalahmadi and Parast, 2016). Sheffi and Rice (2005) argue that investing in flexibility is the most important step in increasing resilience, given that investing in redundancy increases costs. Similarly, Christopher and Holweg (2011) suggest that building flexible options into the design of GVCs is the key in responding to disruptions. Taken together, this suggests that MNCs can increase GVC resilience by refocusing on increasing redundancy and/or flexibility, rather than maximizing efficiency and profits. This is summarized in Figure 16.1 below, suggesting that MNCs should prepare themselves and increase GVC resilience by finding the right balance between GVC efficiency, redundancy and flexibility to minimize their vulnerability.

In the literature, initial efforts have been made to identify strategies and design principles, which can guide MNCs in their efforts to create more resilient value chains and prepare for future foreseeable or unforeseeable events, which can directly affect the operation and stability of GVCs. For example, Tang (2006) proposes nine different strategies to mitigate vulnerabilities in supply chains, including: (1) postponement, (2) strategic stock, (3) flexible supply base, (4) make-and-buy trade-off, (5) economic supply incentives, (6) flexible transportation, (7) revenue management, (8) dynamic assortment planning, and (9) silent product rollover. Christopher and Peck (2004) proposed a number of design principles, for designing more resilient supply chains, including: (1) selecting strategies

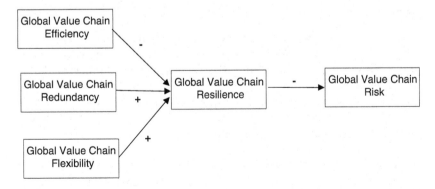

Figure 16.1 Antecedents and Consequences of Global Value Chain Resilience.
Source: The Author.

that keep several options open, (2) re-examining the efficiency vs. re-dundancy trade-off, (3) developing collaborative working, (4) developing visibility and (5) improving velocity and acceleration. Finally, Blackhurst et al. (2011) conclude that companies can increase their ability to quickly and efficiently recover from a disruptive event by combining both tangible (i.e., physical capital resources) and intangible resources (i.e., human capital) and organizational and inter-organizational capital resources. Taken together, these studies suggest that GVC resilience can be generated through many different types of investment that ultimately enhances GVC resilience by increasing redundancy and flexibility in the value chain.

Despite wide recognition that resilience is a key capability for MNCs in mitigating increasing value chain risk, we currently have limited knowledge about what characterizes resilient MNCs and GVCs, with emerging findings being fragmented across the literature (Blackhurst et al., 2011; Kamalahmadi and Parast, 2016). Thus, there are many opportunities for IB scholars to contribute to existing knowledge by exploring resilience as a means to cope with the increased length and complexity of GVCs. In particular, COVID-19 can be used as a natural experiment to either subject hypotheses to empirical testing regarding the antecedents and consequences of GVC resilience for MNCs or to theo-rize from carefully selected case studies. For example, IB scholars are encouraged to identify cases that vary from each other as much as possible in their ability to anticipate, withstand, respond to, and recover from the GVC disruptions caused by COVID-19 in order to explore why some MNCs are better able to reduce the severity and duration of dis-ruptions to their GVCs. Doing so will help us understand why some MNCs perform better than others under conditions of severe disrup-tions. Furthermore, such studies may be undertaken at different levels of aggregation and analysis, including individual, organizational, industry, and national levels.

Conclusion

The nature and characteristics of MNCs have changed dramatically over the past four decades with MNCs increasingly acting as orchestrators of GVCs. Global supply chains and MNCs' heavy focus on increased effi-ciency and cost reduction bring increased risks of disruption. This paper points to possible vulnerabilities of the modern MNE and the global factory as an organizational form, particularly the one-sided focus of the global factory on efficiency maximization.

The basic proposition of this chapter is that most boundary and lo-cation decisions in modern MNCs are primarily made with efficiency considerations in order to maximize efficiency rents. This is done by separating various business functions and activities and locating each function or activity in locations where it can be carried out in the most efficient way. The main lesson to be learned from COVID-19 is that some MNCs have focused too heavily on efficiency in making boundary and location decision, which has caused them and their GVCs to be vulnerable to unpredictable disruptions. Supposedly, this may have far reaching implications for MNCs and the development of IB thinking.

Resilience can be an important strategic weapon in anticipating unforeseen disruptive events, withstanding and responding to disruptions, and recovering from disruptions. Thus, MNCs are encouraged to balance efficiency considerations against risk and resilience concerns, as MNCs that invest in resilient GVCs will be best prepared to respond to and recover from unexpected critical events, such as epidemic outbreaks, natural disasters, trade wars, and strikes. To do so, MNCs must reconfigure their GVCs and rethink their management in order to find the right balance between efficiency and resilience. An excessive focus on efficiency results in GVCs that are efficient under normal conditions, but vulnerable to disruptions, while an excessive focus on resilience creates unprofitable supply chains and causes MNCs to become uncompetitive. Thus, the old dilemma regarding the achievement of efficiency in activities, while managing the risks assumed in carrying out those activities remains just as relevant today as it did three decades ago.

References

Adobor, H., McMullen, R.S., 2018. Supply chain resilience: a dynamic and multidimensional approach. *Int. J. Logist. Manag.* 29(4), 1451–1471.

Aven, T., 2019. The call for a shift from risk to resilience: what does it mean? *Risk Anal.* 39(6), 1196–1203.

Baldwin, R., Tomiura, E., 2020. Thinking ahead about the trade impact of COVID-19. In: Baldwin, R., di Mauro, B.W. (Eds.), *Economics in the Time of COVID-19*. CEPR Press, pp. 59–72.

Blackhurst, J., Dunn, K.S., Craighead, C.W., 2011. An empirically derived framework of global supply resiliency. *J. Bus. Logist.* 32(4), 374–391.

Buckley, P.J., Strange, R., 2015. The governance of the global factory: Location and control of world economic activity. *Acad. Manag. Perspect.* 29(2), 237–249.

Caligiuri, P., De Cieri, H., Minbaeva, D., Verbeke, A., Zimmermann, A., 2020. International HRM insights for navigating the COVID-19 pandemic: implications for future research and practice. *J. Int. Bus. Stud.* Advanced online publication https://doi.org/10.1057/s41267-020-00335-9.

Carvalho, H., Barroso, A.P., MacHado, V.H., Azevedo, S., Cruz-Machado, V., 2012. Supply chain redesign for resilience using simulation. *Comput. Ind. Eng.* 62(1), 329–341.

Centeno, M.A., Nag, M., Patterson, T.S., Shaver, A., Windawi, A.J., 2014. The emergence of global systemic risk. *Annu. Rev. Sociol.* 41(1), 65–85.

Christopher M., Holweg M., 2011. "Supply Chain 2.0": Managing supply chains in the era of turbulence. 41(1). *International Journal of Physical Distribution & Logictics Management*, 63–82.

Christopher, M., Peck, H., 2004. Building the resilient supply chain. *Int. J. Logist. Manag.* 15(2), 1–14.

Christopher, M., Towill, D.R., 2000. Supply chain migration from lean and functional to agile and customised. *Supply Chain Manag.* 5(4), 206–213.

Dolan, D., 2020. Nissan to halt production at Japan factory due to coronavirus. Retrieved from https://www.reuters.com/article/us-china-health-nissan/nissan-to-halt-production-at-japan-factory-due-to-coronavirus-idUSKBN20419A.

Gereffi, G., Fernandez-Stark, K., 2011. *Global Value Chain Analysis: A Primer.* Center on Globalization, Governance & Competitiveness (CHHC), Duke University, North Carolina, USA.

Ghoshal, S., 1987. Global strategy: An organizing framework. *Strategic Manag. J.* 8(5), 425–440.

Goldin, I., Mariathasan, M., 2016. *The Butterfly Defect: How Globalization Creates Systemic Risks, and What to Do About It.* Princeton University Press, Princeton, NJ.

Gunasekaran, A., Subramanian, N., Rahman, S., 2015. Supply chain resilience: role of complexities and strategies. *Int. J. Prod. Res.* 53(22), 6809–6819.

Hamel, G., Välikangas, L., 2003. Why resilience matters. *Harv. Bus. Rev.* 81(9), 52–63.

He, P., Huang, Z., 2020. This industry was crippled by the coronavirus - here's how it's fighting back. Retrieved June 10, 2020, from https://www.weforum.org/agenda/2020/02/coronavirus-china-automotive-industry/.

Hernández, V., Pedersen, T., 2017. Global value chain configuration: a review and research agenda. *BRQ Bus. Res. Q.* 20(2), 137–150.

Ivanov, D., Sokolov, B., Dolgui, A., 2014. The Ripple effect in supply chains: Trade-off "efficiency-flexibility- resilience" in disruption management. *Int. J. Prod. Res.* 52(7), 2154–2172.

Kamalahmadi, M., Parast, M.M., 2016. A review of the literature on the principles of enterprise and supply chain resilience: Major findings and directions for future research. *Int. J. Prod. Econ.* 171, 116–133.

Lee, J., Hyunjoo, J., 2020. Hyundai to halt South Korea output as China virus disrupts parts supply. Retrieved June 10, 2020, from https://www.reuters.com/article/us-hyundai-motor-virus-china/hyundai-to-halt-south-korea-output-as-china-virus-disrupts-parts-supply-idUSKBN1ZY0GG.

Liesch, P.W., Welch, L.S., 2019. *The firms of our times: risk and uncertainty.* Van Tulder R., Verbeke A., Jankowska B. (Eds.), *International Business in a VUCA World: The Changing Role of States and Firms* (pp. 41–53). Bingley: Emerald Publishing Ltd, https://doi.org/10.1108/S1745-886220190000014004.

Pedersen, C.L., Ritter, T., Di Benedetto, C.A., 2020. Managing through a crisis: managerial implications for business-to-business firms. *Ind. Mark. Manag.* 88, 314–322. https://doi.org/10.1016/j.indmarman.2020.05.034.

Ponomarov, S.Y., Holcomb, M.C., 2009. Understanding the concept of supply chain resilience. *Int. J. Logist. Manag.* 20(1), 124–143.

Sharma, A., Rangarajan, D., Paesbrugghe, B., 2020. Increasing resilience by creating an adaptive salesforce. *Ind. Mark. Manag.* 88, 238–246.

Sharma, P., Leung, T.Y., Kingshott, R.P.J., Davcik, N.S., Cardinali, S., 2020. Managing uncertainty during a global pandemic: an international business perspective. *J. Bus. Res.* 116, 188–192.

Sheffi, Y., Rice, J.B., 2005. A supply chain view of the resilient enterprise. *MIT. Sloan Manag. Rev.* 47(1), 41–48.

Sherman, E., 2020. 94% of the Fortune 1000 are seeing coronavirus supply chain disruptions: Report. Retrieved June 10, 2020, from https://fortune.com/2020/02/21/fortune-1000-coronavirus-china-supply-chain-impact/.

Smith, D., Fischbacher, M., 2009. The changing nature of risk and risk management: the challenge of borders, uncertainty and resilience. *Risk Management: An. Int. J.* 11(1), 1–12.

Stecke, K.E., Kumar, S., 2009. Sources of supply chain disruptions, factors that breed vulnerability, and mitigating strategies. *J. Mark. Channels,* 16(3), 193–226.

Strange, R., 2020. *The 2020 Covid-19 pandemic and global value chains, J. Ind. Bus. Econ.* Advance online publication. https://doi.org/10.1007/s40812-020-00162-x.

Tajitsu, N., 2020. Japanese automakers close more plants in Europe, Asia due to virus. Retrieved June 10, 2020, from https://www.reuters.com/article/us-health-coronavirus-toyota/japanese-automakers-close-more-plants-in-europe-asia-due-to-virus-idUSKBN2151FI.

Tang, C.S., 2006. Robust strategies for mitigating supply chain disruptions. *Int. J. Logist. Res. Appl.* 9(1), 33–45.

van der Vegt, G.S., Essens, P., Wahlstrom, M., George, G., 2015. Managing Risk and Resilience. *Acad. Manag. J.,* 58(4), 971–980.

World Trade Organization, 2020. *Trade set to plunge as COVID-19 pandemic upends global economy.* https://www.wto.org/english/news_e/pres20_e/pr855_e.htm#:~:text=PRESS%2F855PRESS%20RELEASE-,Trade%20set%20to%20plunge%20as%20COVID%2D19%20pandemic%20upends%20global,and%20life%20around%20the%20world.

17 The Butterfly Effect of COVID-19

Toward an Adapted Model of Commodity Supply

Laurent Lacroix and Eric Milliot

Introduction

The world of raw materials is with limited coverage by the media. Yet it enriches some and impoverishes others. It secures a country or a continent develop; it also enslaves a country or a continent. History proves this beyond doubt. Thanks to commodity markets new products are created that are ever more resource-intensive.

COVID-19 is presently threatening this economic notion, which has been unsustainable for several decades. Thus, the extractive industry of the last few centuries has heavily damaged the environment, and COVID-19 now endangers humanity by navigating the merchant networks that are vectors of contamination.

It is now a viral risk, in the epidemiological sense of the term, forcing us to rethink our supply chain fundamentals and the quality of supplies. The health concern, which is turning the spotlight on small- and medium-sized enterprises (SMEs) worldwide, calls for a redefinition of the geographical framework referring to the production/consumption interface. Such a redefinition is necessary if we are to avoid a repeat of the history of transnational disasters of recent centuries.

In order to justify the need to adopt a new commodities supply model, this chapter is structured in three parts. The first part focuses on the search for a more sustainable global economic model. The second assesses the impacts of COVID-19 on all supply chains. The third proposes a new supply model for products characterized by their rarefaction and/or strategic nature.

Toward a More Sustainable Economic Model

Since humanity has been organizing exchanges to create value, the flow of products and capital has never ceased to grow. Today, channels and networks that make it possible to cover almost the entire globe in record short time carry them. While this scale has economic and social benefits, it brings transnational dangers.

The Curse of Raw Materials

From ancient times up to the Middle Ages, Christian Europe for theological-cultural reasons was to focus on gold, while the secular world was to move closer to silver. The gold of Ghana was used to pay the Roman legions. The Greeks exploited the silver mines of Laurion to finance their cultural influence. Diamonds and precious stones fueled the conquests across the globe for 15 centuries before the discovery of the South African mines at the end of the nineteenth century.

Thus, the State and merchants were in search of raw materials to finance armies, develop trade and secure their public/private supplies for the expansion of territory or simply to develop national economies. But this economic windfall was associated with a procession of barbarities and inequalities served by slavery, of which the destitute were considered only as an adjustment variable. Such was the curse of raw materials: *Auri sacra fames* (The hunger for gold). In 1949, Braudel (1949) defined the notion of the world economy as an economically autonomous piece on the planet, which, according to him, would be essentially capable of supporting itself and to which its connections and internal exchanges would confer a certain organic unity. At the end of the 1970s, and against the backdrop of the oil crises (1973–1979), the international economy was looking for a new start to keep this Braudelian economic autonomy alive.

The Creation of New Markets

In 1987, and throughout the 1990s, Bourguinat's three 'D's' applied: financial Deregulation, global Decompartmentalization of firms, and Dismantling of the State. As part of the implementation of a policy of economic liberalization, financial deregulation will allow the market economy to produce more money to finance administrations and companies from stock exchanges. The global decompartmentalization of firms has encouraged foreign direct investment, allowing for financial transactions to be carried out between parent companies and their subsidiaries. The gradual dismantling of the State has thus further favored the market and its invisible hand by relieving it of the weight of institutional and regulatory constraints. One of the collateral effects of this sudden deregulation was the creation of financial masses and the decorrelation between its volume of paper (banknotes, Treasury bills, etc.) and the physical world (market and tangible counterparts). This decorrelation had the effect of increasing the prices of commodities and pushing the global extraction of raw materials in an attempt to re-establish equilibrium. This is the reign of liberal economists (Friedman and Friedman, 1980; Hayek, 1988), from the Chicago school; a stream of American economic thought that appeared at the beginning of the twentieth century.

The 1990s and 2000s saw the beginning of the reign of the GAFAMs (Google and its search engine, Amazon and its online shopping mall, Facebook and its global address book, Apple and its communication technologies, Microsoft and its office environment) and their insatiable appetite for rare earths.

The year 2010 also saw the birth of NATU (Netflix, AirBnB, Tesla, Uber), accelerating the race for raw materials essential to the proper functioning of these new technologies. The world is undergoing a demographic, economic, technological and environmental revolution at the same time.

In less than 50 years and with four times as many people in one century, world trade increased tenfold, both in volume (mass of products traded) and in value, from US$2 trillion in 1970 to US$19.475 trillion in 2018 (World Trade Organization, 2019). Global trade now accounts for nearly a quarter of the total wealth as gross world product was expected to reach approximately US$80 trillion in 2017 (International Monetary Fund, 2018). Half of this wealth production is created by fewer than 500 transnational, global and regional firms (International Monetary Fund, 2018). With US$4 trillion in trade, East Asia is the world's second largest trading center after Europe (US$7 trillion), ahead of North America (US $2 trillion) (International Monetary Fund, 2018). The New York Stock Exchange, which is the world's leading financial center, represented circa US$30 trillion in 2019 in capitalization, the equivalent of ten times the Paris Stock Exchange (Py, 2019). Speculation in commodities accounts for 15 percent of the world capitalization (International Monetary Fund, 2018), plus US$12 trillion in the hidden circuits of economic globalization (narcotics, arms, prostitution, counterfeits, etc.) and other contested markets. This whole is technically fed by multiple connections between stakeholders and an internet network that follows the path traced for five millennia by the successive inventions of writing and printing.

In Search of an Economic Model More Adapted to Environmental Requirements

At a time of the third energy shock and the emergence of the leadership of China and India, with their 2 billion 700 million inhabitants with changing purchasing behaviors, global economic governance is becoming increasingly essential. The economy is therefore focused on identifying and managing rarities, growth and development. *The Circle of Economists* (2007) identifies three types of scarcity:

- Scarcity of environmental resources and natural energies (e.g., air, water);
- Scarcity with a strong impact on the economic situations (e.g., crude oil, gas);
- Scarcity of medicines and other subsistence food products (e.g., wheat, millet).

Over the past 15 years or so, one issue has emerged or rather reappeared, that of securing supplies of raw materials. This issue is becoming a major concern for companies and countries wishing to sustain their production and consumption standards. New contingencies upsetting the rules of the game force both companies and governments to reorganize themselves. The latter, insufficiently protected in the face of uncertainties related to strategic metals, agricultural products or fishery resources, are thus progressively exposed to geopolitical risks. This situation is particularly sensitive in times of crisis such as the one caused by COVID-19.

New Thinking on International Risk Management

A decade ago, geopolitical risk was taking the pole position in terms of future risks. In 2020, it was dethroned by the risk of a devastating pandemic. The notion of ecosystem predominates here. It reflects a set of physical elements (geological, climatic), but also biological (biosphere), constituting the natural environment in which we evolve. In addition, for human beings, a cultural and socio-economic dimension also interacts with these natural factors. This contributes to the shaping of an eco-system in perpetual motion.

Thus, from time to time, a zoonosis may affect human populations with a varying degree of severity. The plague is a sad example in this respect. During the medieval plague, rats were responsible for trans-porting these undesirables by running along the gangways and ropes that linked galleons and caravels to the mooring bollards of the loading docks. Many epidemics have an animal origin, from influenza to Ebola. Bats alone have carried 30 different coronaviruses.

The Impacts of COVID-19 on Value Chains

Epidemics result from contagious diseases, often of infectious origin. They are characterized by the virulence and contagiousness of the pathogen, which rapidly and simultaneously affects a large number of people on a continent or worldwide. Thus, they become pandemics, which are out of proportion to an epidemic outbreak. It is also out of proportion with other pandemics that are equally deadly, but whose chronic nature mitigates their effect. These are malaria, AIDS, etc., which are not common with other pandemics that are just as deadly, but whose chronic aspect mitigates their effect.

COVID-19 Weakens the Existing Value Chains

History contains risks, threats and shocks. The emergence of a pandemic similar to the one the world has been facing in 2020 depends on several factors:

- The pathogenicity of certain micro-organisms (bacteria, viruses, etc.).
- The sensitivity and susceptibility of the population to a particular microorganism.
- The rapidity of its propagation according to the modes of transport of the time.

In the fourteenth century, the Black Death took more than a decade to cross Asia and half as long to cross from the Black Sea to the Baltic Sea. At the beginning of the twentieth century, when steam vehicles overtook horses and the internal combustion engine replaced the old rigging, the Spanish flu went into the homes of demobilized soldiers at the end of year 1918. A century later, the COVID-19 has circumnavigated the world in just a few weeks.

The danger, which the speed and intensity of travel and trade make us face during the pandemic, is counterbalanced by the moderate contagiousness of COVID-19 (an individual carrying the virus contaminates about three other individuals, compared to seven or eight in the case of measles).

With COVID-19, we are faced with an unprecedented economic, financial and social upheaval. Globalization, often referred to as a recent phenomenon, in fact draws its history from the time empires or a continents, such as Europe, has wished to give back space to merchant trade across borders as was the case for instance after the Thirty Year War. Even if the globalization of trade is a milestone in history, we have never gone so far in the break-up, or even atomization, of corporate logistics. The vertical breakdown of the value chain, which always tends to produce at the lowest cost, forces supply chain managers to constantly refine their calculations on all the items in the long chain in order to save a bit of money. This approach compresses production costs, but at the same time it weakens multimodal networks that have become increasingly complex and interdependent.

The Impact of the Health Crisis on Raw Materials and the Supply Chain

During COVID-19, it was first the stock exchanges that were devalued, e.g., CAC 40, DAX, IBEX and Borsa Italiana. The issue here is the loss of investor's confidence; as it is still the primary indicator in the eyes of the economists. Almost all commodities have been impacted by this generalized devaluation. Lithium, oil, etc., started being much less in demand. In March 2020, OPEC warned that global storage capacity, equivalent to one billion barrels, could be exceeded by the end of May 2020. By April 2020, more than 70 percent of the world's oil tankers had already been saturated. This led oil sellers to pay buyers to get rid of Light, Brent and even bitumen oil.

Overhauling Logistics

In terms of logistics, this is a transformation that is likely to take place across all value chains many of which will be relocated or even reinvented. At the beginning of 2020, supply chain projections assumed that supply chains would no longer expand, but with a few rare exceptions would remain as they were without contracting. The coronavirus has inverted such forecasts. The trend to relocate certain activities along value chains and, not to say certain industries, has been impacting logistics for some time. Therefore, the strategic vision, in terms of the location, nature, composition and interactions of value chains, needs to be rethought.

The change is likely to be a painful process. Let us take the example of oxigen respirators, which include more than 500 different components. On the one hand, certain raw materials have seen their prices rise sharply to meet a brand new demand, such as Curare (an essential drug for resuscitation). The production is emerging as a one-off need– at least we can hope so – and no country has the capacity to produce such large volumes at competitive prices. It takes 18 months to reorganize a plant. Investing exorbitant finances for a product in a relatively small market would not be economically profitable. A huge amount of investment will be required and nothing will be possible if governments do not provide support to companies with certain accompanying measures such as the creation of a relocation tax credit.

Experts from the Boston Consulting Group have calculated that the total production costs of a regular Chinese firm are now almost equivalent to those of its Polish counterpart. MNEs and government agencies are now thinking in terms of locating geographical areas in order to find regional low cost locations. Re-regionalization movements, therefore, the multiplication of customs barriers, the increase in transportation costs linked to the carbon footprint and, above all, the desire of buyers to consume locally, will force many companies to readjust their policies and location choices if they wish to remain competitive internationally (Lacroix, 2020a). In IT services and call centers, the awareness of over-dependence on India is emerging. Repatriating part of their IT services to Romania could be, for European companies, a probable relocation move.

However, the notion of independence has a limit, that of access to raw materials. During COVID-19 and afterwards, China would remain the world's key producer of rare ores. Indispensable for the technologies of the future, these raw minerals have been integrated into our mobile phones, computers and other ultra-connected traveling objects for several decades. Smith (1776) discussed country specialization as a means to reduce costs and keep them low in view of generating greater profit. At the time, for economic reasons, it was sometimes better to sell your wine to a country that did not have it or at least could not produce it in order to make the most of the supply/demand relationship, rather than to distribute it in your country. Especially if the purchasing country had a much higher consumption of wine than the producing country. However, in the current situation, countries and companies may need to reconsider their specialization and the location of productive activities not only based on the supply/demand relationship and cost reduction, but considering resilience at a time of crisis.

Three Key Sectors: Automotive, Health and Food Processing

Certain sectors seem to be particularly concerned by relocation. It is then a question of which activities along the value chain may be worth relocating. Key sectors in certain advanced countries (France, Germany, Italy, Japan, the U.S., etc.) are the automotive, health and food processing, many of the value chain activities of which are located in foreign markets, well beyond the home countries.

The automotive sector has historically been strategic. It benefits from numerous infrastructures and a large specialized workforce. It is characterized by a number of international suppliers and complex international logistics.

For health care, it is important to avoid tensions in times of crisis on the supply side of medicines for intensive care patients. There is an urgent need for some governments to relocate the production of active ingredients, 60–80 percent of which are manufactured outside Europe. In Europe, Sanofi has already announced the creation of a European champion for active ingredients from its existing plants, whose production could increase by 5–10 percent per year to meet increased demand (Benz, 2020).

In the food processing industry, the issue of relocation is less important than the security of the supply chain. To ensure food security, it is necessary first to ensure the financial security of producers. Moreover, States or even trading blocs must finance storage solutions in order to store products when prices are really low.

Cobots (collaborative robots), artificial intelligence, augmented reality and 3D printing can help certain segments of any industry become highly competitive again. This can be possible with shortening production cycles at reasonable costs. This might be good news for relocation decisions to some areas, although it may not be too good news for employment. Nevertheless, at the dawn of a new era of raw material consumption, we have to arbitrate between priorities that can ensure a successful recovery.

A New Supply Model for Commodities

The antidote to the health crisis is not less globalization, but more globalization (Mahler, 2020). Indeed, information on the virus needs to be circulated faster than the virus itself and research needs to be pooled. It is also necessary to organize the production of protective and care equipment and to cooperate on a worldwide scale to find a vaccine and effective treatments. This invites us to revisit the logic of supplies of all kinds.

Globalization 5.0

The process of globalization is paradoxical (Milliot and Tournois, 2010). The take-off of the countries of the South has tipped industry and jobs toward them, reducing – in a few decades – the wealth gap with the developed countries by more than a third. In Europe, however, we have become aware of the fragility of value chains and supply chains that are overly dependent on certain countries, notably on China. As we have already stated, whole ranges of activities will have to be relocated and re-industrialized. We will have to rethink industrial locations in a coordinated manner because none of the sectors such as luxury goods, aeronautics, defense or food processing could survive by limiting themselves to domestic markets alone. It will also be necessary to rethink the security of strategic products such as pharmaceuticals. Finally, institutions and rules will have to be devised to revive international trade, which is expected to decline significantly due to COVID-19 at least in the short run.

A regionalization of globalization is most probably underway. This is why the international environment will have to be reshaped around poles combining cooperation and competition (coopetition). Digitization and ecological transition will have to be accelerated, while at the same time strengthening the resilience of nations and their economies. Multilateral and transnational coordination is expected to be key to a successful recovery.

2020 Voted Best Year in History to Face a Pandemic

In 2019, researchers from Oxford and Tel Aviv Universities showed that frequent interactions between populations increase resistance to unknown virus strains making mobility a natural vaccination (Mahler, 2020). Out of the 30 countries, 24 most severely hit by COVID-19 are island nations, or cohorts of individuals confined to regional isolation. It was not the conquistadors who decimated the Incas, Aztecs and Mayans, but smallpox imported by settlers.

The big difference in 2020 is that science is also globalized. Never before in history have we given such a rapid response to a new disease. Even despite late communication, the genome sequencing by Chinese scientists was completed within a week; before a Berlin-based company produced screening tests less than two months after the virus began to spread. It took humanity thousands of years to develop vaccines against smallpox. In the face of the coronavirus, there were very quickly nearly 100 research programs on a vaccine capable of stopping the pandemic. Instead of allowing prophets of doom to add to the anxieties of frightened populations who focus defensively on globalization and immigration, we should welcome globalization as a potentially life-saving phenomenon.

Let us recall that in the fifteenth century, the Ming dynasty suspended – for health reasons – maritime explorations by ordering the outright destruction of its fleet, at that time the most powerful in the whole world. This decision prevented China from benefiting from the technological innovations and scientific advances that flourished and spread everywhere else. The Middle Kingdom lost 500 years before regaining a leading position in many fields. In the fourteenth century, the Black Death also caused the Muslim world to turn inward. It broke the Mongol Empire that had allowed the trade along the Silk Road. Since the disease came from elsewhere, foreigners had to be banished and traditional ideas had to be revived.

From the Linear to the Circular Economy

A linear economy is characterized by the extraction of a material from nature, its transformation into a production resource and then its marketing as a product. This product is eventually abandoned by consumers and turned into waste. This applies to almost all sectors of activity: construction, plastics, food processing, textiles, jewelry, metalworking, cosmetics, etc.

The circular economy is an economic concept within the framework of sustainable development. The notions of green economy and industrial ecology, defining all waste as reusable energy, notably inspire it. In the face of soil depletion and widespread impoverishment of the planet, the current global trend is towards economic, social and environmental improvement. In order to respect this triptych, it is crucial to circularize economic activity. The objective is to develop ecosystems/eco-business models that provide economic opportunities (very often through economic partnerships) for more sustainable modes of production. This organizational principle tends to be structured and systematized (Levy and Aurez, 2014). We could give the example of the company Geficca and its vulcanization process designed to recycle at least twice the rubber consumed. A circular strategy can therefore be broken down into three dimensions: reduction of use (of the materials), recycling and substitution. The last vector seems to be the most promising from a technological point of view (Lacroix, 2020a). These three dimensions make it possible to understand that the supply chain must henceforth be at the service of the circular economy.

Decoupling for Better Consumption

The will to decouple has been a worldwide trend for about 15 years. The aim is to decouple economic and demographic growth from the use of resources. In other words, it is a matter of protecting the environment by extending the use of the resources at our disposal. All sectors of activity are involved here.

All waste is a misplaced resource waiting only for the strategic resilience of companies to move out of the linear model and adapt to the circular model. The very notion of the supply chain must therefore be revisited. This can be achieved by reconsidering upstream of the product (eco-design). This involves repair, reuse and recycling loops, while thinking about systems of actors, or ecosystems, with new stakeholders (new transporters, new IT service providers, etc. (Carbone, 2017). Therefore, based on recent work, each sector of activity – and perhaps each product – will have to invent the supply chain best suited to its characteristics and consumption patterns.

The Return of SMEs

In the current crisis, SMEs – often left behind in the globalization of supply – may have a new card to play in the post COVID-19 reality. In the face of the pandemic, many governments had to close large, internationalized factories in a matter of days. These closures have disrupted globalized supply chains in numerous sectors. Currently, the pandemic risk is now en more important than the geopolitical risk offering new opportunities to SMEs that are more flexible than large firms and less subject to state decisions. COVID-19 will perhaps help the most resilient SMEs to reshape their supply chain:

- By forcing them to re-contract their value chains, i.e., by reducing the number of stakeholders in the logistics used;
- By allowing them to relocate some of their operations;
- By offering consumers who are more responsible and more aware of the new challenges and the opportunity to consume more regionally rather than across continents.

A New Supply Model to Help SMEs

SMEs, which import raw materials for processing or semi-processing, anticipate supply risks. This is even more pronounced during crises, which has an impact to a greater or lesser extent on their supply chain management. Not benefiting from a forward-looking strategy, these firms are particularly in need of flexibility and responsiveness. Consequently, we propose a new model for securing the supply of commodities. To develop this model, the managers of 58 companies – representing 15 industry sectors – were interviewed in France (Lacroix, 2020b).

Using the Environment-Strategy-Organization (ESO) framework (see Figure 17.1), developed by Milliot (2013, 2014), we take up the idea that a firm has two ways of acting in relation to the external environment it faces:

- The adequacy approach to adapt to environmental conditions;
- The intention approach (Hamel and Prahalad, 1989) to impact the market.

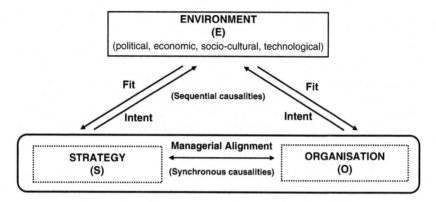

Figure 17.1 The Environment-Strategy-Organization (ESO) Framework.
Sources: Milliot (2013, 2014).

As regards internal operating logic, the managers interviewed revealed that there was a synchronous link – thus confirming the managerial alignment of the ESO framework – between the strategic choice to engage in the reduction of use, substitution or recycling of commodities (S) and the organization put in place to serve this strategy (O). Each of these strategies (reduction, substitution or recycling) has an impact on the structure and managerial profile of the company. At the same time, the organization conditions each of these strategies.

To help SMEs cope successfully with a crisis, the circular strategy must be put at the heart of the analysis. Based on the postulate of Donada and Fournier (2014), this strategy can then be resource-oriented (supply of raw materials) and/or customer-oriented (demand). Sequential interactions with the environment suggest a search for a balance between these two strategies. The appropriate combination of these two strategies is a response to the complexity of supply in the face of sudden changes in the environment. The highlight of this new model is the cursor between resources and customer. In a context characterized by scarcity of raw materials, this cursor makes it possible to appreciate more precisely the options available to SMEs. The resulting flexibility is essential for reacting to changes in the environment in times of crisis. This is done independently of risk management and supply chain management, whose respective and potential value creation is, however, enhanced by their interoperability. The identification of this set of interactions makes it possible to propose a new model for securing commodity supplies (see Figure 17.2).

The model can be transposed to all sectors of activity. It can also be applied, in certain circumstances, to large accounts if they have a lack of supply management.

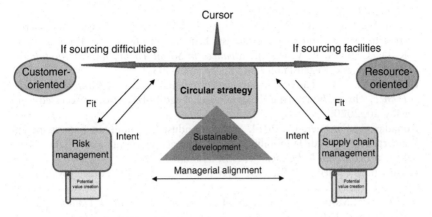

Figure 17.2 A Model for Securing Supplies.
Sources: Lacroix (2020).

Conclusion

Crises bring out the worst in a society and in particular its inequalities accentuating the level of emotional chaos of an entire population. This is the eternal story of the new winners, which will be some companies more agile than others who will come back closer to their consumers and their new purchasing behaviors. It is also some new losers who will see their pearl necklace strategy eroded as post-globalization demands something else (sanitized consumption).

Faced with the disorganization of many supply chains caused by COVID-19, we propose a flexible model for securing commodity supplies. This model integrates the multiple and complex interactions between a company (its strategy and organization) and its environment (the market, standards, rules, technologies, etc.). This flexibility allows an essential re-activity in a context marked by a particularly high level of interdependence of actors and actants (Callon and Latour, 1981). Indeed, with a microscopic organism that partially paralyzes human activities on a global scale, the butterfly effect of chaos theory (Lorenz, 1963) finds its most concrete illustration here.

References

Benz, S., 2020. Relocalisation: Les pistes de Sanofi pour créer un géant européen es principes actifs, *L'Express*, https://lexpansion.lexpress.fr/actualite-economique/sanofi-nous-appelons-la-bpi-et-l-europe-au-capital-du-futur-geant-des-principes-actifs_2124921.html, (Accessed on June 5, 2020).
Bourguinat, H., 1987. *Les Vertiges de la Finance Internationale*. Économica, Paris.

Braudel, F., 1949. *La Méditerranée et le Monde Méditéranéen à L'époque de Philippe II*. Armand Colin, Paris.

Callon, M., Latour, B., 1981. Unscrewing the big Leviathan: how actors macro-structure reality and how sociologists help them to do so. In: Knorr-Cetina, K. D., Cicourel, A. V. (Eds.), *Advances in Social Theory and Methodology*. Routledge and Kegan Paul, London, pp. 277–303.

Carbone, V., 2017. The business models of circular economy. *Conférence Aslog France*, https://www.youtube.com/watch?v=gdR84zPc3No, (Accessed on May 20, 2020).

Donada, C., Fournier, G., 2014. Stratégie industrielle pour un écosystème en émergence: le cas de la mobilité 2.0, décarbonée, intermodale et collaborative. *Rev. d'Economie Industrielle* 4(148), 317–348.

Friedman, M., Friedman, R., 1980. *Free to Choose*. Harcourt Brace Jovanovich, New York, NY.

International Monetary Fund, 2018. *World Economic Outlook Database*. IMF, Washington, D.C.

Hamel, G., Prahalad, C.K., 1989. Strategic Intent. *Harv. Bus. Rev.* 67(3), 63–76.

Hayek, F. A., 1988. *The Fatal Conceit: The Errors of Socialism*. University of Chicago Press, Chicago, IL.

Lacroix, L., 2020a. "Quelle Europe de la *supply chain* et des approvisionnements". *Quest. d'Europe – Fond. Robert Schuman, Policy Pap. 561*, 1–6.

Lacroix, L., 2020b, forthcoming. *La sécurisation des approvisionnements en matières premières des PME françaises par la gestion des risques et la mutation de la chaîne de valeur globale, thèse de doctorat (PhD)*. Université de Poitiers, France.

Levy, J.C., Aurez, V., 2014. Les dynamiques de l'économie circulaire en Chine. *Annales des. Mines, Responsabilité et. Environ.* 76, 13–18.

Lorenz, E. N., 1963. Deterministic nonperiodic flow. *J. Atmos. Sci.* 20(2), 130–141.

Mahler, T., 2020. L'année 2020 est la meilleure dans l'histoire pour faire face à une pandémie. *L'express 3590*, 64–65.

Milliot, E., Tournois, N., (Eds.). 2010. *The Paradoxes of Globalisation*. Palgrave Macmillan, Basingstoke.

Milliot, E., 2013. Book review: Ulrike Mayrhofer (editor) (2013), Management of Multinational Companies. A French Perspective. *M@n@gement 16*(2), 176–194.

Milliot, E., 2014. La segmentation stratégique revisitée. *Rech. en. Sci. de. Gest. – Manag. Sci. – Cienc. de Gest. 100*(1), 23–44.

Py, M., 2019. Wall Street, la première Bourse au monde, *Le Revenu*, https://www.lerevenu.com/bourse/wall-street-la-premiere-bourse-au-monde, (Accessed on May 10, 2020).

Smith, A., 2012. *The Wealth of Nations [first edition, 1776]*. Wordsworth, London.

Smith, A., 1776. *An Inquiry into the Nature and Causes of the Wealth of Nations*. W. Strahan and T. Cadell, London.

World Trade Organization, 2019. La croissance du commerce mondial s'essouffle alors que les tensions commerciales persistent, *News*. WTO, Geneva.

18 Sustainable Global Supply Chain Management Model Post-COVID-19

Sardana Islam Khan and Julian Teicher

Introduction

The unprecedented global COVID-19 pandemic is predicted to leave an enduring impact on demand and firm's operations engaged in international business. This pandemic has exposed the vulnerability of existing supply chains and the need for international businesses to reinvent their global sourcing as well as supply chain management for achieving sustainable competitive advantage and crisis survival. A few possible changes in the world marketplace have been predicted by economists and think tanks immediately after COVID-19 pandemic was recognized (e.g., Baker et al., 2020; McKibbin and Fernando, 2020). At the outset, the World Bank and International Monetary Fund have pre-COVID-19 predicted a global recession, which turned into reality. The pandemic has already hit markets firmly at local, regional and world level and is expected to continue to influence them decisively in the future (Fernandes, 2020; Guerrieri et al., 2020).

At the start of the pandemic, different countries used dissimilar global sourcing policies to deal with the extraordinary COVID-19 situation and related with it challenges. Thus, Japan offered a US$2.2 billion stimulus packages in March 2020 to support Japanese manufacturing firms move production from China back to Japan in order to avoid future disruption in their supply chain (Reynolds and Urabe, 2020). Numerous new opportunities for global sourcing have been emerging during this pandemic such as negative oil price in April 2020, which attracted interest in engaging in global stock piling (Irwin, 2020). The global outsourcing moves originally driven by cost consideration were initially replaced by stability, safety and manageability benefits in local sourcing options during the early stages of COVID-19. Many countries are now trying to mitigate risk by shifting production home via reshoring or at least closer to home (Reynolds and Urabe, 2020; Seifert and Markoff, 2020). However, these speculative and sporadic practices may compromise the economic benefit once enjoyed by international businesses through global sourcing or offshoring (Kilpatrick and Barter, 2020; Seifert and Markoff, 2020).

Facing an unpredictable post-COVID-19 economy, it is crucially important for firms engaged in international business to create a resilient, sustainable and flexible global supply chain management model based on stronger collaboration between carefully selected international supply chain (ISC) partners (Kilpatrick and Barter, 2020). These developments have been preceded by a growing interest in international business concerning the use of sustainable supply chain management (SSCM) as a new archetype with additional value proposition for the businesses.

SSCM comprises the socially and ecologically responsible supply chain management practices that may help extend the competitive advantage by profitably managing both internal and external business activities and relationships (Schaltegger et al., 2014). Closed Loop Supply Chains (CLSC) is one of the SSCM models that uses forward and reverse supply chains to form a closed loop where the focal organization and foreign members of the supply chain work together in an integrated manner to collect and remanufacture the worn out or obsolete parts of a product (Ashby, 2018). Natural resource based view underpins this model which integrates pollution prevention, product stewardship and sustainable development strategies for key resource acquisition to gain sustained competitive advantage (Hart, 1995). Reducing wastage and environmental footprint are the key focus of CLSC that may also reduce the production cost and enhance value addition (Ashby, 2018). Supply management (SM) practices on the other hand are viewed as a structured approach to strengthen relationships with a few suppliers by empowering them and closely coordinating the supply chain activities (Schaltegger et al., 2014). Recent studies have found strong positive associations between SM and SSCM although global sourcing may moderate the relationship or challenge the outcome (Schaltegger et al., 2014).

The need for multiple approaches to global sourcing is worth exploring. For example, the U.S. could be autarkic as this country has a large market though it may have issues to resolve acquiring rare resources for producing semiconductors. Essentially, in the new and unpredictable post-pandemic world economy, one size will not even fit one, let alone all. In a recent survey conducted on 132 Japanese businesses (within the period May 25–28, 2020), 72.1 percent expressed a need to alter their supply chains; of them, 65.3 percent said they want to improve the ability to switch sources with greater flexibility in case of crises and 57.1 percent wanted to switch from a single country to many in order to diversify sources (Hayashi, 2020). Multiple innovative strategies to ensure supply chain agility seems to be of major concern of international businesses during and beyond COVID-19 though how to create those is still to be found out.

In this chapter, we advocate for not only an SSCM but also for an encompassing and flexible yet viable global sourcing model to respond to the unpredictable demand fluctuations of such unprecedented global crisis as COVID-19 and subsequent policy responses.

We argue that integrating and customizing CLSC model and SM practices according to the particular industry's operational context will allow internationalized businesses to enjoy the economic advantages from international operations under normal circumstances, without compromising their ability to produce for focal firms' countries of origin in case of future crises. Similarly, firms' international manufacturing facilities and supply chain partners can also keep producing for their respective home market by using forward and reverse supply chains during crises. SM practices will empower the supply chain partners and improve the coordination and information flow between the stakeholders to sustain the supply process. In addition, the supply chain participants will need to have a variety of contingent models available to them in order to be able to meet a variety of critical scenarios with the most extreme being a long-term disruption to the supply chain.

In this chapter, we initially review the current policy responses of the dominant advanced economies to gain some perspectives on the hard to gauge post-COVID-19 trajectory of international trade. We then predict a range of possible global sourcing scenarios on the other side of COVID-19 crisis. Finally, we explore the possibility of integrating the CLSC model (Ashby, 2018) with some traditional SM practices, e.g., reduction, selection, integration and development of suppliers (Schaltegger et al. 2014), to propose a more sustainable and flexible global supply chain management regime for post-COVID-19 international businesses.

International Trade during COVID-19 Pandemic (January–May 2020)

This section of our chapter explores the challenges faced by firms engaged in international business and the policy directions of some of the most dominant advanced economies based on press releases and World Trade Organisation (WTO) reports in the period January–May 2020 (World Trade Organisation, 2020a). Table 18.1 summarizes the major changes and trends in international markets and government instructions from various regions functioning as either the drivers or barriers to firms' international business operations and their global supply chain management.

International trade partners faced supply chain management issues much earlier than COVID-19 struck as a global pandemic. The pandemic outbreak was initially contained to China with Chinese producers facing global supply chain disruptions and uncertainty in particular in the agro-industrial sector (Zhang and Xiong, 2020). However, as production was set back in China, their Western offshoring partners faced critical stoppages in getting supplies from China. This situation started reversing in March 2020 when Chinese industries started to reopen production facilities while other countries imposed more and more

Table 18.1 Drivers and Barriers for International Business during the COVID-19 Crisis

Timeline	Market/Policy Driven Challenges	Implications for International Businesses	Source
Jan–Feb, 2020	• COVID-19 pandemic became a serious global crisis disrupting the global trade flows and connectivity. • Retailers faced supply shortages due to panic purchase of essential commodities and medical supplies.	• A sharp drop in airfreight capacity • Volatile airfreight increasing the uncertainty for the international businesses and supply chain. • Global disruptions to transports via sea and land, due to enhanced seaports and land border restrictions and suspended port operations.	ABC news
Feb–Mar, 2020	World leaders started to acknowledge the importance of facilitating connectivity and strengthening the global supply chains to effectively respond to the COVID-19 crisis.	The countries depending on each other for the raw materials and other production facilities of essential commodities, especially medical supplies started coming together to jointly facilitate supply chains that straddle multiple like-minded countries.	WTO website
March 20, 2020	Singapore and New Zealand jointly affirmed commitment to ensure supply chain connectivity amidst the COVID-19 situation	• Affirmed commitment to open and connected supply chain. • Both sides decided to work more closely to identify and address trade disruptions with ramifications on the flow of necessities.	WTO report

(Continued)

Table 18.1 (Continued)

Timeline	Market/Policy Driven Challenges	Implications for International Businesses	Source
March 25, 2020	Australia, Brunei Darussalam, Canada, Chile, Myanmar, New Zealand and Singapore jointly affirmed commitment to ensure supply chain connectivity amidst the COVID-19 situation	• The regular air and sea freight trade lines remain open to facilitate especially the flow of essential supplies. • Pause on the export controls or tariffs and non-tariff barriers and remove trade restrictions on essential goods and medical supplies during the pandemic. • Critical infrastructure (e.g., air, seaports, etc.) remain open to support the global supply chains within the like-minded countries. • Same as the March 20, 2020 declaration of Singapore and New Zealand, only extended to more like-minded countries (seven countries). • Like-minded countries seem to include those managing COVID-19 crisis with minimum casualties till date. • Open invitation to join extended to all WTO members.	WTO website

(Continued)

Table 18.1 (Continued)

Timeline	Market/Policy Driven Challenges	Implications for International Businesses	Source
April 14, 2020	Australia, Brunei Darussalam, Canada, Chile, Lao PDR, Myanmar, New Zealand, Singapore and Uruguay jointly affirmed commitment to ensure supply chain connectivity amidst the COVID-19 situation	• Same as the March 25, 2020 declaration, only extended to more like-minded countries (nine countries). • Like-minded countries seem to include those managing COVID-19 crisis with minimum casualties till date. • Open invitation to join extended to all WTO members.	WTO website
April 20, 2020	Australia, Brazil, Canada, Chile, Colombia, Costa Rica, European Union, Hong Kong, China, Japan, Republic of Korea, Malawi, Mexico, New Zealand, Paraguay, Peru, Qatar, Singapore, Switzerland, The Separate Customs Territory of Taiwan, Penghu, Kinmen And Matsu, Ukraine, United Kingdom, U.S., and Uruguay jointly responded to the COVID-19 pandemic with open and predictable trade in agricultural and food products	• 24 countries accounting for 63 percent of global exports of agriculture and agri-food products and 55 percent of global imports of agriculture and agri-food products committed to open, more relaxed and stronger global agriculture supply chain during COVID-19 crisis. • These countries pledged their commitment to timely and accurate provision of information on agriculture and agri-food-related trade measures, levels of production, consumption, stocks, and prices to reduce uncertainty	WTO website

(Continued)

Table 18.1 (Continued)

Timeline	Market/Policy Driven Challenges	Implications for International Businesses	Source
		in the global food supply during pandemic and allow governments, traders, consumers, producers to make informed decisions.	
April 30, 2020	Association of Southeast Asian Nations (ASEAN) in their special video summit declared stronger cooperation between ASEAN and with external countries in crisis management through sharing information and international trade to ensure uninterrupted supplies of essential commodities. ASEAN member countries include Brunei Darussalam, Cambodia, Indonesia, Lao PDR, Malaysia, Myanmar, the Philippines, Singapore, Thailand and Viet Nam.	• ASEAN called for strengthening the resilience and sustainability of regional supply chains, especially for food, commodities, medicines, medical and essential supplies. • Knowledge, resource and information sharing for better crisis management within ASEAN countries and external partners. • Encourage the development of a post-pandemic recovery plan to share knowledge, restore connectivity, tourism, normal business and social activities and prevent potential economic downturns. • Build on existing trade facilitating platforms in ASEAN, such as the	WTO website

(Continued)

Table 18.1 (Continued)

Timeline	Market/Policy Driven Challenges	Implications for International Businesses	Source
May 4, 2020	Members of the Group of Least-Developed Countries pledged commitment to securing LDCs emergency access to essential medical and food products to combat the COVID-19 pandemic	ASEAN Single Window, to promote and support supply chain connectivity. LDC Group requested non-LDC Members not to impose export prohibitions or restrictions on food and medical supplies considering the import dependent LDCs' heavy reliance on the global supply chain.	WTO website
May 5, 2020	Afghanistan; Australia; Barbados; Benin; Cambodia; Canada; Chile; Colombia; Costa Rica; Ecuador; El Salvador; Guatemala; Guyana; Hong Kong, China; Iceland; Israel; Jamaica; Japan; Kenya; Republic of Korea; the State of Kuwait; Liechtenstein; Madagascar; Mauritius; Mexico; Republic of Moldova; Montenegro; Nepal; New Zealand; Nigeria; North Macedonia; Norway; Peru; Saint Lucia; Kingdom of Saudi Arabia; Singapore; Solomon Islands; Switzerland; Ukraine; United Arab Emirates; United Kingdom; and	These 43 countries from different region came together to acknowledge 'A predictable, transparent, non-discriminatory and open global trading system will be essential for broad-based, sustainable economic recovery'. They also agreed to: • support for the rules-based multilateral trading system with WTO playing the central role. • refrain from raising new unjustified barriers to investment or to trade in goods and services between these countries and also the external partners.	WTO website

(Continued)

Table 18.1 (Continued)

Timeline	Market/Policy Driven Challenges	Implications for International Businesses	Source
	Uruguay issues a joint Ministerial statement on COVID-19 and the multilateral trading system.	• recognize the greater challenges faced by developing Member and least developed Members. • pledge extended supports for micro-, small- and medium-sized enterprises for all member countries.	
March–May 2020	• Supply chain disruptions between China and U.S. • Trade war between Australian and China	• Impact on international trade deals: Delays and Uncertainties of supplies • Global politics in play: International trade war between countries over COVID-19	The Conversation and ABC News (2020)
May 16, 2020	• Call for the strategic independence of five eye nations from China • China continued to aggressively seek new investment opportunities in Asia and Africa and increase the trade restrictions on imports from countries such as Australia,	'Breaking the China Chain', published by London-based think tank Henry Jackson Society, examined the import dependence of the 'Five Eyes' intelligence-sharing countries, i.e., Australia, the U.S., United Kingdom, New Zealand and Canada, on China. The findings called for a greater alliance between these nations to break the Chinese dependency for nine critical strategic supplies. These are: artificial intelligence and machine learning, autonomous robotics, computing hardware, cryptographic technology,	The age May 16, 2020

(Continued)

Table 18.1 (Continued)

Timeline	Market/Policy Driven Challenges	Implications for International Businesses	Source
		materials and manufacturing science, nanotechnologies, networking and data communication, quantum technology and synthetic biology	

Source: The Authors.

stringent lockdowns and faced a market-driven crisis of medical supplies and numerous essential commodities (Kuo, 2020). This situation was exacerbated by efforts of some market participants and speculators to profit from actual and forthcoming shortages.

In an effort to manage both artificial and real supply shortages, major retailers in developed economies such as Australia imposed purchase restrictions on highly demanded bulky and low value added retail products and started looking for new suppliers from safer locations. Government and private entrepreneurs started to retool their production facilities by repositioning their offerings to meet the growing market demand for essentials such as toilet paper, medical equipment, personal protective equipment, hand sanitizer and so forth (Hall, 2020). However, due to shortages of resources, port restrictions and travel bans, many producers could not acquire the necessary manufacturing raw materials. As the knowledge and understanding about the coronavirus grew and the pattern of spreading and the damage became clearer, some nations came together through the WTO platform to jointly state their intention to strengthen global supply chains in an effort to better manage the increased market demand for supplies of essential commodities, especially medical supplies (World Trade Organisation, 2020b). The cooperation initially focused on only mutually beneficial international trade between member countries but soon was extended to assisting the least developed WTO member countries that strongly depended on imports for medical and other essential supplies (World Trade Organisation, 2020b). In the meantime, China reportedly sold medical supplies to countries such as Italy at a most favorable price during the peak of this crisis (Everington, 2020; Kuo, 2020).

Certain Western countries have called for an independent investigation into the management of the pandemic by WHO and trace the source of COVID-19. The countries in the forefront of this call are Australia, the U.K. and the U.S. China followed a retributive strategy by issuing a cautionary statement about discouraging Chinese students and tourists from visiting Australia and a possible ban on Australian beef imports with additional tariffs imposed on some Australian imported products such as barley (Mercer et al., 2020; Robinson, 2020). However, as of June 2020, China continues to import vital mining products and high-quality baby formula from Australia (Burke, 2020). How this plays out may lead to new global supply chain alliances or restrictions for these major economies to restore the power balance.

Analyzing the stream of events and policy responses in the period January–May 2020 to the unprecedented challenges arising from the COVID-19, they can be categorized in four major policy response scenarios, each with certain implications for international business (see Figure 18.1). These response scenarios/situations are:

a the unpredictable crisis coupled with trial and error emergency responses;
b emerging pattern of the crisis followed by gradual and short term policy responses based on informed speculations;
c solid pattern of the crisis followed by a regional and global collaborative policy response to achieve the best economic outcomes; and
d a steeping trade war between countries with pre-existing political and economic tensions leading to retributive policy responses.

Alternative Post-COVID-19 Scenarios

Figure 18.1 presents situations c) and d) as alternative policy responses that may lead to either new opportunities for collaboration or unforeseen post COVID-19 challenges for the international businesses. The c) policy response represents the growing collaboration between like-minded nations in a new COVID-19 related global supply chain situation, which facilitates global sourcing of essential commodities and medical supplies during the crisis. This policy is expected to open new opportunities for international businesses and/or strengthen the existing relationships between offshore partners. In contrast, d) situation, i.e.,

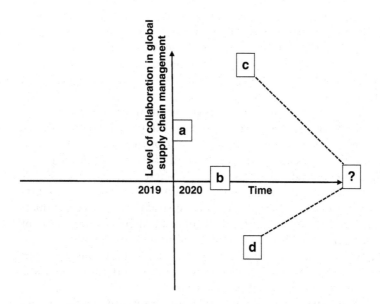

Figure 18.1 Policy Response to COVID-19 Global Supply Chain Management Challenges.
Source: The Authors.
Note: Timeline-Jan–May, 2020.

growing tension between existing global trading partners, challenges many international businesses and may cause short-term or long-lasting supply chain disruptions. However, it is important to note that, even the countries obviously heading toward a trade war (e.g., China versus the U.S. and Australia) have signed the joint declaration of collaboration as WTO member countries to facilitate global sourcing of essential supplies during the COVID-19 pandemic. Amidst such uncertainties, only a resilient and flexible global sourcing policy can ensure a sustainable global supply chain management for firms engaged in international business.

Reconfiguring the Concept of ISC Agility

The ability of a firm to thrive in a continuously changing, unpredictable business environment, otherwise known as 'agility' has never been more important in the context of ISC management as it is now. Prater et al. (2001:3) defined an agile firm as the one that designed its organization, processes and products to promptly respond to changes in a suitable time frame. In a rapidly changing environment, supply chain operations are most affected by changes especially due to the influence of a complex geopolitical, structural and logistical mix in the ISC equation, which may reduce firm's performance. These challenges in ISC management encourage many international firms with limited financial resources and other capacities to undertake counter-agile actions to remain competitive in the market (Prater et al., 2001), which may include increased local or regional sourcing, CLSC and adaptation of some traditional SM strategies.

The agility of supply chains of an international firm depends on the speed and flexibility of change response in three physical components of the supply chain: sourcing, manufacturing and delivery (see Figure 18.2). How these three physical components are configured to ensure speed and flexibility essentially determines the supply chain agility of international operations (Prater et al., 2001). For example, the inflexibility of delivery operation can be compensated by the speed and flexibility of manufacturing or sourcing to maintain the SC agility. Such a strategy could be the most useful way for international businesses to remain agile as delivery and transport of both inbound and outbound logistics is a critical ISC challenge during the global pandemic, lockdowns and border restrictions. However, the traditional notion of flexibility may need to adjust to the COVID-19 new reality, especially because the outbound logistics may only be sold in the local market or limited number of foreign countries.

We therefore argue that in the post-COVID-19 world, supply chain agility for international businesses needs to be redefined and reconfigured by adding the retooling and repurposing capacity as part of flexibility capabilities of international firms. In extant literature, flexibility capabilities of an agile SC are characterized by the promptness to adjust supply chain speed, destination and volumes. Adding retooling capacity to

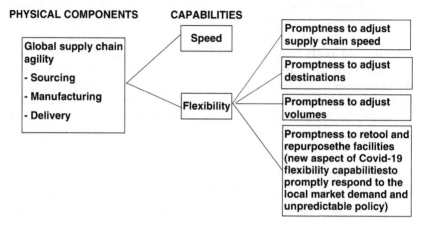

PHYSICAL COMPONENTS   CAPABILITIES

Figure 18.2 Supply Chain Agility in the COVID-19 International Business Context.
Source: The Authors, adapted from Prater et al. (2001).

the mix seems vital in closed border situations to keep production facilities operational by effectively using the available inbound logistics to keep supplying essential products in domestic markets. This capacity will increase the resilience of international businesses during the uncertainties of global pandemics and other crises, and serve the needs of local and international markets (see Figure 19.2). Numerous examples of such retooling and repurposing capacity have been demonstrated by small manufacturers in different countries during a) and b) stages indicated above (see Figure 19.1), while many large multinational businesses struggled to keep afloat or useful despite carefully building the traditional three flexibility capabilities over many years. In situations c) and d), this additional capacity will provide international firms with options of reinventing their products or repurposing their facilities to meet new or localized market demand for essential supplies and/or take advantage of the stronger worldwide SC collaboration during a global crisis. Even in the case of a new unexpected or growing trade war between countries in d) situation repurposing and retooling capacity seems like a vital lifeline for sustainable international operations.

Toward a More Sustainable International SC Management Model Post-COVID-19

We propose the integration of the CLSC model with the traditional SM practices to increase ISC agility (see Figure 18.3). Reusing or recycling production waste or some parts of the used materials may offer an alternative and cheaper source of inbound logistics and a scope to

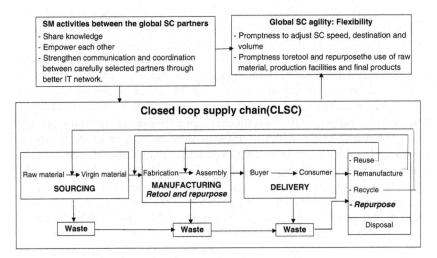

Figure 18.3 Sustainable Global Supply Chain Management Framework for the Post-COVID-19 International Businesses.
Sources: Adapted from *Prater et al. (2001)*, Ashby (2018) and Schaltegger et al. (2014).
Note: The bold-italic words are the additional post-COVID-19 activities/factors for the sustainable global SC proposed in this chapter.

repurpose or retool the manufacturing facilities to produce critical goods for the local or proximate markets if needed. The traditional SM offers a more integrated knowledge sharing and coordination partnership among carefully selected offshore partners during normal times. Integrating the basic premise of these two frameworks may make international businesses more sustainable in the post-COVID-19 reality and in future unpredictable global pandemic or border lockdown situations without having to resort to counter-agility actions for survival. We acknowledge that some of these mechanisms are in fact developed as a tool for counter-agility strategy to improve performance of an organization with limited resources to invest in infrastructure and logistics. However, careful customization of these models according to the capacity of an international business may actually work well to increase their ISC agility facing post-COVID-19 international supply chain management (ISCM) challenges or a similar worldwide lockdown crisis in the future.

Use of CLSC Model

CLSC model prioritizes the collection, reuse and recycling of all existing parts of any product in an indefinite number of closed loops that return most of the raw materials back to the production process in an effort to minimize the environmental impact. This is one of the more climate-focused SSCM models where the manufacturers' roles can largely be transformed into providers of maintenance services as they take the old products and use their parts to produce an upgraded product or use the parts for repair services. Some of the parts that cannot be used in the upgraded products may be repurposed by using other supply chain partners, including international. Even raw materials or inbound logistics can be repurposed. Such models can increase the flexibility of the manufacturing components of ISCs in different countries or locations during global lockdowns to keep production plants operational. Also, it reduces the requirements of global sourcing during widespread lockdowns or where international freight movements are limited or stopped, what was expensed during wars, as much of the supplies can be sourced locally. However, to be agile, each partner in the supply chain should be equipped with a basic infrastructure to repurpose and retool independently during border restrictions or as a well-coordinated chain during normal times and that is where some traditional SM practices and knowledge sharing practices come into play.

Integrating Traditional SM Practices into the CLSC Model to Improve ISC Agility

The traditional SM practices comprise a series of activities to develop long-term relationships with a few carefully and strategically selected suppliers and maintain close communication and coordination to empower the supply chain partners via robust information sharing and networking (see, Chen and Paulraj, 2004; Cousins, 1999). These activities are independent of any environmental and social issues but may directly and positively affect international firms' sustainable performance as argued by Schaltegger et al., (2014). "By sharing information and improving coordination with suppliers, for instance, companies can optimize their inbound transportation flows and reduce the generation of by-products (e.g. packaging, carbon dioxide)" (Plambeck and Taylor, 2007 as cited by Schaltegger et al., 2014: 260). There is a noteworthy opportunity to reduce waste by improving manufacturing and delivery efficiency or quality by sharing best practices and innovation among the global SC partners (see Figure 18.3) for mutual gains (Gimenez et al., 2012; Pagell et al., 2007; Schaltegger et al., 2014). In the COVID-19 b) and c) situations (see Figure 19.1), consolidated partnering policies and integration procedures (Schaltegger et al. 2014) seem well suited to push the sustainability agenda as well.

Based on Hall (2000), an international company can understand its SC partners' operations and capabilities and improve them through well-structured and planned SM activities. Such a level of understanding, sharing innovation and empowering each other to sustain though an unprecedented situation as COVID-19 should increase the global supply chain agility by developing quick retooling and repurposing capacity of all international SC partners (see Figure 18.3). A more synchronized coordination will also help improve the speed of responses in the three physical components of the SCM process when the crisis heads toward the c) situation type of scenarios featured in Figure 19.1 as increased collaboration between countries and more relaxed border restrictions for essential commodities are applied. For example, if a supplier firm can repurpose its facilities to produce an essential commodity that is required by a buyer chain partner, it may empower both parties by providing inbound or outbound logistics for repurposing and retooling for a more efficient and effective supply chain performance. The challenge remains in building trust among sourcing partners worldwide and one way to do it can be achieved by applying the traditional SM practices for mutual benefits.

Conclusion

The integration of CLSC and traditional SM can lead to increased sustainability of ISC by improving the ISCM agility during and post-COVID-19. Economies worldwide have initially focused on strict border lockdowns for public health and safety reasons. However, only retooling and repurposing the country manufacturing failed to effectively handle the heightened demands for critical and essential supplies. The crisis was dire for numerous import -dependent advanced economies and calamitous for import-dependent developing economies. While each country initially took the conservative and self-serving crisis management policy, many of them soon realized that a country has little or no chance to survive through this crisis standing alone. Most of the WTO member countries gradually acknowledged the importance of collaboration and relaxed border and global trade restrictions to meet the unprecedented demand for essential commodities and medical supplies to better handle the dismal challenges of the COVID-19 crisis. Numerous international businesses were unprepared to take advantage of possible collaboration in the conditions of tariff reliefs and relaxed border restrictions, either due to lack of flexible infrastructure to retool or repurpose, inflexible and slow responding supply chain systems, lack of adequate empowerment of SC partners, lose and thinly spread out global networks and resources and consequential lack of understanding and willingness for cooperation between the global sourcing partners. In this chapter, we argue for a more SSCM for the post-COVID-19 international businesses by offering a framework to improve the ISC agility and be better prepared for the forthcoming global crises be them pandemics or of geopolitical nature. Having the capacity to retool and repurpose production facilities and improve efficiency by recycling raw material through a closed-loop supply chain, increased cooperation and coordination, information sharing and empowering the carefully selected partners have all been recommended in this chapter as possible remedies for the suffering of ISCs caused by the economic side effects of COVID-19.

References

Ashby, A., 2018. Developing closed loop supply chains for environmental sustainability: insights from a UK clothing case study. *J. Manuf. Technol. Manag.* 29(4), 699–722.

Baker, S. R., Bloom, N., Davis, S. J., Terry, S. J., 2020. *COVID-induced economic uncertainty, NBER working papers 26983*, National Bureau of Economic Research, Inc.

Burke, K., 2020, China export ban threats could be saved by Australia's baby formula industry. https://7news.com.au/business/finance/china-export-ban-threats-could-be-saved-by-australias-baby-formula-industry-c-1034849, (Accessed on June 3, 2020).

Chen, I. J., Paulraj, A., 2004. Towards a theory of supply chain management: the constructs and measurements. *J. Oper. Manag.* 22(2), 119–150.

Cousins, P. D., 1999. Supply base rationalisation: myth or reality? *Eur. J. Purchasing Supply Manag.* 5(3/4), 143–155.

Everington, K., 8 April 2020. Italy forced to buy back medical supplies it had donated to China. *Taiwan News.* https://www.taiwannews.com.tw/en/news/3912335, (Accessed on May 20, 2020).

Fernandes, N., 2020. Economic effects of coronavirus outbreak (COVID-19) on the world economy. *Available from SSRN 3557504.* https://papers.ssrn.com/sol3/papers.cfm?abstract_id=3557504, (Accessed on May 29, 2020).

Gimenez, C., Sierra, V., Rodon, J., 2012. Sustainable operations: their impact on the triple bottom line. *Int. J. Prod. Econ.* 140(1), 149–159.

Guerrieri, V., Lorenzoni, G., Straub, L., Werning, I., 2020. Macroeconomic implications of COVID-19: can negative supply shocks cause demand shortages? (0898–2937). https://scholar.harvard.edu/files/straub/files/covid19_supply_demand.pdf, (Accessed on May 28, 2020).

Hall, J., 2000. Environmental supply chain dynamics. *J. Clean. Prod.* 8(6), 455–471.

Hall, J., April 16, 2020. Coronavirus: Australian businesses retooling due to virus outbreak. https://www.news.com.au/finance/business/retail/coronavirus-australian-businesses-retooling-due-to-virus-outbreak/news-story/67e03f9c5305cd5cff3dc734acc337eb, (Accessed on May 30, 2020).

Hart, S. L., 1995. A natural-resource-based view of the firm. *Acad. Manag. Rev.* 20(4), 986–1014.

Hayashi, E., June 1, 2020. *70 percent of Japan execs plan changes to supply chain: Nikkei survey. Nikkei Asian Review.* https://asia.nikkei.com/Business/Business-trends/70-of-Japan-execs-plan-changes-to-supply-chain-Nikkei-survey, (Accessed on June 6, 2020).

Irwin, N., April 22, 2020. What the negative price of oil is telling us. *The Economic Times.* https://economictimes.indiatimes.com/markets/commodities/news/what-the-negative-price-of-oil-is-telling-us/articleshow/75293739.cms?from=mdr#:~:text=The%20coronavirus%20pandemic%20has%20caused, States%20fell%20to%20negative%20%2437.63, (Accessed on May 12, 2020).

Kilpatrick, J. and Barter, L., 2020. *COVID-19: Managing supply chain risk and disruption.* file:///C:/Users/Khanis/OneDrive%20-%20CENTRAL%20QUEEN SLAND%20UNIVERSITY/Desktop/Publications%202020/COVID %2019%20IB%20paper%202020%20bk%20chapter/News%20or%20recent %20articles%20on%20covid%2019/gx-COVID-19-managing-supply-chain-risk-and-disruption.pdf, (Accessed on May 20, 2020).

Kuo, L., March 19, 2020. *China sends doctors and masks overseas as domestic coronavirus infections drop. The Guardian.* https://www.theguardian.com/ world/2020/mar/19/china-positions-itself-as-a-leader-in-tackling-the-coronaviru, (Accessed on May 25, 2020).

McKibbin, W. J. and Fernando, R., 2020. The global macroeconomic impacts of COVID-19: Seven scenarios. https://www.brookings.edu/wp-content/uploads/ 2020/03/20200302_COVID19.pdf, (Accessed on May 27, 2020).

Mercer, D., Prendergast, J., Daly, J., May 11, 2020. *China's tariff threats on Australian barley force farmers to pause mid-planting. ABC Rural.* https:// www.abc.net.au/news/rural/2020-05-11/wa-barley-farmers-stop-as-china-threatens-tariffs/12234548, (Accessed on May 20, 2020).

Pagell, M., Wu, Z., Murthy, N. N., 2007. The supply chain implications of recycling. *Bus. Horiz. 50*(2), 133–143.

Plambeck, E. L., Taylor, T. A., 2007. Implications of breach remedy and regeneration design for innovation and capacity,*Manag. Sci. 53*(12), 1859-1871.

Prater, E., Biehl, M., Smith, M. A., 2001. International supply chain agility-Tradeoffs between flexibility and uncertainty. *Int. J. Oper. Prod. Manag. 21*(5/6), 39–58.

Reynolds, I., Urabe, E., April 9, 2020. *Japan to fund firms to shift production out of China. Bloomberg.* https://www.bloomberg.com/news/articles/2020-04-08/ japan-to-fund-firms-to-shift-production-out-of-china, (Accessed on May 20, 2020).

Robinson, L., May 13, 2020. *China beef ban could see thousands of Queensland jobs at risk, premier warns. ABC News.* https://www.abc.net.au/news/2020-05-13/chinese-meat-sales-trade-suspension-queensland-producers/12241440, (Accessed on May 30, 2020).

Schaltegger, S., Burritt, R., Gualandris, J., Golini, R., Kalchschmidt, M., 2014. Do supply management and global sourcing matter for firm sustainability performance? *Supply Chain Management: An. Int. J. 19*(3), 258–274.

Seifert, R., Markoff, R., May 13, 2020. *Digesting the shocks: how supply chains are adapting to the Covid-19 lockdowns. Research & Knowledge.* https://www.imd.org/research-knowledge/articles/supply-chains-adapting-to-covid-19/, (Accessed on May 31, 2020).

World Trade Organisation, 2020a. https://www.sgpc.gov.sg/sgpcmedia/media_ releases/mti/press_release/P-20200325-2/attachment/JOINT%20MINISTERIAL %20STATEMENT%20AFFIRMING%20COMMITMENT%20TO%20ENS URING%20SUPPLY%20CHAIN%20CONNECTIVITY%20AMIDST%20T HE%20COVID-19%20SITUATION.pdf, (Accessed on May 30, 2020).

World Trade Organisation, 2020b. https://www.mti.gov.sg/-/media/MTI/Newsroom/ Press-Releases/2020/03/Joint-Ministerial-Statement-by-SG-and-NZ-Affirming-Commitment-to-Ensuring-Supply-Chain-Connectivity.pdf, (Accessed on June 1, 2020).

Zhang, W., Xiong, T., March 13, 2020. *The coronavirus will delay agricultural export surges promised in trade deal with China. The Conversation.* https://theconversation.com/the-coronavirus-will-delay-agricultural-export-surges-promised-in-trade-deal-with-china-132227, (Accessed on April 12, 2020).

19 COVID-19 and Global Value Chains in South-East Asia and Singapore

Anikó Magasházi

Introduction

The accelerated globalization in the beginning of the 1990s and the rise of emerging economies have led to a new organizational innovation in transnational corporations (TNCs) – the emergence of their global networks. The ICT revolution has allowed firms to coordinate complex networks at a distance. Great differences in wage costs between developed and developing/emerging economies made possible the separation of various production stages and their geographical dispersion. Consequently, TNCs have become capable of vertically fine-slicing their production processes with precision and detail that has never been seen before and thus locate these geographically in various parts of the world based on their location advantages to create the 'global factory' (Buckley 2009). International corporations optimize vast resources worldwide within their borderless networks, while state borders have remained in place. According to the World Trade Statistical Review, more than half of the world trade in goods and services consists of intermediate products and global value chains (GVCs) covered 57 percent of world trade in 2015. In the past decade, the growing domain of the GVC research attracted the attention of scholars from various disciplinary fields such as international business, general management, supply chain management, operations management, economic geography, regional and development studies, and international political economy, extensively reviewed in a recent study (Kano et al. 2020).

Measuring GVC participation in exports, South-East Asia is in the lead as many of its companies operate in 'the middle' of GVCs with equally outstanding participation both upstream and downstream[1] (UNCTAD, 2013, p. 134). Fukinari Kimura argues that "although we observe similar cross-border production sharing and fine slicing of activities in the U.S.–Mexico nexus and in the Western Europe–Central/Eastern Europe corridor, these have not yet reached the level of development that East Asia has accomplished" (Kimura, 2006, p. 326). Modern supply chains have become longer and more complex than ever before. East Asia, which is highly interconnected with Europe and the Americas, is a perfect geographical area to study impacts of global turbulence such as the COVID-19 pandemic on the functioning of the twenty-first century GVCs during the public health crisis and beyond.

Lessons from Past Challenges to GVCs/Supply Chains

The severe acute respiratory syndrome (SARS) emerged in November 2002 in China and spread to more than 20 countries, especially in South-East Asia, in 2002–2003. Seldom have intersections between politics, economic development and public health been more graphically demonstrated.[2] These outcomes were concluded at the academic workshop titled 'Learning from SARS Preparing for the Next Disease Outbreak' held in September 2003 in the U.S. The epicenter of the disease was in the Guangzhou and Shenzhen area – a global hot spot of the electronics industry and a hub for LCD panel and laptop manufacturing. The SARS outbreak pointed to major risk factors within the electronics supply chains. Apart from the critical role of the low cost assembly activities, several electronic components, such as laptop power supply units, that were sourced from China only were seriously affected by production delays and disruptions in air cargo. In another major hub of the electronics industry, Singapore, the impact was also rather negative. For instance, many companies, among which Motorola, suspended production because many of their work force were quarantined with symptoms of SARS.[3]

In 2011, floods in Thailand, earthquake and tsunami in Japan leading up to the Fukushima Daiichi nuclear disaster damaged the automotive supply chains worldwide. The massive floods in Thailand in 2011 showed that while the share of automotive components in the total value of Thai automotive exports represented 35 percent prior the floods,[4] when 80 percent of the producers in Ayutthaya industrial park came under water, global production networks led by Japanese automobile manufacturers incurred enormous losses due to severe import delays and export contraction. Following this, the affected MNCs developed approaches to managing and mitigating supply chain risks. They responded by building redundancy rules and enhanced supply chain flexibility through information exchange and coordination in vertical relationships to ensure resilience against high-impact, low-probability shocks (Chongvilaivan, 2012). As a direct consequence of the catastrophic events in Japan and China, several Japanese companies engaged into corporation-wide detailed analysis of their GVCs, including all their processes and suppliers, and started to purchase critical components from more than one supplier. Unfortunately, supply chain mapping is very costly, and many international companies refrained from following their example. As a Japanese semiconductor manufacturer explained in an interview, it took a team of 100 people more than a year to map the company's supply networks across all supply sub-tiers in 2011 (Choi et al., 2020).

The COVID-19 Challenge to Global Supply Chains in South-East Asia and Singapore

Since 2004, health officials in South-East Asia have been fearing a new, bigger occurrence of a viral infection that could spread quickly across the world.[5] In May 2020, when this book chapter is written, we have been amidst a global pandemic for more than two months and it can be certainly stated that the COVID-19 pandemic has tested global supply chains and production networks in a much more drastic way compared to any adverse events in the three decades of global division of labour. On 27 May, the virus had already spread into 213 countries and territories.[6] Earlier academic research dealt mostly with the effects of localized adverse events on GVCs and their impact on international trade and income, while the effects of a broader pandemic scenario were hardly considered at all.

China's role in the world economy increased substantially by the end of 2019 compared to its contribution at the time of the SARS epidemic outbreak. China accounted for only 4 percent of the world's GDP in 2003, while its share had reached 20 percent of global GDP in 2019. It not only became the 'Factory of the World' giving almost 30 percent of the global manufacturing output in 2018, but it embraced technological innovation across various economic sectors thus challenging the positions of established multinational firms in global markets. GVCs included many manufacturing sites in China run by Chinese private entrepreneurs who engaged as low-cost, efficiency-driven suppliers who became part of the so-called 'bamboo capitalism'. The most prominent sectors were electronics, automotive and pharmaceuticals, all having strong base in the virus epicenter, Hubei province. Thus, the scale and scope of supply chain risk became substantial, as "81 percent of global companies rely on Chinese suppliers", emphasized Alex Capri, researcher of the NUS Business School, citing a February 2020 survey of the German Kloepfel Consulting. Every third company had major Chinese customers and 41 percent of firms delayed their planned project due to the epidemic already in February 2020. In addition, international companies had already started to alternate the dominant tendency of their China-centered supply chains in response to the tariff hikes in the U.S.–China Trade War. To mitigate risks, both international and local companies operating in China cautiously opened alternative smaller plants in other ASEAN countries, mainly in Vietnam, Malaysia, Thailand and Indonesia. Multinational companies have not closed yet their giant Chinese plants that are still unbeatable in large-scale production with the abundant labor supply and accumulated organizational knowledge in combination with the huge domestic consumer market. However, every Asian country has a different set of strengths in manufacturing that could be considered in rebuilding supply chains. The Indian government has been trying to position the country as a global manufacturing hub with wage costs only a third of those in China by building Special Economic Zones and providing tax incentives for FDI as part of the 'Make in India' program. India's micro-, small-, and medium-sized enterprise base is the second largest in the world (after China) and the domestic market is expected to be the third biggest in the world by 2025 after those of the U.S. and China. In the ASEAN region, Vietnam has become a much sought after location choice of multinational corporations as part of their 'China plus one' strategy due to competitive costs, a wide range of FTAs, and liberal investment environment.

Singapore can indirectly benefit from such supply chain shifts as it is one of the region's main financial and logistics hubs. International companies entering into the ASEAN region often need a reliable treasury in the region which can provide funding, cash management and services to new entrants. The strategic position and level of development of Singapore is a key factor pulling companies to invest there. Nevertheless, in the conditions of COVID-19, Singapore – with its small local market and export-oriented economy has felt the effects of the pandemic. For example, the vulnerability of its trade-led economic growth started to show its constraints already in the first quarter of 2019 due to the U.S.–China trade war.

From a macro perspective, the Singapore government is known for its outstanding institutional efficiency. Singapore's economy was badly hit by the SARS outbreak in 2003, therefore the country's institutions were in many respects well prepared for an eventual return of the virus. The last 17 year have brought about a consciously driven preparedness not only by developing the public health sector but by a long-term macroeconomic strategy that restructured the manufacturing sector in order to reduce its strong dependence on electronics. Substantial institutional and financial resources have been dedicated to building biomedical sciences from scratch and attracting biomedical and biotechnological manufacturing into the country with purpose-built, high-quality, sector-specific research and industrial parks such as Biopolis and Tuas Biomedical Park. As part of the strategic vision, Singapore managed to capture all aspects of the biomedical science value chain. These economic restructuring measures led to severe decline in revenue from the country's electronics production in the period January–April 2020 that was counterbalanced by outstanding output growth in the advanced biomedical/pharmaceutical sector with 16.5 percent year-on-year increase as of March 2020 and 13 percent rise of production even during the lockdown in April this year. Nevertheless, overall manufacturing contribution to GDP, constituting about 20–25 percent of the Singaporean economy, shrank. The country's vast trade turnover, tourism and air traffic, accounting for a big proportion of the GDP, contracted dramatically. In May 2020, the government forecasted annual GDP decline of 4–7 percent.

When COVID-19 reached Singapore on January 23, 2020, precautionary measures were put in place immediately not only in relation to public health, but also in respect of business continuity, job support, avoiding mass bankruptcies of SMEs and self-employed persons. The first four stimulus packages announced between February and May amounted altogether to 20 percent of the country's GDP[7]. The government agency Enterprise Singapore along with other government agencies drafted a Business Continuity Plan (BCP) to minimize disruptions already in January 2020, with further editions in February and April. It included advice for companies on HR, business and operational management and communication issues, and working with third parties. Special attention was given to identifying critical operations, critical employees, developing a plan to minimize disruptions, discussing and establishing contact with key customers and suppliers, and developing alternate procurement of supplies and parts. Transparent and timely communication supported businesses through websites of relevant ministries and agencies.

The COVID-19 Challenge to Businesses

On the micro-level of international business, the closure of a number of Chinese plants has disrupted the supply chains since January and has had a major impact on the Singaporean electronics companies. For example, the Singaporean contract manufacturing firm Watson EP Industries reopened its factory in Dongguan, China on February 10, but the management claimed that only slightly more than half of its 350 workers were back at work due to strict regional border controls. Another global corporation, Apple, experienced shortages on its iPhone supply as the company's primary contract manufacturer, Foxconn, needed to shut down much of its production in China, many of its 200 suppliers in multiple geographical locations were impacted, and so was its Singapore-based major semiconductor packaging design and assembly solutions company, JCET StatsChipPAC. Shipments of the smart phone sector suffered the largest year-on-year decline by 11.7 percent globally in the first quarter of 2020 due to supply chain disruptions and stark decline of purchases in China. The market leader Samsung and its global production network in which Singapore is highly integrated experienced similar disruptions on a massive scale.

As COVID-19 grew into a global pandemic by mid-March, the consequences have become far-reaching. Even if companies had drawn contingency plans how to ramp up production in other locations, the rapid spread of the virus around the globe made virtually unpredictable which regions would be least affected in order to seek suppliers in them. Closures of borders and lockdown in countries across the globe hindered the flow of people and goods on and across all continents. On March 17, the Singaporean–Malaysian border saw the rush of 300,000 daily commuter Malaysian workers from Singapore to Malaysia and back to get their necessary belongings for the period of the announced two-week lockdown in Malaysia in order to continue their work in Singapore, whereas the government assisted people with the logistics of securing accommodation.

The dramatic effects can be illustrated by the case of the Singaporean flagship contract manufacturer Venture Corporation. The group provides services from design to manufacturing to its broad customer base through its 30 companies with global clusters in South-East Asia, North-East Asia, America and Europe, employing over 12,000 people worldwide. The company's supply chain ecosystem is developed with suppliers clustered within close proximity – as the company relies on balance between reliable supply, control, flexibility, cost and lead time. It has a large network of key component suppliers and has expertise in streamlining the suppliers' value chain to achieve improved cost savings and operational efficiencies. Nevertheless, revenue fell by 27.5 percent year-on-year to US$673 million and profits shrank by more than a third in the first quarter of 2020 due to disruptions in its supply chain in China, Malaysia and Singapore, the lockdown in China, Spain, the U.S. and Malaysia.[8] It is worth noting that Venture Corporation shifted from electronics to the health sector following two of their major U.S.-based customers, Illumina and Philip Morris, in the last couple of years. Illumina develops, manufactures and markets integrated systems for the analysis of genetic variations and biological functions. Phillip Morris developed the I-Quit-Ordinary-Smoking (iQOS) device for which the U.S. Food and Drug Administration Authority granted a license in 2019. This move helped Venture Corporation's share price to remain above the average level of the Singaporean Composite Index (STI) and to experience a considerably faster recovery following the substantial fall of the STI.

DBS Group's research analyst Ling Lee Keng expects Venture to emerge stronger from the pandemic due to its expertise especially in advanced supply chain management, its strong relationship with customers and its healthy balance sheet. Venture claimed, when filing its Q1 results, that it saw strong demand for their services and products in the diagnostic and research equipment for health area, including ventilators used in treating severely ill COVID-19- patients. They expect some realignment and refocusing of the locations of their global supply chain that would benefit from opportunities in Singapore and Malaysia.

Conclusions and Implications

The Singaporean government took measures to contain the virus and tried to avoid the irreversible disruption of company activities and supply chains in the country. Even during the unavoidable lockdown – called 'Circuit breaker', between April 7 and June 1, companies in sectors which are part of global networks could apply for permission to continue their production activity taking all necessary health precautions. As manufacturers of essential products and services, aside from health care and food supplies, companies and their suppliers in the chemical, semiconductor, pharmaceutical and biomedical science sector were also listed, while companies and suppliers from other major manufacturing sectors of strategic importance such as marine and offshore engineering, aerospace maintenance and overhaul have also been exempt from the lockdown. Singapore participated in the G20 Trade Ministers Meeting in April 2020, where countries agreed to work together to maintain global production systems and trade links, while business leaders planned to diversify their supply chains to boost their resilience. The government expects new opportunities for local businesses to emerge from the shift in global supply chains[9] with the country's eminent position in the evolving Asian regionalism and three decades of expertise in dealing with multinational firms. In effect, this can further upgrade the country's manufacturing and services sector within GVCs in the medium-to-long term. Such opportunities are even more viable and being accelerated by the heating up U.S.–China Trade War and political rhetoric. Singapore-based companies started to realize that risks associated with highly fragmented production processes, including single-sourced, low-cost nodes, were ignored or underestimated at best.

Moreover, it has become clear that:

- Companies should map their supply chains with attention to detail. Digital technologies offer real-time visibility with novel supply network data analysis tools developed by specialized service providers to calculate optimal inventory allocations in order to respond swiftly to market demand (e.g., Elementum, spin off from Flextronics, Llamasoft and Resilinc).
- Lead firms should coordinate upstream and downstream suppliers and cooperate with the entire industry chain to find quick responses to disruptions. Suppliers of all tiers should reconsider their supply models. To this end, international business research has explored relational/collaborative governance forms within GVCs (Kano, 2018) and intersections between GVCs and policy engagement (Gereffi, 2019).
- Companies could recover faster after the crisis by keeping critical expertise and maintaining full or partial pay to workers during the

VENTURE CORPORATION LIMITED (V03) 2.6%
STRAITS TIMES INDEX (STI) -20.1%

Relative Price Performance
2019-05-30 to 2020-05-29   SGinvestors.io

Figure 19.1 STI and Share Price of Venture Corporation.

crisis period. Investment promotion agencies should also focus on business and talent retention during the crisis and beyond.

- OEMs, contract manufacturers and advanced suppliers with unique capabilities could establish more flexible, geographically diversified, if proximity of customer base necessitates, shorter regional supply chains on different continents in order to mitigate risks and build resilience, a move from robust global supply chains to internal 'micro supply chains'.
- Companies should focus on upgrading their manufacturing efficiency with plant automation, introducing industry 4.0 and smart factory solutions. It can contribute to faster and efficient reshoring/backshoring of certain activities to the home-country region, while others remain close to the customer base.

COVID-19 brought up another important question: how values and organizational culture may change in the post-COVID-19 era as individuals, organizations and societies across the globe were forced to become much more inward looking. It seems that collective values and teamwork, communication and connectivity, better home/work balance and cross group virtual collaboration may expand their significance and thus organizations will have to embrace these in order to enhance their resilience in a business reality where GVCs might change their structure, location and relationships.

Notes

1 In the case of upstream flows, we look backward and in the case of downstream flows, we look forward along the global value chain.

2 https://www.ncbi.nlm.nih.gov/books/NBK92462/. Learning from SARS Preparing for the Next Disease Outbreak workshop summary held by the U.S.-based National Institute of Health, the largest biomedical research agency in the world. Washington (DC): National Academies Press (U.S.); 2004.
3 Motorola temporarily suspended production at a Singapore facility after 305 workers were quarantined for SARS exposure.
4 Chongvilaivan, 2012, p. 14.
5 Source: John Overby, Mike Rayburn, Kevin L Hammond, David Wyld: China Syndrome: the impact of the SARS epidemic in South-East Asia Asia Pacific Journal of Marketing and Logistics 16(1):69–94 March 2004.
6 Source: www.worldometers.com.
7 Reuters 26th May 2020 Facing biggest downturn, Singapore's virus relief reaching 20% of the GDP.
8 https://www.businesstimes.com.sg/companies-markets/venture-q1-profit-down-336. May 08, 2020.
9 The Strait Times, April 06, 2020.

References

Buckley, P. J., 2009. The impact of the global factory on economic development. *J. World Bus.* 44, 131–143. DOI: 10.1016/j.jwb.2008.05.003.

Choi, T. I., Rogers, D., Vakil, B., 2020. *Coronavirus as a wake-up call for supply chain management.* Harvard Business Review, March 27, 2020.

Chongvilaivan, A., 2012. *Thailand's 2011 flooding: Its impact on direct exports and global supply chains, ARTNeT working paper series no.* 113/May 2012, Bangkok. ESCAP available from artnetontrade.org.

Gereffi, G., 2019. Global value chains and international development policy: bringing firms, networks and policy-engaged scholarship back in. *J. Int. Bus. Policy* 2(3), 195–210.

Kano, L., 2018. Global value chain governance: a relational perspective. *J. Int. Bus. Stud.* 49(6), 684–705.

Kano, L., Tsang, E. W., Yeung, H. W.-C., 2020. Global value chains: a review of the multidisciplinary literature. *J. Int. Bus. Stud.* 51, 577–622. https://doi.org/10.1057/s41267-020-00304-2.

Kimura, F., 2006. International production and distribution networks in East Asia: eighteen facts, mechanics and policy implications. *Asian Econ. Policy Rev.* 1, 326–344. doi: 10.1111/j.1748-3131.2006.00039.

Magashazi, A., 2020 forthcoming. *Singapore Globally Entangled – Lessons for Central Europe?* Monograph.

Hertel, T., Hummels, D., Walmsley, T. L., 2014. The vulnerability of the Asian supply chains to localized disasters. In: Ferrarini, B., Hummels, D. (Eds.), *Asia and Global Production Networks: Implications for Trade, Incomes and Economic Vulnerability.* Edward Elgar, Cheltenham, UK, pp. 81–112.

UNCTAD World Investment Report, 2013. *Global Value Chains: Investment and Trade for Development.* United Nations, New York and Geneva.

Xing, L., 2007. *East Asian regional integration: from Japan-led "flying-geese" to China-centred "bamboo capitalism".* Working Paper no 3., Aalborg

University Center for Comparative Integration Studies, http://vbn.aau.dk/files/ 13003157/CCIS_wp_no._3.

Yeung, H. W., 2016. *Strategic Coupling. East Asian Industrial Transformation in the New Global Economy.* Cornell University Press, Ithaca, US.

Dezan, Shira & Associates, 27/4/2020 *India Briefing: Can India Takeover China's Position as a Global Manufacturing Hub?.*

Part V

COVID-19 and International Business Ethics

20 Corporate Social Responsibility Response Strategies to COVID-19

Leonidas C. Leonidou, Bilge Aykol, Pantelitsa Eteokleous, and Angeliki Voskou

Introduction

The recent coronavirus pandemic crisis, apart from impacting public health worldwide, has resulted in an uncertain socio-economic climate with serious implications for the business community at large. These implications have been more profound among firms operating internationally, because: (a) they have to cope with the idiosyncratic conditions of the pandemic prevailing in the various countries in which they operate; (b) they are confronted with different stakeholder groups in each of these countries, which exert pressures of different nature and intensity; and (c) they are immediately visible to a wider global audience with regard to their specific actions taken to accommodate and mitigate the coronavirus crisis. All these necessitate a careful crafting of a set of response strategies, with corporate social responsibility (CSR) strategies playing a particularly crucial role (Ham and Kim, 2019).

By demonstrating a socially responsible behavior in this crisis situation, international firms aim to preserve a favorable image and enhance their reputation by helping their various stakeholders (e.g., employees, customers and suppliers) to reduce various negative emotions (e.g., anxiety, uncertainty and helplessness) and by providing solutions to various social problems (e.g., poverty, job losses and health risk) caused by the adversities of this unprecedented phenomenon (Pearson and Clair, 1998; Zyglidopoulos and Phillips, 1999). Indeed, the widespread presence, abundance of resources and considerable power of multinational firms has increased pressures on them by governments, organized groups and individuals to provide assistance to members of the society in these difficult and obscure times (Dillard and Murray, 2012).

An effective CSR strategy under a crisis situation necessitates the proper management of stakeholder interdependence, as firms need to interact and improvise with each of their stakeholder groups during the crisis development process and its aftermath (Pearson and Clair, 1998). Moreover, the uncertainty associated with the crisis also increases the need for firms to disseminate timely, accurate and comprehensive information regarding their socially responsible actions. In fact, if the firm fails to communicate effectively with its stakeholders, the latter will have to use other information sources (e.g., traditional media, social media or even rumor) to obtain this information, which may neglect, undervalue or even distort its socially responsible character (Pearson and Clair, 1998; DuFrene and Lehman, 2014).

In light of the above, the objective of this chapter is to conceptualize how international business firms have pursued specific internal and external CSR initiatives as a response strategy to the coronavirus crisis, in order to create a positive image and achieve a favorable reputation. In doing so, we first set the theoretical foundations of our analysis, which centers on the situational crisis communication theory. This is followed by an analysis of the internal and external CSR initiatives undertaken by international business firms during the coronavirus pandemic. Finally, we close this chapter with conclusions and guidelines for managers.

Background Theory

Situational crisis communication theory represents a prescriptive system for matching crisis response strategies to crisis situations with the aim of preserving a favorable reputation that will translate into an organization's legitimacy (Sellnow and Seeger, 2013). This is because a crisis, as in the case of the current coronavirus pandemic, not only potentially inflicts physical, emotional and financial harm to organizational stakeholders, but also menaces its reputation and relationships with its various stakeholders by providing the latter with reasons to have negative thoughts (Coombs, 2007). Hence, firms need to embark on a responsible crisis communication to protect their reputational capital immediately after they effectively address the physical and psychological concerns of the stakeholders exposed. This is because the uncertainty inherent in a crisis situation gives rise to concerns by various stakeholder groups about what socially responsible actions were taken by firms during the current crisis, as well as what actions are expected to be taken against similar crises in the future (Coombs, 2007).

To achieve an effective response to the crisis problem, firms need to assess the reputational threat associated with it, which is a function of three key factors: (a) *initial crisis responsibility*, which shows the extent of stakeholder attributions of organizational control for the crisis; (b) *crisis history*, which denotes whether and how the organization had experienced a comparable crisis in the past; and (c) *prior relational reputation*, which indicates how well the organization treats its stakeholders in other settings. Having experienced comparable crises, coupled with a poor reputation of treating stakeholders in the past, intensifies the crisis responsibility attributions to the organization and increases the reputational threat. In fact, a crisis responsibility attributed to the organization leads to negative emotions and a tarnished reputation, which may have a harmful impact on the firm's market (e.g., negative word-of-mouth) and financial (e.g., drop in sales and profits) performance (Coombs, 2007).

Situational crisis communication theory categorizes the firm's response strategies to a crisis situation into three groups: (a) *instructing information*, that is, helping stakeholders to physically protect themselves from the crisis (e.g., using protective equipment), preventing them in this way from becoming victims; (b) *adjusting information*, that is, providing stakeholders with the psychological support needed (e.g., reducing stress levels) to cope with the crisis; and (c) *reputation repair*, that is, actions (e.g., offering assistance to vulnerable groups) addressed to reducing any negative impact of a crisis on an organization's reputation and associated assets (Coombs, 2008; Coombs, 2015). These response strategies comprise information transmitted to stakeholders aiming to enhance and/or restore the reputation of the organization during and/or after the crisis. These firm's communication efforts are vital during the crisis situation and cover both the management of information (i.e., gathering, analyzing and dissemination of crisis-related information) and the management of meaning (i.e., taking measures to manage perceptions about the crisis; Coombs, 2008).

Internal CSR Initiatives

Internal CSR initiatives comprise all those aspects of the firm's socially responsible behavior that address the needs of stakeholders existing within the organization, such as workers, managers and shareholders. Being responsive to social issues dealing with internal matters is indicative of an organization that truly adheres to a CSR philosophy and really cares about the well-being of its own people (Tang et al., 2012). During the coronavirus pandemic, international firms have adopted various internal CSR initiatives, which can be categorized into protecting employee rights, preserving employee health and safety, taking care of diversity issues and acting in a transparent way.

Protecting Employee Rights

Employees are always the first and foremost stakeholders that should be addressed during a truly committed effort by the company to show evidence of its CSR practice. This is because if the rights of their employees are respected, the latter are expected to be: (a) more engaged and committed to their organization and willing to undergo any sacrifices; (b) more productive and motivated to carry out their jobs, even under difficult situations; and (c) more willing to adjust to new working conditions and to implement new practices (Farooq et al., 2017; Mory et al.,

2016). A crisis situation, as in the case of the coronavirus pandemic, gives rise to uncertainty and anxiety among many employees because of the fear of losing their jobs, of their salaries being reduced or their mode (or type) of work changed. Hence, managers should be careful to understand these employees' worries and take actions that will minimize any physical and psychological effects on them caused by the crisis (Coombs, 2015). Hence, respecting employees' rights and understanding their catalytic role in generating an ability and willingness to adjust to the new state of affairs created by the crisis is vital. For example, the CEO of Nestlé publicly thanked its employees for responding with great passion, dedication and patience during the adjustment period and the new job requirements assigned to them, while Unilever's management stated that for three months it would safeguard its employees from experiencing a high level of reduction in their salary, stemming from swings in market demand for specific products or inability to complete their tasks (Askew, 2020). In another case, Lululemon Athletica (a company dealing with technical athletic apparel) announced that, despite the fact that its stores around the world were temporarily closed because of the pandemic, it would continue to pay a regular salary to its employees, while funding generated from savings incurred from salary cuts of its management team and its board of directors were allocated to a special fund to support its employees (Ballard, 2020). Similarly, Netflix, the biggest online streaming service worldwide, created a fund to financially support people in its production studios, including cast and crew around the world, affected by the crisis (Hartmans, 2020).

Preserving Employee Health and Safety

By its very nature, the coronavirus crisis poses a high risk to the health and safety of employees, and any failure to safeguard this can damage not only an organization's reputation, but can also put it under scrutiny from government bodies and the media (Carroll, 2009). In fact, preserving the health and safety of employees should be the ultimate goal of organizations under the coronavirus pandemic and should include, among others, using appropriate equipment to protect them from any harm caused by the execution of their tasks, providing paid leave or other benefits in cases of sickness and maintaining a normal mental status which may be disrupted by reasons of fear (Regan et al., 2016). All these prophylactic measures are expected to enhance customer trust and satisfaction, particularly in cases where the company's efforts exceed the minimum health and safety standards required (Mandl and Dorr, 2007). There are many examples of international firms that have taken effective measures to protect the lives of their employees from the harmful effects of the coronavirus disease. For example, Coca-Cola, which runs production/distilleries, distribution and retail facilities around the world, guided their local management teams into abiding by local and global regulations, and receiving advice from health authorities to ensure that all employees are safe and the company remains free from COVID-19 reported cases. Procter and Gamble has also collaborated with medical professionals in order to introduce measures in their factories focusing on the cleaning and sanitation of all production areas, taking personnel's temperatures at regular intervals, ensuring that social distancing is kept and providing their employees with the option of staying at home should they not feel well. Many other international firms, such as Amazon, Microsoft, Apple, Ford and Starbucks, urged their employees (especially those in positions where this would be feasible) to work remotely (de Leon and Geller, 2020). Since the coronavirus pandemic can harm not only physical, but also mental and psychological health, some firms have taken additional measures in this direction. For example, Panasonic has developed a program in which some of its employees have become 'ambassadors', with the task of periodically contacting their peers in order to ensure that they remain mentally well and safe in these difficult times (Hasan, 2020).

Taking Care of Diversity Issues

Even though employees' health and safety must be the first and foremost consideration of international business firms during the coronavirus pandemic, it is also important for them to understand the negative impact of the coronavirus crisis on specific employee groups relating to gender, age, ethnicity, race and other diversity issues. As Lloyd W. Howell, Jr., chief financial officer and treasurer at Booz Allen Hamilton (a global technology and management consulting firm) argues, one of the greatest challenges of business leaders during this crisis is to understand the needs and circumstances of employees, who themselves are diverse and are also affected by widely varying life, work and family conditions (Howell, 2020). According to data collected by the Institute of Fiscal Studies – Economic and Social Research Council, women and young people are those who are most negatively affected by the coronavirus pandemic crisis, due to the fact that: (a) they are more likely to work in a sector that has been forced to suspend trade; (b) they are more likely to work in lower-paid jobs; and (c) they are at greater risk of becoming unemployed (Joyce and Xu, 2020). Certain groups of employees may also be in need of greater attention and care by internationals firms, mainly because of their greater sensitivity (e.g., feeling weak and helpless) and vulnerability (e.g., excessive family obligations) to the problems caused by the coronavirus crisis (Byron and Post, 2016; Mallin and Michelon, 2011). For example, Laura Hay, the Global Head of Insurance at KPMG stressed the negative impact of government lockdown measures on women's mental health as they struggle to find a work–life balance, as well as on those employees who live alone and feel socially isolated. Another example is that of Facebook, which collaborated with the child and elder care provider 'Bright Horizons', to give the opportunity to women to share advice and thoughts regarding issues associated with the coronavirus crisis, such as tips for styling their hair at home and exchanging recipes for preparing healthy home meals (Umoh, 2020). Starbucks has also put into effect various benefits and grants (e.g., 'catastrophe pay') for those employees who may need to take extra precautions, such as those who have underlying health conditions (e.g., suffer from diabetes), or worry or feel unsafe about coming to work (e.g., feelings of stress).

Acting in a Transparent Way

Transparency represents the reputation of an organization for sharing relevant, timely, understandable and reliable information with its stakeholders, demonstrating in this way the clear visibility of its actions to the general public (Auger, 2014; Kim et al., 2014; Schnackenberg and Tomlinson, 2016). A transparent organization is characterized by integrity, respect and openness with respect to its various stakeholders (Rawlins, 2008). For an organization, being transparent during a crisis is particularly crucial because: (a) it increases its accountability by clarifying complaints, problems and responsibilities associated with the crisis; (b) it provides sufficient information to stakeholders (e.g., shareholders, suppliers and distributors) for them to be able to make informed decisions; and (c) it denotes an honest interest and commitment toward taking actions to combat the adversities resulting from the crisis (Rawlins, 2008; Schnackenberg and Tomlinson, 2016; Sisson and Bowen, 2017). Many multinational firms (e.g., Coca-Cola, Unilever, Johnson and Johnson, Apple, Nike and Amazon) have comprehensively reported through their websites, social media and other communication means, their social practices and the specific measures taken to combat the coronavirus pandemic worldwide. In addition, the CEOs of many of these firms have become the 'media representatives' and 'company spokespersons', communicating regularly to the public concerning their organizational efforts taken to deal with the effects of the pandemic worldwide. An important dimension of transparency has to do with the company's financial resources, which for many firms have been seriously damaged by the coronavirus crisis. For example, Apple was among the first to announce openly to its investors that it will not reach its financial targets in terms of revenues for the year when the pandemic erupted, attributing this to the temporary closure of its main partner Foxconn factory in China, which resulted in a significant drop in the production of its iPhone smartphone devices (Hawkings and Abergotti, 2020).

External CSR Initiatives

External CSR initiatives refer to all those socially responsible activities taken by the firm, focusing on the concerns and problems of its various external stakeholders (e.g., customers, regulators and community), which are publicly visible and have a direct effect on its reputation (Tang et al., 2012). These initiatives comprise the firm's engagement in philanthropic activities, acting in an ethical manner, demonstrating product/service responsibility and exhibiting solidarity to weak parties of the business community. All of these are particularly important during the coronavirus pandemic in order to clearly demonstrate the firm's commitment to a better, safer and healthier world.

Engaging in Philanthropic Activities

Although crises are responsible for limiting the firm's access to resources, there is a need for it to engage in various forms of philanthropic activities, in order to meet social expectations (e.g., helping the society at large) and instill positive attitudes (e.g., showing corporate citizenship) among stakeholders (Bundy and Pfarrer, 2015). Such engagement will also help to improve reputational capital, facilitate access to scarce resources and compensate the diminished shareholder value because of the crisis (Muller and Kräussl, 2011; Ducassy, 2013). During the coronavirus crisis, the majority of the philanthropic actions of international firms concern donations to the society in general and to the health care sector in particular. At the society level, international firms provided aid to countries suffering mostly from COVID-19 (e.g., China, Italy and Spain). For example, L'Oreal and LVMH altered their manufacturing process to produce sanitizer gels, while Pernod Ricard (a French company producing alcoholic beverages) has donated 70,000 liters of pure alcohol to a health company manufacturing hand sanitizers (Lakritz, 2020). Food and beverage corporations, such as McDonalds, Starbucks and Kraft Heinz, have also embarked on donating free meals and beverages to support local communities in need and the medical personnel fighting the pandemic (Callahan, 2020; Hines, 2020). Johnson and Johnson has also introduced a 'scientific approach' to corporate philanthropy, by involving its scientists in a project aiming to produce a vaccine that would prevent the spread of the coronavirus disease. With regard to health care, many companies, including Apple, Amazon, Facebook, JPMorgan Chase and McDonalds, offered money, consumables (e.g., masks, gloves and sanitizers), or equipment (e.g., ventilators) to health care providers, organizations and professionals (Hines, 2020; Lakritz, 2020; Nickelsburg, 2020; Peters, 2020).

Acting in an Ethical Manner

During a crisis situation, the demonstration of ethical behavior by firms is vital in order to be sensitive and responsive to the anxieties and special circumstances of exposed stakeholders and the public at large (Xu and Li, 2013). Although some firms during the coronavirus pandemic encountered serious financial problems (with some being on the verge of closing down), others found this an opportunity to make excessive profits (Levenson, 2020; Thompson, 2020). For example, Clorox, a leading multinational manufacturer and marketer of consumer and professional goods, reported unexpectedly high profits during the crisis period, resulting from the extraordinarily high demand for its products (e.g., disinfectant wipes) in the U.S. and Europe (Barro, 2020). However, there were incidences of profits being made unethically, as in the case of an unauthorized reseller of 3 M, which was selling masks and sanitizers at incredibly high prices to exploit people's need to protect themselves (Lee, 2020). This phenomenon of excessive prices was the result of: (a) shortages in certain products because of people's 'panic buying', due to the coronavirus lockdown and disruptions in supply chains that were not prepared to accommodate this unexpected situation; (b) the abnormally high levels of demand for specific product categories, particularly those relating to personal hygiene and health care, packaged foodstuffs and day-to-day household essentials; and (c) export and import restrictions imposed in some countries during lockdown periods to limit the spread of the coronavirus pandemic (Ro, 2020). Another example of business unethicality has to do with various companies selling their products on Amazon, which sought to make excessive profits by overcharging for products highly demanded during the coronavirus pandemic. In fact, even though Amazon declared that it was against this price overcharging, products such as hand sanitizers and respiratory masks were sold at more than 2,000 percent above normal retail prices! As part of its CSR strategy, Amazon has taken measures to remove from its platform more than one million product listings, as these were providing misleading product information relating to the coronavirus disease (Lee, 2020).

Demonstrating Product/Service Responsibility

Product/service responsibility has to do with providing customers with what they were promised at the correct quality level and with the right safety standards (Pandey and Hassan, 2020). Showing such responsibility during a crisis situation is vital, due to increasing concerns by stakeholders (especially customers) about defective or counterfeit products, misleading product information, overcharging and other unethical marketing practices that find fertile ground to develop (Bowen and Zheng, 2015). Of particular importance during the current coronavirus pandemic was the need: (a) to maintain constant product availability (particularly for food, beverages and personal hygiene) to satisfy basic consumer requirements, especially under lockdown conditions; (b) to ensure product safety by maintaining hygiene conditions to produce, handle and distribute products to end users; and (c) to demonstrate commitment that prices will remain at normal levels, avoiding in this way the possibility of taking advantage of the difficult situation in which buyers are caught to make excessive profits (FDA, 2020; Lee, 2020). An example of a company that has shown evidence of product responsibility is Coca Cola, which took extra steps in their production facilities to ensure that all of its employees use hand sanitizers and masks at work, as well as pass through regular checks to monitor their state of health in relation to COVID-19. The reason was that the company wanted to prevent the spread of the coronavirus on its products and transfer this to end-users, as well as avoid an interruption in its supplies to the market as a result of factory closures due to contaminated production facilities. During the coronavirus pandemic, we have also witnessed unique cases of responsible behavior among service firms. For example, Starbucks gave its customers the option of ordering online or on a 'grab and go' basis, while additional locations for delivery of its food and beverages were made available. Another example is that of Netflix, which compromised its 'streaming quality' to enable enough internet capacity for users of its services in Europe, due to rising requirements for remote working, student attendance of online classes and people's need to use social media to communicate during lockdowns (Hartmans, 2020).

Exhibiting Solidarity to Weak Parties of the Business Community

During the coronavirus pandemic, a number of international firms embarked on efforts (e.g., funding, training and information) to assist weaker and smaller firms to overcome problems stemming from the crisis situation. Such actions denote solidarity to vulnerable members of the business community and improve the firm's reputation not only among other firms, but also among other stakeholders (Heide and John, 1992). Here are some examples of such altruistic behavior. JPMorgan Chase (an American multinational investment bank and financial services holding company) committed millions of dollars to support its existing nonprofit partners who are responding to COVID-19 and to assist vulnerable small businesses in the U.S., China and Europe (Hines, 2020). Amazon donated US$5 million to small businesses around its Seattle headquarters that will be impacted by thousands of tech workers telecommuting. This 'Neighborhood Small Business Relief

Fund' will provide cash grants to businesses near Amazon's offices in Seattle and Bellevue (Peters, 2020). Google allocated also US$50 million to support organizations working on COVID-19 relief from multiple angles, including educational resources and small businesses (Hines, 2020). Facebook initiated a US$100 million grant program for small businesses to cover for operational costs, such as paying their workers and covering rents. Instagram created the application 'Support Small Business' sticker, which can help businesses reach new customers and stay connected to the people they serve, such as entrepreneurs in their community (Instagram, 2020). Finally, Facebook created the 'Business Hub' with tips and resources for businesses trying to survive during the outbreak and hosted virtual trainings.

Summary and Conclusions

In this chapter, we have examined CSR initiatives as response strategies to the coronavirus crisis by international business firms (see Table 20.1).

Using the situational crisis communication theory as our theoretical lens, we have explained how these firms can usefully take a socially responsible stance in relation to the challenges faced by the coronavirus crisis, in order to maintain and even enhance their reputation. The way firms address these challenges is closely observed by various stakeholder groups in multiple countries and therefore any signal of inappropriate or inconsistent social behavior is very likely to generate skepticism, erode trust and damage their image. In fact, this can be done nowadays at an exponential progression, due to the widespread use of the internet, and in particular of social media.

Our analysis has shown that international firms should see CSR as a holistic framework, incorporating both inward-looking and outward-looking initiatives, and that having in place a strong CSR strategy is of paramount importance to respond effectively to the many adversities associated with the crisis situation (see Figure 20.1).

Indeed, firms that were well prepared to grasp the nuances of the new socio-economic situation created by the coronavirus pandemic and act accordingly in a socially responsible way have managed to enrich their reputation capital, as opposed to those that have not taken any actions at all. This is particularly important when operating on an international scale, where the coronavirus crises impacted stakeholder groups in a different way and intensity across countries.

Although a crisis situation may impose limitations on the amount of resources that the firm can devote to CSR activities, its stakeholders still expect it to take socially responsible initiatives that will help to somehow alleviate some of the financial, social and other problems associated with the crisis *per se*. We have also demonstrated that for an international

Table 20.1 International Business CSR Initiatives in Response to the Coronavirus Crisis

CSR Dimension	Company Initiative *Internal CSR activities*
Health and Safety	• Coca-Cola: cooperated with local management teams and regulators to ensure that it complies with requirements set forth by each country related to COVID-19. It also provided personal protective equipment to its staff aiming to have zero COVID-19 cases in its facilities/distilleries. • Procter and Gamble: adopted all precautionary measures, such as social distancing, rotation of shifts, temperatures control and personal protective equipment, while cooperating with its medical staff for providing advice on how to ensure health and safety within the workplace. • Microsoft: established remote working routines to be continued as long as possible until the coronavirus problem is removed. • Panasonic: offered to its employee's mental support through a program named 'HR Ambassadors' dedicated to assure psychological stability. This initiative was based on a regular calling of other peers to ask them how they were coping while working remotely and if they were safe or sick. • Starbucks: in an attempt to ascribe value and importance to its employees, it created a mental health support scheme through dedicated programs (e.g., cooperating with 'Lyra Health' in the U.S., providing to employees and their families 20 free sessions with a coach for mental support.
Employee Rights	• Starbucks: created two different plans for employees pay, 'service pay' and 'catastrophe pay'. While the former gives employees the opportunity to receive an extra US$3 per hour if s/he returns to work, provided s/he is healthy, the latter deals with all those employees who were diagnosed/exposed to the pandemic and need to be in self-isolation. • Netflix: did not fire employees and cast because of closing down production studios as a result of the coronavirus pandemic, but instead created a fund to support them. • Nestlé: provided sick pay for employees infected with the virus and to all employees (hourly and salaried) full payment even in places where factories closed down for at least twelve weeks. • Lululemon Athletica: committed itself to the continuous payment of its employees, despite the fact that its stores remained closed for a long period of time. To support employees in need, the company

(Continued)

Table 20.1 (Continued)

CSR Dimension	Company Initiative
	set a fund which was backed up by payment cuts of the management team and board of directors.
Diversity	• Lockheed Martin: supported women in the workplace during the coronavirus pandemic according to its Diversity & Inclusion policies. • Facebook: collaborated during the crisis period with child and elder care provider 'Bright Horizons' to give an opportunity to women to share advice and thoughts. • Starbucks: initiated various benefits and grants for their employees during the coronavirus era, such as 'catastrophe pay', 'Starbucks service pay', 'hardship grants' and 'Care@Work program'. • Verizon and AT&T: suspended overage caps and fees for home usage, waiving late fees and not canceling services.
Transparency	• H&M: awarded first place among other companies in the fashion industry in transparency index by disclosing information about its supply chain during COVID-19 pandemic. • Apple: publicly reported to its shareholders the negative impact of the coronavirus pandemic on its sales and profits. • Unilever: made its website available to everyone, updated with the activities of the company regarding its actions on COVID-19, on issues such as workplace conditions, health and well-being, supply chains, etc.

External CSR activities

Philanthropy	• Amazon: donated millions of masks to health professionals in the U.S. and Europe. • Apple: donated more than one million items (e.g., medical-grade protective masks, isolation suits and disposable gloves) to health care professionals in China. • Facebook: donated their emergency reserve of 720,000 masks. • Johnson & Johnson: donated one million surgical masks, one electrosurgical generator and other medical devices to hospitals, over 1,300 packs of contact lenses to medical workers, and a team of company scientists is working on a potential vaccine. • JPMorgan Chase: committed US$5 million to fight the coronavirus pandemic including health care provision.

(Continued)

Table 20.1 (Continued)

CSR Dimension	Company Initiative
	• L'Oreal: produced hand sanitizers and hydroalcoholic gels (instead of makeup and cosmetic creams) and donated one million Euros to provide hygiene kits for volunteers.
	• LVMH: manufactured hand sanitizer gels and provided free delivery of the products to French health care authorities.
	• Pernod Ricard: donated 70,000 liters of pure alcohol to a health company manufacturing hand sanitizers amid shortages due to the coronavirus pandemic.
	• Google: committed US$50 million to support organizations working on COVID-19 relief from multiple angles, including educational resources and small businesses.
	• Starbucks: donated free coffee for police officers, firefighters, paramedics, doctors, nurses, hospital or medical staff members or medical researchers.
Ethical Conduct	• 3 M: some of its unauthorized resellers sharply increased prices in its masks and hand sanitizers.
	• Google: ethical concerns regarding sharing collective data on people's movements during the coronavirus pandemic.
	• Amazon: its sellers sought to make profits by increasing/hiking prices on products like face masks and hand sanitizers, even though Amazon declared that it is against it.
Product Responsibility	• Coca Cola: in an attempt to ensure product safety in its facilities it ensured that employees wear personal protective equipment and are regularly checked for their health condition in order to prevent any contamination of their production facilities.
	• Starbucks: used its application to add an online ordering feature so that its customers put their order online and 'grab and go' to a Starbucks location or had their order delivered at home.
	• Netflix: in an effort to free internet capacity due to heightened demand by students and employees proceeded in reducing its streaming quality in Europe.
Business Solidarity	• Amazon: offered US$5 million to small businesses around its Seattle headquarters that will be impacted by thousands of tech workers telecommuting in response to the COVID-19 outbreak. The 'Neighborhood Small Business Relief Fund' will provide cash grants to businesses near Amazon's offices in Seattle and Bellevue
	• Capital One: committed US$50 million to help its

(Continued)

Table 20.1 (Continued)

CSR Dimension	Company Initiative
	non-profit partners to respond to changing needs within the communities they serve, including assisting small business
	• Facebook: initiated a US$100 million grant program for small businesses for operational costs (e.g., paying workers and paying rent), created the Business Hub with tips and resources for businesses trying to survive during the outbreak, hosted virtual trainings and found ways to help people connect and learn to use technology through Blueprint, a free e-learning training program.
	• Google: committed US$50 million to support organizations working on COVID-19 relief from multiple angles, including educational resources and small businesses.
	• Instagram created the application 'Support Small Business' sticker, which can help businesses reach new customers and stay connected to the people they serve
	• JPMorgan Chase: committed US$2 million to support its existing nonprofit partners who are responding to COVID-19, US$8 million to assist vulnerable small businesses in the U.S., China and Europe.

Source: The Authors.

firm to maintain (and even enhance) its reputation and legitimacy in foreign markets under a crisis situation, it is vital to:

(a) craft CSR response strategies proportionately with the stakeholders' expectations from the firm in a specific foreign market;
(b) focus on CSR initiatives (e.g., health and safety, product/service responsibility and donations) that are better suited to the requirements of the specific crisis; and
(c) disseminate information about the results of the CSR activities taken to various interested parties, such as customers, pressure groups and governments.

Managerial Implications

Our previous analysis of the CSR strategies adopted by international firms in response to the coronavirus crisis has several managerial implications. First, it is important for managers to adopt a socially responsible approach to the new conditions generated in each country by the coronavirus pandemic. Among others, this requires protecting the health of people inside and outside the organization, being transparent

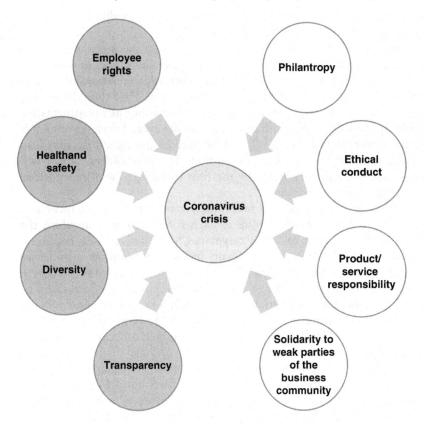

Figure 20.1 Types of CSR Initiatives under the Coronavirus Pandemic.
Source: The Authors.

among various groups (e.g., customers, shareholders and governments) about the effects of the crisis on the company's business activities, and avoiding any unethical or derogatory conduct that would place the firm in the spotlight. Although the intensity and variety of these actions may vary across countries, according to the harmful effects of the crisis, they should be characterized by altruism, transparency and honesty in order to gain stakeholder trust and enhance company reputation.

Second, in shaping their CSR strategies, international firms should first clearly understand how stakeholders in different countries perceive the hurdles of the crisis situation and what they expect their firms to do in response. In shaping their CSR response strategies, it is crucial to avoid any stakeholder manipulations and set clear objectives, aiming to preserve and even ethically further improve their reputation in each foreign market. It is also advisable for firms, through their subsidiary managers, to be in close contact with host governments and provide assistance to overcome the crisis whenever this is feasible, thus facilitating their operations in the aftermath of the crisis.

Third, international firms should also note that the way they respond to the current coronavirus crisis will determine assessments of their crisis history, as the way they manage their stakeholder relationships today will shape their relationship reputation tomorrow. They should therefore regard their CSR initiatives not as expenditures, but as investments for building both reputation and confidence in the eyes of their stakeholders in the future. In fact, low levels of CSR activity during a crisis may lead to the formation of negative perceptions by stakeholders, which will require a much greater effort by the firm to change them into positive once the crisis is over.

Fourth, it is important to take into consideration the nuances and needs of each stakeholder group in each foreign country in which the firm operates in order to clearly target its CSR initiatives. This requires a sound coordination between company headquarters and its subsidiaries in order to accurately understand the specific problems of stakeholders in each foreign market. Moreover, any socially responsible actions taken by the firm before the crisis period will serve as a 'reservoir of goodwill' and 'insurance-like protection', so that similar actions during the crisis period are done in good faith and not opportunistically in order to make a good impression.

Finally, it is important to understand that adopting proper CSR strategies under crisis conditions will help to build long-lasting relationships with various groups, especially those who have benefited directly from the firm's socially responsible actions. Such a practice will not only preserve the firm's reputation (and even survival) during the difficult crisis period, but will also help to improve its future business performance by creating loyal employees, enthusiastic customers and legitimacy in host communities, while at the same time building trust and confidence among investors in the company's future operations.

References

Amazon, 2020. Neighborhood small business relief fund. Retrieved from: https://www.aboutamazon.com/job-creation-and-investment/neighborhood-small-business-relief-fund.

Askew, K., 2020. Nestlé, Unilever respond to coronavirus pandemic. *Food Navigator,* Retrieved from: https://www.foodnavigator.com/Article/2020/03/26/Nestle-Unilever-respond-to-coronavirus-pandemic?utm_source=copyrightandutm_medium=OnSiteandutm_campaign=copyright.

Auger, G. A., 2014. Trust me, trust me not: an experimental analysis of the effect of transparency on organizations. *J. Public. Relat. Res.* 26(4), 325–343.

Ballard, J., 2020. 5 Reasons Lululemon Athletica is uniquely positioned to survive COVID-19. *Nasdaq*. Retrieved from: https://www.nasdaq.com/articles/5-reasons-lululemon-athletica-is-uniquely-positioned-to-survive-covid-19-2020-04-05.

Barro, J., 2020. The companies that stand to profit from the pandemic. *New York Intelligencer*. Retrieved from: https://nymag.com/intelligencer/2020/04/the-companies-that-stand-to-profit-from-the-coronavirus.html.

Bowen, S. A., Zheng, Y., 2015. Auto recall crisis, framing, and ethical response: Toyota's missteps. *Public. Relat. Rev. 41*, 40–49.

Bundy, J., Pfarrer, M. D., 2015. A burden of responsibility: the role of social approval at the onset of a crisis. *Acad. Manag. Rev. 40*(3), 345–369.

Byron, K., Post, C., 2016. Women on boards of directors and corporate social performance: a meta-analysis. *Corp. Governance: An. Int. Rev. 24*(4), 428–442.

Callahan, C., 2020. Starbucks, Uber Eats and more are giving out free food and drinks to medical workers. *Today*. Retrieved from: https://www.today.com/food/food-companies-give-away-meals-medical-workers-offer-free-delivery-t176164.

Carroll, C., 2009. Defying a reputational crisis – Cadbury's salmonella scare: why are customers willing to forgive and forget? *Corp. Reput. Rev. 12*(1), 64–82.

Coombs, W. T., 2007. Protecting organization reputations during a crisis: the development and application of situational crisis communication theory. *Corp. Reput. Rev. 10*(3), 163–176.

Coombs, W. T., 2008. Situational theory of crisis: Situational crisis communication theory and corporate reputation. In: Carroll, C.E. (Ed.), *Handbook of Communication and Corporate Reputation*. John Wiley and Sons, Inc, West Sussex, pp. 262–268.

Coombs, W. T., 2015. The value of communication during a crisis: insights from strategic communication research. *Bus. Horiz. 58*(2), 141–148.

de Leon, R., Geller, J., 2020. Here's how every major workforce has been impacted by the coronavirus pandemic. *CNBC Workforce Wire*. Retrieved from: https://www.cnbc.com/2020/03/13/workforce-wire-coronavirus-heres-what-every-major-company-is-doing-about-the-pandemic.html.

Dillard, J., Murray, A., 2012. Deciphering the domain of corporate social responsibility. In: Haynes, K., Murray, A., Dillard, J. (Eds.), *Corporate Social Responsibility: A Research Handbook*. Routlegde, Oxon, pp. 10–27.

Ducassy, I., 2013. Does corporate social responsibility pay off in times of crisis? An alternate perspective on the relationship between financial and corporate social performance. *Corp. Soc. Responsibility Environ. Manag. 20*, 157–167.

DuFrene, D. D., Lehman, C. M., 2014. Navigating change: Employee communication in times of instability. *Bus. Professional Commun. Q. 77*(4), 443–452.

Farooq, O., Rupp, D. E., Farooq, M., 2017. The multiple pathways through which internal and external corporate social responsibility influence organizational identification and multifoci outcomes: the moderating role of cultural and social orientations. *Acad. Manag. J. 60*(3), 954–985.

FDA 2020. FDA's Perspective on Food Safety and Availability During and

Beyond COVID-19: A conversation with Frank Yiannas. Retrieved from: https://www.fda.gov/food/conversations-experts-food-topics/fdas-perspective-food-safety-and-availability-during-and-beyond-covid-19.

Ham, H., Kim, J., 2019. The role of CSR in crises: Integration of situational crisis communication theory and the persuasion knowledge model. *J. Bus. Ethics* 158, 353–372.

Hartmans, A. 2020. Netflix is reducing its streaming quality in Europe to avoid straining the internet during COVID-19. *World Economic Forum.* Retrieved from: https://www.weforum.org/agenda/2020/03/netflix-is-reducing-the-quality-of-its-streams-in-europe-to-avoid-straining-the-internet-during-the-coronavirus-outbreak/.

Hasan, A. 2020. How companies are helping employees in response to COVID-19. *People Matters, C-Suite.* Retrieved from: https://www.peoplemattersglobal.com/article/c-suite/how-companies-are-helping-employees-in-response-to-covid-19-25301.

Hawkings, D. and Abergotti, R. 2020, Apple says the coronavirus will cause it to miss its revenue goals. Retrieved from: https://www.washingtonpost.com/technology/2020/02/17/apple-said-it-wont-meet-its-quarterly-revenue-goals-because-coronaviruss-impact-production-demand/.

Heide, J. B., John, G., 1992. Do norms matter in marketing relationships? *J. Mark. 56*(2), 32–44.

Hines, M. 2020. At the height of a pandemic, these corporations are giving back. *Built In.* Retrieved from: https://builtin.com/company-culture/enterprise-companies-giving-back-coronavirus.

Howell, L. W. 2020. Coronavirus: Why diverse leadership matters more than ever. *Weforum.* Retrieved from: https://www.weforum.org/agenda/2020/03/why-leadership-diversity-matters-in-handling-crises-like-covid-19.

Instagram 2020. Supporting small businesses on Instagram. Retrieved from: https://business.instagram.com/blog/supporting-small-businesses-on-instagram.

Joyce, R., Xu, X., 2020. *Sector shutdowns during the coronavirus crisis: which workers are most exposed?*Institute of Fiscal Studies. Economic and Research Council,https://www.ifs.org.uk/publications/14781, Accessed on 30/06/2020.

Kim, B., Hong, S., Cameron, G. T., 2014. What corporations say matters more than what they say they do? A test of a truth claim and transparency in press releases on corporate websites and Facebook pages. *Journal. Mass. Commun. Q. 91*(4), 811–829.

Lakritz, T., 2020. 12 innovative ways companies are helping people affected by the coronavirus. *Business Insider.* Retrieved from: https://www.businessinsider.com/coronavirus-companies-donations-helping-people#louis-vuittons-parent-company-will-use-its-cosmetics-and-perfume-manufacturing-facilities-to-make-free-alcohol-based-sanitizer-amid-the-global-shortage-4.

Lee, D., 2020. Amazon battles sharp price rises of coronavirus products. *Financial Times.* Retrieved from: https://www.ft.com/content/8db033ac-5d11-11ea-b0ab-339c2307bcd4.

Levenson, M., 2020. Price gouging complaints surge amid Coronavirus pandemic. *The New York Times.* Retrieved from: https://www.nytimes.com/2020/03/27/us/coronavirus-price-gouging-hand-sanitizer-masks-wipes.html.

Mallin, C. A., Michelon, G., 2011. Board reputation attributes and corporate social performance: An empirical investigation of the US Best Corporate Citizens. *Account. Bus. Res. 41*(2), 119–144.

Mandl, I., Dorr, A., 2007. *CSR and Competitiveness. European SMEs' Good Practice.* Consolidated European Report, Vienna.

Mory, L., Wirtz, B. W., Göttel, V., 2016. Factors of internal corporate social responsibility and the effect on organizational commitment. *Int. J. Hum. Resour. Manag. 27*(13), 1393–1425.

Muller, A., Kräussl, R., 2011. Doing good deeds in times of need: a strategic perspective on corporate disaster donations. *Strategic Manag. J. 32*, 911–929.

Netflix 2020. Emergency support for workers in the creative community. *Netflix Official site.* Retrieved from: https://media.netflix.com/en/company-blog/emergency-support-for-workers-in-the-creative-community.

Nickelsburg, M., 2020. Amazon will donate $5M to help small businesses near its headquarters mitigate coronavirus losses. Retrieved from: https://www.geekwire.com/2020/amazon-will-donate-5m-help-small-businesses-near-headquarters-mitigate-coronavirus-losses/.

Pandey, J., Hassan, Y., 2020. Effect of board- and firm-level characteristics on the product responsibility rating of firms from emerging markets. *Benchmarking: An. Int. J. 27*(4), 1433–1454.

Pearson, C. M., Clair, J. A., 1998. Reframing crisis management. *Acad. Manag. Rev. 23*(1), 59–76.

Peters, H., 2020. Now is the time: Corporate citizenship amidst Covid-19. Hill and Knowlton Strategies. Retrieved from: https://www.hkstrategies.com/now-is-the-time-corporate-citizenship-amidst-covid-19/.

Rawlins, B., 2008. Give the emperor a mirror: toward developing a stakeholder measurement of organizational transparency. *J. Public. Relat. Res. 21*(1), 71–99.

Regan, A., Raats, M., Shan, L. C., Wall, P. G., McConnon, A., 2016. Risk communication and social media during food safety crises: a study of stakeholders' opinions in Ireland. *J. Risk Res. 19*(1), 119–133.

Ro, C., 2020. Can price hikes by businesses ever be justified? BBC, Worklife. Retreived from: https://www.bbc.com/worklife/article/20200427-coronavirus-can-price-hikes-by-businesses-ever-be-justified.

Schnackenberg, A. K., Tomlinson, E. C., 2016. Organizational transparency: a new perspective on managing trust in organization-stakeholder relationships. *J. Manag. 42*(7), 1784–1810.

Sellnow, T. L., Seeger, M. W., 2013. *Theorizing Crisis Communication.* John Wiley and Sons, Inc, West Sussex.

Sisson, D. C., Bowen, S. A., 2017. Reputation management and authenticity: a case study of Starbucks' UK tax crisis and "SpreadTheCheer" campaign. *J. Commun. Manag. 21*(3), 287–302.

Starbucks, 2020a. At a glance: What customers need to know about Starbucks response to COVID-19. Retrieved from: https://stories.starbucks.com/press/2020/what-customers-need-to-know-about-starbucks-response-to-covid-19/.

Starbucks, 2020b. A letter to partners: Comprehensive partner care as we adapt to COVID-19. Starbucks Official Website. Retrieved from: https://stories.starbucks.com/stories/2020/a-letter-to-partners-comprehensive-partner-care-as-we-adapt-to-covid-19/.

Tang, Z., Hull, C. E., Rothenberg, S., 2012. How corporate social responsibility engagement strategy moderates the CSR–financial performance relationship. *J. Manag. Stud.* 49(7), 1274–1303.

Thompson, R. 2020. Coronavirus: Hand sanitiser and face masks overpriced or out-of-stock as COVID-19 spreads. Euronews. Retrieved from: https://www.euronews.com/2020/03/13/coronavirus-hand-sanitiser-and-face-masks-overpriced-or-out-of-stock-as-covid-19-spreads.

The Coca-Cola Company, 2020. How the Coca-Cola company is responding to the coronavirus outbreak. Retrieved from: https://www.coca-colacompany.com/news/how-the-coca-cola-company-is-responding-to-the-coronavirus-outbreak.

Umoh, R., 2020. How diversity heads are steering their companies through the COVID-19 crisis. *Forbes.* Retrieved from: https://www.forbes.com/sites/ruthumoh/2020/04/15/how-chief-diversity-officers-are-steering-their-companies-through-the-covid-19-crisis/#3dae4b5b65a9

Xu, K., Li, W., 2013. An ethical stakeholder approach to crisis communication: a case study of Foxconn's 2010 employee suicide crisis. *J. Bus. Ethics* 117, 371–386.

Zyglidopoulos, S., Phillips, N., 1999. Responding to reputational crises: a stakeholder perspective. *Corp. Reput. Rev.* 2(4), 333–350.

21 Is Irresponsible Business Immune to COVID-19? The Case of Modern Slavery

Snejina Michailova

By early 2020, a viral particle of the size of 60–140 nm has brought the world economy to its knees. The impacts of the COVID-19 pandemic have been and will be multiple encompassing: health, economic, social, and environmental aspects, to mention but a few. The media is bombarding the world population with not only news stories on COVID-19 here and now; media also overwhelms us with projections and predictions regarding the environment, economy and work-life issues, concerning the future of work. Whilst these concerns are pertinent, we have not heard as much about the human rights problems that the virus has caused and exposed. I am yet to see human rights specialists and experts on responsible/irresponsible business dissecting the issue at a briefing or press conference along with health specialists.

Let me cut to the chase and offer my answer to the question I posed in the title – yes, irresponsible business[1] is immune to COVID-19, and to all other pandemics, and to crises in general. Unfortunately, irresponsible business is not only immune to such impacts; if anything, it will only grow stronger. It has survived numerous exogenous shocks in the past and is expected to survive others in the future, be those global health crises, severe financial downturns, political upheavals, or environmental disasters.

In this essay, I focus on modern slavery. Modern slavery is an umbrella term that includes slavery, forced labor, bonded labor, human trafficking and other forms of exploitation (Lake et al., 2016). Dangerous, impossible, often inhumane working conditions, meagre (if any) wages, unstable (or non-existent) contracts are not elements of what constitutes 'work' – these all comprise modern slavery. The latter is "the total control of one person by another for the purposes of economic exploitation" (Bales, 2012: 6). Craig et al., (2007: 12) call it "severe economic exploitation". Its enabling conditions lie in five key macro-institutional contexts: industry, socioeconomic, geographical, cultural and regulatory (Crane, 2013).

Slavery operates both within and across borders in a hidden form in the complex supply chains of producers, labor contractors and global retailers. Admittedly, the statistics for modern slavery are ambiguous. Slavery is largely covert but underreported; in 2013, close to 30 million people were enslaved; whereas in 2014, this figure exceeded 35 million (Koslowska, 2017). In 2016, more than 40 million people were enslaved (International Labour Organization (ILO) and Walk Free Foundation and International Organization for Migration (IOM), 2017) – more than eight times the population of Ireland, or of New Zealand, or of Croatia. Modern slavery has become a part of business life not only in developing countries but also in well-developed, advanced economies that pride themselves for their enforced institutions and sound business practices. In fact, developed economies are far from immune to modern slavery (Lake et al., 2016). Moreover, modern slavery thrives not only in labor-intensive industries like agriculture, farming, and construction; it is very much part of high fashion, information technology, and electronics. The pressure intensifies as one travels down the supply chain, eventuating in an employer or multiple employers, not only exploiting their workers, they enslave them.

Modern slavery has been, is, and will likely continue to be a business. Multiple actors are involved in it – the victims, exploiters, intermediaries and (typically) large corporations that are the face of it all. And then there are you and I, the consumers. We are all implicated, knowingly or not – when we buy our tuna in the supermarket or the latest mobile phone in the tech shop. It could be that many consumers are not aware of the risk of purchasing and consuming products tinned with slavery. After all, we are told it is healthy to eat fish! But even those who know slavery labor is implicated in their cell phones, would they refuse to buy them? Most likely not. A colleague of mine experimented with a simple question in the classroom. After she introduced the audience to the issue of modern slavery and alerted every one of the possibility their phone has components that are mined in exploitative conditions, she asked whether they would buy one next time. 98 percent responded with a definite yes. Comfort and technology 'dependency' seem to be much stronger motives than the suffering of those working for our comfort and luxury addictions.

I find it rather astonishing that international business researchers have largely disregarded the issue of modern slavery despite continuously claiming the field is pursuing the examination of grand challenges. In fact, a number of articles have appeared inviting international business scholars to engage in tackling such challenges (e.g., Buckley, 2002; Buckley et al. 2017; Buckley and Lessard, 2005). But not many have actually done it (see, Dörrenbächer and Michailova, 2019).

Here is just one grand challenge. The United Nations' Sustainable Development Goal 8.7 is: "Take immediate and effective measures to eradicate forced labour, end modern slavery and human trafficking and secure the prohibition and elimination of the worst forms of child labour, including recruitment and use of child soldiers, and by 2025 end child labour in all its forms".

With colleagues of mine, I made the observation that international business research is behind many disciplines in investigating issues related to modern slavery. I have done so several times (e.g., Michailova and Stringer, 2018a, 2018b, Michailova et al. 2020). It seems to me that it will take some time until the international business scholarly community warms up to the idea (and the need) of contributing more significantly in this area, both in international business research field and in the classroom where we teach international business disciplines. The term is historically heavily loaded, and many may feel uncomfortable using it, but modern slavery is out there, often at our doorstep, whether we realize it or not, whether we acknowledge it or not. And it is really a global problem (Nolan and Boersma, 2019).

While I am not overly optimistic at this point in time about international business scholarship embracing the opportunity to study and investigate modern slavery, I do wonder whether the COVID-19 crisis would play a role in at least increasing the awareness, if not the understanding, of it in general and of modern slavery as a business in particular. And as an international business phenomenon. Although sad, a global health crisis may be the one to prompt the investigation of modern slavery and irresponsible business. Further, I shall elaborate on this issue.

In his 2019 article published in *Critical Perspectives on International Business*, Ahen developed the argument that there are undeniably strong links between international business and global health. According to him, three factors are at play in these links. One, "vector-borne parasitic diseases, international travel, tourism, international production and commerce go hand in hand" (Ahen, 2019: 160). Two, the World Bank, International Monetary Fund, and World Trade Organization are major players in both international business and global health; add to this mighty Troika national governments, supranational and international organizations, and multinational enterprises, and the links become indissoluble. Three, it is these actors that define and decide "which problems actually matter and those which will not merit financing", shape institutions and "in the end, have systemic effects on billions of people" (Ahen, 2019: 160).

One would be stretched to dispute that businesses around the world are under the immense financial strain caused by COVID-19. Supply chains have rarely been under such an enormous strain, as consumerism dwindles. The lockdown measures (read working from the luxury of your home for some and huge trouble and excruciating conditions for many, including acute hunger) in several countries around the world have clearly decreased the demand for numerous commodities. While it can be tempting to think that removing key players (consumers) from the equation will bring modern slavery to a grinding halt, a lack of consumerism has instead placed even more pressure on global supply chains. Far too many companies had to reduce cost, and this amplifies as one moves down the chain of production and supply.

A major consequence is massive job losses across industries and countries. Demand for work has collapsed; so, demand for labor has, too. The economic collapse caused by the pandemic will push millions of people into extreme poverty. A complicating factor is that COVID-19 has struck everywhere at once – this has eliminated all earlier established and well learned and applied 'coping mechanisms' in terms of how poor and vulnerable people could at all deal with the calamity and its consequences. As put bluntly by *The Economist* (2020, May 23–29: 46), "Covid-19 imperils one of the greatest achievements of recent decades – the stunning reduction in global poverty". The statistics are grim, the expectations even grimmer. According to the same source, "[f]rom 1990 until last year [2019] the number of extremely poor people – those who subsist on less than $1.90 per day – fell from 2bn, or 36 percent of the world's population, to around 630m, or just 8 percent. Now, for the first time since 1998, that number is rising – very fast" (ibid.). 'Progress undone' reads the heading of the graph supplementing the text of that article.

It is not unlikely that dismissed workers, in desperation, would turn to work that entails exploitative conditions. Sadly, I foresee that the number of enslaved people worldwide would have increased during this pandemic. After all, slavery is related to poverty. Amidst this crisis, part of the narrative has often been (at least in some countries) that we are trying to protect our most vulnerable. And these were thought to be the elderly, people with pre-existing medical conditions, and sick people. But what about when our most vulnerable are hidden? Would they gain from the so-called cost-benefit analyses of the lockdown and other measures, no matter how large or small the margin of error in these so-called calculations? They most obviously would not.

Moreover, I seriously doubt that there are any protective measures such as physical distancing adopted in diamond mines, cocoa plantations, or electronic and clothing factories. And in slaughterhouses, construction sites, and fruit orchards. It is often migrants who work there and it is they who collapse by the end of their 'shift' in overcrowded accommodations with no hygiene standards whatsoever. Not only are victims subject to horrific slavery conditions, now their health is likely at even more risk due to COVID-19. Numerous Romanian migrant workers in German and French slaughterhouses (BBC, 2020) are just one example of many, actually far too many.

One can ask – what about governments? Whether people trust their government or not, they are tasked with protecting their citizens. Protect them from what? The focus has been very much on their health and combatting the virus. This is understandable and even justifiable. The COVID-19 crisis has shown that governments did not seem to have the time, not to mention the resources, to focus on the hidden populations in their countries. And often, they would not know where the enslaved workers actually are. Governmental agencies that are leading in combatting modern slavery have had to divert their attention to immediate issues, in which every move is scrutinized and dissected on a daily, if not hourly, basis. Other governments who pre-COVID-19 started warming up to the idea of issuing anti-slavery legislation, seem to have placed this on the backburner. Either way, the ones who lose are the ones who did not have a say anyway – whether it be on the government or on their lives.

Corporate players' role has not decreased while eyes were turned to governments. This seems to have been the case not only in countries where low trust in governments has been exposed, but also in those where large parts of the population preferred to rely more on disinformation at the cost of expert-based health guidelines. In such environments, businesses have an even bigger role to play. In fact, a recent study by Edelman (2020) revealed that the most credible source is employer communications. The 2020 Edelman Trust Barometer conducted the survey in ten countries: Brazil, Canada, France, Germany, Italy, Japan, South Africa, South Korea, the U.K., and the U.S. Employers were found to be most trusted, ahead of nongovernment organizations (NGOs) ahead of government and media. In eight of the ten countries, respondents viewed their employers to be better prepared than their country. This level of trust came in conjunction with high expectations of business to act: 78 percent of the respondents expect business to act to protect employees; 79 percent suppose adaptation of business operations, and 73 percent count on businesses to acclimatize their human resources policies.

How companies deal with the COVID-19 crisis will determine, to a great extent, whether they at all will survive and sustain their businesses. Maybe the crisis time is a good one to realize that businesses that have not been turning a blind eye on slavery and human rights are the ones best and most robustly prepared to not only respond to, but actively manage the challenges of the crisis.

There are many evils in the contemporary business landscape. Corruption, creative tax avoidance, nepotism have been present in the international business landscape for a very long time, actually have always been with us. But none of these can compare with modern slavery in terms of how ugly and persistent the evil is. And how immune to exogenous shocks it is. COVID-19, though unique in its nature and causalities, is but one and the latest example.

Globalization has always been in the driver's seat when it comes to the growth in the number of the enslaved people (Bales, 2012). But it might also be the one to save the world post-COVID-19 pandemic. No actor can address universal issues and grand challenges alone and this includes the outbreak of the COVID-19 coronavirus pandemic. A key finding by the 2020 Edelman Trust Barometer, to which I referred earlier, showed that governments and businesses are expected to team up if they are to combat COVID-19 successfully and there is twice as much trust in combined efforts than any of the actors fighting the corona virus alone. And rich countries will not solve the issue until the virus is alive and deadly in the poor ones.

Will closing national borders lower the risk? May be, maybe not. In my mind, there seems to be two key paths down the road post COVID-19. One is that companies will delay or cancel orders with their suppliers and subcontractors. Divesting is typically also on the cards when there is a crisis. A second one would be companies continuing doing business as usual, profiting from slavery. Which one is more likely?

My worry is that no matter which path the involved actors will choose, the losing party will be the enslaved people. My even bigger worry is that the effects of the COVID-19 pandemic on sustaining modern slavery will be long-lasting, very long lasting. And so, while health experts and scholars both argue and collaborate on gaining better data and developing improved models and predictions, I wonder until when will we, as international business scholars, stand by and not go full speed ahead to address the best way we can the crime of modern slavery and irresponsible business.

Note

1 For the purposes of the essay, I define irresponsible business as business doing wrong in relation to the community, society and/or business practices.

References

Ahen, F., 2019 Global health and international business: new frontiers of international business research. *Crit. Perspect. Int. Bus.* 15(2/3), 158–178.

Bales, K., 2012 *Disposable People: New Slavery in the Global Economy.* Berkeley, CA: University of California Press.

BBC, 2020 Coronavirus: virus outbreaks push Germany to clean up abattoirs. May 20. Available from: https://www.bbc.com/news/world-europe-52738356 (accessed04.06.20.).

Buckley, P. J., 2002 Is the international business research agenda running out of steam? *J. Int. Bus. Stud.* 33(2), 365–373.

Buckley, P. J., Lessard, D. R., 2005 Regaining the edge for international business research. *J. Int. Bus. Stud.* 36(6), 595–599.

Buckley, P. J., Doh, J. P., Benischke, M. H., 2017 Towards a renaissance in international business research? Big questions, grand challenges, and the future of IB scholarship. *J. Int. Bus. Stud.* 48(9), 1045–1064.

Craig, G., Gaus, A., Wilkinson, M., Skrivankova, K., McQuade, A., 2007 *Contemporary Slavery in the UK: Overview and Key Issues*. New York, N.Y.: Joseph Rowntree Foundation

Crane, A., 2013 Modern slavery as a management practice: exploring the conditions and capabilities for human exploitation. *Acad. Manag. Rev. 38*(1), 49–69.

Dörrenbächer, C., Michailova, S., 2019 Societally engaged, critical international business research: A programmatic view on the role and contribution of *cpoib* (Editorial). *Crit. Perspect. Int. Bus. 15*(2/3), 110–118.

Edelman, 2020 Edelman Trust Barometer. https://www.edelman.com/research/edelman-trust-covid-19-demonstrates-essential-role-of-private-sector (accessed 30.05.20.).

International Labour Organization (ILO) , Walk Free Foundation & International Organization for Migration (IOM), 2017 *Global Estimates of Modern Slavery: Forced Labour and Forced Marriage*. Geneva: ILO.

Kozlowka, H., 2017 One of the biggest problems in rescuing people from modern-day slavery is counting them. Quartz. https://qz.com/1081852/modern-day-slavery-one-of-the-biggest-problems-in-rescuing-people-is-counting-them (accessed 29.05.20.).

Lake, Q., MacAllister, J., Berman, C., Gitshaw, M., Page, N., 2016 *Corporate Approaches to Addressing Modern Slavery in Supply Chains: A Snapshot of Current Practice*, vol. 29. Ethical Trading Initiative and the Ashridge Centre for Business and Sustainability at Hult International Business School.

Michailova, S., Stringer, C., 2018a Modern slavery as an international business: an old institutionalism perspective. Paper presented at ANZIBA (Australia and New Zealand International Business Academy) Annual Conference, 2018.

Michailova, S., Stringer, C., 2018b Studying modern slavery: It is time for IB scholarship to contribute. *AIB Insights 18*(2), 21–22.

Michailova, S., Stringer, C., Mezias, J., 2020*Studying modern slavery: How IB scholarship can contribute. Special issue commentary and introduction. AIB Insights*, forthcoming.

Nolan, J., Boersma, M., 2019 *Addressing Modern Slavery*. Sydney: UNSW Press.

Stringer, C., Michailova, S., 2018 Why modern slavery thrives in multinational corporations' global value chains. *Multinatl. Bus. Rev. 26*(3), 194–206.

The Economist, 2020 The greatest reversal. May 23–29: 46–48.

Part VI

Small and Medium-Sized Firms and Social Enterprises in COVID-19

22 Effects of COVID-19 on the Export Operations of Smaller Manufacturing Enterprises

George Tesar

The effect of the current global pandemic, (Coronavirus or COVID-19), on international business operations is enormous. In modern times, no other systemic interruptions, including wars, ideologies, or dictatorship have hindered international operations of enterprises as much as the current global pandemic. In contrast to previous global pandemics, today the international business community is much more complex, international transactions are mostly assumed to be long standing and routine, assisted by extensive telecommunication capabilities, and almost without systemic interruptions. The existing theory of international business, as it was formulated by academics over the past several decades, is based on an assumption of a stable and transparent international business climate, only seldom disturbed by governmental trade disputes or protectionist attempts to limit international business operations. The current global pandemic clearly indicates that the international business theory, including tentative formulations of strategies, and operations have, in the past, been expressed without consideration of the possibility for large future systemic interruptions—such as a global pandemic.

A range of responses to a new global pandemic requires that governments become actively involved, cooperate with international health organizations, and direct a variety of regulatory agencies to minimize the effect of a modern pandemic on their constituencies. One of the constituencies impacted by a new pandemic are enterprises involved in international business operations. During a global epidemic, such enterprises quickly discover that government actions can interrupt their daily routine, by issuing shelter at home directives, declare production to be essential or nonessential, or even stop international transactions including their logistical support. Such leave enterprises with major challenges, operational discontinuities, and eventually lead to financial predicaments. Governments may declare a national state of emergency, close borders, or shut down entire economies. The current pandemic suggests that when governments deploy emergency directives, many enterprises, domestic and international, are not prepared for an unexpected phenomenon and the resulting systemic discontinuities.

Larger enterprises have advantages during a global pandemic. Typically, they have the financial resources, cash reserves, and abilities to borrow to survive. Smaller enterprises do not. However, managers and bankers point out that it is not just financial issues that loom over international enterprises; human resources are also affected. From government initiated shutdowns, enterprises temporarily lose technological knowhow and expertise in the global marketplace, because their key employees leave, are dismissed, or are unable to function for health reasons. Governments may limit or deny entry to foreign workers—executives, managers, engineers, skilled or unskilled workforces; these are major interruptions for any enterprise regardless of its size. As a global pandemic spreads, smaller manufacturing enterprises are faced with existential threats. In the past such threats have not been extensively studied by academics or management consultants. At the incipiency of the current pandemic exploratory studies are emerging without comprehensive and conclusive results.

Global Pandemic and Smaller Manufacturing Enterprises

Governments have shut countries during the current global pandemic. Smaller manufacturing enterprises have been shut and then divided into essential and nonessential enterprises. Those classified as essential in lowering the spread of an epidemic, or accelerating its demise, continue to function. These are mostly high technology enterprises specializing in manufacturing technologically advanced medical equipment, supplies, or related medical products needed by the health care community, including research and development of necessary for other pharmaceutical products. In some countries, this may not be an advantage for some of the enterprises designated as essential. If an enterprise is designated as essential, it may be subject to government intervention or even nationalization.

During a global pandemic, an enterprise might be required to manufacture medical equipment, personal protection items, or other products considered by a government as essential. In some countries, government intervention is designed to temporarily take over enterprises that provide benefits to society, including infrastructural elements such as hospitals or locally owned public facilities; transportation companies such as airline, mass transportation providers, or ambulance services, and food production facilities, among others.

During a global pandemic, the major challenge that smaller manufacturing enterprises face is the nature of the pandemic itself. The current pandemic is not homogeneous everywhere. In some regions the pandemic is phasing out while in other regions it is just starting. Its inconsistency and unpredictability present major challenges in international business management and operations. Market demand fluctuates; consumer spending is down; and physical retailing is confronted with shifts towards online buying, credit purchases only, increasing shipping costs, and limited inventory. Because demand for consumer products is weak, distribution channels close temporarily. Suppliers worldwide want to ship products, but clients in economies that are shutdown are not able to accept them. The notion of global markets and globalization is in question (The Economist, 2020).

A realistic assessment of smaller manufacturing enterprises suggests that their managers and key decision makers were not prepared for systemic discontinuities in international business operations caused by the current global pandemic. They find it difficult to focus on critical decisions and formulate necessary contingency strategies for near-term survival and long-term preparedness for eventual future pandemics. One reason is that smaller manufacturing enterprises do not have the financial or human resources to divert from day to day international operations to potentially existential activities.

Over the years, mostly due to globalization, many smaller manufacturing enterprises became integral parts of international supply and distribution chains—mainly through direct exporting. Regardless of whether an enterprise is operated by a craftsman simply responding to unsolicited orders from abroad, an enterprise managed by an entrepreneurial promoter who expediates solicited or unsolicited opportunistic export orders, or is an enterprise that is rationally managed and directs well established portfolio of international operations it is, to some degree, dependent on exports. (Tesar et al., 2010: 67–72)

Nevertheless, a major systemic disturbance such as a global pandemic disturbs even the most stable international operations—more specifically, export operations.

Smaller manufacturing enterprises tend to be local and offer products manufactured from locally sourced raw materials, component parts and even subassemblies. If they manage international operations it is because of their geographic proximity to their foreign customers, reputation of quality that precedes them, have a substantial technological advantage, or offer favorable prices. Managers find it essential, in the current global context, to post a website and inform existing and potential customers about their identity, products and support services they provide. Smaller manufacturing enterprises operated by craftsmen type managers consider exports important but do not generally seek export orders. Opportunistic or rationally managed enterprises typically establish international relationships and receive most of their export orders over the Internet. Locally established enterprises have an inherent advantage—they source, manufacture and distribute products domestically first and export second. Accordingly, during a global pandemic, local smaller manufacturing enterprises are subject to a single business environment with its laws, regulations, social and economic burdens; but also to the same government with its own subsidies and incentives.

However, increasingly smaller manufacturing enterprises manufacture or assemble products in foreign countries, maintain distribution hubs, and provide customer and technical support centers in strategic locations abroad. Such enterprises manage their export functions and perform export operations from their head office in their home countries. During a global pandemic they are subject to multiple governmental jurisdictions, and consequently, on different operational levels and in different countries, their export operations may be interrupted.

If smaller manufacturing enterprises have a unique resource base, especially technical expertise, and operate in several countries, they may be required by a country government to produce pandemic related products needed in that country. Local government may confront the local branch of an enterprise with unexpected financial burdens such as paying local employees full wages during shelter at home periods. They may experience their products to be seized and diverted for the use in the pandemic. Economically and socially challenged countries may let exporters operate during a global pandemic because they depend on foreign exchange from exports or when the exported products have strategic considerations for the country's government. For many smaller manufacturing enterprises, these are difficult challenges that expose their managers to a portfolio of economic and social environments touched by the current global pandemic, on different levels of risk and consequences.

Smaller manufacturing enterprises that contract for components or even finished products manufactured abroad and imported to the home country for eventual export are confronted with another set of challenges. Manufactured components or finished products, depending on built-in tax and price advantages, are fully or partly assembled, modified, or repackaged to project the image of the home country and subsequently exported. Such enterprises are not generally classified as traditional exporters, but rather as re-exporters—they import components or products from one country and export them to other countries. Their primary objective is to maintain a global presence and favorable country image. Enterprises that are dependent on imports of their own components or products operate in foreign business environments that approach the current global pandemic differently at different points in time. They may have greater flexibility sourcing from suppliers abroad even under the current pandemic conditions. However, due to local pandemic conditions, they may not have the ability to import their own products from abroad to their home country and generate the image they need for their foreign made products.

When countries and systems shut down, international operations stop. Depending on the duration of the shut down and the nature of the pandemic, managers of smaller manufacturing enterprises inevitably deplete financial resources needed to cover fixed costs, operating expenditures, or funds needed to retain employees. They may not be able to secure loans and they quickly move towards liquidation. Many smaller manufacturing exporters operate internationally on open accounts, give credit to their customers, or use foreign country deposits. All these forms of payments, among others, tend to become dysfunctional during a global pandemic. In the meantime, the value of foreign currencies fluctuates and importers are reluctant to pay more. These are additional challenges that contribute to financial instability of exporters. Exporters of commodities, generic products, or products with diminishing consumer demand do not benefit from a global pandemic.

Most factors above impact individual exporters and are considered operational factors manageable and influenceable by export specialists. There are additional factors mandated or regulated by governmental or even international regulatory agencies that directly influence export operations and are considered noncontrollable or influenceable. A country may decide to impose an embargo on products imported from another country where the pandemic is out of control (textile or processed agricultural products). Governments of several countries, states, provinces, or regions may join in an emergency actions to trade together during a pandemic (essential consumer products including personal protection equipment). Countries may place temporary tariffs on nonessential consumer products (automobiles, appliances, or home maintenance products). In addition, personal communication is affected by denying sales personnel or service technicians entry into a country from those regions of the world where a pandemic is still active (international airlines become responsible for checking passengers' destinations).

Customers and Exporters

Foreign customers dependent on products exported by technologically advanced enterprises, frequently provide financial assistance to their suppliers during a pandemic to assure that they will be able to receive the products they need in the future. It is not only private enterprises engaged in manufacturing of high technology products such as medical instruments and equipment used during a pandemic, but also computer components and computers, telephones, and electronic equipment. Foreign customers with strong financial reserves typically assist smaller manufacturing enterprises during a pandemic to stabilize their post pandemic future.

Relationships between customers and smaller manufacturing enterprises are further complicated during a pandemic because some smaller manufacturing exporters are, for the first time, confronted with purchasing regulations of governments. Exporters perceive these relationships reluctantly and with a great deal of caution. Although most such arrangements, and large scale orders appear genuine, some are speculative and conditioned for many smaller exporters. Governmental agencies tend to place large orders with smaller manufacturing exporting enterprises that they cannot fill because they simply do not have the manufacturing flexibility or capacity and become subject to unrealistic and enormous penalties set by governmental agencies. A foreign customer (enterprise or governmental agency) may perceives an advantage to take over a weak exporter-supplier in another country and thereby gain a competitive position in the market.

The role of smaller manufacturing exporting enterprises during the time of a pandemic is tenuous. Managers of smaller manufacturing enterprises frequently perceive export operations, especially direct exports, as relatively high risk operations, although experience indicates that there is less risk involved in exports than in routine domestic operations. Smaller export enterprises operated by craftsmen and promoter type entrepreneurs are reluctant to make their products more suitable for exports, they frequently ignore foreign product standards, and often are averse to directly communicate with their foreign customers. Although they maintain websites and have direct communication channels open to them, their attitude is passive towards direct contact with foreign customers. During a pandemic, however, direct communication becomes essential.

Rationally managed exporters, with longer track records in export operations, have more skilled approaches for communicating with customers. Many established strong communication ties before the current pandemic and rely extensively on telecommunication technology. Experienced international managers and export specialists have fewer difficulties during a pandemic and continue to communicate directly and formally or informally with their foreign customers. They continue communicating from home offices to maintain solid communication ties with customers. Experienced exporters also suggest that a global pandemic with all the challenges it presents changes not only how exporters communicate with foreign customers, but the current pandemic also changes the patterns of export operations, their structure, and management. A new export function is evolving among the more experienced exporters. Some of the operational problems outlined above are illustrated by three short scenarios below. These short scenarios were developed for illustration purposes only. Any similarity to actual smaller manufacturing enterprises is coincidental.

1   A small manufacturer of garden equipment, mainly for do-it-yourself gardeners, including watering hoses, hand-held watering devices, garden tools, and other equipment. Most products are manufactured in the home country facility, but some products are assembled in a facility abroad. Specialized products intended for specific markets are also sourced abroad. Products intended for exports are shipped to a warehouse maintained in a conveniently located country for sales and

export into global markets. It maintains a sales force in its home office and an international sales force attached to the warehouse location. Early in its international operations it opened a website designed to communicate directly with consumers and users and offers technical support and repair services (in some markets gardening equipment is purchased by hired gardeners not by do it yourself homeowner gardeners).

Although sales of gardening equipment increased during the current pandemic, mostly because people shelter at home policies and want to be outside in their gardens, their entire exporting function shut down. The home office was subject to the shelter at home directive; the warehouse operations were left open for curb pick up and Internet sales. Managers responsible for exports in the home country continued to work from home but could not make arrangement to ship products, primarily because the products were not designated as essential during the pandemic. Their international operations were interrupted. Some of their export markets were open and some were closed. Customers in open markets switched to other products available locally or from other open markets. Since their exports account for a major portion of the total revenue, it is time to rethink the entire export effort and consider future international involvement.

2   A small manufacturer of medical equipment used in monitoring and displaying vital body functions in post-operative procedures in research hospitals. It engineers and assembles each medical equipment to order. It maintains a protected webpage for its clients. Specification of versions of the product are listed on the website and technical support is provided to assure that the equipment is optimally and safely used. During the pandemic demand for its equipment increased substantially and the product is classified as essential for pandemic related medical applications. Installation of the equipment in a hospital setting requires medical and technical expertise. Each product is personally delivered and installed by technicians who provide training for the medical personnel who will use it.

Because the equipment is classified as essential it can be internationally shipped after a routine technology related export license is issued. However, since international travel is restricted during the current pandemic, the technicians cannot deliver and install the equipment and train the operators. Technicians are subject to international quarantine, airline stoppages and other pandemic travel related health problems. The shipping delays are extensive, custom clearances are long, and timely domestic deliveries are unreliable. At the same time, the equipment is used in scientific studies; it is indispensable.

The manufacturer is introducing two innovations. First, it is training potential users of the equipment via the Internet by organizing training sessions; and second, it is developing user networks abroad where current users of the equipment would train potential user nearby. The first approach appears to be marginally successful, despite language technicalities and lack of 'hands on' examples. Managers responsible for export operations and client service are exploring more efficient and client friendly options.

3   A craftsman-type enterprise fabricates custom made electrical components and wire harnesses for old car enthusiasts whose hobby it is to restore antique automobiles all over the world. The owner-manager maintains a website which is irregularly updated. Product reputation among antique car restores and clients is remarkably high. The owner-manager believes that there is no need for advertising or promotion of his skills. Five employees perform several tasks including order taking (in English, Spanish and Polish), fabricate components, and expedite orders. The revenue generated from domestic sales is about 45 percent and is increasingly dependent on orders from abroad. The enterprise has low overhead expenses and keeps minimal inventory. It is short of cash because of the current pandemic.

The enterprise was forced to shut down and employees were required to shelter at home at the start of the pandemic. The entire operations, including communications with clients, were centered at the small management office consisting of one main computer, a single line telephone extension network and a privately owned cell (mobile) telephone. Employees involved in order taking could only do so at the central office and do not have the opportunity to work from home.

After sheltering at home several weeks with pay, the owner-manager informed the employees that he will not be able to cover their salaries and was seeking a government sponsored loan from a local bank. After several days of trying, it became obvious that he could not secure a loan due to administrative obstacles.

The pandemic came quickly, the enterprise has several unpaid orders, a substantial inventory of new orders and material ordered for scheduled fabrication. Unless the owner-manager can obtain a loan, the enterprise will have to liquidate, five employees will lose their jobs and clients all over the world will be without a source for their automotive restoration hobby.

Major Developments

During global pandemics, smaller manufacturing enterprises must assess and restructure their international operations which are export operations in most instances. Before the global pandemic, smaller manufacturing enterprises were reluctant to consider external factor such as global pandemics or other systemic discontinuities. For them, many noncontrollable factors were to a degree influenceable and did not directly impact export operations. It was the importer's, or typically, the customer's responsibility to deal with local conditions in their home countries. Import regulations such as tariffs, duties, or embargos of certain products were their responsibility. Even basic requirements such as local electrical, construction, or lifestyle standards were ignored by smaller exporters. Involvement of governments during the global pandemic has changed all that—they closed countries, stopped export and import operations, declared products essential or nonessential, and modified or restructured entire marketing systems. All for the benefit of expediting the progress of ending their own pandemics.

On an enterprise level, the current global pandemic introduced unprecedented problems for individual smaller manufacturing enterprises ranging from loss of market opportunities, erosion of technical knowhow, trained employees, and issues of survival. Depending on how important export revenue is to an enterprise, export operations may not even be a part of the decision concerning its future. However, in a global interconnected world of commerce, exports account for a major portions of total sales revenue for most smaller manufacturing enterprises.

To make a sound decision about export operations, smaller manufacturing enterprises must develop an understanding of the entire framework in which they operate—a framework that consists of all the external factors including economic, technological, social and lifestyle issues. Each enterprise must evaluate and weigh each relevant factor in making strategic decisions. These sets of external factors must be understood both in domestic and international contexts. Each country has its own external business environment made up of various factors. Managers and decision makers managing export operations for smaller manufacturing enterprises must understand them and factor them into future strategic decisions. Based on these factors, they must understand the extend and dispensability of their resources and the role of these factors in both domestic and export operations.

The key questions for theory and practice of international strategy and operations are: as managers of smaller manufacturing enterprises, how do our export opportunities relate to our overall enterprise mission? What infrastructure do we need to continue operating or entering international markets during a global pandemic? And finally, what are our objectives in foreign markets? Managers of smaller manufacturing enterprises need to better understand the fundamentals of international strategies and operations, specifically, export operations under the constraints of governmental intervention. Managers need to conduct analyses to identify certainties and uncertainties for each export market. In the future they must recognize the dangerous potential of global pandemics before they happen and be able to respond to the inevitable uncertainties of future export strategies and operations.

Smaller manufacturing enterprises formulate export strategies and conduct export operations in the context of international business and thus they are an integral part of international business theory. However, most managers and decision makers of smaller manufacturing enterprises are less concerned about export strategies than they are about export operations. Nevertheless, before the current global pandemic, international business theory failed to recognize the entire external business environment, including government interventions in which such enterprises function. Under these conditions, the validity of theory of international business must be reconsidered.

The contemporary international business theory generally assumes that the possibility of closing entire countries by governmental directives, under any conditions, is not likely. The theory also assumes that political actions and social initiatives will not be likely, for whatever reason, to take over enterprises. Or that governments will force enterprises to produce products needed to combat another global pandemic. A new comprehensive analytical framework must be conceptualized to recognize that the community of international business managers and decision makers do not operate outside external technological, economic, social, or lifestyle forces (Tesar et al., 2010: 159–169).

Reconceptualization of export operations within the context of international business theory is essential. Decision makers in smaller manufacturing enterprises must understand that relatively low export risk combined with extensive and effective international logistical support, and a well-established international clearing function for export and import documentation, is not subject to absolute collapse for various external reasons. Although these functions operate in relatively stable economic, political and technological environments, such enterprises cannot ignore external risk factors that the current pandemic has triggered.

Smaller manufacturing enterprises that are well connected to the Internet, maintain regular direct communication with their customers, and even use video conferencing capabilities, may continue these activities, and survive a systemic shutdown. It is the reluctant passive exporters that need to adjust their understanding of export operations and develop new and effective future strategies; if they hesitate, their future in a post global pandemic is questionable.

Surviving and competing will require a new generation of managers and management styles. New perspectives on the world are needed for managers of international business to understand the indispensable interrelationships and interdependencies in the external business environments. On a smaller scale, managers and decision makers must understand the role their enterprises play in the global context. At the same time, they need to be proactive in identifying, recognizing and assessing incipient trends that may interrupt their international strategies and operations.

The new imminent managerial styles must include a realization that traditional physical organizational structures will change because of the constraints of the current global pandemic—shelter at home means work and manage from home. Managerial supervision and instantaneous decision making practiced by autocratic managers must be replaced by remote consensus management. Teleconferencing capabilities are not homogeneously distributed worldwide and may not be accessible worldwide to employees of enterprises. All these challenges, among others, resulting from the current global pandemic will change how international managers will manage, make decisions, and how international operations will be implemented in the post global pandemic and beyond: also how international business theory, including export operations among smaller manufacturing enterprises, will be reconceptualized, how new constructs will be tested, and how the resulting findings will be implemented by a new cadre of international business managers.

References

The Economist, 2020 *Goodbye glocalisation: the dangerous lure of self-sufficiency.* 435(9194), May 16th–22nd, 7.

Tesar, G., Moini, H., Kuada, J., Sørensen, O.J., 2010.*Smaller manufacturing enterprises in an international context: A longitudinal exploration.* Imperial College Press, London.

Tesar, G., Moini, H., Sørensen, O.J., 2018. *Mapping managerial implications of green strategy: A framework for sustainable innovation.* World Scientific Publishing Europe Ltd, Hackensack, New Jersey.

23 COVID-19
Challenges to the Internationalization of SMEs

Ernesto Tapia Moore

Introduction

COVID-19 pandemic has stricken the worldwide marketplace. Most countries have put an actual end to freedom of movement of people, while maintaining freedom of trade. Most people have been forced into confinement and businesses they worked for came to a jarring halt during the confinement period. Many consumers suffered searing reductions of income with the extent depending on the countries' unemployment programs. The economy at large came to a crawl. Numerous industries and their subcontractors have been hit hard, except for the agribusiness, health essentials, and energy recently, among others. Most services, with the notable exception of health, sanitation, basic retail, and telecommunications were shut down. The non-essential primary sector businesses have closed.

The price of crude oil has plummeted with difficult to predict future. Stock market indexes have receded strongly. A minimum 8 percent recession in the world has been announced. Some propose that the world economy is expected to return to its 2019 levels only sometime after 2022, which indicates that the COVID-19 impact has been sudden, unprecedented and massive.

Businesses would be returning little by little to activity in the post-confinement world. Severe market contractions are expected and explained by the efforts to maintain trade. Businesses have faced restricted freedom of movement coupled with sharp reduction in consumer income. Several possible scenarios emerge, yet all tend to forecast firms reverting their efforts to domestic markets. In doing so, they aspire to sustain local economies and make themselves available for government subsidies beyond the blanket economic measures implemented during the initial stages of the Covid-19 pandemic and the post-confinement period. In this situation the smaller businesses are the most exposed ones.

Small and Medium-Sized Enterprises (SMEs)

Large businesses represent somewhat under 5 percent of the number of the world business population and employ about 30 percent of the world labor. They are also deeply rooted in international business. Focusing on businesses representing 95 percent of the overall number of firms in the world, the emphasis of this chapter is on SMEs in accordance with the definition given by the European Union (EU)[1].

Reference is made circuitously to manufacturing SMEs, as they are ones of the most exposed and dependent on MNEs as well as political interventions. By their very nature, SMEs are fragile firms and would most likely be the utmost affected by Covid-19. These firms would have to withstand the slump of market demand and subsequent volatility and turbulence of the business environment as firms disappear and governments intervene sometimes unpredictably. Germany's recent departure from its long-standing opposition to sharing public debt amongst the EU member countries is an example of such unanticipated decisions.

Most struggling SMEs consider compensating lost domestic sales by foreign market initiatives. Not many bridge the gap for reasons associated to firm size. Nonetheless, firm size only limits the number of markets served by a firm (Campbell, 1996).

Turbulence

The aftereffects of the COVID-19 pandemic affect all businesses, however, unequally. Additional environmental pressure would make poor performers fail more frequently than average performers. The latter would fail more frequently than better performers, regardless of the size of their businesses (Denrell and March, 2001). Environmental hostility impacts growth, then growth impacts performance (Wolff and Pett, 2006).

Turbulence, nevertheless, offers avenues for exploiting opportunities (Préfontaine and Bourgault, 2002), including international ones (Johanson and Johanson, 2006). The effects of environmental turbulence on performance appear to be key factors, even if they have been studied under the pre-COVID-19 conditions.

A careful consideration of the influence of the dramatic environmental changes on decision-making processes during and post-COVID-19 pandemic generates new insight on the processes and provides a basis to propose adapted foreign-market analytical tools for SME internationalization.

Processes at Stake

SMEs' International Performance

While the fundamental building blocks of globalization remain the foundations of the post-confinement period, 'market confinement' measures are appearing in the form of local product preference, economic nationalism and protectionism. The COVID-19 caused recession is expected to impact weaker firms the most. Nonetheless, one should not discard SME involvement in internationalization. SMEs have consistently sought alternative growth avenues in foreign markets. In doing so, they have shown a better survival rate when they are young and coping with limited resources than their older and wealthier counterparts (Meschi et al., 2017; Schrader et al., 2000).

Recent research obtained evidence suggests that this is also the case for first-time exporting SMEs (Meschi et al., 2020). What the new evidence suggests is that *aspiration-level performance*, a model that explains firms' behavior by observing the difference between firm's performance and aspirations (March and Shapira, 1992), in the form of *social* and *historical aspiration performance*, determines post-internationalization performance measured as earnings yield. *Social aspiration performance* refers to the performance of a firm relative to its peers; *historical aspiration performance* focuses on one firm's performance record over time (Meschi et al., 2020).

Social and historical aspiration performances appear to overshadow classical factors of IB theory. The main findings of Meschi et al. (2020), confirm that underperforming firms in their pre-internationalization period outperform all others in their post-internationalization period. Performance is measured relative to SMEs' peers in their specific industry. This outperformance is particularly salient for younger firms implementing an *international new venture* (INV) process executed in a speedy and decisive manner. INV process describes internationalization implemented from a firm's establishment until the end of the first four years of its internationalization. Extant literature suggests that INV firms possess specific organizational advantages. These include focus, decisiveness, adaptability and reactivity (Meschi et al., 2017; Oviatt and McDougall, 2005). Given the major alteration of the economic environment, many internationalizing SMEs could qualify as INVs.

Firms implementing an incremental internationalization approach suggested by Internationalization Process Model (Johanson and Vahlne, 1977), (IP model) hereafter, do not succeed as well as their peers during their post-internationalization period.[2] However, SMEs allocate resources in an incremental fashion and combine unique competitive advantages with deep-niche strategies (Rieskamp et al., 2003; Schrader et al., 2000).

It has been documented that pre-internationalization outperforming firms become post-internationalization underperforming ones. Domestic pre-internationalization underperforming SMEs have been found best positioned to outperform their competitors during their post-internationalization period.

Post-internationalization performance is somewhat better for SMEs having adopted a Limited Liability and Private company forms, managed by non-shareholding executives and generating good cash flows (Meschi et al., 2020).

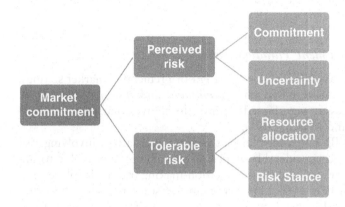

Figure 23.1 Market Commitment Variables of the Internationalization Process Model.

Source: The Author, based on Johanson and Vahlne (1977).

This points directly at Agency Theory (AT) in that *"no manager has control rights over decisions for which he has management rights"*(Jensen, 2003: 142), that *"risk-sharing benefits forgone when residual claims are restricted to one or a few decision agents are less serious in a small noncomplex organization than in a large organization, because the total risk of net cash-flows to be shared is generally smaller in small organizations"* (Jensen, 2001: 180). It also points at the effects of Jensen's Resourceful Evaluative Maximizer (REM) model in that *"people have a positive rate of discount for future as opposed to present goods and that they value .../... self-realization"* (Jensen, 2001: 37). Bearing directly on the process of internationalization, the *market commitment* variables of Johanson and Vahlne's 1977 IP model (see Figure 23.1) provide a valuable canvas for analysis, although the IP model *per se* does not appear to yield the results expected in extant literature. Combining Agency theory (AT) with the IP model yields substantial explanatory value in decision-making SMEs (Tapia Moore, 2008).

In SMEs, *perceived* and *tolerable* risk variables of the 1977 IP model are directly linked to *decision* and *control* rights of AT. Additionally, according to AT, *perceived* and *tolerable* risks constructs are inversely correlated. Also, the component variables of each of these two constructs (see Figure 23.1) interact in an inversely correlated, zero-sum relationship. In other words, the *perceived* and *tolerable* risks constructs reflect a trade-off between their component variables (Schrader et al., 2000).

In addition, underperforming SMEs tend to show a positive correlation between environmental turbulence and performance (Lichtenthaler,

2009), while outperforming SMEs tend to show a negative one (Jansen et al. 2006).

'Market Commitment' Paradigm Shift

During the pre-COVID-19 pandemic era of predictable market settings, decisions were made based on *commitment* and *resource allocations*. Learning processes were biased against alternatives that required practice (Denrell and March, 2001).

In the COVID-19 pandemic, bias against alternatives involving risk has strengthened considerably as negative outcomes appear due to unpredictable market conditions. Decision-making rationale places *uncertainty* at the core of decision-making processes. Firms' *risk stance* has moved from risk-neutral to risk-averse (Denrell and March, 2001; Wiseman and Gomez-Mejia, 1998). *Uncertainty* and *risk stance* have become the basis on which decisions are made. This constitutes a paradigm shift in *market commitment*. The shift depends on companies' social and historical aspirations: Firms having ambitious aspirations and considering themselves as underperforming relative to their peers charge better. The alignment of relative present underperformance and future ambitious aspirations makes sense for firms' members and insures the success of the firm (Devos et al., 2007; Fiegenbaum et al., 1996). These firms do not experience a paradigm shift, as their REM managers base their decisions on *commitment* and *resource allocations*. Their *problemistic search* routines (March and Shapira, 1992) are focused. A change for the worse in the market environment would have less consequences for such firms than for most other firms (Cao, 2011; Préfontaine and Bourgault, 2002). *"Because the bias against risky and new activities is a product of the tendency to reproduce actions that have been successful, the bias will be reduced whenever failures are more likely to be produced"* (Denrell and March, 2001: 535).

Over-performing firms tend to become complacent and dwell in cognitive laziness (McKelvie et al., 2011). When facing an unexpected and sudden change in the market conditions, they implement risk-averse decisions in an attempt to abate losses and often find themselves in a vicious cycle that produces misalignment: instructions are poorly implemented, objectives misunderstood, change is insecure and threatening (Fiegenbaum et al., 1996; Beer et al., 2005; Devos et al., 2007). Such firms are fully exposed to the market commitment paradigm shift; they tend to focus on *uncertainty* and hence adopt a *risk averse* stance. Their information processing routines are plagued with *conceptual drift* where non-adapted information-searching routines generate irrelevant information (Nebus and Chai, 2014). As these firms become overwhelmed, they begin to experience *information overload* (Auster and Chun Wei, 1993; Herriot et al., 1985).

Information Overload (IO)

A generalized definition of IO is still to be agreed upon (Roetzel, 2019). However, authors describe it as a form of cognitive overload, generating anxiety, provoked by personal and organizational-related causes (Sund et al., 2016). For our purposes, the cause of IO results from a sudden and dramatic change in market conditions, rendering inadequate most of the information-acquisition models and processes used by firms before March 2020.[3]

Moreover, turbulence in markets blurs information. *Context-awareness* and *context-saliency*, a fundamental part of information interpretation, are particularly affected (Nebus and Chai, 2007, 2014). *Context awareness* is the ability to identify relevant contextual data. *Context saliency* allows data disambiguation. Under turbulent settings, such as those created by COVID-19, *context-awareness* is exacerbated, impairing fact segregation; *context-saliency* is exalted by volatility, undermining fact discernment. Indiscriminately absorbed, all information becomes important. This confusion prompts organizations to regain control and reduce uncertainty through 'urgent' decision-making. 'Urgency' generally leads to disorderly action. *"Disorderly action [occurs] under conditions in which the 'noise' swamps the 'signal.' Goals may be ambiguous, attention problematic, memory incomplete, causality confusing"* (March and Shapira, 1992: 275).

Causality confusion leads managers to mechanically revert to 'tried and true' anterior models and best practices. Not being adapted to the situation at hand, these produce more uncertainty, more risk aversion, higher risk perception, lower tolerance to risk, and a general inability to take corrective action. The implemented market models do not provide coherent feedback loops. They impair learning processes and absorptive capacity, which is a firm's ability to absorb information and learn simultaneously (Camic, 1992; Auster and Chun Wei, 1993; Jansen et al., 2005; Lichtenthaler, 2009; Tapia Moore, 2017).

When information-seeking activities increase, they moderate the effects of causality confusion. As information influx increases, the feeling of uncertainty decreases and the feeling of control over events is heightened as well (Devos et al., 2007). As information influx increases, the interpretation of events becomes polarized into clear-cut opportunities or threats (Sund, 2015). Because of event polarization, the effects of IO worsen, and the absorptive capacity deteriorates.

Absorptive Capacity

In pre-COVID-19 markets, all variables of the absorptive capacity construct had a positive and significant impact on absorptive capacity (see Figure 23.2). In COVID-19 and possibly in the post-pandemic markets, this no longer holds true. IO tends to impair *recognition* and

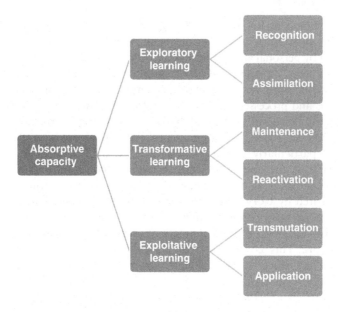

Figure 23.2 Absorptive Capacity Construct.
Source: The author, based on Lichtenthaler (2009).

assimilation (*exploratory learning*), *reactivation* (*transformative learning*), and *transmutation* (*exploitative learning*) variables. On the other hand, IO tends to promote *maintenance* (*transformative learning*) and *application* (*exploitative learning*).

All in all, absorptive capacity is negatively impacted by IO: innovation is reduced to its simplest expression; performance capacity is severely handicapped (Jansen et al., 2005; Lichtenthaler, 2009). Consequently, firm's willingness to change decreases dramatically. It seems 'mentally blocked' by a situation that, at this point, appears beyond control and understanding (Devos et al., 2007).

Perceived Environmental Uncertainty (PEU)

The underlying cause of the effects above is the firm's perception of uncertainty due to environmental turbulence. Pre-COVID-19 PEU literature focuses on the turbulence caused by the changes in market and technological dimensions. Admittedly, in the pre-pandemic, steady, globalized market, these two dimensions fluctuated significantly. During COVID-19, political, economic, monetary, fiscal, infrastructural, technological, market and competitive dimensions of environmental uncertainty would be unreliable (See Table 23.1).

Table 23.1 Dimensions and Variables of Three Perceived Environmental Uncertainty Models.

Dimensions and Variables of 3 Perceived Environmental Uncertainty Models		
PEU 1 (Miller, 1993)	PEU 2 (Werner et al., 1996)	PEU 3 (Tapia Moore, 2012)
Political/Government policies	**Political/Government Policies**	**Political/Government Policies**
Ability of the party in power to maintain control of the government	Ability of the party in power to maintain control of the government	Ability of the party in power to maintain control of the government
Threat of armed conflict	Threat of armed conflict	Threat of armed conflict
Tax policies	Tax policies	Tax policies
Monetary policies	Monetary policies	Monetary policies
Prices controlled by the government	Prices controlled by the government	Prices controlled by the government
National laws affecting international business	National laws affecting international business	National laws affecting international business
Legal regulations affecting the business sector	Legal regulations affecting the business sector	Legal regulations affecting the business sector
Tariffs on imported goods	Tariffs on imported goods	Tariffs on imported goods
Enforcement of existing laws	Enforcement of existing laws	Enforcement of existing laws
Public service provision	Public service provision	Public service provision
Macroeconomics	**Macroeconomics**	**Macroeconomics**
Inflation rate	Inflation rate	Inflation rate
Exchange rate against the USD	Exchange rate against the USD	Exchange rate against the USD

(Continued)

Table 23.1 (Continued)

Dimensions and Variables of 3 Perceived Environmental Uncertainty Models		
PEU 1 (Miller, 1993)	PEU 2 (Werner et al., 1996)	PEU 3 (Tapia Moore, 2012)
Interest rate	Interest rate	Interest rate
Results of economic restructuring	Results of economic restructuring	Results of economic restructuring
Resources and Services Used by the Company	**Materials/Infrastructure**	**Materials/Infrastructure**
Availability of trained labor	Quality of inputs, raw materials and components	Quality of inputs, raw materials and components
Labor and union problems	Availability of inputs, raw materials and components	Availability of inputs, raw materials and components
Quality of inputs, raw materials and components	Transportation systems within the country	Transportation systems within the country
Availability of inputs, raw materials and components	Transportation systems to foreign countries	Transportation systems to foreign countries
Prices of inputs, raw materials, and components	**Product Market and Demand**	
Transportation systems within the country	Client preferences	
Transportation systems to foreign countries	Product demand	
Product Market and Demand	Availability of substitute products	
Client preferences		

(*Continued*)

Table 23.1 (Continued)

Dimensions and Variables of 3 Perceived Environmental Uncertainty Models

PEU 1 (Miller, 1993)	PEU 2 (Werner et al., 1996)	PEU 3 (Tapia Moore, 2012)
Product demand		
Availability of substitute products		
Availability of complementary products	Availability of complementary products	
Competition	**Competition**	
Changes in competitors' prices	Changes in competitors' prices	
Changes in the markets served by competitors	Changes in the markets served by competitors	
Changes in competitors' strategies	Changes in competitors' strategies	
Entry of new firms into the market	Entry of new firms into the market	
Domestic competitors	Domestic competitors	
Foreign competitors	Foreign competitors	
Technology in your industry		
Product changes		
Change in product quality		
New product introductions		
Changes in the production process		

Source: The Author.

Uncertainty stems from firm's inability to predict future events; to forecast the impact and/or the effect of changes; the inability to formulate response options, values, and the utility of courses of action (Ashill and Jobber, 2001).

The perception of uncertainty, augmented by the effects of IO, would affect firms. Leadership charisma can influence overall performance, as this is often seen in SMEs: When environmental uncertainty increases, charismatic leadership will federate and stimulate SMEs. This fact brings in better performance. Inversely, an increase in environmental certainty tends to result in poorer performance (Waldman et al., 2001). Environmental certainty occurs when a firm's competitive/technological advantage is strong and the market trends are reasonably predictable.

Market Outlook

A firm's present (p) versus future (f) market outlook has a direct impact on the effects of *uncertainty* and *certainty*. Four possibilities are offered: Negative (+p/-f)[4], positive (-p/+f), pessimistic (-p/-f), and optimistic (+p/+f). Negative and positive outlooks tend to generate *uncertainty*, while pessimistic and optimistic outlooks tend to produce *certainty*. Concurrent to the degree of unpredictability and volatility, *certainty* generates organizational inertia, whereas *uncertainty* produces organizational flexibility (Helfat et al., 2007).

When SMEs experience organizational inertia, the market commitment paradigm shift takes place and goes unnoticed. IO is regarded as a necessary evil; information-gathering routines increase and concentrate on market and technological PEU dimensions, further contributing to the certainty of an unwelcome outcome.

When SMEs experience organizational flexibility, the market commitment paradigm shift is either acknowledged as an involuntary consequence (negative outlook), or voluntarily refused (positive outlook). Until information-gathering routines are adapted to digest the new multiple and relevant environmental uncertainty dimensions, these organizations will suffer substantial IO. This is when the effects of charismatic leadership become essential: negative outlook organizations fight to ensure survival; positive outlook organizations rally to guarantee success. Both types of organizations implement adaptive learning routines, reducing ambiguity and maintaining openness to change (March, 1989; Camic, 1992; Auster and Chun Wei, 1993; Johanson and Johanson, 2006; Devos et al., 2007; Nebus and Chai, 2014). Using proven PEU tools, further reduces IO.

Tools

Perceived Environmental Uncertainty (PEU) Models PEU1 and PEU2

Miller's PEU1 model (1993) was the first to specifically address the international business dimensions in a comprehensive manner. It is structured in six environmental dimension (See Table 23.1), connects strategy with international management in a disaggregated approach, and is based on the foreign direct investment notion picturing firms as seekers, exploiters of imperfections and internalizers.

Redundancies and difficulties with overlapping concepts among the variables of the PEU1 were identified (Werner et al., 1996). These shortcomings are of lesser importance when the results aim at qualitative analysis promoting context awareness and context saliency.

The PEU2 encompasses both quantitative and qualitative methods. It retains all PEU1 features and integrates four of the original dimensions and variables (See Table 23.1). Overall integrity, inter-rater reliability and internal consistency are improved (Lewis and Harvey, 2001; Werner et al., 1996).

Like the PEU1, the PEU2 is a self-administered questionnaire of one item per variable. Both models are for internal use and are meant for multiple respondents in larger organizations. Some MNEs include PEU2 variables in their reporting procedures. In addition, the PEU2 data-gathering methodology is flexible.

A version of the PEU2 was successfully adapted, implemented, and validated in a very turbulent environment. It was done for a French MNE that was in the first stages of extending their activities to the Ukraine during the 2008–2009 global crisis. The French MNE needed to validate the timing for an opportunistic move to enter the Ukrainian market and position there.

Instead of internal qualitative questionnaires, a quantitative time-series item-occurrence approach was used. Vector Auto-Regressions (VAR) for data analysis was adopted. One person foreign to the French MNE and the Ukraine conducted the data-gathering. Access to internal data was not available to populate the *product market and demand*, and *competition* dimensions. This was an extreme-case scenario and a departure from the endogenous problem-solving routines implemented in that MNE. It also yielded surprisingly good statistical results. This applied research was very helpful for the MNE. It prevented the firm from entering that country's market at a very turbulent time and gave clear indications of which specific conditions in the Ukrainian market had to be met, and when those conditions were most likely to be met later. The MNE has entered the Ukrainian market later and presently holds a dominant market position there (Tapia Moore, 2012). This study has become the starting point of our PEU2 adaptation efforts.

Adapting PEU Models and Procedures for SMEs

Implementing the PEU2 unadapted could be damaging for SMEs: If the PEU2 were effectively carried out in its initial qualitative form, it would increase IO, generate more uncertainty, and decrease absorptive capacity, the latter being key in maintaining SMEs' proactivity and adaptability, their real competitive advantages. Nonetheless, the PEU models can be used as environmental monitoring checklists. The PEU1 would be best suited for this purpose: It is most comprehensive and allows room for interpreting variables along organizational culture. Care should be taken to avoid conceptual overlap by clearly defining variable semantics first.

With SMEs in mind, the PEU2 reduced-dimensions model has been experimented. A French SME provided the context. Specifically, the SME requested help in providing information on the appropriateness of their foreign market activities and identifying alternative internationalization strategic priorities. They were aware that they needed to adapt to the new market conditions, but did not know how.

SMEs have numerous limitations including manpower. Consequently, PEU quantitative procedures have been administered by a third party foreign to the SME's organizational culture. Quantitative methods are used because the third party unfamiliar with the organizational culture would not know how to interpret and translate signals in a qualitative form valuable to the SME. Inversely, although SMEs usually do employ qualified marketing talent, it may be a challenge for resident marketing teams to implement PEU quantitative procedures and easily interpret the statistics.

In 2012, four countries in different degrees of turbulence were monitored: Argentina, Spain, South Korea, and the Ukraine. Data were gathered by a team of eight people of different nationalities, all foreign to the studied countries, the SME, and its industry.

The results were statistically robust reflecting more than 95 percent of the studied phenomenon. Regarding the prediction capacity of VARs, it was found that a minimum data input of 45 observations were necessary before reaching acceptable results. More than 90 observations allowed for better results.

Using Varimax rotated Factor Analysis for each dimension allowed for better context awareness, context saliency, and a comprehensive understanding of the situation. The results allowed to express the decision-making. Different from the PEU2 in procedure, method, and content, the applied model became the PEU3 (Tapia Moore, 2013).

The SME was able to adapt its international activities by successfully exiting Argentina and entering Spain due to country specificities. It modified the form of its market presence in South Korea due to changes in the legislation concerning foreign investors. The SME has since then consistently outperformed its competitors.

During the 45 to 90 day PEU3 data-collection period, SMEs must still adapt to deal with the effects of uncertainty prompted by environmental turbulence in the SME's management processes and procedures as explained above.

Conclusion

Young, underperforming, ambitious, internationalizing SMEs tend not to experience bias against risky and new activities as a result of re-producing actions that have been successful. The bias experience tends to be reduced whenever failures are more likely to occur. Older, internationalizing outperforming SMEs tend not to share competence gained from experience via internalizing. They have a better chance that a potentially good risky alternative would become extinct before their potential is discovered (Denrell and March, 2001).

The main warning sign of what is now at hand related to COVID-19 pandemic is the *market commitment* paradigm shift depending on the SMEs' *market outlook*. REM managers would implement adaptive learning routines preventing mental blocks in organizations (Jensen, 2001).

The turbulent and highly unpredictable COVID-19 situation in international markets has reset organizations' decision-making and performance. After reset, numerous decisions are required before firms begin to yield new results with a positive impact on performance (Musaji et al., 2020).

SMEs have faced and will continue to face severe needs for changes due to drastic challenges. Environmental turbulence might offer opportunities for those SMEs that could identify and would be able to exploit them.

Having outlined some of the tasks at hand and conditions for success in the internationalizing efforts of SMEs during and post COVID-19, it could be concluded that the COVID-19 pandemic in parallel to causing problems might create some opportunities that have to be well analyzed, identified and pursued appropriately following the above recommended experimented approaches together with other relevant methods.

Notes

1 European Commission recommendation 2003/361/CE: May 3rd, 2003.Statistical criteria: 10 to 249 employees.
2 Neither the INV nor the IP model give indications relative to the way the models are implemented.
3 Date of the arrival of the pandemic in Europe
4 (+p/-f) = Positive past versus negative future = > Negative outlook

References

Ashill, N. J., Jobber, D., 2001. Defining the domain of perceived environmental uncertainty: an exploratory study of senior marketing executives. *J. Mark. Manag.* 17(5/6), 543–558.

Auster, E., Chun Wei, C., 1993. Environmental scanning by CEOs in two Canadian industries. *J. Am. Soc. Inf. Sci.* 44(4), 194–203.

Beer, M., Sven, C., Voelpel, M. L., Eden, B.T., 2005. Strategic management as organizational learning: developing fit and alignment through a disciplined process. *Long. Range Plan.* 38(5), 445–465.

Camic, C., 1992. The matter of habit. In: Zey, M.(Eds.), *Decision Making*. Sage, Newbury Park, VA.

Campbell, A. J., 1996. The effects of internal firm barriers on the export behavior of small firms in a free trade environment. *J. Small Bus. Manag.* 34(3), 50–58.

Cao, L., 2011. Dynamic capabilities in a turbulent market environment: empirical evidence from international retailers in China. *J. Strategic Mark.* 19(5), 455–469.

Denrell, J., March, J.M., 2001. Adaptation as information restriction: the hot stove effect. *Organ. Sci.* 12(5), 523–538.

Devos, G., Buelens, M., Bouckenooghe, D., 2007. Contribution of content, context, and process to understanding openness to organizational change: two experimental simulation studies. *J. Soc. Psychol.* 147(6), 607–630.

Fiegenbaum, A., Hart, S., Schendel, D., 1996. Strategic reference point theory. *Strategic Manag. J.* 17(3), 219–235.

Helfat, C. E., Finkelstein, S., Mitchell, W., Peteraf, M., Singh, H., Teece, D., Winter, S.G., 2007. *Dynamic Capabilities: Understanding Strategic Chance in Organization*. Blackwell Publishing, Oxford.

Herriot, S. R., Levinthal, D., March, J. G., 1985. Learning from experience in organizations. American economic review. *Pap. Proc. 97th Annu. Meet. Am. Economic Assoc.* 75(2), 298–302.

Jansen, J., Frans, J. P., Van Den Bosch, A. J., Volberda, H. W., 2006. Exploratory innovation, exploitative innovation, and performance: effects of organizational antecedents and environmental moderators. *Manag. Sci.* 52(11), 1661–1674.

Jansen, J., Frans, J. P., Van Den Bosch, A. J., Volberda, H. W., 2005. Managing potential and realized absorptive capacity: how do organizational antecedents matter?*Acad. Manag. J.* 48(6), 999–1015.

Jensen, M. C., 2001. *Foundations of Organizational Strategy*. Harvard University Press, Cambridge, MA.

Jensen, M. C., 2003. *A Theory of the Firm*. Harvard University Press, Cambridge, MA.

Johanson, J., Vahlne, J.-E., 1977. The internationalization process of the firm -a model of knowledge development and increasing foreign market commitments. *J. Int. Bus. Stud.* 8(1), 23–32.

Johanson, M., Johanson, J., 2006. Turbulence, discovery and foreign market entry: a longitudinal study of an entry into the Russian market. *Manag. Int. Rev.* 46(2), 179–205.

Lewis, G. J., Harvey, B., 2001. Perceived environmental uncertainty: the extension of miller's scale to the natural environment. *J. Manag. Stud. 38*(2), 201–233.

Lichtenthaler, U., 2009. Absorptive capacity, environmental turbulence, and the complementarity of organizational learning processes. *Acad. Manag. J. 52*(4), 822–846.

March, J. G., 1989. *Decisions and Organizations*. Basil Blackwell, Oxford.

March, J. G., Shapira, Z., 1992. Behavioral decision theory and organizational decision theory. In: Zayed, M. (Ed.), *Decision Making*. Sage, Newbury Park, VA. pp. 273–303.

McKelvie, A., Haynie, J. M., Gustavsson, V., 2011. Unpacking the uncertainty construct: implications for entrepreneurial action. *J. Bus. Venturing 26*(3), 273–292.

Meschi, P.-X., Ricard, A., Tapia Moore, E., 2017. Fast and furious or slow and cautions? The joint impact of age at internationalization, speed, and risk diversity on the survival of exporting firms. *J. Int. Manag. 23*(3), 279–291.

Meschi, P.-X., Ricard, A., Tapia Moore, E., 2020. Pre-internationalization conditions & performance of fist-time exporting SMEs. *Management 24*(4), forthcoming).

Musaji, S., Schulze, W. S., De Castro, J. O., 2020. How long does it take to get to the learning curve? *Acad. Manag. J. 63*(1), 205–223.

Nebus, J., Chai, K. H., 2007. *Overcoming contextual barriers in knowledge transfer: making the 'invisible' salient*. Paper presented at the Academy of Management Annual Meeting Proceedings, Philadelphia, PA, the U.S.A.

Nebus, J., Chai, K. H., 2014. Putting the "psychic" back in psychic distance: awareness, perceptions, and understanding as dimensions of psychic distance. *J. Int. Manag. 20*(1), 8–24.

Oviatt, B. M., McDougall, P. P., 2005. Defining international entrepreneurship and modeling the speed of internationalization. *Entrepreneurship: Theory Pract. 29*(5), 537–553.

Préfontaine, L., Bourgault, M., 2002. Strategic analysis and export behavior of SMEs: a comparison between the United States and Canada. *Int. Small Bus. J. 20*(2), 123–134.

Rieskamp, J., Busemeyer, J. R., Laine, T., 2003. How do people learn to allocate ressources? Comparing two learning theories. *J. Exp. Psychology: Learning, Memory, Cognition 29*(6), 1066–1081.

Roetzel, P. G., 2019. Information overload in the information age: a review of the literature from business administration, business psychology, and related disciplines with a bibliometric approach and framework development, *Business Research 12*(2): 479–522.

Schrader, R. C., Oviatt, B. M., McDougall, P.P., 2000. How new ventures exploit trade-offs among international risk factors: lessons for the accelerated internationalization of the 21st century. *Acad. Manag. J. 43*(6), 1227–1247.

Sund, K. J., 2015. Revisiting organizational interpretation and three types of uncertainty. *Int. J. Organ. Anal. 23*(4), 588–605.

Sund, K. J., Galavan, R. J., Huff, A. S., 2016. *Uncertainty and Strategic Decision Making*. Emerald Group Publishing Ltd, Bingley.

Tapia Moore, E., 2008. *Théorie de l'Agence et internationalisation incrémentale des PME managériales*. Dissertation, Cret-Log, Ecole Doctorale de Sciences Economiques et de Gestion d'Aix Marseille, Faculté des Sciences Economiques, Université de la Méditerranée (Aix-Marseille II), Aix en Provence.

Tapia Moore, E., 2012. *Foreign market entry in turbulent countries: extending the perceived environmental uncertainty 2 measure*, Paper presented at 38th EIBA, Brighton, December 12–14.

Tapia Moore, E., 2013. *Reproducing the Perceived Environmental Uncertainty 3 measure*. 39th European International Business AcademyBremen, Germany, December.

Tapia Moore, E., 2017. Information overload and the internationalization process model: an implementation attempt. *J. Bus.* 9(1), 119–142.

Waldman, D. A., Ramirez, G. G., House, R. J., Puranam, P., 2001. Does leadership matter? CEO leadership attributes and profitability under conditions of perceived environmental uncertainty. *Acad. Manag. J.* 44(1), 134–143.

Werner, S., Brouthers, L. E., Brouthers, K. D., 1996. International risk and perceived environmental uncertainty: the dimensionality and internal consistency of miller's measure. *J. Int. Bus. Stud.* 27(3), 571–587.

Wiseman, R. M., Gomez-Mejia, L. R., 1998. A behavioral agency model of managerial risk taking. *Acad. Manag. Rev.* 23(1), 133–153.

Wolff, J. A., Pett, T. L., 2006. Small-firm performance: modeling the role of product and process improvements. *J. Small Bus. Manag.* 44(2), 268–284.

24 The Power of Social Enterprises

Cooperatives as Partners of Multinational Firms in the Post-Pandemic Recovery

Andrei Kuznetsov and Olga Kuznetsova

The last few years have been marked by growing skepticism in the wide strata of the population across the world towards the process of internationalization and its consequences reinforced by concerns caused by the depletion of natural resources and human-induced climate change. The UK leaving the European Union following a national referendum, President Trump pushing forward a populist protectionist agenda in the U.S.—these are just two conspicuous manifestations of the prevalence of this mood in different parts of the world. COVID-19 has been the latest development that in the minds of many has emphasized the dark side of internationalization leading to greater uncontrollable consequences of interdependence between territories and nations and exposing people within nation-states to forces that appear as alien, overpowering, and therefore sinister and threatening.

These changes create a challenge to multinational corporations (MNCs) that are seen by many as the main protagonists and beneficiaries of globalization. The economic crisis caused by the COVID-19 pandemic is likely to change the business environment in countries around the world in a way that is difficult to predict with any certainty. There is a strong opinion among analysts that the COVID-19 pandemic will re-write the growth scenarios for all national economies, rendering the recovery of regions and well-being of economies and individuals dependent on solutions requiring cooperation and grassroot-level sources of resilience and initiative (OECD, 2020a, 2020b). Taking this argument as a starting point, in this essay we consider a category of economic agents whose role and influence in the economy and society may increase, making them an important component of the business environment, and yet until now, they have remained mostly ignored by the mainstream international business (IB) literature, even though their impact can be powerful (UN, 2013; Stiglitz, 2009; WCM, 2018). They are organizations that originate in the cooperative sector or prioritize social solidarity and community-focused commitments, e.g., workers' cooperatives, mutual benefit societies and social enterprises. In many countries, the unprecedented societal disruptions from COVID-19 have highlighted the prominence of these organizations, as they have been able to provide a particularly prompt response to the economic and social calamities of the pandemic (International Labor Organization, 2020). On many occasions, as pointed by Vieta and Duguid (2020), they responded sooner and more concretely than the national or local leaders, as well as large businesses. In Canada, for example, grocery cooperatives innovated employee safety and salary top-up while workers' cooperatives quickly shifted to producing medical products, and credit unions offered far-reaching grants to community groups, loan deferrals and even zero-interest credit cards (Vieta and Duguid, 2020). These organizations proved to be especially efficient in terms of the mobilization and creation of community assets to boost the resilience of local economies. The COVID-19 crisis has destroyed many of the 'givens' of our social and economic structures and societal fabric, leaving a knowledge gap as to how they can be replaced. The argument of this chapter is that MNCs and governments may turn the current challenge into an opportunity by recognizing the role and potential of these organizations, constituting the so-called social and solidarity economy, within the changing business environment.

Following an influential paper by Johanson and Vahlne (2009), there is growing recognition in the IB literature that the business environment should be viewed as a web of relationships, a network, rather than as a neoclassical market with many independent suppliers and customers. This perspective emphasizes the key role of the surrounding business environment, the importance of identifying and joining existing networks and creating new ones. This may be a serious challenge considering that networks of relationship that constitute the modern business environment are complex, exist at different levels (national, regional, local) and have various patterns. What follows from this analysis is the prominence of both general and market-specific knowledge as a means to identify relevant networks. A recent development in research on the business environment within the IB field is the appearance of papers that attempt to achieve a more nuanced understanding by unpacking the local, subnational context (Monaghan et al., 2014). This perspective is going to gain in importance, in our opinion, because of the evidence of local communities in different parts of the world seeking to increase their role and take back control to ensure that they have a fair share of the benefits of local growth.

One prominent example of this trend may be found in the United Kingdom in the form of the so-called Preston model named after a city in England. It is a regional development program led by the Preston city council, anchor institutions (the term refers to large, typically non-profit organizations like hospitals and universities, unlikely to move once established) and other partners. At its heart is a procurement policy that requires local authorities and the anchor institutions to prioritize local supplies, in particular small and medium firms, to prevent the wealth created being siphoned out of the locality by profit-seeking external commercial actors. This is achieved, for example, by splitting large orders into smaller lots that these firms can handle. Thus, the local university, one of the anchor institutions, required non-local contractors to sub-contract to local firms to develop its GBP200 million campus masterplan. In so doing, the university applied its spending power to advance community wealth building within Preston and the wider Lancashire area. Overall, spending by the institutions that signed to the project increased from GBP38 million in 2012–2013 to GBP112 million in 2016-2017 in the city of Preston and from GBP289 million to GBP489 million in the wider district of Lancashire (Sheffield, 2019).

The Preston model has attracted much attention and scrutiny in the country and abroad (there was even an article in The New-York Times) as an example of a city taking back control but the trend it represents is not limited to the UK. In fact, the Preston council has reproduced the ideas and principles first developed and implemented in Cleveland, Ohio by the organization The Democracy Collaborative. This strategy has two noteworthy characteristics relevant to the operation of MNCs. First, redirecting local spending on area businesses in order to keep more money in the community rather than sending it away to big corporations and international retailers with no vested local interest. Second, the focus on creating collaborative, inclusive, sustainable, and democratically controlled local economies. This has resulted in strengthening of the importance and influence of certain categories of local players such as cooperatives and their networks as well as other organizations based on principles of participatory economy. The Preston model, for example, envisages the creation of a network of worker-owned cooperatives in the catering, tech, and digital sectors to fill the supply side gap where the anchor institutions are unable to spend locally for lack of local providers.

Although almost two hundred years in existence, cooperatives have mostly managed to avoid the attention of IB scholars. Our search of two leading IB journals, the Journal of International Business Studies and the Journal of World Business, has failed to identify any publications dealing with cooperatives in the last 20 years. This contrasts with the substantial presence of cooperative enterprises in the world economy. According to the latest available data, at least 12 percent of people on earth is a co-operator of any of the three million cooperatives in existence. Cooperatives provide jobs or work opportunities to 10 percent of the employed population, and the 300 largest co-operatives or mutuals generate US$ 2,034.98 billion in turnover (International Cooperative Alliance, no data). Cooperatives are prominent in agriculture, food processing, banking and financial services, insurance, retail, utilities, health and social care, information technologies and crafts, and are widely present on both developed and developing countries. The rate of growth of the cooperative sector is ascending and their share in the global economy is reaching 15 percent. In the EU, for example, co-operatives have a 60 percent share in the processing and marketing of agricultural commodities. Overall, there are nearly 180,000 cooperative enterprises in Europe with more than 4.5 million employees and more than €1,000 billion in annual turnover (Cooperatives Europe, 2016). In the U.S., the cooperative sector represents over US$500 billion in revenues and employs about two million people (Deller et al. 2009). The cooperative enterprises are feeders into many global supply chains. In spite of such prominence, the cooperative business model has been 'off the research radar' for some years. This created gaps in a systematic scholarly analysis of this form of entrepreneurship, its dynamics and the place that it occupies in international business relations. Encouragingly, there are modern thinkers and public intellectuals, including Nobel Prize laureates, who argue in favor of market plurality and endorse the cooperative model as a viable and promising alternative to market orthodoxy.[1]

According to the Statement of Cooperative Identity (SCI) endorsed by the International Cooperative Alliance, an apex body of the cooperative movement, a cooperative is an autonomous association of persons united voluntarily to meet their common economic, social and cultural needs and aspirations through a jointly owned and democratically controlled enterprise. There are different types of cooperatives of which consumers' cooperatives and worker cooperatives are the most widespread. Consumers' cooperatives operate as a form of mutual aid and often take the form of retail outlets owned and operated by their consumers. Worker cooperatives are essentially businesses in which the employees contribute both capital and labor. Cooperatives are not a charity and cannot survive for long without a profit. For this reason, they should not be viewed as a 'not-for-profit' entity. Importantly, though, the cooperative is an association of persons and not of capital. Consequently, the cooperative differs from the conventional investor-owned business through its focus on delivering economic and social benefits to members according to the values of solidarity and social justice (Mazzarol, 2012), which makes them more than a commercial enterprise. Their organization and governance are defined by adherence to the internationally agreed principles of participatory democracy embodied in the SCI—voluntary and open membership, democratic member control; member economic participation; autonomy and independence; education, training, and information; cooperation among cooperatives; and concern for the community. Their purpose is to meet the needs of the members and the community rather than to maximize the wealth of shareholders. This is reflected in how co-operatives are managed: all members have equal voting rights regardless of the amount of capital they put into the enterprise. Together with mutual societies and many other association-based economic entities co-operatives operate business activities with the specific objective of promoting the wider well-being of society (Ridley-Duff and Bull, 2015; UN, 2013).

Driven by values and not just profit, cooperatives display characteristics that make them distinctive and secure a strong position at the local and regional levels. The central tenet of cooperative ethos is stake holding. Cooperative members benefit from their participation in the organization and how they use its assets rather than from income on invested capital. This changes the balance of values that influences decision-making and shifts focus towards aspects that normally are not prioritized by public corporations. To begin with, there is a strong sense of local identity and belonging. To join a cooperative all members must contribute some seed capital, but there are no absentee owners as in most cases cooperative members are also the employees of the cooperative. Because cooperatives are not owned by shareholders, the economic and social benefits of their activity stay in the communities where they are established. Profits generated are either reinvested in the enterprise or returned to the members. In some countries, e.g., Italy, the legislation does not allow cooperatives to operate in multiple areas and thereby force them to remain locally focused, bringing cooperatives close to the community, which they serve and of which they are a part. This is most evident in the case of social cooperatives in Italy, 'general interest cooperatives' in France and social solidarity cooperatives in Portugal where the primary purpose is to benefit the community through the delivery of essential services in interaction with the local authorities, including social, educational and work integration services (Borzaga et al. 2017).

Cooperatives tend to be small. This makes them face difficulties familiar to many other small and medium enterprises (SME), for example, acquiring financing from banks, who tend to see SMEs as high risk and prefer larger businesses with a long track record of profitability (Canales and Nanda, 2012). The fact that they are not strictly profit-oriented makes it difficult for cooperatives to access financial markets. In addition, they often face prejudice and misunderstanding on the part of mainstream businesses, which narrows their opportunities to have dealings outside the cooperative sector. Cooperatives, however, have an advantage over other types of SMEs: the shared values that create a strong foundation for solidarity within the wider cooperative movement. This naturally directs cooperatives to establish regional and national networks often formalized as federations and associations so that they can remain small and locally based but have the economies of scale and specialist services to make them competitive. In Italy, the apex organization Legacoop and numerous associations offer a range of services including accountancy consulting, training and marketing. On the other side of the globe, Cooperative Business New Zealand provides its members assistance with education and training, advocacy and lobbying, cooperation among cooperatives and starting up a cooperative. In Latin America, cooperatives are a leading force in fair trade producer networks (Moore, 2004).

The power of the participative economy and cooperative networking is illustrated by the example of the Mondragon Cooperative Corporation in the Basque Country in Spain. It currently consists of 102 federated cooperatives employing over 73,000 people. The vast majority of these worker-owners are in the industrial and distribution segments of the economy, competing successfully in global markets. In addition, the Mondragon cooperative system owns its own bank, university, a social welfare agency, several business incubators and a supermarket chain. This makes Mondragon the largest employer in the region and one of the largest companies in the country, breaking the mould of traditional assertions that portray cooperatives as small, marginal and inefficient. In 2017, it had annual revenues of over €12 billion—equivalent to those of Kellogg's or Visa. It is active in mechanical engineering, automotive, finance, retail and infrastructure construction. Despite its size, the network is managed on the same principle – one member one vote – as any organization subscribing to the International Cooperative Alliance's Statement on the Cooperative Identity. This helps all employees to maintain a bond with the organization and the cooperative economy as whole, making it strong and resilient. This principle of inter-cooperation when cooperatives help and support each other through networking plays an essential role in the cooperative sector and is one of its strengths. When in the wake of the 2008 financial crisis, Fagor Electrodomésticos, the largest of the industrial cooperatives in the Basque Country, had to be liquidated, most of its 1,800 worker-owners were relocated to other cooperatives within the Mondragon federation. This is just one example of the major contribution of the social and solidarity economy in preserving employment and the well-being of local communities and thus preserving conditions for own existence and growth. This explains to an extent their vitality: Canadian research shows that after five years, 62 percent of cooperatives are still in business compared with only 35 percent of traditional businesses (MEDIE, 2008).

There are also changes in the structure of the market to be considered that increase the economic role of the organizations composing the social and solidarity economy. These changes are associated with an increase in demand for health, social and cultural services against the background of a decline of the welfare state in many countries. Such services are often labor intensive, while at the same time it is difficult to reduce the cost of labor through technological innovation and automation. As a result, conventional firms often find the provision of these services commercially unattractive. Cooperatives and other social solidarity organizations operate on different principles. For them, this is an opportunity for growth. Over the past few years, these organizations have been extremely dynamic, growing faster than the rest of the economy in many countries and demonstrating a good capacity for innovation, as evidenced by their ability to find new solutions to social problems (Borzaga et al., 2017).

There is another feature of modern cooperatives of particular relevance to the current economic slump caused by the COVID-19 pandemic: the well-documented anti-cyclical pattern of the economic behavior of cooperatives, as evidenced by their resilience in times of economic crisis (Birchall and Ketilson, 2009; Stiglitz, 2009). The analysis of the impact of the financial crisis of 2007–2008 reveals that worker and social cooperatives in Europe overall showed more resilience than conventional enterprises of a similar size, active in the same sectors and present in the same communities and regions (Roelants et al., 2012). This is because, entre alia, these organizations will strive to maintain employment and quality of service for their members and customers, even by reducing their profits as social economy organizations tend to give precedence to people and labor over capital in the distribution of incomes (Borzaga et al., 2014). Another reason is the reduced dependence of these organizations on the financial markets and the socialized nature of its capital, which has allowed them to suffer a lower pressure in the financial crisis. In fact, research shows that during and after crises the number of c-operatives increases (Roelants et al. 2012).

In many countries cooperatives, therefore, are staples of the local economy; they generate productive and social fabric in their areas and communities (Bretos and Marcuello, 2017). The innate focus on societal good, community well-being and social capital building embedded in the cooperative business format grants the cooperative economy legitimacy, which big corporations only aspire to achieve spending millions on Corporate Social Responsibility and self-promotion. Cooperatives are no universal remedy and have their issues and contradictions. However, what matters in the context of IB research is this: as a business model, cooperatives are everything that MNCs and their usual business counter-agents are not. Cooperatives are locally anchored, egalitarian and democratic, adhere to the distribution of wealth based on solidarity, strongly networked, collaborative. MNCs are footloose, bureaucratic and hierarchic; they prioritize creating wealth for shareholders.

MNCs can exploit these differences when looking for a response to the challenges of post-COVID-19 business environment which is likely to demand a more local and regional modus operandi in terms of supply chains and business models reflecting the need of a new balance between efficiency and resilience.[2] One key element of resilience is increasing diversity (Nieuwenhuis and Lammgård, 2013; Walker and Salt, 2012). By forging relations with locally rooted and community-oriented organizations such as cooperatives, they can improve their image and better integrate into the economy, in particular at the local level, expand and diversify the cohort of business partners and, accordingly, the spectrum of business opportunities. This will mitigate the risk of alienation caused by the anti-global and pro-local sentiment in host countries, and open new routes to establishing contacts with important existing grassroots networks, which might be a path for MNC to overcome the 'liability of foreignness' by becoming 'more local'.

Notes

1 Among them are N. Chomsky, A. Sen, J. Stiglitz, E. Olsen. For details, see Stiglitz, J. D. 2009. Moving beyond market fundamentalism to a more balanced economy. Ann. Public Coop. Econ. 80(3): 345–360.
2 Toyota, often presented as an example of efficiency due to its lean manufacturing system, was forced to rethink its procurement strategy after the 2011 earthquake and tsunami in Tohoku. A supply chain audit revealed that Toyota's supply chain actually had several potential vulnerabilities due to the prioritization of efficiency. It turned out, for example, many single suppliers of key components were located in high-risk earthquake zones. At the same time, there were no backup provisions because of the desire to eliminate all duplication and redundancy in the production process. Source: Matsuo, H. 2015. Implications of the Tohoku earthquake for Toyota's coordination mechanism: supply chain disruption of automotive semiconductors. Int. J. Prod. Econ. 161, pp. 217–227.

References

Birchall, J., Ketilson, L. H., 2009. *Resilience of the Co-operative Business Model in Times of Crisis*. International Labour Organisation, Geneva.

Borzaga, C., Bodini, R., Carini, C., Depedri, S., Galera, G., Salvatori, G., 2014. Europe in transition: the role of social cooperatives and social enterprises. Euricse Working Papers No. 69|14.

Borzaga, C., Salvatori, G., Bodini, R., 2017. Social and Solidarity Economy and the Future of Work. Euricse Working Paper for the ILO/ International Labor Office. Geneva: International Labor Organization.

Bretos, I., Marcuello, C., 2017. Revisiting globalization challenges and opportunities in the development of cooperatives. *Ann. Public. Cooperative Econ.* 88(1), 47–73.

Canales, R., Nanda, R., 2012. A darker side to decentralized banks: market power and credit rationing in SME lending. *J. Financial Econ. 105*(2), 353–366.

Cooperatives Europe, 2016. The power of cooperation – Cooperatives Europe key figures Brussels. Available from: https://coopseurope.coop/sites/default/files/The %20power%20of%20Cooperation%20-%20Cooperatives%20Europe%20key %20statistics%202015.pdf (accessed 07.05.20.).

Deller, S., Hoyt, A., Sundaram-Stukel, B. H. R., 2009. *Research on the Economic Impact of Cooperatives*. University of Wisconsin Centre for Cooperatives, Madison, WI.

International Cooperative Alliance, (n. d.). *ICA facts and figures*. Available from: https://www.ica.coop/en/cooperatives/facts-and-figures (accessed 09.06.20.).

International Labor Organization, 2020. *Cooperatives and wider SSE enterprises respond to COVID-19 disruptions, and government measures are being put in place.* ILO Office, Geneva. Available from: https://www.ilo.org/global/topics/cooperatives/news/WCMS_740254/lang--en/index.htm.

International Labor Organization, 2013. *Resilience in a downturn: The power of financial co-operatives.* ILO Office, Geneva.

Johanson, J., Vahlne, J. E., 2009. The Uppsala internationalization process model revisited: From liability of foreignness to liability of outsidership. *J. Int. Bus. Stud.* 40(9), 1411–1431.

Mazzarol, T., 2012. Co-operatives and social enterprise: are they a replacement for mainstream capitalism?. Available from: https://theconversation.com/co-operatives-and-social-enterprise-are-they-a-replacement-for-mainstream-capitalism-10520 (accessed 11.06.20.).

MEDIE, 2008. Survival rate of co-operatives in Québec. Available from: https://ccednet-rcdec.ca/files/ccednet/pdfs/2008-Quebec_Co-op_Survival_Report_Summary.pdf (accessed 09.01.20.).

Monaghan, S., Gunnigle, P., Lavelle, J., 2014. Courting the multinational: subnational institutional capacity and foreign market insidership. *J. Int. Bus. Stud.* 45(2), 131–150.

Moore, G., 2004. The fair trade movement: parameters, issues and future research. *J. Bus. Ethics* 53(1–2), 73–86.

Nieuwenhuis, P., Lammgård, C., 2013. Industrial ecology as an ecological model for business: diversity and firm survival. *Prog. Ind. Ecology, an. Int. J.* 8(3), 189–204.

OECD, 2020a. *OECD Interim Economic Assessment Coronavirus. The World Economy at Risk.* Available from: https://www.oecd.org/berlin/publikationen/Interim-Economic-Assessment-2-March-2020.pdf. (accessed 30.05.20.).

OECD, 2020b. Tackling the coronavirus (COVID-19): contributing to a global effort. Available from: <http://www.oecd.org/coronavirus/en/> (accessed on 30.05.20.).

Ridley-Duff, R., Bull, M., 2015. *Understanding Social Enterprise: Theory and Practice.* SAGE Publications Ltd, London.

Roelants, B., Dovgan, D., Eum, H. and Terrasi, E., 2012. The resilience of the co-operative model. How worker cooperatives, social cooperatives and other worker-owned enterprises respond to the crisis and its consequences. Available from: https://www.ess-europe.eu/sites/default/files/report_cecop_2012_en_web.pdf (accessed 09.06.20.).

Sheffield, H., 2019. A British town's novel solution to austerity. *The Atlantic.* Available from: https://www.theatlantic.com/international/archive/2019/05/british-town-local-economy/588943/ (accessed 12.04.20.).

Stiglitz, J. D., 2009. Moving beyond market fundamentalism to a more balanced economy. *Ann. Public. Cooperative Econ.* 80(3), 345–360.

UN, 2013. Co-operatives in social development and the observance of the International Year of Co-operatives. Report of the Secretary-General A/68/168. Available from: http://daccess-dds-ny.un.org/doc/UNDOC/GEN/N13/402/80/PDF/N1340280.pdf?OpenElement (accessed 20.03.20.).

Vieta, M., Duguid, F., 2020. Canada's co-operatives: helping communities during and after the coronavirus. Available from: https://theconversation.com/canadas-co-operatives-helping-communities-during-and-after-the-coronavirus-135477 (accessed 09.03.20.).

Walker, B., Salt, D., 2012. *Resilience thinking: sustaining ecosystems and people in a changing world.* Island press, Washington, D. C.

WCM, 2018. The 2018 world cooperative monitor. Available from: https://monitor.coop/sites/default/files/publication-files/wcm2018-web-803416144.pdf (accessed 09.03.20.).

Part VII

Geographic Perspectives of COVID-19 Impacts on International Business

25 China Gets Triple Hit by COVID-19

Shuquan He, Maria Elo, Xiaotian Zhang, and Julia Zhang

Introduction

After its outbreak in late 2019, COVID-19 has spread across the world. It has had a huge multidimensional influence on the world economy and international business. Being one of the world leading economies and a major player in international business, China itself was the first to start experiencing the harsh consequences of the health pandemic. In this chapter, we argue that China has been triple hit by the COVID-19 pandemic as it has caused a major trade shock, an investment shock and a business environment shock.

To date, the globalized economies are interconnected by international trade, which makes trade an important vehicle for international contagion (WTO, 2020). Globalization and economic shocks are underpinned by a variety of forces affecting economic and societal changes creating a domino effect in global production networks (Dicken, 2007; Hertz, 1999; Rodrik, 2018). The shock in the Chinese trade triggered by COVID-19 came directly and indirectly. The direct shock came in the first two months of 2020 when COVID-19 broke out in China. Initially, it caused a massive confusion that was quickly followed by the mobilized response of the country's highly organized system of healthcare provision. The second wave came as COVID-19 started spreading in Europe and America, followed by almost all other regions and countries in the world.

Apart from international trade, inward or outward foreign direct investment (FDI), has been another important channel connecting the global economy and driving the remarkable Chinese economic growth (Dicken, 2007; UNCTAD, 2020b). The impact of the COVID-19 pandemic on China's overseas investments has been rather negative as FDI and other overseas investments substantially decreased in the first quarter of 2020 (OECD, 2020b).

The COVID-19 pandemic is changing the way business is conducted worldwide. As a result, Chinese companies are now confronted with a new international business environment that is moving away from globalization that had been creating opportunities for firms from emerging economies to grow their presence in global markets. Instead, there is a rise of institutional constraints, greater role of government regulation and restrictions of FDI, and resurgence of nationalism in assessing the activities and role of FDI. For instance, there are nine countries, including the U.S., modifying their laws and regulations on restricting inward FDI mostly targeting FDI from Chinese companies. Such a change in the FDI investment climate represents a big challenge to the Chinese economy, which for several decades has been export and outward FDI oriented and this orientation has been the source of revenue, but more so of new technologies and know-how, market and product/service development knowledge, capacity development and learning in international networks and partnerships. This change will account for the most serious blow to the Chinese economy that will be deeper and last longer than the other two thumps.

COVID-19 has exposed the vulnerability of the world economy to external systemic shocks. It is undisputable that the virus affects the immune system and cells in human beings and as such, it knows no geographical borders. Hence, it has hit one of the most important capitals for each economy, the human one. This blow has affected human capital not only in terms of health, but even more so in terms of its provision of labor for the production and delivery of products and services; its travel, socialization and psychological needs, consumption patterns, and the fundamental need for own survival. While the 2008–2009 financial crises hit the financial capital in a dramatic manner and thus affected the lives of millions of people, the magnitude and effects on human beings of the current pandemic is by far much greater. As a consequence, the economic recession from the pandemic is global and will prove to be rather severe with consequences for all countries and regions in the world.

In an interdependent and connected global economy with global production networks and supply chains so far driven by the search for efficiency gains, no country has been and could be self-sufficient – no matter how powerful or advanced it may be. Thus, despite of the massive decoupling of production, logistics and capital flows it seems that the needed solutions to the pandemic and to economic recovery must be international and global, or at least regional.

China's position as a global work bank and a central actor in global production networks puts high pressure on its actions. Confronted with the trade conflict with the U.S. and the Covid-19 pandemic, Chinese response has been unswervingly to expand its opening up to the outside world thus contributing to the recovery of the world economy. Diverse estimations on global trade and investment show how the great economic uncertainty and vulnerability of global manufacturing chains and the collapse of a diverse range of service provisions have led to substantially lower dynamics, value and volume of global trade and investment flows. Moreover, the recent environmental dynamics have changed views on distance and national interests, which will have a long-term effect on the Chinese economy. Next, the chapter will review the developments regarding different types of shocks.

International Trade Shocks

The outbreak of COVID-19 has badly hit global trade. IMF's recent economic outlook projected that the global economy would contract sharply by at least 3 percent in 2020 (IMF, 2020). In addition, in May 2020, WTO predicted that the world merchandise trade would plummet by between 13 and 32 percent and nearly all regions would suffer a double-digit decline in trade volumes in 2020 (WTO, 2020). Such predictions are also indicative of the direct and indirect shocks to China's international trade. In the first months of COVID-19 in China, the domestic supply was disrupted due to business shutdown, which dramatically affected the existing supply capacity to international markets and in effect led to a massive cancelation of international orders. Cancellation of orders had a snowball effect, especially for companies entirely oriented towards exporting. Subsequent restrictions on the movement of people, goods and services, as well as containment measures such as factory closures emaciated manufacturing and domestic demand (OECD, 2020a). Furthermore, as COVID-19 hit Europe, the U.S. and the rest of the world, it shut down a large range of economic activities. The widely introduced national measures to control the spread of COVID-19 accompanied by business lockdown constricted international demand for Chinese products. As countries across the world are still in the heart of the COVID-19 pandemic, Chinese businesses that have started gradually to resume production have faced dwindling demand for their output and fewer international orders compared to pre-COVID-19 levels.

The indirect blow of COVID-19 on the Chinese economy is attributed to the interconnected global supply chains (Haddad, 2007). When trade patterns are simple, the transmission vectors are also simple. A drop in one nation's income will reduce imports from its trading partners, and a supply disruption in one nation's production shows up as a reduction in its exports to its trade partners. However, world trade is not simple anymore. Since the mid to late 1980s, global supply chains have multiplied into complex networks, which complicates the propagation of shocks. Direct supply disruptions have hindered production and supply dramatically since COVID-19 burst in the world's manufacturing heartland and spread fast to the other industrial giants. Supply chain contagion has amplified the direct supply shocks as manufacturing sectors in less-affected nations find it harder and/or more expensive to acquire necessary imported industrial inputs from the hard-hit nations, and subsequently from each other. An example of this is the situation in the global automotive industry. It has been sourcing parts from China and as a reaction to COVID-19 had to close down factories in South Korea and across Europe and the Americas for several weeks as it was unable to receive parts needed for production, thus, spreading this effect on closures of supplier plants across the world. Meanwhile, sales of cars to end consumers and business customers largely collapsed.

Consequently, Chinese trade has faced a 'two-sided shock' on both the demand and supply side. On the one hand, export orders have been decreasing or canceled as almost all of China's trading partners are suffering from the pandemic and international demand has shrank. On the other hand, global supply chains are blocked; there are difficulties in importing raw materials and spare parts; and the international supply capacity for various inputs in a diverse range of sectors is significantly undermined. A survey by the magazine 'Import and Export Managers' in March and April 2020 showed that:

"– 45.6 percent of the companies engaged in international trade were heavily affected by the COVID-19 pandemic and just managing to survive,

– 27.2 percent of the firms were seriously affected, suffering immense economic losses from their operations, and

– only about 25.3 percent of the companies claimed that they were less affected, but still experiencing difficulties in operation (Li, 2020)".

The massive demand, supply and sourcing problems have brought about significant negative effects on Chinese exports and imports. According to Chinese customs' statistics, only during the first four months of 2020, the total value of China's imports and exports was US$1.3 trillion, with a decline of 7.5 percent as compared with the same period in 2019. Exports decreased by 9 percent, while imports decreased by 5.9 percent. The trade surplus reached only US$58.23 billion, a decrease of 32.6 percent. (Ministry of Commerce of China, 2020c).

Looking from a firm-level perspective, Chinese exporters across various sectors are suffering from a series of unexpected fluctuations and hurdles in their cross-border activities. Their internationalization patterns are nonlinear with a series of both voluntary and involuntary de- and re-internationalizations. Previous research (Zhang and Larimo, 2013; Zhang et al. 2020) indicates that Chinese firms, particularly export-intensive ones, adopt different strategies when faced with radical changes affecting their internationalization process. Chinese firms with accumulated foreign market experiential knowledge in general perform better financially and can cope more successfully with unexpected fluctuations of orders from foreign clients (Zhang, 2013; Tsukanova and Zhang, 2019). Compared with the previous global financial crisis in 2008, the current COVID-19-related impact on Chinese exporters is immediate and radical. It is too early to evaluate the cumulative final impact, however, it is already evident that Chinese firms with higher level of foreign market experiential knowledge are preparing for foreign market selective re-entry; while the rest are more likely to adopt a strategy of re-focusing on the demand for their products and services in the Chinese domestic market.

International Investment Shock

The global spread of COVID-19 is strongly affecting foreign direct investment (FDI). The recent Global Investment Trends Monitor, published in April this year, predicted a drastic drop in global FDI flows – up to 40 percent in 2020–2021, thus, reaching the lowest level in the past two decades. (UNCTAD, 2020b)

International inward and outward FDI has been a key pillar of Chinese economic growth in the last few decades. The impact of the COVID-19 pandemic on China's overseas investment is manifold. In the first quarter of 2020, the contract value of service outsourcing undertaken by Chinese enterprises was RMB237.3 billion, and the executed value was RMB161.04 billion, showing a decrease of 18 percent and 10.6 percent respectively, while the executed value was RMB99.12 billion – down by 17.9 percent and 6.7 percent year-on-year change. In USD, the contracted value of offshore service outsourcing was US$21.58 billion and the executed value was US$14.53 billion – down respectively by 19.9 percent and 7.6 percent year-on-year change (Ministry of Commerce of China, 2020b, 2020d). According to data released by the Chinese Ministry of Commerce in April 2020, China's non-financial FDI in the first quarter was US$24.22 billion, a 3.9 percent decrease on year-on-year basis. In 2020, the novel coronavirus pandemic affected FDI and the actual use of foreign capital in the first quarter was RMB216.2 billion, a decrease of 10.8 percent, which is equivalent to US$31.2 billion or a decrease by 12.8 percent compared to the same period in 2019. In March, the actual use of foreign investment in China was RMB81.78 billion, i.e., a fall by 14.1 percent year on year. (Ministry of Commerce of China, 2020a)

International Business Environment Shock

Already before the COVID-19 ignited pandemic, there have been several debates in the World Trade Organization and on national levels, e.g., in the U.S., regarding the increasingly important role of China in international trade. As part of these debates there have been heated discussions about the extent to which global supply and production depends on China, what vulnerabilities have been created and what this kind of vulnerabilities mean for global production and consumption, as well as for nation states. The role of China as a context and a major source of world inputs for many industries is now debated and being reconsidered as industries have realized the critical exposure of their manufacturing and sourcing operations and have come to evaluate anew national pressures on macro-meso- and firm-level strategy (Costantino and Pellegrino, 2010; Xu and Meyer, 2013). Reflecting on the disadvantages of offshoring, re-shoring and near-shoring have been promoted as solutions alleviating distance-related disruptions and improving sustainability aspects (Ashby, 2016; Bock, 2008; Ellram et al., 2013).

It is clear that the COVID-19 pandemic will change the way businesses behave. Chinese businesses are exposed to the changing international business environment as perceptions on China's roles are shifting. Looking back to the past months, the initial instinctive reaction to COVID-19 in most countries was to look inwards and mobilize re-sources and actions nationally. For example, France and Germany banned sales of vital hospital equipment outside their national borders in March. Export protectionism has become a dominant COVID-19 re-sponse measure. The United Kingdom, South Korea, Brazil, India, Turkey, Russia and dozens of other countries have restricted or even banned for a while foreign sales of medical supplies, pharmaceuticals, agricultural produce and even food. As an outcome of the pandemic, borders have been closed, supply chains have been disrupted, and re-gional economic activity has fallen. These made nation states inward-looking and closed, which coupled with the other effects of COVID-19 lead to a deep economic recession in the whole world (United Nations, 2020). While measuring human mobility and migration can be useful for tackling COVID-19, the measures also extend to the mobility of entrepreneurs and business people, in the long-term influencing their ability to conduct business, venture and generate economic development (e.g., Elo et al., 2019; Sirkeci and Yücesahin, 2020). The business environment shock extends beyond COVID-19 measures altering the nature of transnational activities, human mobility, business- and poli-tical strategizing. In order to prevent foreign countries from 'taking the opportunity to acquire key national assets and technologies', many countries and regional integration blocs, such as the European Union (EU), Australia, India, Spain and so on, have recently introduced in-vestment regulations on FDI, many of which refer to China. This hap-pens at a time when Europe's biggest economy, as well as the EU as a whole, is reconsidering relations with China in the face of increased investment in critical sectors of the European economy by Chinese state-owned enterprises (Kraemer and Rinke, 2020). On March 25, 2020, the European Commission issued guidelines on FDI and the free flow of capital extending the protection of EU strategic asset acquisition to all Member States. The guidelines are supposedly novel coronavirus-justified, and are aimed at the acquisition of strategic assets by foreign investors before the possible implementation of the EU foreign investment review ordinance. The EU foreign investment review regulation has a direct effect on all EU member states and will be enforced on October 11, 2020.

Australia took action on March 29, 2020 by lowering the key acquisition threshold from a \$1.2 billion (US\$736 million) to zero to ensure that any foreign acquisition offer is reviewed by federal officials. The countries covered by this reviewed threshold include China. Australian media said that the rule will be imposed on the occasion of a sharp fall in the Australian stock market and public concerns over predatory acquisitions. On April 18, 2020, Canada issued a policy statement saying that, as in the case of other major economies, the epidemic has reduced the valuation of many Canadian enterprises. This may lead to 'opportunistic investment behavior' and hence FDI into Canada will require approval.

On April 18, 2020, India announced that it would revise its foreign investment policy, stipulating that 'any investor from a country bordering India' could only invest under the government access path, which greatly increased the difficulty of investment in India by enterprises from a country bordering India, including China. The announcement explains the purpose of the revised legislation: to curb the acquisition of Indian enterprises in the context of the COVID-19 epidemic. As of December 2019, China's cumulative investment in India exceeded US\$8 billion, which was far greater than the combined value of the FDI in India by several other countries with a border with India.

The impact of this policy on Chinese investors is self-evident. The newly erected FDI barriers to investors in specific countries not only violate the non-discriminatory principles of WTO, but also run against the general direction of trade and investment liberalization and facilitation. They do not conform to the consensus of the G20 leaders and trade ministers on safeguarding a free, fair, non-discriminatory, transparent, predictable and stable trade and investment environment, and maintaining market openness. This will be a big challenge to the Chinese economy, which will need a thorough review of its positioning and strategies. As the largest trade partner of China is the U.S., the U.S. Department of Commerce has made a series of amendments to the relevant articles of Export Administration Regulations (EAR). The new rules deal with military and civilian dual-usage equipment, technologies and products, strengthening export restrictions on some products related to U.S. national security. These rules have affected many Chinese companies, among which is the non-state owned Huawei. These new regulations will further aggravate the difficulties for China's imports and even for the production of related products, and bring a severe test to the development of China's related industries. In order to implement export controls, the U.S. has formulated a 'commerce control list' (CCL) according to law. CCL is divided into ten categories, including nuclear materials, chemicals and microorganisms, material processing, electronic products, computers, communication and information security, sensors and lasers, navigation and avionics, ocean exploration, aviation and propulsion systems. In addition to CCL, the U.S. has also prepared an 'entity list'. Companies and enterprises included in the list of entities will be subject to more stringent and extensive export controls than those stipulated by CCL. Since 2019, Huawei and its 114 related enterprises have been included in the entity list. It is for this reason that some American companies no longer sell software and parts to China, which has forced Huawei to adopt a strategic reorientation and start relying on domestic or other countries' software and parts. On May 22, 2020, the U.S. added 20 more Chinese companies to the entity list (Zhu, 2020).

In addition, the U.S. issued three new rules, aimed at the policy of China's military civilian integration and tightened the control on China's exports, including the activities of Huawei and its related companies. The new rules add provisions for China's military end users as previously, there were no export restrictions for them. Under the new rules, if the products are exported to China's "military end-users" or if there is a risk of being acquired by China's 'military end-users', then these exports will also be subject to U.S. export controls. The new rules remove a series of license exceptions for civil end-users enjoyed by the importing countries, including China, Russia and Venezuela. In other words, even if these products are exported to China for civil use, the exporter now needs to obtain an export license before exporting the products. Previously, semiconductor production equipment, computers, telecommunications equipment, acoustic and optical equipment and materials, ship systems and civil aircraft engine production equipment exported to China could have license exceptions. Now that these exceptions have been removed, exporters of these products will need to apply for export licenses and obtain approval before they can export to China. The new regulations, set especially for Huawei and its related enterprises, expand the scope of application of the 'provisions on foreign direct products'. According to the new regulations, if Huawei or its related enterprises (including Hisilicon) listed in the 'entity list' use software and technology regulated by the U.S. to directly produce semiconductor design and other products, or other overseas companies (mainly Taiwan Semiconductor Manufacturing Company (TSMC)) use American production equipment to produce products (including chips) designed by Huawei and related enterprises (including Hisilicon), these products can only be re-exported, exported from abroad, or transferred to China after obtaining an export license from the Industrial Security Bureau of the Ministry of Commerce.

The upsurge of these recent measures is a stark reminder of the ban imposed by the U.S. Congress in 1947 on technology exports to the

Soviet bloc countries, which in the 1950s came to incorporate similar bans from all allied and non-allied Western countries. In the 1970s the ban was followed by the Bucy Report, as a result of which more than 3,000 Western products and technologies were put on the export ban list for the Soviet bloc countries. Thus, from an initial embargo on military technology exports, it grew into a fully-fledged ban imposed on the Council for Mutual Economic Assistance (SMEA) countries by the Coordinated Committee for Mutual Export Controls (CoCom). Consequently, almost all technology transfers and exports to the Soviet bloc were banned in order to contain its technological development and 'cultural preparedness' (Berend, 2014; Mastanduno, 1992).

China's Reaction: Promoting a Higher Level Opening to the World

China has been severely hit by the trade, investment and business environment shocks, which highlights China's need to find solutions for alleviating the consequences of these shocks and reducing their spillover effects. China has responded by further opening up to the outside world, trying to find new stability for industrial supply chains across the world, and by promoting reform and development while opening up. In his speech at the third annual session of the 13th National People's Congress (NPC), which opened at the Great Hall of the People in Beijing on May 22, 2020, Chinese Premier Li Keqiang said that China would promote a higher level opening to the outside world and stabilize the basics of foreign trade and foreign investment. In order to facilitate foreign trade, China is focusing on supporting enterprises to increase orders and stabilize employment, to increase credit, to expand export credit insurance coverage, as well as to reduce the cost of import and export compliance (Li, 2020). As external demand has declined for the past few months, China is now supporting the transfer of exported products to the domestic market to generate sales and promote domestic consumption, as well as accelerate the development of new trade modes such as cross-border e-commerce, and enhance transport capacity for international goods. As services are becoming increasingly important in economic deployment and manufacturing development, China has committed to a more open services industry with comprehensive pilot projects. There will be a new round of pilot projects for service trade innovation and development. Import serves the same role as export to propel economic development. As a major event for the international economic cooperation, China's International Import Expo has greatly enhanced the ability of trade to nurture global economic development. China is organizing the 3rd Import Expo as previously scheduled, in order to actively expand imports and develop a larger market for the world as the WTO predicts that world merchandise trade is set to plummet by between 13 and 32 percent in 2020 due to the COVID-19 pandemic (WTO, 2020a).

While a 2021 recovery in trade is expected, it depends on the duration of the outbreak and the effectiveness of the policy responses. The policies China is to implement are aimed to help the trade recovery in the world. Though the downward pressure for FDI could be -30 to -40 percent as projected by UNCTAD (2020b), China is actively attracting foreign capital with significant reduction of the items in the negative list of foreign capital access and introducing cross-border services. In addition to the negative list in FDI, China is reducing the items included in the negative list for trade.

Free trade zones and free trade ports are the emphasis and the main platform for China to provide a more open environment. China will give the Pilot Free Trade Zone greater autonomy for reform and opening up, and speeding up the construction of Hainan free trade port. Moreover, China is to speed up the establishment of free trade pilot zones and comprehensive bonded zones in the central and western regions. In April, the State Council approved the establishment of Inner-land Open Economy Pilot Zone in Jiangxi Province. In addition, the newly established Yangshan Special Comprehensive Bonded Zone in Shanghai Free Trade Zone marks another major step forward in China's commitment to a much greater level in its opening-up. The governance of international economic collaboration initiatives requires innovation as the business and natural environment for business activities in the COVID-19 pandemic has called for fast responses. The 'Belt and Road Initiative' (BRI) provides opportunities for participation – as Guterres (2019) mentions, there is a unique opportunity to build a new generation of climate resilient and people-centered cities and transit systems, and energy grids that prioritize low emissions and sustainability. He highlighted the aspirations of China to act as one pillar of international cooperation and multilateralism where other countries can build their own pillars. Meanwhile, China has confirmed its commitment to strengthening economic and trade cooperation with various countries and achieving mutual benefits based on a win-win principle. It is also actively promoting trade and investment liberalization and facilitation by maintaining and insisting on the need for a multilateral trading system. It is also actively involved in WTO reforms and promoting regional comprehensive economic partnerships such as the China-Japan-Korea free trade negotiations. All these efforts are juxtaposed to the drive towards closing access to national markets and technologies by rising nationalism, which can lead the world to new confrontations.

Discussion and Conclusion

Beyond national COVID-19 measures, strategic long-term solutions to the pandemic could stand a chance to be internationally co-constructed, which might prove to be essential for the global economic recovery.

The most important policy to reconnect the economic flows is to keep the global economy open and to support sustainable reconnection of the disrupted international supply chains and global productions networks.

On a global business level, the multinational enterprises, together with all other smaller businesses that depend on Chinese supply-networks, had to react to the pandemic effects that showed a lack of alternative options. In recent decades, the globalization of business has largely been built on global efficiency, which has created complicated, wide-spread and fine tuned systems of supply, trade and manufacturing. This systemic development focusing on efficiency and profits had largely disregarded issues such as national-level production capacity and supply safety during a global crisis. As sourcing strategies built on dual and multiple sourcing have been criticized for their inefficiencies, reshoring and near-shoring debates are likely to continue as a result of the COVID-19 crisis.

In short, the supranational and national layers of interdependencies have become intertwined and in this COVID-19 crisis the discussions have reached the political level while business actors have been struggling on the operational level. The strategy of businesses, previously seen as an aspect of private sector interest, has recently gained public attention. For example, discussions have to continue on how to diversify pharmaceutical-health care businesses as they have proven to be rather dependent and fragile and thus, unsustainable. Such discussions need to involve not only businesses, but also politicians who need to undertake actions and allow for new safety regulations to emerge. In the current debates, China's low cost production is being seen through a more negative lens, i.e., as an instrument of dominance or 'colonial aspirations' and not as a means to achieving greater economic efficiency.

The United Nations have underlined the need for countries to beat the virus together, and in parallel, to tackle its profound consequences in a sustainable manner. The underlying challenge here is to tackle climate change and other global challenges while dealing with the economic impacts of COVID-19. "Everything we do during and after this crisis must be with a strong focus on building more equal, inclusive and sustainable economies and societies that are more resilient in the face of pandemics, climate change, and the many other global challenges we face", Guterres (2020) notes.

Therefore, an open and collaborative world is much more needed now than ever before as the indirect effects can turn into populist and negative developments on all sides, if not carefully considered. China, as one of the major players in the world economy, is playing its role in making the world economy flourish again and increase peoples' prosperity with a higher level of opening up to the world. The policymakers need to consider all aspects of society and environment, multinational enterprises as well as small businesses and entrepreneurs, and human mobility when developing new approaches to organizing global production, trade, investment, and international entrepreneurship. As pandemics may reoccur, the lessons from the diverse shocks caused by COVID-19 need more research to support future crises governance.

References

Ashby, A., 2016. From global to local: reshoring for sustainability. *Oper. Manag. Res. 9*(3–4), 75–88.

Baldwin, R., di Mauro, W., 2020a. *Economics in the Time of COVID-19. a VoxEU.org ebook*, CEPR Press.

Baldwin, R., di Mauro, B. W., 2020b. *Mitigating the COVID economic crisis: Act fast and do whatever it takes. a VoxEU.org ebook*: CEPR Press.

Baldwin, R., Freeman, R., 2020. The COVID concussion and supply-chain contagion waves. VoxEU.org. https://voxeu.org/article/covidconcussion-and-supply-chain-contagion-waves (accessed 01.04.20).

Bock, S., 2008. Supporting offshoring and nearshoring decisions for mass customization manufacturing processes. *Eur. J. Operational Res. 184*(2), 490–508.

Costantino, N., Pellegrino, R., 2010. Choosing between single and multiple sourcing based on supplier default risk: A real options approach. *J. Purchasing Supply Manag. 16*(1), 27–40.

Dicken, P., 2007. Global shift: Mapping the changing contours of the world economy. Sage, London.

Ellram, L. M., Tate, W. L., Petersen, K. J., 2013. Offshoring and reshoring: an update on the manufacturing location decision. *J. Supply Chain Manag. 49*(2), 14–22.

Elo, M., Täube, F., Volovelsky, E. K., 2019. Migration 'against the tide': Location and Jewish diaspora entrepreneurs. *Regional Stud. 53*(1), 95–106.

Guterres, A., 2019. United Nations poised to support alignment of China's Belt and Road Initiative with Sustainable Development Goals, Secretary-General says at opening ceremony. United Nations. https://www.un.org/press/en/2019/sgsm19556.doc.htm (accessed 30.04.20).

Guterres, A., 2020. Speech, 31.3.2020. https://www.un.org/sg/en/content/sg/secretary-generals-speeches (accessed 24.04.20).

Berend, I., 2014. Industrial policy and its failure in the Soviet Bloc. In: Grabas, C., Nützenadel, A. (Eds.), *Industrial policy in Europe after 1945: Wealth, Power and Economic Development in the Cold War*. Palgrave Macmillan, London, pp. 279–299.

Haddad, M., 2007. Trade integration in East Asia: The role of China and production networks. World Bank Policy Research Working Paper No. 4160. https://ssrn.com/abstract=969237 (accessed 26.04.20).

He, S., 2020. Shanghai working for post-pandemic economic recovery. http://www.china.org.cn/china/special_coverage/2020-05/19/content_76062076.htm (accessed 19.05.20).

Hertz, S., 1999. Domino effects in international networks. *J. Business-to-Business Mark. 5*(3), 3–31.

IMF, 2020. World economic outlook, April 2020: the great lockdown. https://www.imf.org/en/Publications/WEO/Issues/2020/04/14/weoapril-2020 (accessed 14.04.20).

Kraemer, C., Rinke, A., 2020. Germany tightens rules on foreign takeovers. https://www.reuters.com/article/us-health-coronavirus-germanymergers/germany-tightens-rules-on-foreign-takeovers-idUSKBN21Q0VI (accessed 25.05.20).

Li, K., 2020. Government work report at the third annual session of the 13th National People's Congress (NPC). http://www.gov.cn/zhuanti/2020lhzfgzbg/index.htm (accessed 22.05.20).

Li, Q.2020. A survey on the COVID-19 and Chinese exporting companies. http://www.tradetree.cn/content/7811/20.html (accessed 14.04.20).

Mastanduno, M., 1992. Economic Containment: CoCom and the Politics of East-West Trade. Cornell University Press, Ithaca, NY.

Ministry of Commerce of China, 2020a. A briefing on FDI in China of the first quarter 2020. http://www.mofcom.gov.cn/article/ae/sjjd/202004/2020040 2955393.shtml (accessed 15.04.20).

Ministry of Commerce of China, 2020b. A briefing on overseas investment of the first quarter 2020. http://www.mofcom.gov.cn/article/ae/sjjd/202004/20200 402957267.shtml (accessed 15.04.20).

Ministry of Commerce of China, 2020c. A briefing on foreign trade of Jan-April 2020. http://www.mofcom.gov.cn/article/ae/sjjd/202004/20200402955393. shtml (accessed on May 9, 2020).

Ministry of Commerce of China, 2020d. A briefing on offshore service of Jan-April 2020. http://www.mofcom.gov.cn/article/ae/sjjd/202005/20200502966 667.shtml (accessed 20.05.20).

OECD, 2020a. Coronavirus: the world economy at risk. OECD economic outlook. Interim Report March 2020. https://www.oecd.org/economic-outlook/ (accessed 25.05.20).

OECD, 2020b. Foreign direct investment flows in the time of COVID-19. https://read.oecd-ilibrary.org/view/?ref=132_132646-g8as4msdp9&title=Foreign-direct-investment-flows-in-the-time-of-COVID-19 (accessed 30.05.20).

Rodrik, D., 2018. Populism and the economics of globalization. *J. Int. Bus. Policy* 1(1–2), 12–33.

Sirkeci, I., Yucesahin, M. M., 2020. Coronavirus and migration: analysis of human mobility and the spread of Covid-19. *Migr. Lett.* 17(2), 379–398.

Tsukanova, T., Zhang, X., 2019. Early and rapid internationalization of firms from emerging economies: understanding the heterogeneity of Chinese exporters. *J. East-West Bus.* 25(2), 194–224.

UNCTAD, 2020a. Investment policy monitor. https://unctad.org/en/Publications Library/diaepcbinf2020d1_en.pdf (accessed 03.04.20).

UNCTAD, 2020b. Investment policy monitor: special issue - investment policy responses to the COVID-19 pandemic. https://unctad.org/en/PublicationsLibrary/ diaepcbinf2020d3_en.pdf (accessed 04.04.20).

United Nations, 2020c. Covid-19 response. https://www.un.org/en/un-coronavirus-communications-team/launch-report-socioeconomic-impacts-covid-19 (accessed 03.04.20).

Wang, W., 2018. Nine countries revise regulations and laws on FDI. https://mp. weixin.qq.com/s/g4W7qrvW1IcPw0EsYXlF2A (accessed 27.04.20).

WTO, 2020. Trade set to plunge as COVID-19 pandemic upends global economy. https://www.wto.org/english/news_e/pres20_e/pr855_e.pdf (accessed 08.04.20).

Xu, D., Meyer, K. E., 2013. Linking theory and context: Strategy research in emerging economies after Wright et al. (2005), *Journal of Management Studies*, *50*(7), 1322–1346.

Zhang, X., Aman, R., Zhang, J. H., Xi, Y., 2020. Serial nonlinearities in firm's internationalisation process: case evidence from China. *Int. J. Export. Mark.* *3*(3), 219–244.

Zhang, X., 2013. *Internationalization Processes of Chinese Firms: The Role of Knowledge*. Doctoral dissertation. University of Tartu Press, Tartu.

Zhang, X., Larimo, J., 2013. Longitudinal internationalization processes of born globals: Three Chinese cases of radical change and the global crisis. In: Marinov, M.A. (ed.) *Emerging Economies and Firms in the Global Crisis*. Palgrave Macmillan, Basingstoke, pp. 334–366.

Zhu, He, 2020. US make modifications to Export Administration Regulations (EAR). https://mp.weixin.qq.com/s/QQVlCyG1hmdh0G91Jc9L9g (accessed 19.05.20).

26 Rebuilding Chinese International Business during and Post-COVID-19

Shuquan He and Xiaoying Wang

Introduction

There have been several pandemics and economic recessions in the recent history that caused serious economic downturns. However, the COVID-19 pandemic differs in many aspects from pandemics such as the Spanish flu of SARS, as the global economy is interdependent and COVID-19 affected rather negatively the economies that are most active in international business. Unlike any previous economic shocks caused by economic or financial imbalances crises, COVID-19 is external to the economic system, which supposedly may indicate a less serious impact on the economy itself (He, 2020a). Nevertheless, the ways in which governments have reacted by raising spending and debt to unprecedented levels and the serious blow to unemployment, combined with company closures and business lockdown, have sent shock waves throughout national, regional and global supply, demand, production, logistics and finance (Baldwin and di Mauro, 2020a; 2020b). Parts of various global production networks were destroyed, which in effect produced a snowball contagion effect worldwide causing huge economic loss to suppliers and clients, but also to indirectly related parties (Baldwin and Freeman, 2020; Watts, 2020).

Leaving China is Easier Said than Done

The trade conflict between China and the U.S. amplified calls in the U.S. and elsewhere for reducing dependence on China in global supply chains. The disruption of global supply chains during the past months has politicians vowing to take decisive action. The U.S. officials have talked repeatedly about bringing supply chains home from China, and calling on companies involved in global supply chains to leave China (Taylor, 2020). Consequently, 'To stay or not to stay in China?' has become a key question for many multinational companies (MNCs), although the other side of this question is 'Is it easy to rule China out of global supply chains?' The likely answer is 'Perhaps not as easy as it may seem to some, if you apply business logic'.

A recent survey by the American Chamber of Business in China reveals that in contrast to some global narratives, the majority of its members will not be leaving China anytime soon (He, 2020c). Although some companies in certain industries may diversify or expand manufacturing operations outside China, the reality is that a major manufacturing shift away from China is easier said than done as it will be rather costly, time and effort consuming, and most likely an irreversible process. It is relatively easy to move a single production task out of China, but it is difficult to have essential supporting activities in the new host country. Some companies with diversified production are finding it hard to break away from their well-developed supply chain in China. For example, Nintendo, the Japanese video game producer, which moved the manufacturing activity of its blockbuster gaming console to Vietnam in 2019, find there is a shortage of switch consoles because of the lack of essential components flowing to the company's Vietnamese factories from Chinese suppliers (Mirchandani, 2020).

In addition, from the demand side, the Chinese market is huge enough to persuade MNCs to stay in China. MNCs are attracted to big markets and are convinced of China's increasing market demand and its growing future potential as a major market for most consumer products employing advanced technologies such as robotics, autonomous vehicles and smart devices. With nearly 350 million people in China's middle class and still growing, China is likely to be MNC's biggest consumer target market over the next 20 years where proximity to customers is essential (He, 2020c). As manufacturers examine their supply chains post-COVID-19, they will review and balance the imperative for greater supply chain resilience and the attractiveness of China as a manufacturing location and tech-forward early adopter consumer market. To leave China is not as simple as to pack up a shop, lock the doors, turn out the lights, and move back home.

It is also worth noting that China is ahead of the global curve when it comes to economic recovery after months of lockdown. The IMF's latest World Economic Outlook growth projections released in late June 2020 suggest that China is the only economy in the world likely to enjoy positive growth in 2020 (IMF, 2020). Instead of leaving China, most MNCs are focusing on operational improvements, digital transformation and strategic supply chain transformation by investing in new technologies to automate manufacturing and improve competitiveness (Mirchandani, 2020). In addition, the improvements in China's regulatory environment is another issue to take into consideration when MNCs decide whether to stay in or leave China. Among other changes, the 2020 version negative list for foreign investment from July 23, 2020 will improve the level of openness in the service, manufacturing and agricultural sectors, in comparison with the 2019 list. Foreign investors in the piloted free trade zones (FTZs) now have 30 listed items, down from 37 items in last year's list, and the rest of the country is required to implement 33 items instead of the 40 items in the previous version (He, 2020c). As an important part of the services industry, the financial sector is accelerating its opening-up. China began to allow some foreign financial entities to increase their minority stake to a majority of 51 percent from January 2020. This will be a major step in establishing Shanghai into a global financial hub.

Over the past 20 years or so, the pattern of global supply chains has typical regional characteristics with a three-center pattern at the core – the U.S., China and Germany. The Chinese industrial chains are driven by urban agglomerations and exhibits regional characteristics. The centers are Beijing-Tianjin-Hebei, Yangtze River Delta, Guangdong-Hong Kong-Macao Greater Bay Area, Chengdu and Chongqing. From the demand side, China is closely connected with the ASEAN economic bloc with China, Japan and South Korea at the core, and the network is self-circulating with China in the middle and lower reaches of the network. China's digital talents and key areas of the digital industry are clustered in several major urban agglomerations that are far ahead in digital convergence. The ASEAN economic network with China, Japan and South Korea at the core and the three major urban clusters in the north, and Shanghai and Guangzhou as the fulcrum, have focused on cross-border digital trade and have accelerated China's development in the field of industrial chain digitalization. Along this, China should attach great importance to market size and the dominance of digital trade rules in the digitization of industrial chains as the bridgehead for China to move from the East Asian regional industrial chains to the global industrial chains and design an open strategy around this.

The COVID-19 pandemic and rapidly changing business environment have forced companies to relocate and diversify their supply chains. Some MNCs have already adopted 'China plus one' supply chain strategy with China as the primary supplier while also establishing a stand-by supplier (Venkatesh, 2020). Several factors will give China advantages to keep its position in global supply chains. First, China has been able to proceed at a relatively high speed in terms of scope, scale and dynamics of commercial operations. Second, the 'flexible working hours' system in China gives a favored link for most global supply chains. In addition, China's good relations with ASEAN and Africa are a source of another competitive advantage in maintaining a stable global supply chain.

To sum up, with its economic growth and stability, China has been the factory of the world for almost 30 years. While the calls for relocating supply chains out of China due to the COVID-19 pandemic and the China - U.S. trade tensions have been repeatedly echoed by a number of U.S. allies, the aspiration to find an alternative to China may not be as effective as claimed, and hence might prove to be 'easier said than done'.

Shanghai and its Role in Boosting the Economy

In addition to the policies at the national level to propel economic growth, province-level measures are developed and released across the country. Shanghai is one of the cities actively fueling economic growth in the areas of domestic consumption, new infrastructure, foreign investment and international trade. On May 16, 2020, Shanghai officially unveiled Yangshan Special Comprehensive Bonded Zone, marking another major step forward in China's commitment to greater openness to the world. Located in the Lingang Special Area of China's Shanghai Pilot Free Trade Zone, Yangshan was approved to be upgraded into the first special comprehensive bonded zone by the State Council on January 17, 2020. Such a zone will be of great significance for MNCs to ensure that they can tackle more effectively and efficiently the adverse effects of the pandemic (He, 2020b). The Zone will be guided by a special supervision guideline to implement opening-up policies and mechanisms, which are competitive worldwide. One of the measures is to eliminate unnecessary trade supervision, permits and processes while prioritizing safety and efficiency. In addition, the customs declaration system will be simplified to a great extent to enable management freedom. The customs statistical methods will be upgraded to make more room for the development of international transfer services.

The launch of Yangshan Special Comprehensive Bonded Zone is only one initiative amongst many others. Shanghai has also approved an action plan to promote development of the online new economy, focusing on 12 key aspects that include unmanned factories, industrial internet and online health care. The outbreak of COVID-19 has disrupted production and changed the way people live. By implementing the action plan for the new online economy, Shanghai aims to develop the online economy as a new driver to boost economic recovery after the pandemic. One of the goals is to attract more than 100 innovative companies to invest and relocate in Shanghai in 2020. These companies should be those with core technologies, independent intellectual property rights and strong international competitiveness. The action plan includes 23 items to develop the city's new online economy, employing an array of technologies such as artificial intelligence, 5G networks and big data to transform and empower traditional industries (He, 2020b). For example, on May 5 ('Double Five') Shanghai launched a Shopping Festival as part of the immediate measures to boost consumer spending, which slowed down and contracted dramatically in February, March and April. The two-month-long shopping festival is expected to stimulate consumption and reduce the economic impact of the COVID-19 pandemic and will run until the end of June featuring more than 800 online and offline activities. Another example is the newly introduced shopping carnival, which is the first of its kind initiated by the municipal government. It has helped online and offline retailers to achieve total sales of RMB15.68 billion (US$2.22 billion) only within the first 24 hours after it was launched. New product consumption was one of the highlights during the shopping festival, with 73 new products released by 52 brands only by the end of May. Consumption of imported goods is also encouraged to benefit foreign companies. For instance, the Japanese department store Takashimaya has provided discounts of up to 45 percent for designated products. Bright Food Group has released a number of high-protein foods while Wine Exchange Shanghai has offered discounts on wine imported from Italy and France.

With the global economy being in turmoil, China is in a unique position in leading the post-COVID-19 recovery. Shanghai, the most dynamic city in the country, has boosted its economic confidence and rolled out a series of economic stimuli packages. There are policies to promote consumption in areas such as leisure activities, automobiles, information and home refurbishment, and various measures to bring the economy back to normal and increase economic openness. More importantly, adapting to the changed economic environment, Shanghai has been carrying out action plans to promote directions for new economic growth, focusing on the development of 'new infrastructure', such as 5G networks, NEV charging stations, energy efficiency programs, and other initiatives that will help build China's economy of the future. Relying on huge domestic consumption and openness to the world, China and its major cities are placing themselves as the locomotive of regional and global economic development (He, 2020b).

Chinese Companies Rebuilding their Business

In 1993, 10 years before SARS, the Chinese government's Golden Projects laid an important foundation for online payments. As the Golden Bridge Project built out internet networks, the Golden Card Project established a unified payment card system, while the Golden Customs Project linked customs points through a national electronic data interchange (EDI) system to promote paperless trade. When SARS hit in 2003, the basic infrastructures for digital payments were in place. Nearly 67 million people, or 5.2 percent of the population, had access to the internet and 500 million payment cards were in circulation. Alibaba launched Taobao, its first consumer-facing e-commerce website, and soon after created Alipay, now the dominant third-party payment system in China, to help solve payment and trust problems that inhibited the growth of online shopping. As SARS has shown, the world after COVID-19 most likely will become even more digitized. Countries lagging in digital payments should proactively build out their identity, Internet and banking infrastructure, as China did, to take advantage of these advancements (Bourdinière, 2020c).

Chinese companies are well prepared for the oncoming changes. For instance, the contactless delivery has been widely introduced (Bourdinière, 2020a). The most innovative addition in the customer journey is contactless delivery and driverless delivery. Contactless delivery orders make up over 80 percent of total orders, and more than 66 percent of users have already adopted touchless delivery for every order, which was in response to the immense pressure on shipping capacity caused by the demand spike. Alibaba, JD, Meituan and Suning launched driverless delivery programs to cover services in a 5 km radius. JD Logistics was the first to complete a driverless delivery order during the quarantine in Wuhan on February 6. Soon, driverless deliveries accounted for over half of their deliveries to Wuhan's hospitals. Following JD, other retailers adopted similar techniques, such as Suning, which partnered with Carrefour to launch a 'same-city-delivery' service in more than 51 cities. In 2003, the SARS outbreak contributed to the surge of e-commerce adoption in China. For similar reasons, but on a much bigger scale and at a higher level of technology maturity, touchless retail might just become China's new way to shop and pave the way for the rest of the world to follow.

Chinese companies are speeding up digitalization to invent new customer experiences (Bourdinière, 2020b). During the COVID-19 crisis, the lockdown accelerated the digitalization of marketing and sales in the auto industry at a speed and scale that nobody could have predicted. OEMs, dealers and platforms have introduced multiple innovations to engage their customers and, ultimately, continue to sell cars. Cloud launching is common in China. Almost all auto brands have devoted their efforts to using live streaming as the main marketing method during this difficult period. On March 9, Chery launched its newest model the Tiggo 7/7 PRO exclusively via live stream. According to the official data, this online event attracted more than 700,000 viewers, and guaranteed the company more than 7,000 sales deals.

Tesla China has started offering 'contactless trial driving' options to customers in Beijing and Shanghai (Bourdinière, 2020b). Customers can make an appointment by phone and sign e-agreement online. A sales assistant would unlock the car remotely and customers could watch in-car video instructions on the center screen, while mitigating any transmission risk throughout the whole process.

Dealers in China are also advancing their online marketing development schedules to maintain customer relationships, improve their teams' capabilities and prepare for market recovery (Bourdinière, 2020b). A Subaru 4S shop in Fuzhou resumed work on February 10 and quickly devoted its activities to online marketing, focusing on live after-sales interactions. This included special offers for medical personnel, free warranty extension, free disinfection of vehicles, and other promotions. The dealer has attracted approximately 200–300 viewers per online streaming event, which is equivalent to visitors normally expected at a large offline event. By the end of March, the shop's after-sales business had recovered about 70–80 percent of the initial sales volume.

Major platforms such as Tmall, Weibo, AutoHome, BitAuto, Kuaishou, and DongCheDi have quickly launched digital marketing online services to support businesses in their online marketing efforts (Bourdinière, 2020b). For example, the short video app Kuaishou launched a solution specifically for automotive brands featuring a special account combining marketing videos on demand, live stream functions, social interaction and lead management tools to help with attracting and retaining customers.

AutoHome has been using big data systems to analyze changes in customer behavior during the pandemic to understand consumer needs (Bourdinière, 2020b). Taking the 'Smart Car Cloud' product as an example, it provides car companies with three major services: intelligent early warning, intelligent diagnostics and intelligent suggestion. In addition, through the creation of smart showrooms and online virtual stores, AutoHome provides the four major functions of car viewing, selection, ordering and buying online.

New flexible human resource management is being developed. Already recognized for its innovations in retail, Alibaba introduced a 'resource leasing model' designed to share manpower (Wang and Bourdinière, 2020). For their grocery chain Hema, which faced a massive increase in demand, Alibaba started ad hoc resource sharing to fill gaps in manpower and serve online orders. In fact, while Hema experienced staff shortages, traditional restaurant chains whose outlets were closed struggled with excessive costs on under-utilized employees. Hema therefore partnered with these chains to share their human resources and thus soften the impact of salary and job losses experienced by other businesses.

Having introduced this resource leasing model during the crisis, Alibaba is now preparing to digitize and industrialize it further. In April, they introduced a digital platform to manage shared manpower and integrate the resource leasing model into their ongoing operations. According to Hema, data analytics will be applied to categorize employee profiles such as years of experience, specialization and matching roles. There are several benefits to human resource management from this new approach. Firstly, a digital approach to the flexible sharing of resources will clarify employers' responsibilities when pooling employees and resolve questions about legal accountability and insurance. Secondly, the real-time flexibility it provides will accommodate variations in the speed of recovery, helping to match resources and demand. It may provide new opportunities for digital commerce in relation to other big events in China such as the Chinese New Year, international championships, etc.

Concluding Remarks

COVID-19 and the pandemic will change the way in which people engage with business offers, innovate business models, and accelerate policy changes countries adopt. While globalization will not end but will change, evolve and continue in new ways, the national and international business environment will be different. However, the fundamentals of globalization processes will not change, but may face decoupling or even re-coupling of financial flows, existing supply chains, movement of people and goods. These changes will force companies to innovate their businesses and governments to adjust their legislation. Chinese companies are fast rebuilding their national restructuring and commercial innovation potential, preparing to launch innovative service and delivery solutions internationally in by leveraging emerging technologies to their businesses response to the changing environment.

References

Baldwin, R, di Mauro, B.W., 2020a. *Economics in the Time of Covid-19*. a VoxEU.org eBook: Centre for Economic Policy Research Press: London.

Baldwin, R., di Mauro, B.W., 2020b. *Mitigating the Covid economic crisis: Act fast and do whatever it takes*. a VoxEU.org eBook: Centre for Economic Policy Research Press:London.

Baldwin, R. and Freeman, R. 2020. The Covid concussion and supply-chain contagion waves. VoxEU.org. https://voxeu.org/article/covid-concussion-and-supply-chain-contagion-waves (accessed 03.04.20.).

Bourdinière, J. 2020a. Touchless retail: What the rest of the world could learn from China's new ways to shop. https://www.capgemini.com/gb-en/2020/04/preparing-for-tomorrow-touchless-retail-chinas-new-way-to-shop/ (accessed 16.04.20.).

Bourdinière, J. 2020b. How China's automotive industry is digitalising to invent new customer experiences. https://www.capgemini.com/gb-en/2020/04/how-chinas-automotive-industry-is-digitalising-to-invent-new-customer-experiences/ (accessed 16.04.20.).

Bourdinière, J. 2020c. How digital innovations enabled supply chains remained operational during the COVID-19 outbreak. https://www.capgemini.com/gb-en/2020/06/how-digital-innovations-enabled-supply-chains-to-remain-operational-during-the-covid-19-outbreak/ (accessed 26.06.20.).

He, S. 2020a. Post-COVID-19 recovery needs an open world to reconnect the economic fuel line. http://www.china.org.cn/opinion/2020-05/07/content_76015165.htm (accessed 07.05.20.).

He, S. 2020b Shanghai working for post-pandemic economic recovery. http://www.china.org.cn/china/special_coverage/2020-05/19/content_76062076.htm (accessed 19.05.20.).

He, S. 2020c. Multinationals favor China as world economy begins to revive. http://www.china.org.cn/opinion/2020-07/11/content_76258202.htm (accessed 11.07.20.).

IMF 2020. World economic outlook update, June 2020: A crisis like no other, an uncertain recovery. https://www.imf.org/en/Publications/WEO/issues/2020/06/24/WEOUpdateJune2020 (accessed 26.06.20.).

Mirchandani, M. 2020. Reducing global supply chain reliance on China won't be easy. https://www.greenbiz.com/article/reducing-global-supply-chain-reliance-china-wont-be-easy (accessed 05.05.20).

Taylor, C. 2020. Companies will shift supply chains away from China after coronavirus crisis, Mark Mobius predicts. https://www.cnbc.com/2020/04/21/supply-chains-will-move-away-from-china-after-coronavirus-mark-mobius.html (accessed 17.04.20.).

Venkatesh, P. 2020. Repositioning global supply chains out of China will not be easy. https://www.firstpost.com/business/repositioning-global-supply-chains-out-of-china-will-not-be-easy-beijing-will-enjoy-an-advantage-even-post-coronavirus-8459011.html (accessed 20.06.20.).

Wang, C. and Bourdinière, J. 2020. Prepare for tomorrow: perspective from China. https://www.capgemini.com/gb-en/2020/04/lessons-learnt-for-grocery-and-fresh-food-distribution/ (accessed 01.04.20.).

Watts, W. 2020. Here's what China's coronavirus shutdown did to global supply chains. https://www.marketwatch.com/story/heres-what-chinas-coronavirus-shutdown-did-to-global-supply-chains-2020-05-12 (accessed 13.05.20.).

27 Danish Companies in China during COVID-19

Staying Afloat and Post-Pandemic Trends

Dmitrij Slepniov

Introduction

Flashing back to BC (Before Coronavirus), many Danish companies operating in China and oriented toward the local Chinese market were well on track to reach new heights in terms of market share and revenue growth. Since 1978, when the period of new reforms and opening-up began, China had been experiencing tremendous economic growth and economic transformation, which initially led to China's ascendancy in global manufacturing and more recently to significant growth of China's middle class with its purchasing power. Combined with the Chinese government policy incentives centered on innovation and quality-oriented sustainable growth, these factors influenced the increasing importance of China and the Chinese market for many Danish brands. Some of the brands even defined China as their 'second home market' and declared their long-term commitment to it.

A survey of 71 Danish companies in China carried out at the end of 2019 found many signs of confidence and optimism expressed by the Danish business community about the role of their activities as well as the outlook for their operations in China (Hoppe et al., 2020). 79 percent of respondents in that survey indicated that their activities in China were essential for the global performance of the Danish MNCs. 75 percent of companies believed that the global turnover by the company's entities in China would increase in the next five years, while 72 percent planned to increase their capacity in China in the same period. Furthermore, 58 percent of companies reported on established strategic collaborations in China and almost half placed their global or local bases for various functions in China. It seemed that despite numerous challenges and liability of foreignness that any overseas player was likely to face in the Chinese market, the overall sentiment of the Danish business community was rather positive or at least cautiously optimistic.

In mid-January 2020, as managers and employees were celebrating the successes in the previous year and preparing for the fast-approaching Chinese Spring Festival, few could have imagined how devastating the news that had started coming out of Wuhan, a city of 11 million in South Central China, would turn out to be. Shortly after, it became increasingly clear that the crushing effects of COVID-19 would have a profound impact on companies all over the world, including Danish companies located in China. However, it was not entirely clear what those impacts would be. In early March, the world was witnessing the end of the initial supply shock coming out of China, as the country started its recovery from the health crisis and the lockdown of the economy. At the same time, the global spread of the virus caused a significant demand shock. Subsequently, structural and strategic implications for the Chinese economy and foreign companies operating there became inevitable.

Notwithstanding a few studies and reports (e.g., Aslam and Hussain, 2020; Craven et al., 2020; Crick and Crick, 2020; Donthu and Gustafsson, 2020; Jorda et al., 2020), as we were in the middle of the crisis no one had reliable data and we were ill equipped to understand any immediate and long-term effects of the crisis. This situation prompted
a dialogue with Danish companies operating in China, the first country struck by the outbreak. The remainder of the chapter discusses the experiences of the companies during the outbreak and reflects on the emerging contours of a new normal in the international operations of Danish companies in the AC (After Coronavirus) era.

Inflection Point and China's First in First out (FIFO)

In the period when the first interviews were conducted in late February, the outbreak reached the inflection point: the situation in China started showing signs of stabilizing while beginning to deteriorate elsewhere. Under these circumstances, several interviewees assessing the prospects of China's speedy economic recovery pointed to a high likelihood of FIFO scenario, meaning that China would most likely recover first, ahead of its Western counterparts. One interviewee commented.

> *"For the last 2–3 days, the situation in China is getting more controlled and people are more relaxed than before. But the problem is that the virus has spread to other countries. So now, we also see tendencies of some provinces to apply special measures for people coming back from Western countries. That can also bring us challenges."*
> (Interview with a General Manager, February 25, 2020)

In hindsight, the prediction for new challenges to international companies dependent on foreign employees returning to China proved to be prophetic. A month later, given the rapid spread of COVID-19 across the world, the Chinese government decided to temporarily suspend entry by all foreign nationals into China. Reciprocal measures by many other countries followed. Whether this restriction on movement of people will become a significant driver of economic separation and decoupling remains to be seen. For now, it merely illustrates the effects of 'chained globalization' (Farrell and Newman, 2020) and shows how deeply dependent companies are on what takes place in other parts of the world and how difficult it is to decouple without causing havoc to company operations, at least in the short run.

China's FIFO demonstrated the country's ability to show the way forward in combating the outbreak.

"China is now in a better condition, if we look at the whole world, because they are ready and most factories are increasingly up and running, while in Europe and the U.S., we have not even started seeing the effect yet."
(Interview with a General Manager, March 12, 2020)

However, China's FIFO and the end of the economic turbulence were too early to celebrate. Demand for the country's many export-oriented sectors was rapidly dwindling as the world economy was coming to a standstill.

From Supply Disruption to Demand Squeeze

To create a more comprehensive overview of the challenges created by COVID-19 and to outline the main coping measures, a survey was carried out among 84 members of the Danish Chamber of Commerce in China in May 2020. The survey resulted in a 50 percent response rate, with 42 companies answering the online questionnaire. Figure 27.1 outlines the top five challenges posed by the COVID-19 crisis.

COVID-19 challenges are primarily linked to limitations on internal operations, supply-side disruptions and squeeze on demand in China and overseas. Of the surveyed companies, 66 percent indicated limitations on regular business operations as a challenge, making it the most commonly experienced challenge. This challenge, which is echoed in the interviews,

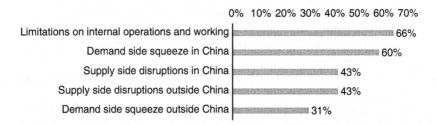

Figure 27.1 Challenges Caused by COVID-19 for Danish Companies in China.
Source: The Author.

seemed to be symptomatic for many, especially at the initial stages of the crisis. A head of production noted this as follows.

"We did not have our people at work for some time until we established a system to make sure that nothing is contaminated. Now, everything is checked before it enters the factory. We are checking people's whereabouts, so we know exactly where they have been, from when they have been home and their temperature. We are providing them with masks and we are working according to all regulations issued by the government."
(Interview with a Head of Production, March 10, 2020)

As many Danish companies focus on the Chinese market with their subsidiaries located there and performing market server role (Ferdows, 1997), it was predictable that the COVID-19 crisis would negatively affect the demand-side figures. As one general manager said:

"I estimate that there will be in total around three months of disrupted operations, and we are preparing for approximately 10–15 percent drop in revenue. However, I still hope that we will be able to keep at least a small growth compared to 2019".
(Interview with a General Manager, March 5, 2020)

Those companies whose operations were geared towards an arbitrage strategy in China (Ghemawat, 2017) took a hit from the overseas demand squeeze.

Although in mid-March, the interviews showed the overall shared sense of optimism about the situation in China getting back on track, some expressed concern about the overall impact of the crisis on the economy and especially on small businesses.

"In 2008, many small shops didn't get that much affected..., but in the current situation, the small shops are directly affected and losing money every day because they need to pay rent and salaries but are not making any money. So they are running out of cash. And where this money is supposed to come from, nobody knows right now. We also don't know anything about the unemployment rate right now.... It could be that millions of people already lost their jobs in the past couple of weeks, but nobody is talking about it."
(Interview with a General Manager, March 12, 2020)

The rescue and recovery packages offered by the Chinese government made this concern go away at least in the short run as the country continued to bounce back.

Meeting the Challenges

In many respects, the COVID-19 crisis became a catalyst for enhancing the tendencies that were in place before. One point worth dwelling upon is the role of government in the COVID-19 crisis. 'Understand the market, but work with the state' has always been a well-known rule of the game for doing business in China (Paine, 2010). However, this rule was further reinforced and greatly aided by the fact that the orderly reopening of businesses in spring 2020 was highly dependent on active coordination and engagement with the local government. As some interviewees recalled.

> *"We started to take actions quite quickly going into the Chinese New Year. Following that and acting local, we assembled a team of people to gather the information and resources and engaged with the local government."*
> (Interview with a VP Operations, March 12, 2020)

> *"We have been able to run the factory throughout the whole period. We had only small disruptions and that was right after the Chinese New Year when all this broke out. I managed to get a meeting with the local vice-mayor, and we agreed on how he could accept that we run a safe operation and which rules and regulations we have to apply".*
> (Interview with a Head of Production, March 10, 2020)

Turning back to the results of the survey of Danish companies conducted in China in May, Figure 27.2 includes examples of other coping measures that companies put in place in dealing with the challenges in the aftermath of the outbreak.

The silver lining to COVID-19 can be new opportunities that the crisis has revealed. Acting as a dynamic agent of change, it forced many companies to experiment. Some of these forced experiments were related to new ways of organizing work. With 71 percent of respondents

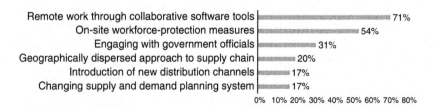

Figure 27.2 Measures Implemented by Companies to Deal with COVID-19 Challenges.
Source: The Author.

implementing remote work measures, we witnessed a huge real-life experiment involving working from home. Although the debate about the death of the traditional office and working from home has for quite a while been a sign of our times in the West, the interviews showed how rather groundbreaking and refreshing the idea appeared in China.

> *"I think this is something that we have learned. Our Chinese employees have never before tried the freedom of working from home. This was a big learning for all of us and some people really blossomed."*
> (Interview with an Executive Business Director, June 1, 2020)

Digitalization was also crucial for some in keeping the business running while the offline channels got shut. A total of 17 percent mentioned that they turned to the new digital means of doing business.

> *"We are not completely in the dark because for the last 4–5 years we have already started the digitalization of our business. So we do have an APP that we use for the leftover products, and we may make use of that platform to help our sales."*
> (Interview with a General Manager, February 25, 2020)

In this regard, COVID-19 has manifested itself not only as an agent of change but also as an accelerator of change—and in the business world in China, this acceleration might have been especially pronounced in the e-commerce industry.

> *"The acceleration of e-commerce is also an important lesson from COVID-19. China has already gone very far in this area and had the logistics systems to support that. However, the lockdowns with the narrative of 'stay at home and shop at home' accelerated this even further."*
> (Interview with a VP for Asia, June 3, 2020)

The investigation also showed that there was no 'one size fits all' in how the road to recovery and post-recovery might look like in different sectors. The service sectors may face loss and unrecoverable demand, while others may see delayed demand and the recuperation of temporary loses, as a general manager commented.

> *"It is very much case-by-case … industry-by-industry…. I am sure if we are talking retail industry, there will still be a long period in which people will be hesitant to go out at the same level as they did before. But in terms of manufacturing, once things are up and running again, there is a big backlog. So, the wheels will be turning*

really, really fast. So, there will be industries that will be able to catch up, but others will have a long-term dislocation."
(Interview with a General Manager, February 21, 2020)

The challenges caused by COVID-19 proved to be a real test for many companies. While some started showing a dent, others highlighted opportunities for improving their position on the market.

"We know that our competition is under pressure, some more than others. Of course, we all are, but I think we can walk a longer mile under this pressure than some of our competition and that may bring an opportunity, meaning picking up customers from our competition."
(Interview with a CEO, May 28, 2020)

Adjusting and Recalibrating for the Future

In China, for China

In the survey questionnaire, the Danish companies were asked to give up to three reasons for their presence in China. Market-seeking motive seemed to dominate, and for 86 percent of companies, the access to the Chinese market was by far the most prevalent reason for their presence in China now as well as in the future. A managing director reflected in a follow-up interview as follows.

"We see a clear tendency that the companies that invest in China for the purpose of providing goods and services in China for the Chinese market are actually the ones that perform best and are most optimistic. While the companies that are typically manufacturing for the markets outside China are probably the ones that are now looking at how to reduce their exposure to China by creating the supply chains that are not so dependent on China."
(Interview with a Managing Director, June 2, 2020)

Looking ahead, we can expect that localization strategy may become a new normal in China in the post-COVID-19 world, replacing arbitrage that has already been under pressure for some time due to wage inflation and growing competition from new emerging low-cost destinations in South-East Asia.

The Crucial and Growing Role of Subsidiaries in China

When asked to assess the overall importance of China for their business, 74 percent of respondents agreed or strongly agreed that their company's activities in China were crucial for their overall global performance. Some managers commented as follows.

"China has a key place on our global map and that is why we have three factories here."
(Interview with an Executive Business Director, June 1, 2020)

"Going forward, the site has very high importance. Our ambitions are high and we expect a large impact on the group's consolidated figures from our company in China."
(Interview with a CEO, May 28, 2020)

In times of worry for international business, when we have seen countries close borders and implement (hopefully temporary) restrictive measures, the role of companies' subsidiaries in China may increase further.

"Being present in China now is more important than it has ever been. If walls are erected for one reason or another, you need to be inside that wall or you cannot survive."
(Interview with a VP for Asia, June 3, 2020)

Conclusion

The chapter revisited the experiences of Danish companies in China during the first several months of the COVID-19 crisis. It took stock of challenges that the companies faced and discussed some of the coping measures we saw implemented to stay afloat and be prepared for the post-pandemic world.

Limitations on working combined with supply and demand shocks meant that the companies were forced to rethink the old normal and try new things. These include new modes of operating a factory, new ways of planning and coordinating supply and demand, and new approaches to reaching their customers through e-channels or by developing a new product remotely using digital tools. The jury is still out on which changes are here to stay in the long run. However, based on the insights from the study, we can paint the contours of some strategic moves that are likely to enter the strategy documents of Danish (and possibly other Western) companies in China. Among those who see potential in the Chinese market, we are likely to see an increasing emphasis on localization and on 'In China, For China' strategy. For others, who focus on the markets outside China and only use it as an offshore low-cost destination for manufacturing, COVID-19 may be a turning point in the radical rethinking of their supply chain and reduced exposure to China.

On the one hand, the period of COVID-19 in the minds of many is associated with distancing and isolation. On the other hand, it is also the period of intense communication and reliance on networks and innovation. If COVID-19 changes anything irreversibly, let us hope it is not the natural human propensity to seek dialogue, connection and cooperation in moving forward in the AC (After Corona) world.

References

Aslam, H., Hussain, R., 2020. *Fighting COVID-19: Lessons from China, South Korea and Japan*. Sustainable Development Policy Institute Report.

Craven, M., Liu, L., Mysore, M., Wilson, M., 2020. *COVID-19: implications for business. McKinsey Quarterly*, March, 1–8.

Crick, J. M., Crick, D., Jul. 2020. Coopetition and COVID-19: collaborative business-to-business marketing strategies in a pandemic crisis. *Ind. Mark. Manag. 88*, 206–213.

Donthu, N., Gustafsson, A., Sep. 2020. Effects of COVID-19 on business and research. *J. Bus. Res. 117*, 284–289.

Farrell, H., Newman, A. L., 2020. *Chained to globalization: why it's too late to decouple. Foreign Affairs*, January/February, 70–80.

Ferdows, K., 1997. Making the most of foreign factories. *Harv. Bus. Rev. 75*(2), 73–88.

Ghemawat, P., 2017. Globalization in the age of Trump. *Harv. Bus. Rev. 95*(4), 112–123.

Habel, J., Jarotschkin, V., Schmitz, B., Eggert, A., Plötner, O., Jul. 2020. Industrial buying during the coronavirus pandemic: a cross-cultural study. *Ind. Mark. Manag. 88*, 195–205.

Hoppe, T., Slepniov, D., Boyer, M., Nielsen, M., 2020. *Danish in China: Challenges and Opportunities*. Royal Danish Embassy in Beijing, Danish Chamber of Commerce in China, Sino-Danish Center for Education and Research, Beijing, China.

Jorda, O., Singh, S. R., Taylor, A. M., 2020. *Longer-run economic consequences of pandemics. National Bureau of Economic Research*. Report no. w26934.

Paine, L. S., 2010. The China rules. *Harv. Bus. Rev. 88*(6), 103–108.

28 Investment Attractiveness of Central and Eastern Europe for Western Multinational Firms in the Post-COVID-19 Era

Arnold Schuh

Introduction

Enormous economic downturns have always been triggers to testing the basic assumptions of business models that guided the firm in the preceding no crisis times. The 'going east' strategy of Western multinational companies in the late 1990s and early 2000s underwent such a review during the global financial and economic crisis of 2007–2009. The Great Recession abruptly stopped the catching-up process of the economies of Central and Eastern Europe in 2009 and a seven year long boom phase with average annual growth rates of 6 percent (Bruegel, 2010). The economies of the region were among the hardest hit worldwide and it took them five years on average to return to the pre-crisis gross domestic product (GDP) levels. The origin of the crisis in 2007 was the subprime residential mortgage market combined with weak regulatory oversight in the U.S. that spread to the rest of the world through exposure to risky and complex financial derivates and was followed by a collapse in global trade and systemic banking crises in many countries. From a Central and Eastern Europe (CEE) point of view, the crisis was to a large degree imported via collapsing export markets and a drying up of credits and foreign direct investment (FDI) from abroad. In addition, 'home-grown' causes such as stretched public budgets and excessive borrowing in foreign currency by households and firms reinforced the negative effects.

Among Western investors[1], the crisis shattered the perception of CEE[2] as a global growth region and led to a discussion of the original 'CEE business model' that was based on fast growth, skilled labor at lower costs and an investor-friendly business climate. In the aftermath of this crisis, the CEE region lost its status as a growth region. Unsurprisingly, Western multinationals became more selective and cautious in their investment behavior. A reduction in Western FDI in general, the withdrawal from peripheral country markets, product portfolio rationalizations, and inward-oriented focus towards the optimization of existing group activities were major outcomes of this strategic reorientation (Schuh, 2012).

A decade later, the COVID-19 pandemic confronts the CEE economies with a drastic external shock again. This time, the cause was the SARS-CoV-2 virus that spread from China across the globe incredibly fast and led to immediate government-induced lockdowns of the economies across the world. This unique combination of a public health crisis, global supply chain interruptions and collapse of demand resulted in an enormous economic downturn. The dire social effects due to increasing unemployment, expanding poverty and inequality are hard to imaging at this stage. The International Monitory Fund (IMF) forecasts a sharp GDP contraction in the range of –3.1 percent for Hungary to –9 percent for Croatia in 2020 (IMF, 2020). While larger economies, having the following forecasts, e.g., Poland –4.6 percent and Romania –5 percent, might be less affected, small export-oriented economies e.g., Slovenia is expected to contract by -8 percent, Lithuania by –8.1 percent and Slovakia by –6.2 percent. They will feel the collapse of international supply chains and foreign demand much stronger. For many CEE countries, the projected declines in their economic outputs will be more severe than those in 2009 (wiiw, 2020).

So how attractive will CEE be for Western multinationals in the post-COVID-19 times? While it is too early to document longer lasting re-orientations, we can make informed guesses on how structural business challenges that Western multinationals already faced before will change under the impact of the COVID-19 pandemic. Since 2014, the CEE economies have been on the catching-up path with decent GDP growth rates, outperforming the EU-28 average by 1.3–2.3 percentage points per year (wiiw, 2019a). Consequently the strong household consumption and rapidly rising wages following 2014 till the pre-COVID-19 pandemic backed this upswing and lifted up the firms' mood in CEE. While satisfied with the sales side, rising labor costs dimmed profitability and labor shortage hampered business expansion. The lack of labor in general and of skilled workers in particular, mirrored in extremely low unemployment rates of below 3 percent in the Czech Republic, Hungary and Poland, became a major challenge for companies operating in the region. Rapidly rising labor costs have questioned the sustainability of the low-cost business model – although in absolute terms labor costs are between 15 percent in Bulgaria and 50 percent in Slovenia of the Austrian and German level. This might partly explain the stagnating FDI inflows into EU-CEE 11 in the recent years at a level of €35 billion (wiiw, 2019b). A less investment-friendly climate due to capricious political interventions may be the other reason why Western investors shy away from further investments. However, ignoring those structural issues for a moment, the CEE economies were at the end of 2019 in a better shape than before the global financial crisis back that started in the region in 2008 with unprecedented low unemployment rates, fast rising wages fueling strong consumption and a sound macro-economic performance.

Which changes can we expect in the aftermath of the COVID-19 pandemic on structural issues such as labor shortage, ambiguous attitudes of local governments towards foreign investors, deteriorating institutions, and the needed transition from an efficiency-driven to an innovation-driven economy? The developments in these areas will strongly influence the attractiveness of the CEE economies for foreign investors.

Impact on Labor Shortage

Due to the lockdown and the collapse of demand, unemployment rates sharply increased in across the CEE region in March, April and May 2020. As some firms have started filing bankruptcies and business performance is not expected to get back to pre-COVID-19 levels quickly, the current unemployment will stay high for quite some time. Foreign production plants of Daimler, Bosch and Audi in Hungary restarted operations again in April but with one-third of their pre-COVID-19 staff. Meanwhile, global industry leaders, which scored high in best employer rankings in CEE, will be careful not to compromise their reputation by laying-off large numbers of staff. Moreover, they will try to keep their key personnel and talents throughout the difficult times of COVID-19. However, hard hit industries such as hospitality, airlines and non-grocery retailing, will not be able to keep all their personnel and so will feed the labor supply. This means a short-term relief for companies on the labor market.

The question is to what degree firms will find candidates for occupations in high demand such as skilled trades, IT staff, engineers and technicians. The lack of staff with the right skills was the main barrier to investment for businesses in EU-CEE (EIB, 2019: 33). Additionally, the expectations of employers towards the skills of their staff or job candidates will continually increase in areas such as specific technical qualifications, language skills and IT literacy (Wölfer, 2018: 19). The pandemic's impact on skills shortage might be weaker as key staff is not readily laid-off and the effect of a reversed brain drain is hard to gage. Although net migration rates have moderated in recent years, the continuing emigration lowers labor supply and hampers future growth. Dissatisfaction with life at home and the desire for higher incomes, a well-functioning social infrastructure and better career opportunities drive people, particularly young and educated ones, abroad. Italy and Spain were centers of the pandemic and have been only slowly lifting the lockdown restrictions what hurt their economies further and let unemployment soar. That might drive back home large numbers of Romanians, the most important immigrant group in both countries, but for how long? As the United Kingdom has lost in attractiveness as an emigration destination post-Brexit, some of the 1.3 million migrants from CEE might return too – or try to find a job in another high-income

Western EU member country. At the same time, the pandemic seems to have prepared the path for more lasting changes such as flexible and remote working arrangements and digital collaboration. That might open the labor market to highly sought after skills in the knowledge economy (e.g., IT and professional services, higher education), and the inclusion of otherwise difficult to reach groups living outside metropolitan areas.

In the mid- to long-term perspective, the projected dramatic demographic decline seems untouched by the pandemic and therefore will remain a crucial challenge for the CEE economies. Bosnia and Herzegovina, Bulgaria, Croatia, Hungary, Latvia, Lithuania and Romania are expected to see their populations decline by more than 15 percent by 2050 and the working-age population will shrink much faster reaching 25–30 percent in Bulgaria and Romania (UN, 2020). When investors have difficulties staffing their facilities then they will look for alternative destinations for their business expansion.

Impact on Politics and Institutions

Politics and institutional environment rank high among the criteria multinationals consider when making a FDI decision. In CEE, both areas are even more important given the outstanding role of economic policy and its pervasive influence even on a micro-level. German firms operating in CEE perceive economic policies as least satisfactory among three composite indicators used to measure the overall business climate in the region. While the overall satisfaction with the 16 countries in Central and Southeastern Europe hovers around a medium satisfaction value, the firms rate the operational environment and labor market more favorably than the factors related to the policy framework. Although there are noteworthy differences between these countries, the satisfaction in areas such as tax authorities, legal security, predictability of economic policies, corruption, transparency of public procurement and bureaucracy stay at inadequate levels – with corruption remaining the most severe problem across the region (Wölfer, 2018: 24). The Czech Republic, Poland, Estonia, Slovakia and Slovenia have been leading the overall ranking with a slightly better than average satisfaction value since 2011, whereas Romania and Hungary stabilized in the last years in terms of their ranking.

Anti-corruption organizations warned that the large amounts of money that are infused into the economies, especially in the health care sector, to alleviate the effects of the COVID-19 outbreak and the accompanying concentration of powers have exposed societies to considerable corruption risks. Scandals in several CEE countries around the rushed procurement of personal protective equipment have highlighted how deeply rooted corruption is in the region. The accusations range from bypassing open tender procedures over personal interventions from ministers for placing contracts with specified companies not active in healthcare yet and intermediaries close to public officials capturing excessive margins.

The negative political development in several EU countries such as Hungary and Poland has been the subject of heated debates in recent years. Holding the status of consolidated democracies back in 2010, Poland declined in the meantime to semi-consolidated democracy status. Hungary following an 'illiberal democracy' path under the Orban government, dropped even out of the group of democracies and became a transitional/hybrid regime – joining Serbia, Albania and the Ukraine (Freedom House, 2020: 3). Taking a stance from the perspective of institutional development, we get a similar picture. The Worldwide Governance Indicator covering among other dimensions the regulatory quality, rule of law and control of corruption it becomes apparent that over the last ten years there have been positive developments for the Czech Republic and Baltic countries but a reversal in the development, namely, a decline of the quality of institutions in Hungary, Poland and Slovakia (WGI, 2020). Good governance is commonly regarded as a precondition for a successful economic development, particularly when moving to a more complex, network-based knowledge economy. A deteriorating and low quality of institutions mirrored in rigged public tenders, a politically biased judiciary, discrimination against foreign firms and pervasive corruption may discourage firms from investing in a particular country.

Will the COVID-19 pandemic further add to the trends of authoritarianism, state capture and interference in the independence of institutions in CEE? Unfortunately, the overall picture is pointing in this direction. The pandemic brought the 'political imperative' back. Governments imposed lockdowns on societies and economies to safeguard their citizens against a disease unseen before in peacetime. They often came with emergency decrees and legislation expanding their power during the crisis. In Hungary, Prime Minister Orban declared emergency in March what gave him the power to sidestep parliament and suspend existing laws. The problem lies in the fact that governments with authoritarian traits might use this phase to change laws in their favor at the expense of opposition parties, media, and civil society, and might prolong emergency legislation after the crisis to consolidate their regimes.[3] It is very tempting to cling to the new won powers, especially in times when citizens recognize and largely accept the notion that a strong government and its interventions avoided the worst outcome in health and economic terms. Hence, the pandemic fosters conservative-nationalist governments that are working on reconfiguring the political and economic system into one that puts national interests first and is less dependent on investments made by foreign firms. They broaden the definition of 'strategic sectors', which inhibits dominant foreign influence or ownership nourishing state-owned or state-controlled businesses to expand the state's influence on the economy.[4] For instance, in May 2020 the Polish government announced that it considers its entry into the grocery retailing business. The government sees it as a chance to exercise control 'from the field to the table' and to guarantee the farmers fair margins on their products. Coincidentally, the big grocery retailers in Poland are all in foreign hands: the leading one, the discounter Biedronka, is owned by the Portuguese Jeronimo Martins Group; Lidl and Kaufland, Auchan and Tesco are the other leading grocery retailers all owned by foreign investors.

On a positive note, what might impress foreign investors are the quickly imposed and strict containment measures that helped the countries to keep the toll on human lives low. When comparing the deaths per 100,000 inhabitants internationally, then CEE countries are at the low end of the ranking (Johns Hopkins, 2020): Slovakia with a ratio of 0.5, Bulgaria with 1.9, Poland with 2.6, Czech Republic with 3 and Hungary with 5 compare very favorably with Western European countries such as Sweden with 39.3, Italy with 54.3 or Belgium 81.3. The governments can argue convincingly that they handled the public health crisis better than most other countries worldwide.

Despite all negative political news that made it to the headlines in the last years, according to the AHK study (Wölfer, 2018: 32) more than 80 percent of the foreign businesses stick to their investment decision and do not plan to exit the country where they have invested. Furthermore, the foreign multinationals appreciated the relative political and macroeconomic stability in CEE – at least those that have not been targeted by special taxes, unilateral contract conversions and re-nationalization (How, 2019). Particularly, the Central European governments are pampering job creating, export-oriented and R&D bringing investors with low corporate income taxes – Hungary leads in the EU with a rate of 9 percent access to government support (and EU funds) through 'strategic partnerships', flexible labor laws, and special economic zones with tax reliefs. Surprisingly enough and unnoticed by the public, some of the foreign multinationals have found ways to benefit from and coexist with the politics of national-populist governments.

For foreign firms a decisive moment will come, when the governments present their plans on how to cover the extraordinary expenses. One important lesson learnt from the recent global financial crisis is that populist-nationalist governments in CEE will turn to sectors where foreign ownership is high such as financial services, grocery retailing and telecommunications to foot the bill. They have plenty of experience in levying special taxes ('bank tax') from multinationals or take other discriminatory regulatory action. As the European Court of Justice recently did not object in its verdict progressive, turnover-based taxes on retailers and telecom firms in Hungary, large firms can expect to pay proportionally higher taxes than smaller firms in the future.

Impact on the Transition to an Innovation-Driven Economy

One obvious lasting outcome of the COVID-19 pandemic may be further penetration and acceleration of the digitalization of numerous areas of our life. These range from remote working, digital collaboration and virtual teaching to business operations and supply chains. CEE economies have been struggling with the transition from the prevalent low-cost economic model to an innovation-driven economy. They are looking for new growth models that go beyond imitation and the import of technology. Productivity increase is expected to come from further specialization, 'home-grown' innovations and internationalization of local firms. Digitalization will play a pivotal role in these plans, as digitalization is associated with better firm performance and management practices, higher innovativeness and faster growth (EIB, 2019). The COVID-19 pandemic has objectively emphasized the necessity and relevance of a broader adoption of digital technology.

How well are now the CEE economies prepared for the digital age? In a recent report McKinsey (2019) considered ten EU-CEE countries as 'digital challengers' as they demonstrate strong potential for growth in the digital economy – Estonia is even rated as a 'digital forerunner' together with the leading Nordic countries. Major reasons for this positive appraisal are good educational systems reflected in leading PISA scores – Estonian, Polish and Slovenian students are among the best in the world from a large STEM/ICT talent pool with over 230,000 graduates. A high-quality digital infrastructure and a vibrant digital ecosystem with innovative and internationally active firms are other assets. Successful firms, which demonstrate the huge potential, can be found in the fields of internet security (Avast, Eset, Bitdefender), game development (CD Projekt, Invictus Games), mobile payments (Fortumo, TransferWise), e-commerce (Alza, Mall Group, Allegro) and software solutions (Assecco, Comarch, YSoft). However, a better cooperation between scientific and business sectors and international collaboration is needed. Right now, the innovation performance depends often on isolated initiatives of inventors and visionary founders. CEE governments have begun to tackle these weaknesses with national innovation programs (often supported by EU funds) and by cooperating with global industry leaders. In May 2020, Microsoft announced a comprehensive US$1 billion investment plan with its strategic partner, the Polish cloud provider Chmura Krajowa, to accelerate innovation and digital transformation. This includes the opening of a new Microsoft datacenter in Poland as part of its global-scale cloud to provide the country's startups, firms, and public institutions access to secure, high-level cloud services. This project is part of the government's plan to accelerate Poland's transformation into a technological hub for the CEE region. In

Hungary, the government opened a test track for self-driving vehicles in Zalaegerszeg, the 'Zala zone', in 2019. They intend to assist the strong local automotive industry in validation tests for autonomous and electric vehicles. In this way, the Hungarian government responds to the current needs of the transforming local automotive industry (among them BMW, Audi, Daimler, Bosch, and Continental) and brings them together with Hungarian technical universities, research centers and startups. It was one the reasons why BMW chose Hungary for the location of its new plant in Debrecen in 2019.

Conclusion

The COVID-19 pandemic interrupted a positive economic development in the EU-CEE 11 member states that was the case in the last years. The pandemic led to a severe economic downturn as in the rest of Europe but the governments were quite effective in handling the situation in many of these countries so far. While the exposure of individual countries to the lockdown have varied, the overall attractiveness of the countries has so far remained rather stable, especially when seen in relation to other countries and regions. If the CEE economies are among the relative winners or losers in the aftermath of the pandemic largely depends on the degree on the economic development in Germany and Western Europe as a whole based on a close integration demonstrated via international trade, tourism, supply chains, and people's migration. The clear de-globalization trends might benefit CEE economies as low-cost production destinations in Europe. The intention to bring in the region strategically sensitive sectors such as medical supplies and equipment, pharmaceuticals and critical products (e.g., batteries) could lead to further investments in CEE countries. At the same time, the threat of intensifying trade wars between the U.S., China and EU may lure investors from China and the U.S. into the region, wanting to secure their participation in the EU single market at competitive costs.

The stronger role of the state that is on the rise due COVID-19 pandemic is likely to stay in the long run. Nationalist-populist governments can easily justify massive state interventions as long as the pandemic endures and later when the funding of the recovery and budget deficits is brought up. Domestic market-oriented foreign multinationals have to prepare for this situation, as they will be a primary target for footing the bill. However, this will be a delicate balancing act for the governments, which want to keep existing investors in core industries such as automotive, electronics or business process outsourcing services and attract new ones that rely heavily on R&D. There will be a need for cooperation with global multinationals to drive forward the transformation of CEE countries to knowledge economies and their digitalization. This effort requires not just capital but access to state-of-the-art technology, education and international research networks. The biggest challenge remains the labor and skills shortage. Although the situation might be easing in the short-term thanks to the rising unemployment caused by government responses to COVID-19, finding the needed amount of staff with the right skills will haunt foreign investors. Whereas higher automation in existing facilities may reduce the strain, the Western Balkans, the Ukraine and Turkey already present themselves to EU-CEE 11 investors as attractive alternative low-cost locations for business expansions. This constellation will help investors that provide important contributions to the national economic development in their bargaining with CEE governments. In any case, foreign multinationals will have to pay more attention to individual country specifics, upgrade regional management competencies in their organizations and consider a more comprehensive use of political strategies and business diplomacy to protect the sustainability of their local businesses in the CEE.

Notes

1 The main foreign investors in CEE come from Western Europe. In 2017, companies from the EU-28 held about 88 percent of the total stocks of FDI in EU-CEE 11 and those from the 'old EU-15' accounted for 78 percent (wiiw, 2019).
2 The focus lies on the EU-CEE 11 countries although some of the mentioned reports refer to a larger group of countries.
3 Hungary's government announced on May 26 that it will end a coronavirus-related state of emergency on June 20.
4 Here it is fair to mention that the EU issued guidelines in March to protect companies in strategic sectors from takeovers by non-EU entities. However, the difference lies in the fact that nationalist governments often use such extraordinary situations to advance their conservative-nationalist agendas.

References

Bruegel, 2010. *Whither Growth in Central and Eastern Europe? Policy Lessons for an Integrated Europe, vol.XI*. Bruegel Blueprint Series, Brussels.
EIB, 2019. Who is prepared for the new digital age? European Investment Bank investment survey. https://www.eib.org/en/publications/who-is-prepared-for-the-new-digital-age (accessed 25.05.20).
Freedom House, 2020. Nations in transit 2020. https://freedomhouse.org/report/nations-transit (accessed 16.05.20).
IMF, 2020. *World Economic Outlook – The Great Lockdown*. International Monetary Fund, Washington, D.C., April.
How, M., 2019. *How many straws to break a camel's back? How do illiberal economies attract so much FDI*. bne-intellinews, October 15, 2019.
Johns Hopkins, 2020. Covid-19 case tracker. Johns Hopkins Coronavirus Research Center. https://coronavirus.jhu.edu/ (accessed 18.05.20).
McKinsey, 2019. *The rise of digital – How digitization can become the next growth engine for Central and Eastern Europechallengers*. McKinsey Central Europe.

https://www.mckinsey.com/~/media/mcKinsey/Featured%20Insights/Europe/
Central%20and%20Eastern%20Europe%20needs%20a%20new%20engine
%20for%20growth/The-rise-of-Digital-Challengers.ashx (accessed 18.05.20).

Schuh, A., 2012. Strategy review for central and eastern Europe: strategic
responses of foreign multinational corporations to the recent economic and
financial crisis. *J. East-West Bus. 18*(2), 185–207.

UN, 2020. *World Population Prospects 2019.* United Nations. https://population.
un.org/wpp/ (accessed 14.05.20).

World Bank, 2020. *Worldwide Governance Indicators.* WGI database. https://
datacatalog.worldbank.org/dataset/worldwide-governance-indicators (accessed
19.05.20).

WGI, 2020. *The Worldwide Government Indicators.* Washington, D. C.: World
Bank Group.

wiiw, 2019a. *Handbook of Statistics 2019 - Central, East and Southeast Europe.*
Vienna Institute for International Economic Studies, Vienna.

wiiw, 2019b. *FDI Report 2019.* Vienna Institute for International Economic
Studies, Vienna.

wiiw, 2020. wiiw further cuts its forecast for economic growth in Eastern Europe
to below 2009 level and seeks weaker recovery. https://wiiw.ac.at/wiiw-
further-cuts-its-forecast-for-economic-growth-in-eastern-europe-to-below-
2009-level-and-sees-weaker-recovery-n-442.html (accessed 22.05.20).

Wölfer, D., 2018. *AHK Investment Climate Survey 2018.* German-Hungarian
Chamber of Industry and Commerce, Budapest, May.

29 Large Firms and COVID-19

Insights from Brazil

Thomaz Wood Jr., Jorge Carneiro, and Maria Tereza Leme Fleury

Introduction

COVID-19 has already affected the business arena in similar ways across most of the world. Considering these there may be implications concerning the ways with which to deal with the current and future challenges of the COVID-19 crisis specific in particular countries. In this chapter, we explore the case of Brazil, one of the hardest-hit countries by the pandemic.

The evidence presented comes from direct information presented by senior executives who are either students at executive programs offered by FGV Sao Paulo School of Administration or participate in the School's research projects on the internationalization of Brazilian firms. Besides, we also build from the opinions and perceptions voiced by top executives at webinars held in the period from March to May 2020. Most of the annotations apply both to Brazilian domestic and international firms, and we have also tried to draw some specific consequences for doing business in the international arena.

How COVID-19 Changed the Brazilian Competitive Landscape

COVID-19 has caused a major shock to the Brazilian economy, which before pandemic was little by little recovering from a recession. As in other countries, restrictions on mobility have led to the disruption of almost all sectors of their economies. Table 29.1 exemplifies how the pandemic changed the competitive environment and the competitive factors in Brazil, and how different types of companies are expected to be affected.

Currently, Brazil is experiencing a political crisis, which introduces new effects or amplifies the COVID-19 pandemic effects on firms. While the combination of negative and positive effects of the crisis can range from a strong survival threat to a significant growth opportunity, many Brazilian companies would, in the medium and long term, discontinue

Table 29.1 Competitiveness Factors and Pandemic Impacts

ECONOMY

Competitiveness Factors	Pandemic Impacts
Natural resources: high availability, favoring especially mining and agribusiness	No direct influence of COVID-19 pandemic; however, the government's environmental policy, out of line with global trends, may harm the business of Brazilian companies, mainly exporting and agribusiness
Labor: relatively scarce technical labor, especially in high-tech areas, but good pool of managerial force; low-skilled labor abounds	COVID-19 increased unemployment, with effect on wages, lowering costs for companies; however, recovering may suffer from bottleneck of qualified technical labor; escape of high-level talent
Capital availability: greater availability of venture capital, due to the reduction in interest rates (in Brazil and abroad) accelerated by the pandemic	Impact by COVID-19 on the access to venture capital, for investments to expand capacity, improve processes, automate and digitize.
Income: unemployment and salary reductions, especially affecting the lower income classes	Numerous industries witnessed reduction in demand due to COVID-19.
Foreign investment: capital outflow due to the pandemic and the political crisis	COVID-19 has lowered availability of capital for foreign investment.
Exchange rate: very intense devaluation of the Brazilian currency in the beginning of the pandemic; recovery trend not expected to reach the level prior to the crisis	Increased competitiveness and margins for exporting companies, with the resulting increase in their capital for investments.
Basic infrastructure: deficient, mainly outside large urban centers and more developed	COVID-19 has caused negative impact on costs and risks; reduction in

Table 29.1 (Continued)

Competitiveness Factors	Pandemic Impacts
regions; political difficulty to carry out privatizations and reforms	competitiveness. However, increase in home office and use of remote means of communication did not represent apparent stress in the telecom system.
Technology: technological developed concentrated in some sectors	Technological acceleration of exporting sectors, agribusiness; improvements in retail and some services.

POLITICS AND INTERNATIONAL RELATIONS

Political situation: increased political instability, with crises between the three powers (legislative, executive and judiciary) and conflicts between the federal and state levels	COVID-19 has caused increased perception of uncertainty, inhibiting investments.
International relations: erratic movement; crises with important trading partners	Potential negative effects of COVID-19 (independent of the pandemic) on businesses, especially Chinese investments and sustainability-related businesses.

NATIONAL STRATEGIES AND PUBLIC POLICY

Economic policy: firm neo-liberal trend, including deregulation and privatization, with strong business support for reforms	Reforms postponed due to the COVID-19 pandemic, with the adoption of economic measures to mitigate the effects of the recession; continuation of reforms is uncertain due to the political crisis and the approaching municipal elections.
Commercial trade: reduced import tariffs since the 1990s, but the country maintains	Reduction in trade due to the COVID-19 pandemic; trend of heterogeneous

(*Continued*)

Table 29.1 (Continued)

Competitiveness Factors	Pandemic Impacts
a relatively low degree of integration with global value chains	resumption as large trading partners resume activities.
Monetary policy: declining interest rate, reaching unprecedented levels in the country's history	Due to COVID-19 discouragement to fixed income investments and speculative capital; incentive to allocate capital to risky assets, favoring investments and new businesses.
Tax system: complex system, penalizing the business environment; reform initiatives dependent on political coalitions	COVID-19 and political crisis postponing and putting reforms at risk; discouragement to foreign capital investment.

INDUSTRIAL DYNAMICS AND STRUCTURE

Competitiveness Factors	Pandemic Impacts
Industrial structure: many industries with low rivalry	COVID-19 and political crisis postponed reforms to modernize the regulatory system and stimulate competition.
Ownership: many companies under family control, with low degree of professionalization and management	COVID-19 pandemic tends to penalize more strongly companies with poorly developed management practices.
Informal economy: pervasive throughout the economy	Informal economy tends to grow during the pandemic, with negative effects on the economy as a whole.

MANAGEMENT, ORGANIZATIONAL STRUCTURE AND ORGANIZATIONAL CULTURE

Competitiveness Factors	Pandemic Impacts
Strategy and business models: great heterogeneity of strategic and business practices, across industries and across companies within industries	COVID-19 tends to favor companies with better strategic practices, especially scenario analysis; opportunities for countercyclical strategic actions arise

(*Continued*)

Table 29.1 (Continued)

Competitiveness Factors	Pandemic Impacts
Organizational models: still significant presence, in some sectors, of hierarchical and functional structures	COVID-19, together with digitization and automation processes, should accelerate the adoption of leaner and more agile organizational models
Management models / managerial practices: great heterogeneity between sectors and between companies within sectors, with significant gaps in terms of planning, control and operational management	COVID-19 pandemic tends to favor companies with more advanced models and practices and greater capacity to adapt to unpredictable and turbulent environments
Organizational culture: high power distance, reduced autonomy and low degree of initiative; but softened by a nascent entrepreneurial or intrapreneurial culture	Potentially COVID-19 contributes to the acceleration of cultural change, favoring values and behaviors more oriented towards results, flexibility, agility, cooperation and autonomy.

Sources: The Authors, based on Caldas and Wood (2007); Coutinho and Ferraz (2002).

experiencing the effects of the pandemic. Naturally, favorable outcomes would materialize if managers interpret correctly the pandemic environment and make appropriate strategic decisions.

The next section shows an illustrative picture of how large Brazilian firms are dealing with the COVID-19 crisis. While the overall feeling is of great concern, there is in general a positive outlook for the future. In order that this outlook would materialize, companies would have to change and upgrade appropriately their managerial decision-making processes.

How Large Brazilian Firms Have Dealt with COVID-19

While companies operating in Brazil acknowledge *the seriousness and 'novelty' of the crisis,* they express *serene attitudes and positive outlooks for the future.* The most experienced senior executives mention various local and global crises that have already been experienced and successfully overcome. Several firms have sought scientific knowledge and engaged more in evidence-based management. Although some companies say that they manage on a daily basis and other indicate that it has been difficult to engage in long-term planning, many companies admit that they work with scenarios, albeit changing them almost on a daily basis as new information is incorporated. Even in the face of the very high degree of uncertainty (or maybe because of it), these companies deem scenarios as essential to guide decisions (although their leaders are quite laconic in terms of advancing their visions of the future).

Overall, companies stress *trust and support for ongoing health-related and economic measures.* In the first weeks of the COVID-19 crisis in Brazil, businesspersons believed that the sanitary measures adopted were the most suitable and they were clearly opposed to premature relaxation of the lockdown. They have recognized that social isolation measures would have a strong economic impact but understood that their early relaxation would be even worse. Some senior executives have mentioned the need for more aggressive economic measures, in order to withstand the difficulties that would be faced by companies, especially by the small and medium enterprises (SMEs). As the economic crisis deepened, some business associations started pressing the government (at the federal, state and municipal levels) to relax isolation gradually, while enforcing sanitary precautions in work facilities and consumer services.

Business leaders emphasize the importance of *preserving jobs and the morale of their workforce.* Virtually, all companies mobilize resources quickly – in about a week – to make remote work possible for a large part of their staff – in some cases for tens of thousands of employees. Quickly, though, work-related commitments have increased sharply because leading in a volatile, uncertain, complex and ambiguous environment implying unplanned events and disruption in schedules requires investing more resources and time in order to prioritize matters and keep things under control. When things (work, family) get mixed up, people become stressed out. So, the challenge is how to keep work teams engaged (mentally and physically) and productive. Leadership skills become critical. Companies that have kept closer contact with employees (e.g., frequent informal virtual meetings, including talks with CEOs) perceive that it helps keep employees motivated and connected with the company.

Companies claim to have adopted one or more of the following *measures to soften the burden on their employees:* frozen layoffs, usually for sixty days, to give their employees peace of mind; special care for employees in health risk segments (e.g., the elderly); anticipation of payment of thirteenth salary (which is legally due only in December). Some companies also sent computers to employees' homes and provided legal, financial and psychological support remotely (including, in some cases, artificial-intelligence systems to assist employees in health-related cituations). Companies have acknowledged huge diversity across the country and implemented measures appropriate to each reality. They also have adopted the best practices of subsidiaries located in countries that were more advanced in experiencing the COVID-19 crisis. Most companies have reduced their capital investments and operational disbursements, and several have adopted legal measures – such as reduction in employee compensation and respective workload as well as vacation anticipation – as a way to reduce current costs and prepare to face the challenges of the future. They believe that it is important to retain employees since sales are expected to grow after the crisis. Companies that have understood the distress of their employees and have taken measures to help them overcome the distress perceive that employees recognize these efforts and are grateful for them. All in all, they recommend greater emphasis on the human aspects of work relations with a change from a bureaucratic and legal approach to a tenderhearted and cultural one. Interestingly, one company indicated that there may be an opportunity to recruit elderly workers who have retired but would still be productive; as long as they have digital expertise, they could engage very well in remote part-time hours. So, there could be a reversal in the unspoken prejudice against elderly people in the workplace. However, such workforce may accept lower salaries, which may bring down employee related cost in general.

Companies have also tried to *reinforce customer relations and care for the financial health of their suppliers.* For example, banks have changed terms of payment for loans or payment for purchases on credit. Several executives, especially those from retail firms, have declared that they are concerned with their supply chains, composed of numerous SMEs without buffers to overcome the crisis. Some large companies are taking firm action to protect their chains, by means of credit lines, as well as managerial, financial, legal and labor advice. Since a great number of companies, which buy from or sell to other larger companies, do not have home-office culture/experience, the largest of them have brought their IT teams to help by providing infrastructure and training (e.g., VPNs - virtual private networks). In addition, more transparency over costing and pricing can be witnessed, so that companies should be able to secure their contracts based on quality, availability and flexibility. The focus seems to be shifting from saving costs to driving value (sharing knowledge, solving problems, optimizing each other's networks and going beyond). By being empathetic, companies hope to strengthen relationships, already planning for post-crisis times. Some have stressed the importance of personalization of contacts with customers.

Interestingly, *cooperation initiatives among competitors for mutual support and support to the society* have been encouraged. The crisis seems to have brought competitors closer together. They have learned (or have improved), first, sharing experiences about each other's actions to face the crisis. Second, they have triggered joint actions towards government agencies, be it pleading for support or offering help. Third, they have conducted social actions – such as donation of financial resources and production equipment as well as materials for hospitals – financial support to small and local companies and donation of food to the poor, as a way to live up to their promised commitment to society. The federal government has also come in: "The Brazilian financial system is solid and supports companies", says the CEO of a large private bank.

Boards of directors need to incorporate even greater responsibilities regarding firm risk management, establishment or reinforcement of crisis management committees, precautions towards cyber security, managing internal and external communication – particularly with investors whose activism seems to has raised, with pressures for short-term profits and better long-term environmental, social and governance (ESG) standards.

The COVID-19 crisis has been a catalyzer of *change from anachronistic patterns of behavior to innovation* by breaking resistance and encouraging new attitudes. Interestingly, some senior executives have stated that communication, even in isolation, has improved significantly, and the decision-making process has become more agile. Productivity levels of administrative activities have indeed increased in several companies, with meetings being much more directly to the point and actions shortly following decisions. The crisis has taught people and companies to be more agile and deal with divergent opinions for the sake of implementing changes quickly. Some companies noted that remote work has shown to be more efficient than office hours. Interestingly, numerous companies are already expecting that some of their employees will prefer to work remotely some days per week after the crisis. Such possible changes might open up the opportunity for co-working spaces in offices and corresponding reduction in space rental. Several public services have improved efficiency by moving their employees to their home offices, while others almost stopped serving the clients.

Digitalization, a process that has already started in many organizations prior COVID-19, has been mentioned by many senior executives as essential to enable companies to respond positively to the challenges imposed changes they face. Born digital companies, nonetheless, have to improve their management since the cash-burning spree is over and the ecosystem has changed, as stated by the CEO of born digital company. One of the authors of this chapter, has just conducted a study of the digitalization of Brazilian MNEs covering the manufacturing and services industries as well as the new breed of born digital companies. She noted a model in which digital transformation involves five capabilities: data management, people management, digital technical capability, organizational capability, and cultural crafting capability. The more advanced the company is in terms of digital transformation, the more agile its decision-making process and the better its capacity to manage the value chain and be part of the eco-innovation system. It has been found that he COVID-19 pandemic has accelerated the digital transformation process of numerous companies. The initiatives address six focal targets: employees, communities, customers, new products, production processes, and strategy formulation and implementation.

A Typology to Help Understand How Large Brazilian Firms Deal with COVID-19

In the sections above we have discussed how the competitive environment and the factors of competitiveness have been strongly altered by the COVID-19 pandemic in Brazil, and how companies have reacted to this crisis. We have seen that the effects are multiple and complex and can affect different firms in diverse ways. We have also revealed that the reactions of large companies show some discernible patterns.

In this section, we argue that the core of company reactions to the crisis lies in managers' ability to realize the competitive factors in a comprehensive way and look for appropriate solutions to be implemented flexibly according to the unfolding phases of the crisis.

To support the analysis and for didactic purposes, we use the typology by Caldas and Wood (2007), which considers two dimensions for the classification of firms: the external factors and internal factors. The former can be classified as favorable or unfavorable, and the latter as articulated or disarticulated. As a result, there are four 'typical types' of firms, each corresponding to a quadrant of a 2 × 2 matrix (see Figure 29.1).

EXTERNAL FACTORS		
	Unfavorable	**Favorable**
INTERNAL FACTORS — **Articulate**	**(A)** **Restricted company:** environmental factors hinder or limit the development of competitive advantages; managers articulate effective responses to contextual problems	**(B)** **Successful company:** environmental factors favor the development of competitive advantages; managers adequately articulate internal factors to take advantage of context
Disarticulate	**(C)** **Threatened company:** environmental factors hinder or limit the development of competitive advantages; managers are unable to internally articulate an effective response to contextual problems	**(D)** **'Wasted' company:** environmental factors favor the development of competitive advantages; managers are unable to articulate an adequate configuration to take advantage of the favorable context

Figure 29.1 Company Typologies.
Source: The authors. Adapted from Caldas and Wood (2007).

The typology presented in Figure 29.1 allows speculation of possible movements of companies between the quadrants due to the impacts of COVID-19 on the competitive environment. Let us look at some illustrative examples. Successful companies (quadrant B) can quickly perceive that external factors have overall changed from favorable to unfavorable, which then would place them in quadrant A with risk of downgrading to quadrant C, therefore requiring readjustment actions. Alternatively, threatened companies (quadrant C) may suddenly perceive that the external factors have changed from unfavorable to favorable, which would move them first, to quadrant D. Such companies may remain in this quadrant or carry out internal adaptation actions to migrate to quadrant B, the one of a successful company.

Most of the companies depicted previously are located in quadrant B. They maintain that the COVID-19 pandemic would be only a short-term challenge and also see it as presenting opportunities for business growth in the medium term. Their managers seem to believe in a careful 'riding' of the crisis, coupled with actions to prepare for a recovery in which their privileged conditions would enhance their competitive advantages.

Reflections and Conclusion

Brazilian Specifics

While many impacts of COVID-19 are common to all countries, there are some particularities in the Brazilian case.

First, the *devaluation of the Brazilian currency*, not only in relation to the U.S. dollar and the euro, but also relatively to the currencies of other emerging economies, has increased the country's competitiveness (regarding factor costs) and improved opportunities for exporting. In addition, the liquidity of markets after the U.S. and EU poured money into their economies as well as the low (or even negative) return of low-risk assets in those markets opens up opportunities for acquisitions by foreign companies in Brazil and for investments in infrastructure projects. The question that remains is whether Brazil would continue to be a low labor cost country instead of investing to upgrade its technical, marketing and managerial capabilities.

Second, the *high tax burden and highly complex tax system* deepens the difficulties faced by many firms. The pandemic has delayed reforms and the political crisis has made these reforms uncertain.

Third, the *inflexible labor laws* have been somewhat relaxed before COVID-19 pandemic and temporally further relaxed to deal with the challenges of the crisis. However, overall Brazil has rather high labor charges and regulations (Carneiro, 2019). The delays of pandemic delayed reforms have created uncertainties.

Fourth, there are *deficiencies in the telecommunication infrastructure*, precarious in many parts of the country, which limit the appropriateness of responses to COVID-19. Moreover, the digital readiness of Brazil is low (Yoo et al., 2018), which means that the country has a long way to go in providing adequate digital literacy and infrastructure, as well as to overcome over-regulation and red tape.

Fifth, the *culture of close social contacts* in Brazil by which people value personal relationships higher than professional interactions is another type of specificity to be considered in relation to COVID-19. Nevertheless, companies and people have adapted surprisingly well to the new conditions imposed by the pandemic. Precautions regarding possible future lawsuits on the grounds of overtime and moral harassment are in the radar of certain companies.

The Cases of Brazilian Multinationals and Foreign Multinationals in Brazil

The COVID-19 pandemic has also had an impact on Brazilian multinationals and foreign multinationals operating in Brazil. These companies constitute an elite group, as they have adopted more sophisticated management practices than their non-internationalized counterparts. They are generally positioned in quadrant B (successful company) as indicated in Figure 29.1.

At first, all of these companies were strongly affected by the pandemic imposed problems of global value chains. It is expected that in the medium term, multinationals in different industry sectors may face different scenarios. Commodity-exporting multinational firms (e.g., grain, ores, pulp) will continue to benefit from the country's favorable climatic conditions, abundance of natural resources and technology, with their competitiveness leveraged by the favorable exchange rate for exporting of the Brazil real, and their performance moderated by the (expected) resumption in their major markets expecting a rapid recovery. Multinationals that export industrial goods (e.g., automobiles, buses and airplanes) may experience a slower recovery due to the market retraction for their products, with special concerns for the air transport sector. Computer service multinationals are facing a historic opportunity for expansion, as the pandemic related crisis can greatly accelerate investments in digitalization. An especially worrying case is the export of oil derivatives and petrochemical products since the pandemic is compounded by a specific crisis of excess supply in the market.

Final Remarks

By June 10, 2020, Brazil had worrying numbers of people contaminated and killed by COVID-19. In addition to the pandemic crisis, a political crisis is also worrying with demonstrations against or in favor of the government across the country.

Short-term urgencies certainly make it difficult to build medium and long-term scenarios. Many Brazilian firms, especially SMEs, would probably not survive the pandemic crisis. The consequences for the level of employment and for the society in general would be significant.

This chapter presents an account of the way in which large Brazilian companies, more robust and capable of dealing successfully with the pandemic deal with its challenges. We hope that their corporate citizenship practices, their initiatives to support value and supply chains, and their digitalization projects should assist them getting successfully through the COVID-19 challenges. Their contribution would certainly be remarkable to mitigate the effects of the crisis on the Brazilian society and contribute to the creation of a more conducive business environment post pandemic.

References

Caldas, M.P., Wood Jr., T., 2007. Por que as Empresas Brasileiras Não São Globalmente Competitivas? (Why Brazilian Firms Are not Competitive Globally?). *EG Economia e Gestão* 7, 178–193.

Carneiro, J., 2019. Managing Multinationals in Brazil – Opportunities and Challenges. In: Grosse, R., Meyer, K. (Eds.), *Oxford Handbook of Management in Emerging Markets*. Oxford University Press, Oxford, 677–703.

Coutinho, L., Ferraz, J. C., (Eds.). 2002. *Estudo da Competitividade da Indústria Brasileira*. (Brazilian Industry Competitiveness Study) (4th Edition). Papirus Editora, Campinas.

Yoo, T., de Wysocki, M., Cumberland, A. 2018. *Country Digital Readiness: Research to Determine a Country's Digital Readiness and Key Interventions*. https://www.cisco.com/c/dam/assets/csr/pdf/Country-Digital-Readiness-White-Paper-US. (Accessed on June5, 2020).

Part VIII
Conclusive Chapter

30 Disrupting Globalization

Prospects for States and Firms in International Business

Svetla Marinova

Change of Era

The COVID-19 pandemic has led the world to a crisis that has grasped countries simultaneously in spite of geography, level of economic development or socio-political system. The blow was swift and hefty; the economic effects were instantaneous – businesses closed, bankruptcies loomed, supply chains fell apart, and unemployment soared. Predictions for unimaginable drop in countries' gross domestic product (GDP) came true and grim prospects for quick economic recovery kindled. In this regard, the COVID-19 pandemic has acted as a critical juncture igniting an abrupt process of change (see Figure 30.1), the consequences of which are still to unfold. Their extent will be disparate for countries, industries, companies and individuals, and almost impossible to outline in detail with certainty.

The de-globalization process, which was triggered by the 2008–2009 financial crisis and engrained by the election of President Trump, started a change of the era of globalization. The discontinuity could be as a result of gradual transformation or breakdown and replacement. The scale, speed and scope of the COVID-19 pandemic have acted as a critical juncture that has accelerated the abrupt change process. In this change process, some actors adamantly supporting globalization are aiming to achieve survival and return to hyper-globalization, while others standing for nation-led and regionally centered power reconfiguration are adopting a strategy of breakdown and replacement of previous socio-political and economic relationships (see Figure 30.1). The juxtaposition of these forces is causing an extreme tension between the attempts to drive change processes to survival and return to the old normal and those pushing it into breakdown and replacement.

COVID-19 has just hastened the changes leading to breakdown and replacement leading to de-globalization. Political forces undermined hyper-globalization as a neoliberal model of globalization, which favored the global market as the dominant business exchange regulating mechanism in which multinational companies (MNCs) formed a supranational system operating beyond and above most nation states. Thus, MNCs were exposed

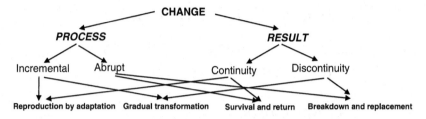

Figure 30.1 Process and Result of Change: Possible Consequent Actions.
Source: The Author, adapted from Streeck and Thelen (2005).

to few institutional regulating mechanisms, enjoyed high bargaining power vis-à-vis most national governments, and created a thorough system mitigating national government regulatory limitations, therefore, reducing the role of the nation state as governing the access to national resources and their use for enhancing public welfare. COVID-19 is now forcing national governments to employ new national polity, and re-instatement of national borders is only one aspect of the political re-focus on national interests based on health and economic benefits.

The desperate need for medical equipment and medication across the world has demonstrated the limitations of globalization and the regulating power of global market transaction mechanisms, thus exposing the inability of national health systems with lower bargaining power to access scarce medical resources in comparison with global influencers who employed in some cases ethically questionable supply behavior. Moreover, the concentrated production of pharmaceutical industry inputs in countries such as China and India, which was motivated by seeking greater efficiency based on lower labor and production costs, exposed the inability of such a model to respond to sudden increases in demand of unprecedented scale and scope across the globe.

The battle to ensure protective equipment, medicines, medical supplies and ventilators exposed the limitations of the neoliberal market-driven globalization model as a force for economic and social development, mostly in its ability to address global needs and simultaneously protect national interests. This seemingly resolved by the globalization of markets and production chasm was dramatically exposed as a rigid dichotomy. Consequently, nations closed down and only a few cases of nation-to-nation (state-to-state) support based on socio-cultural, historic, ideological or integration commitments at a time of extreme hardship became possible. The drive for nation-centered supplies and nation-focused access to limited resources has not only exposed the flaws of the neoliberal globalization, but has also opened up deep societal fissures embedded in the past experiences of nations.

The failure of the neoliberal globalization model at a time of a sudden crisis has also opened up opportunities for nation states to swiftly mobilize own resources in order to deliver a national response to the crisis.

Countries such as China, South Korea, Japan, Israel, Russia, Germany, Vietnam, Singapore and Denmark, among others, have excelled in their national collective response to this crisis. Here, the maturity of institutions as per international comparisons and all the arguments about strong and weak institutions arguing that emerging economies have huge voids in their institutional fields, have given ground to and been questioned by the crisis-imposed reality check. Countries such as China, Vietnam, South Korea and Russia, to name just a few, despite being classified as emerging economies with institutional voids, have shown huge resilience and ability to quickly mobilize and structure their national response to the pandemic. Thus, at a time of a global crisis when the role of a supranational institution was questioned (i.e., the World Health Organization – WHO), efficiency-based health systems in some countries with mature institutions have failed to tackle a crisis of such a magnitude. Unlike these, the ability of national governments to act swiftly by mobilizing resources and organizing a targeted effective response to the crisis has proven most valuable and effective. In this regard, it has become evident that some countries with a sound social contract have fared much better than certain individualistic states. Hence, the COVID-19 pandemic has stressed the importance of the government as a key institutional actor with its ability to organize national policies and strategies, define effective governing mechanisms, and design fast, resource mobilizing and efficient operational responses.

The COVID-19 pandemic has questioned the role of supranational institutions such as the WHO and the World Trade Organization. The pressure on them has increased by limiting their importance via unilateral impositions driving forward the agenda of marginalizing supranational organizations and the role of competitor nation-states. Because of such actions, the competition, juxtaposition, contradictions and various conflicts among nation-states have flared up. Parallel with these, the key challenge to advanced nation states has become the reshaping of their national economy and the main task is reinforce their ability to compete in the post-technological era by boosting their industrial and financial capital, and limiting the access of their competitors to markets and technology. This gives a clue about the recent calls for sanctions, embargoes, tariffs and other type of limitations that the U.S., the EU, the U.K., Canada and Australia, among others, have initiated and/or imposed. COVID-19 is just an accelerator of this juxtaposing by paralyzing international trade, border closures, imposing quarantine and consequently, decoupling the movement of goods, services and people, decoupling production, supply and technology chains, which in the globally interconnected and interdependent economy is bringing businesses to extreme hardship leading to an unprecedented collapse beyond the borders of any nation-state. Subsequently, predictions for a drastic fall of GDP, continuous loss of personal income and lack of jobs, serious threat of bad loans that borrowers cannot return, altogether start bursting the growth-oriented economic bubble and may in the end direct resources to powerful industrial and technological giants that would ensure new levels of technological and industrial leadership.

Decoupling of Production, Supply Chains and Technology

The polity changes are altering the balance between foreign direct investment (FDI) and national investment, thus, re-shaping economic strategies. The global production networks and supply chains that had largely diminished the role of product specialization and trading models between countries had managed to improve production efficiency and provided a stimulus for consumption-driven development, benefiting producers and consumers in developed and emerging markets alike. However, the rise of emerging economies and their increased collective bargaining power, their ability to quickly copy existing and catch-up with extant technologies, and the newly developed innovation and market-oriented potential of their MNCs have challenged the positions of developed-country MNCs and their access to limited resources, markets and production sites as desired location advantages. Consequently, the current pandemic has justified major shifts in global supply chains. For example, Japan set up a government US$2 billion fund to cover the costs of Japanese companies that would backshore their production from China. The U.S. is considering the use of financial stimuli to compensate for any losses of American firms that wish to return their production from China to the U.S. The U.S. has adopted an approach to new regionalization by joining the advantages of the U.S., Canada and Mexico in order to stimulate backshoring and the so-called 'China +1' relocation of production to other Asian states, such as Taiwan, India and Vietnam. India, on its turn, announced attracting foreign investment from Western MNCs currently located in China as their national priority. The U.S. and the EU are installing legislation to filtering FDI in order to stop Chinese companies acquire any European companies experiencing financial difficulties or facing bankruptcy. The U.S. has initiated a strategy of working closely with allies by developing closer partnerships that can promote not only greater political alignment, but also forge U.S. business interests and oust Chinese and other non-allied business investment.

One of the first sectors that has been targeted by the nation-state relocation measures is unquestionably the pharmaceutical and medical technology sector, which in countries such as China, Russia, the U.S. and in the E.U. is being directly supported in its relocation and development by nation-state government regulation and direct purchases. Such a measure is so much needed as, e.g., more than 70 percent of the production of medicines and medicine ingredients used in the U.S. were produced overseas in 2019, and out of that about 13 percent in China.

Similar is the situation in Europe where more than 80 percent of some medicine inputs are produced in Asia, and for example, China produces more than 90 percent of the penicillin used in the world. Hence, the EU Commission has recognized its dependence on medicine supplies from China and India and has now launched an import-substitution program supported by the EU budget. Furthermore, more than 50 percent of the input and production of personal protective equipment was concentrated in China, which became a real problem at the start of the COVID-19 pandemic and caused a huge crisis in the health systems of developed and emerging economies alike.

A movement toward a nation-state-centered economic policy has been adopted by big emerging economies as well. For example, the new program 'Independent India' has been built on a polity associated with state-owned enterprises in economic sectors defined as strategic. These sectors would require that at least one company would be within the control and interest of the government, while private enterprises can also operate in it. Russia has also defined a number of priority sectors for the future development of the national economy, and adopted a strategy for achieving food and agricultural independence. Thus, COVID-19 has also pushed forward national economic agendas in emerging economies that strive to a greater independence and self-sufficiency, moving away from their dependency on lower value added activities in global supply chains. Such a push for national economic independence and global supply chain decoupling is much more feasible for countries that have favorable demographics, substantive internal demand, potential for developing of infrastructure and their own knowledge base. In view of these, China is refocusing its economic potential to knowledge-driven sectors in order to achieve technological decoupling from the U.S., while the latter have introduced rigid limitations on technology export and sharing with China. Such an approach will eventually make international R&D investments a lot more industry-specific, restricted, national-interest driven and at best – regionalized, eventually ensuring substantive technological decoupling in a battle for achieving technological supremacy.

Toward a New Regionalization

The key argument in Child and Marinova (2014) was that the globalization of firms calls for an analysis that considers the implications for the management of FDI arising from *different combinations* of home and host country characteristics. This is of great importance as the institutions and political systems in those contexts not only set requirements for both institutional and resource capital on the part of the overseas-investing firm, but more importantly set *the rules of access* to specific location and ownership advantages. Of course, we recognize the moderating effects of other factors such as firm ownership and sector membership, which impact both on their motives for FDI and on how they can accommodate to host country conditions. Thus, international business and FDIs can only be understood by taking account of the 'triangle' of resource, institutional and political factors that apply in *the combinations* of home and host country contexts. This means that in order to understand FDI, we have to understand types of advantage. To truly appreciate the 'bundling' of easy and difficult to negotiate resources (Hennart, 2009, 2012; Hennart et al., 2015), we need to revisit the bargaining power of actors (governments and firms) in international business and appreciate the role of *access* to resource and institutional capital. Thus, the international business theory and practice has to draw upon insights from resource-based, institutional and political perspectives *simultaneously*.

Consequently, when the political underpinning of the globalization doctrine of economic organization promoting global interdependence are changing, we can expect changes in the access of companies to institutional and resource capital in host and home countries that poses new requirements for their learning and adaptation in foreign markets. Moreover, the global interdependence is retreating to give way to a much more regional interdependence, which will lead, among other transformation processes, to major changes and restructuring of the host market portfolio of firms engaged in FDI.

This is politically determined as we are currently witnessing a period of fundamental realignment of a world that previously pushed forward globalization in the context of predominantly nationally defined institutions. Toulan (2020) argues that COVID-19 is the embodiment of globalization showing its extreme effect on humanity by triggering the most severe reversal of globalization. In effect, governments will exert pressure on foreign firms and imports and on home companies to choose foreign markets where firms can operate politically in a safe place. Depending on the government orientation, companies will be faced with new positioning challenges. For example, U.S. firms will be seeking new opportunities in the UK, Germany, Australia, Canada, Japan and aligned with them emerging markets. Chinese firms will withdraw to the domestic market and seek markets that are aligned with them. The trade war between China and the U.S. is squeezing the markets for Chinese firms in the U.S., UK, Australia and Canada, while new opportunities are created in the domestic market and in other markets that are favorably aligned with the Chinese political and socio-economic paradigm. The priority of cost-reduction and cost-leadership is giving ground to systemic risk minimization and resilience. Perception of lower systemic risk will be used to justify higher production and transaction costs incurred by business actors.

The type of regionalization in sight is lead-nation centered. It drives redistribution of markets and production sites defined by governmental alignment around a core of a lead nation enacting certain political, economic and moral paradigms. For instance, the U.S. is at the center of the Anglo-Saxon core, Germany is at the core of the EU regionalization, Russia – in the CIS and its allies, while China is central for those where its investment and economic influence is particularly strong, e.g., some Asian, African and Latin American states. Nation states and their governments are starting to define which companies can have access to host country institutional and resource capital, based on criteria such as national security, home-country business interests, risk reduction and resilience.

This new regionalization is not a move back to the old imperial divisions, or to another 'Cold War' era, which actually was just supressed, but never finished. It is simply a continuation of old spheres of influence and redefinition of the world landscape in terms of political, economic, technological, sociological and moral doctrines.

What Lies Ahead for International Business?

The changes epitomized above would most probably have long-lasting effects on the global political and economic conjuncture and on international business as theory and practice. However, it is difficult to predict the exact dimensions, extent and significance of the forthcoming changes.

The Strategic Lead of the Nation State

The reinforced power of the nation state is highly likely if the economic consequences prove to be most severe and long lasting. The nation-state is to set priorities using foresight and pivotal alignment. This is the most plausible outcome for big countries that will be recovering and shaping a pivot, meanwhile assisting other aligned with them countries to survive and recover. Actually, the success of the smaller countries will only strengthen the pivot. Such a development reminds of the importance of national resources and the ability of governments to utilize and develop them, as well as their foresight in defining economic priority sectors. Each big state will be able to define these for itself. Financial, knowledge and technological resources will be channeled to enhance the strategic sectors, while the latter may alter over time depending on the nation state's strategic priorities. The companies in the strategic economic sectors will be rather diverse in ownership, including domestic and foreign (Panibratov, 2014; see Figure 30.2).

However, this requires government stability and ability to decisively mobilize and channel resources in sectors with high government interest and varying degree of government control. National economic continuity would facilitate the process, while abrupt discontinuity would significantly jeopardize it. We may see rechanneling of financial flows by the state through selected banks and companies that are essential for

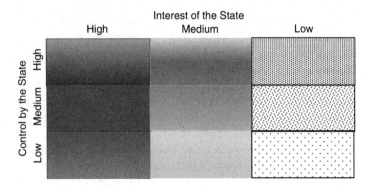

Figure 30.2 Control and Interest of the State in Economic Sectors.
Source: The Author, based on Panibratov (2014).

meeting domestic demand, while relying on increased exports in areas where other nations may experience serious shortages.

MNCs as Power Engines for Economic Recovery

The depth and scale of the global economic downturn as a direct consequence of the COVID-19 pandemic will lead to severe economic slump in many countries, to company bankruptcies and layoffs of unprecedented scale. Recovery might start in 2020, but will most probably take time. Those MNCs that are financially sound and supported by private conglomerate or state interest and control may incur some losses. Through the national (in the case of the EU supranational) recovery measures and targeted financial support, developed country MNCs may well find new investment opportunities, concentrate investment in technologically upcoming sectors and develop innovative solutions to meet demand, while their emerging market presence will be restructured. They will take over market spaces freed by bankrupt companies in developed markets. However, their resurgence will be faced with stringent government requirements and many of them will become mostly regional (leading within their regional pivot) rather than global. They will restructure value chains and markets looking for risk minimization and resilience, which in some cases may lead to changing suppliers and relocating supply operations while simultaneously transforming the portfolio of foreign markets and clients.

Emerging economy MNCs (EMNCs) will face more severe host government-imposed limitations on their operations in developed economies and much of their investment will be pushed out. A stark example of this unfolding pattern is the push against Chinese MNCs in terms of their overseas investments, export reach, access to technology and supply input in global value chains. This will create new growth business space for developed country MNCs in their regional pivots. In spite of this, EMNCs will develop stronger business presence and innovation capacity in their regional pivots by accelerated technological independence, expanding market presence and infrastructure investment in countries within their pivot and in other regions receptive to their political, economic and social paradigm.

Collaborative investment among firms from similar pivots might be possible in some cases of mutual interest. Such a disposition will increase competition and the juxtaposing of regionalized pivots that would engage MNCs in breakthrough innovations, collisions for resource access and drive competition into entirely new areas, such as space projects, genetics, digitalization and robotics. Around these MNCs (both developed and EMNCs), we shall see the emergence and resurgence of new SME clusters.

The Role of Small and Medium-Sized Enterprises (SMEs)

Some predictions are that SMEs will be the fastest to recover from the economic crisis and drive economic recovery as a whole. While SMEs could be smaller and more agile, in adapting to changing external shifts, some of them might be better equipped than others to survive the pandemic. Niche SMEs in the biotech and health or in the IT and food production sectors may fare quite well. The survival of those in tourism, entertainment, hospitality, travel services and restaurant business is seriously threatened. The fate of SMEs in global supply chains will very much depend on the situation with end demand and global logistics, but most are likely to experience dire consequences. Thus, survival will be sector-specific and the economic configuration of countries with a rather high share of SMEs will change. If the majority of SMEs are in endangered sectors and their contribution to GDP is paramount, the need for economic restructuring will become vital, but the availability of financial resources for it may be domestically scarce albeit possibly extended by the pivot.

Although business entrepreneurship is a powerful force driving economic growth in most developed market economies and often a survival mechanism for people in the developing world, the scale and depth of the pandemic's health and economic impact is likely to act as a deterrent to the ability of SMEs to rise as Fenix from the ashes. The length of the pandemic might completely deplete the resources of many SMEs and if government recovery support is not available, they would struggle to survive. In countries with explicit social contract (Wraight, 2008) and especially in those where SMEs account for a huge part of business activity, governments are supposed to create a new or reinforce existing support systems to enable their fast recovery. The real question is about the extent to which SMEs will be able to cocoon or delay bankruptcy. Alternatively, entrepreneurial SMEs could strengthen existing or carve new niche market positions in a variety of upcoming knowledge-intensive or subsistence sectors.

Conclusive Remarks

Any of these developments will apply to a different extent and in a different combination in various countries. The specifics of recovery will depend on the strategic foresight of the nation state combined with country size, resources, type and diversity of economic sectors, company size, agility and exposure to global production and supply networks.

Firm-level international operations would seriously change post-COVID-19. Decoupling of production, technologies and supply will not be easy, but will chart its course. Some companies that had moved operations to China for efficiency reasons will move production back home and/or diversify suppliers. In this process, countries such as Turkey, India, Vietnam and Malaysia would attempt to reposition and attract preferred FDI. Firms seeking to expand market presence in big host markets will need to organize localized production, supply and distribution, while innovation will take place primarily at home. In the case of a small domestic and big foreign market, internationalizing firms will have to localize production, supply and distribution in few big markets turning them into second home market, but most exploratory innovations will be at home or within own pivot. Internationalized firms from big domestic markets will focus on and expand production and innovation at home, thus, deglobaliize and re-gionalize. Most challenging is likely to be the position of internationalized companies with a small home and host market. Unless such firms are in

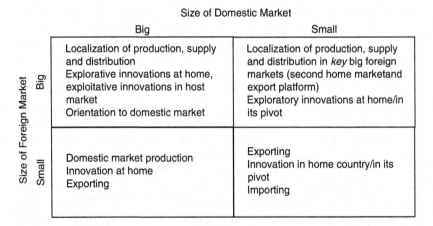

Figure 30.3 International Involvement of Firms based on Size of Home and Host Market.
Source: The Author.

unique niche markets or market leaders in a small high-value added niche market, they are most likely to rely on imports, attempt some exports and co-innovate at home or within their own pivot (see Figure 30.3).

Certainly, all these options are not universal and there is likely to be sector and country specificity. For example, while Chinese firms will be forced to retract, restructure foreign markets and orientate much more toward the domestic market, Russian firms may be forced to co-coon, innovate and grow at home by using national innovation and entrepreneurial potential, which coupled with fundamental science and technological leadership could provide a unique opportunity to install a thriving knowledge economy. Indian firms may largely benefit from their entrepreneurial spirit and big family conglomerates, and their access to know-how and markets in countries from the Anglo-Saxon pivot. For relatively big Central and Eastern European countries, pivot alignment has not been cleared yet. As they are generally of a smaller size and their firms do not have substantial explorative innovation potential, they might be drawn into different pivots with the EU one being most important with its free movement of goods, people and capital, while experiencing pressure from the U.S.-led pivot.

Finally, one of the interesting spillover effects of the COVID-19 pandemic has demonstrated huge differences in the moral orientation of different countries and has opened up moral paradigm rifts. Some

Dimensions / Levels	Economic / Utility	Psychological / Emotional	Sociological / Social significance	Ecological / Environmental
User	Value for money	Happiness	Belonging	Footprint
Organization	Profit, new market and product expansion, new utility creation.	Core and aspirational values	Social fit (e.g. legitimacy), contribution and responsibility (e.g.CSR)	Eco-effectiveness
Ecosystem	Mutual economic gains	Shared drivers	Mutuality and reciprocity	Sustainability
Society	Wealth and income security	Wellbeing and safety	Meaningful life in a social context	Environment and living conditions

Figure 30.4 Dimensions and Levels of Internationalized Business Impact on Human Life.

Source: The Author, Based on Marinova, S., Freeman, S. and Marinov, M. (2019). Value creation in context: A value chain locus perspective, in M Marinov (ed.), *Value in Marketing: Retrospective and Perspective Stance*. Routledge, New York, pp. 180–210; Holbrook, M.B. (1999). *Consumer Value: A Framework for Analysis and Research*. New York: Routledge; Boztepe, S. (2007). User value: Competing theories and models. *International Journal of Design*, 1(2): 55–63; Den Ouden, E. (2011). *Innovation Design: Creating Value for People, Organizations and Society*. Springer Science & Business Media.

countries have focused on saving every human life, others have been fixated on saving economic activity, while others have cautiously tried to merge the two. Whatever the approach, it has become clear that *homo sapiens*' life should be brought in the center of international business with a thoughtful redefinition of its economic, psychological, sociological and environmental effects on individual, organization, ecosystem and societal levels (see Figure 30.4).

The unprecedented disruption in international business has highlighted the need for a better balance between domestic and foreign business activity, and ultimately – for a more critical view on globalization. The pressure for financial resources during and post-COVID-19 has exacerbated the key question about the morality of MNCs receiving rent from selling their goods and services across nation markets and paying taxes on the rent. Not of a lesser importance is the question of why access to foreign markets and hence customer resources should be free, why resources such as knowledge, technology and know-how should be readily available to foreign MNCs, how tariffs could be used more effectively by nation-states to encourage domestic production and employment, and how bilateral agreements can serve national agendas. All these require re-thinking globalization beyond its economic value and aligning international business with its greater sociological, psychological and environmental worthiness. Consequently, internationalized firms will have to draw from and attach to important cultural and socially based ecosystems at home and abroad, and engage in multidimensional value co-creation activities.

References

Boztepe, S., 2007. User value: Competing theories and models. *Int. J. Des.* 1(2), 55–63.

Child, J., Marinova, S., 2014. The role of contextual combination in the internationalization of Chinese firms. *Manag. Organ. Rev.* 10(3), 347–371.

Den Ouden, E., 2011. *Innovation Design: Creating Value for People, Organizations and Society.* Springer Science & Business Media, Berlin.

Hennart, J.-F., 2009. Down with MNE-centric theories! Market entry and expansion as the bundling of MNE and local assets. *J. Int. Bus. Stud.* 40(9), 1432–1454.

Hennart, J.-F., 2012. Emerging market multinationals and the theory of the multinational enterprise. *Glob. Strategy J.* 2(3), 168–187.

Hennart, J.-F., Sheng, H.H., and Pimenta, G. 2015. Local Contemporary inputs as drivers of entry mode choices: The case of US investments in Brazil, *International Business Review*, 24, 466–475.

Holbrook, M.B., 1999. *Consumer Value: A Framework for Analysis and Research.* Routledge, New York.

Marinova, S., Freeman, S., Marinov, M., 2019. Value creation in context: A value chain locus perspective. In: Marinov, M. (ed.), *Value in Marketing: Retrospective and Perspective Stance.* Routledge, New York, pp. 180–210.

Panibratov, A. 2014. Classifying the roles of government in the expansion of Russian MNEs. *The European Financial Review,* June 19, https://www. europeanfinancialreview.com/classifying-the-roles-of-government-in-the-expansion-of-russian-mnes/ (Accessed on July 10, 2020).

Streeck, W., Thelen, K., 2005. Introduction: institutional change in advanced political economies. In: Streeck, W., Thelen, K. (Eds.), *Beyond Continuity: Institutional Change in Advanced Political Economies Oxford.* Oxford University Press, UK, pp. 1–39.

Toulan, O., 2020. *Globalization after COVID-19: What's in store?* https://www. imd.org/research-knowledge/articles/Globalization-after-COVID-19-Whats-in-store/ (Accessed on July 10, 2020).

Wraight, C.D., 2008. *Rousseau's The Social Contract: A Reader's Guide.* Continuum Books, London.

Index

Printed in the United States
By Bookmasters